SMOKE ON THE WATER

GLOBAL AMERICA

GLOBAL AMERICA

Edited by Jay Sexton and Sarah B. Snyder

Columbia University Press's Global America series pushes the history of U.S. foreign relations in new directions, sharpening and diversifying our understanding of the global dimensions of American history from the colonial era to the twenty-first century. Books in the series explore America's global encounters, including how external forces have shaped the development of the United States and vice versa; why American encounters with the wider world have produced volatility, ruptures, and crises; the shifting contours of U.S. power over time; and the impact of hierarchical attitudes regarding identity in shaping U.S. foreign relations. Taken together, the series analyzes the global history of the United States; its authors employ a diverse range of methodological, chronological, disciplinary, geographical, and ideological perspectives.

Robert B. Rakove, *Days of Opportunity: The United States and Afghanistan Before the Soviet Invasion*

M. Todd Bennett, *Neither Confirm nor Deny: How the Glomar Mission Shielded the CIA from Transparency*

DARIO FAZZI

SMOKE ON THE WATER

Incineration at Sea and the Birth of a Transatlantic Environmental Movement

Columbia University Press / *New York*

Columbia University Press
Publishers Since 1893
New York   Chichester, West Sussex
cup.columbia.edu
Copyright © 2023 Columbia University Press
All rights reserved

Cataloging-in-Publication Data is available from the Library of Congress.

ISBN 9780231212427 (hardback)
ISBN 9780231212434 (trade paperback)
ISBN 9780231559379 (e-book)
LCCN 2023024108

Cover design: Chang Jae Lee

Cover image: Picture taken by Greenpeace's Stephen McAllister onboard the *Vulcanus II* on October 1, 1983. Courtesy of Greenpeace Media Library.

*To Leonardo and all those who,
like him, love the sea and swim*

CONTENTS

Introduction   1

1   The Disposable Frontier   21

2   The Military-Chemical-Industrial Complex   45

3   Translocal Activism   71

4   Relentless Commitment   101

5   Ban the Burn   131

6   Quitting Smoking   159

Conclusion   185

Acknowledgments 195

Notes 201

Index 271

SMOKE ON THE WATER

INTRODUCTION

On a wintry morning in early December 1983, while at her home in Harlingen, Texas, Sue Ann Fruge received an unexpected phone call. The voice on the line invited her to Washington, DC, to testify before the House Committee on Merchant Marine and Fisheries. Surprised and excited, Fruge packed her bags with scientific reports, medical records, pictures, and dozens of letters from fellow citizens of the Lower Rio Grande Valley—just a tiny portion of the material she had collected as coordinator of the Gulf Coast Coalition for Public Health (GCCPH). Fruge's goal was to challenge the U.S. Environmental Protection Agency's (EPA) support for and investments in a new method for the disposal of toxic industrial wastes: ocean incineration.[1] Ocean or at-sea incineration meant the offshore destruction of the chemical by-products of industry aboard ships equipped with burning chambers and smokestacks. In theory, this process was safe, disposing of tons of poisonous waste at sea, far from inhabited land. In practice, it released tons of dangerous compounds directly into the sea, contaminating the seawaters' biochemical structure and jeopardizing entire coastal communities.

It was Fruge's first time in such a high-profile setting as a congressional hearing. She had joined the fight over environmental issues only two years

INTRODUCTION

earlier, having led her life as a homemaker with no experience in social activism. By the time she went to Washington, however, Fruge had become a different person. She was well versed, informed, and prepared. She had interviewed people and listened to experts. She had noted down personal stories and concerns. She had collected and analyzed data. Months of campaigning had helped her interiorize why ocean incineration represented such an urgent threat to her family and community. When she embarked on her trip to DC, she had a zeal for social justice and a feeling of responsibility for thousands of fellow coastal residents. Fruge hoped that the politicians could grasp how vital the ocean—a healthy ocean—was for thousands of families who depended on fisheries, shrimping, and seasonal tourism. She wanted them to understand the beauty and abundance of the surrounding marine environment. Above all, knowing that the actions mushrooming around the country against waste facilities were being characterized as "hysterical cries," she wanted her community's concerns taken seriously.[2]

The main object of Fruge's criticism was ocean incineration, but through it she wanted to denounce the highly discriminatory nature of America's hazardous-waste policy. The ways in which the U.S. government managed the disposal of toxic industrial by-products systematically endangered the health of the most disadvantaged people in the country. Fruge saw, in other words, a consistency in how marginalized communities such as Native Americans, African Americans, Latinos, and poor people like the ones living in the Lower Rio Grande Valley were sacrificed on the altar of American industrial capitalism, and she thought that "enough was enough." In fact, she was determined to use her testimony as a clarion call to say that modern industrialism, in complicity with inattentive public regulatory bodies, was inextricably bound to the use and production of deadly substances. Without intervention, these deadly substances would cause irreversible degradation to both human and environmental health, especially in those places that seemingly lay outside of national elites' main concerns.[3] Perhaps even more importantly, she thought that U.S. citizens had to step in, play their role in environmental policy making, and prevent the interests of

FIGURE 0.1 Sue Ann Fruge sporting a T-shirt that shows her opposition to the burning of hazardous waste in the Gulf of Mexico, 1985.

Source: © *Houston Chronicle*, April 26, 1985. Courtesy of the Houston Chronicle Library.

private businesses and industrial conglomerates from prevailing over the needs of the people.

Fruge's indignation and the story behind it—the rise and fall of ocean incineration—are treated here as emblematic of the constraints that the U.S. government faced from the second half of the 1970s onward. In those years, the consistent application of deregulation measures, which affected crucial economic, financial, and industrial sectors, was central to the transformation of America's capitalism and the reaffirmation of Washington's worldwide ascendancy. As Gary Gerstle has recently shown, these neoliberal efforts were instrumental in laying the foundations of a new global order in which U.S. economic and industrial power could still be pivotal after the decline of the previous Keynesian, state-centered model.[4] Such a design, however, as the experience of ocean incineration proves and this book argues, found some of its main limits *translocally*—that is, in a system of interdependent interests, shared governance, grassroots initiatives, widespread pressures, and multichannel advocacy that was able to affect the outcomes of U.S. (environmental) policies at both the domestic and the international levels.[5]

An interpretation of this sort, centered on the role that bottom-up pressures played in limiting the actions of the U.S. government both at home and abroad, allows this book to contribute to a growing scholarship that conjoins social history with international relations, diplomatic history, and the history of the United States in the world.[6] Furthermore, the nature of the topic places it in the field of international environmental history, which has blossomed in the past few decades with studies on multilateral environmental politics and policies, global ecologies, transnational networks, and the relationship between state and nonstate actors.[7] This book adds to this conversation not only by providing the first comprehensive historical account of ocean incineration and its reverberations on U.S. political, military, and economic power but also by juxtaposing ocean incineration with the rise of global interdependence and a critical approach toward America's international leadership, the establishment and expansion of a system of multilateral environmental governance, and the growth of a varied and transboundary environmental constituency.[8] These developments concurrently

INTRODUCTION

contributed to thwarting the U.S. government's ambitions of furthering ocean incineration and eventually prompted it to renounce such a controversial practice mainly on socioecological grounds.

Ocean incineration thus represented one of those environmental processes that throughout the second half of the twentieth century tested the efficacy of America's influence on a global stage.[9] Given Washington's vested economic and security interests in the management of hazardous waste, the international discussions on at-sea incineration fully exposed the contradictions between the theory and the practice of U.S. environmental policy.[10] Washington's idealistic rhetoric of environmental engagement hid an underbelly of practical decisions based on (industrial and military) self-interest. As Paul Harris argues, safeguarding U.S. national interests, "particularly the most vital ones," often translated into unilateral actions that compromised multilateral environmental protection.[11] This was exactly the case of at-sea incineration, an instance in which the U.S. government proved relentlessly committed to the defense of its own military and commercial priorities even when these priorities clashed with rising concerns over human and environmental health. For this reason, the practice came to be seen as the latest manifestation of one of Washington's oldest imperial practices, the unrestrained use of natural resources to its own aggrandizement.[12] The U.S. government was blamed for looking at the oceans simply as an immense frontier to be colonized by its ever-growing petrochemical industry.[13] Ocean incineration became a symbol of exploitation, an attempt by the U.S. government to impose its own national agendas, priorities, and exigencies on the vastness of the oceans.[14]

The responsibility of managing and regulating ocean incineration put the spotlight on the EPA and slowly transformed the agency into a booster for U.S. imperial entanglements. This practice, indeed, progressively projected EPA's mission onto the globe, as had previously happened to the U.S. Department of the Interior.[15] The EPA supported the acquisition of at-sea incineration technology by heavily subsidized U.S. companies and defended the technology's worldwide commercialization and loose regulation. In so doing, the agency favored the creation of patterns of neocolonial dependency on U.S.-owned know-how and capabilities and contributed to

INTRODUCTION

reinforcing a system of "hierarchy, discipline, dispossession, extraction, and exploitation" that, as Paul Kramer has argued, was at the core of U.S. imperial endeavors.[16] In truth, the EPA was just following a pattern that from 1945 had been applied successfully by several other U.S. governmental agencies and institutions in such varied fields as civil aviation, economic development, finance, and trade.[17] The agency sought, almost obsessively, to align the international regulation of the marine environment to U.S. domestic legislation. But the obstacles it encountered in eliciting the necessary domestic and international support for this practice eventually testified to the definitive transformation of America's leadership in the era of global interdependence.[18]

Ocean incineration was also being negotiated and regulated internationally within a growing system of multilateral environmental governance, which further constrained the U.S. government's actions and policies. Whereas Washington initially maintained a highly discretionary power and could impose its will against international control of the practice, its main Western allies progressively isolated it and looked for their own path. This was possible because of the rapid institutionalization of international environmental law from the early 1970s onward. The protection of the natural environment—and especially of watery ecosystems—against exploitative national policies and private interests became one of the main goals of the United Nations (UN) Environmental Program, which was established in the aftermath of the UN Conference on the Human Environment in Stockholm in 1972. At the same time, widespread concern over the health of the seas resulted in the adoption of the first-ever binding international treaties on marine pollution: the Convention on the Prevention of Marine Pollution by Dumping of Wastes and Other Matter (London Dumping Convention) and the International Convention for the Prevention of Pollution from Ships, more familiarly known as MARPOL. The UN conference in Stockholm also served as a springboard for a moratorium on whaling, the launch of the Ramsar Convention on Wetlands, and the establishment of different regional frameworks, such as the Convention for the Prevention of Marine Pollution by Dumping from Ships and Aircraft (Oslo Convention) and the Convention for the Prevention of Marine Pollution from

INTRODUCTION

Land-Based Sources (Paris Convention).[19] Hence, when confronted with America's obstinate defense of ocean incineration, those who criticized and opposed it could resort to a series of international organizations and set up stricter procedures, guidelines, and systems of control that de facto prevented the U.S. government from further interfering with the regulation of this practice beyond its own territorial waters.[20]

The trajectory of ocean incineration further invites political and diplomatic historians to reckon with the transformative potency of an environmentally aware public opinion, which affected U.S. domestic and foreign policies.[21] As a U.S. Information Agency report stated in 1977, by the mid-1970s people's engagement with ecological issues represented an insurmountable constraint on the management of environmental policies. The report, emblematically titled *The Rising Significance of World Opinion*, noted that "the worldwide explosion of communication facilities" had contributed to an unprecedented "tide of public awareness [of] and involvement" in both local and global environmental issues and that people fully understood the various implications of governmental policy in this field.[22] Environmental concerns magnified the growing influence of world public opinion on both global and national governance. U.S. policy makers had to negotiate between, on the one hand, a public opinion that was "strikingly committed" to the protection of the environment and, on the other hand, industrial and financial leaders who "consistently under-estimate[d] the strength of the public's sense of urgency about environmental issues," as a follow-up report explained.[23] No longer capable of dismissing people's growing environmental consciousness, the U.S. government began requiring private companies "to set out their plans and discuss the reasons for their mode of operations at public hearings to determine the effect on the environment of their activity."[24] In the case of ocean incineration, this change of approach empowered critics of the U.S. government even more. Ironically, it also limited U.S. federal agencies' room to maneuver everywhere around the globe, including at home.

What makes the outcry over ocean incineration particularly noteworthy and historically relevant is its translocal nature. In this movement, transnational activism and the nongovernmental organization (NGO) lobby combined with grassroots mobilization and bottom-up protests.[25] The campaign against ocean incineration saw the involvement of a plethora of transnational environmentalist groups and organizations. These groups were financially, structurally, and organizationally able to mobilize communities across multiple national contexts. They served as clearinghouses for information and commissioned, distributed, and popularized studies on the technical flaws and health hazards of the practice. With their global reach, they helped debunk the myths surrounding ocean incineration, effectively countering industry's overly optimistic narrative.[26] Furthermore, and perhaps even more important, the transnational organizations that sustained the effort against ocean incineration were able to bridge the gap between local and global governance. These groups helped the communities on the front lines of the struggle gather the evidence and support they needed to influence local and national policy makers. At the same time, these transnational organizations used their leverage in the supranational regulatory bodies to which vulnerable groups had no direct access. Their active and influential participation in those settings was fundamental to the success of the whole anti-incineration campaign.

At the local level in the United States, the struggle against ocean incineration intersected with the emergence of a popular antitoxics and environmental-justice movement, which provided this new campaign with arguments, slogans, leadership, membership, and protests methods and repertoires. To many U.S. environmentalists, the wreckage of America's hazardous-waste policies was just one of the manifestations of a broader "toxicity crisis," as Sarah Vogel puts it, which went hand-in-hand with the consolidation of neoliberal practices driving both petrochemical and plastic production.[27] For decades, the unaccountable overproduction of hazardous waste had been a structural reality of the U.S.-driven affluent society. By the late 1970s, a radical critique of both modern industrial processes and regulatory practices had gained ground and become mainstream.[28] Scandals and accidents had exposed the industry's lack of compliance with environmental regulation, and its widespread disregard for the consequences of toxic contamination had spurred anger. The glaring failure of public systems of prevention and control had become unmistakable.[29] Hazardous waste became a matter of domestic public concern and climbed to the top of the U.S. environmentalist agenda.[30]

The campaign against ocean incineration, thus, was translocal not only because it was carried out simultaneously by transnational and local groups but also because it was characterized by a series of exchanges of roles, information, networks, and resources and by a close cooperation between local and transnational actors that further complicated U.S. environmental policy both at home and abroad. Anti-ocean-incineration campaigners set up a common strategy that worked efficiently across different levels of sociopolitical action and governance. This strategy constituted a new challenge to the U.S. government, which up to that point had to balance its own strategic and economic priorities with demands for environmental-policy changes coming from either domestic or transnational nonstate actors.[31] The regulatory approach that U.S. policy makers had been devising and embracing from the early 1970s as an attempt to cope with these pressures did not work in the case of ocean incineration.[32] The translocal commitment to the protection of coastal and marine environments could not be easily reconciled with the interests of a seemingly omnipresent military-industrial complex, and U.S. environmental diplomacy short-circuited. In fact, the U.S. government tried to salvage ocean incineration, though unsuccessfully, even when the practice's environmental unviability became apparent.

THE HAZARDOUS-WASTE CRISIS AND ITS DISCONTENTS

Fruge's testimony and the campaign it represented hit a raw nerve in America's modern industrialism. America's industrial production, indeed, was bound to grow in order to keep high standards of living, yet in doing so it was also doomed to generate an exorbitant amount of toxic waste, which ended up exacerbating environmental risk, alienating popular support, and isolating Washington internationally.[33] What the historian Alfred Chandler Jr. has defined as the "polymer/petrochemical revolution" had a dark

INTRODUCTION

side that from the late 1960s onward started confronting the United States—and other industrialized democracies of the world—with an out-of-control hazardous-waste crisis.[34] In those years, the United States was the world's main generator of hazardous wastes, and finding a method for the safe disposal of such toxic substances had become one of the most urgent domestic and international priorities. Ultimately, the decade-long struggle over the fate of ocean incineration revolved around how the main protagonists of this story—several U.S. governmental agencies and different private companies, on the one hand, as well as several international agencies, grassroots movements, and environmental organizations, on the other—sought to balance all the factors in the complex equation of hazardous-waste management.

To the EPA and to several U.S. waste generators and waste-management companies, ocean incineration offered a beacon of hope. Hazardous waste—a broad legal category codified by the U.S. Congress in 1976 as all those ignitable, corrosive, reactive, or toxic by-products of industrial processes able to jeopardize human health—was easy to generate but extremely difficult to dispose of.[35] Every year, the U.S. petrochemical industry alone was spawning roughly 60 million tons of toxic waste, disposing of it substantially in two ways: ocean dumping and landfilling. Ocean dumping had been by far the most common method for the disposal of a variety of hazardous materials, including dredge spoil, sewage sludge, solid and industrial wastes, construction and demolition debris, radioactive wastes, and an unspecified amount of obsolete munitions.[36] Landfilling, too, had been widely employed for decades. In 1980, the EPA revealed that there were more than 27,000 landfill sites scattered across the country.[37] Both of these practices, however, had dire environmental consequences, and from the early 1970s onward they came under public scrutiny. With the rise of environmental concerns and the implementation of both national and international regulations meant to safeguard the marine environment, ocean dumping's viability and popularity faded away.[38] The practice was eventually outlawed both domestically and internationally in 1972.[39] Landfilling, too, was fueling widespread concerns. Burying toxic waste underground entailed the risk of seepage into water sources and the subsequent

INTRODUCTION

contamination of the surrounding areas. These risks, especially after tragic events such as the one that occurred at Love Canal, New York, hit the headlines throughout the country and ignited local protests and widespread discontent.[40]

Though environmentally legitimate and understandable, the decline of ocean dumping and landfilling further aggravated the hazardous-waste crisis insofar as waste generators were left with few alternatives for the disposal of ever-growing amounts of toxic waste.[41] The treatment of chemical waste, in particular, had become extremely expensive—up to $260 per ton when the safest available options were used, which would be multiplied by millions of tons.[42] Public management of such waste was so engulfed that even the EPA came to recognize in the early 1970s that the way in which the nation was grappling with the hazardous-waste crisis was largely inconsistent and "inadequate."[43] For all these reasons, Washington's policy makers fostered research on alternative methods for the disposal of hazardous waste in the hope of perfecting new technologies that could be simultaneously environmentally safe, economically affordable, and socially acceptable. Between 1972 and 1975, while passing a flurry of legislation that was meant to regulate the management of hazardous wastes throughout their life cycle ("from cradle to grave"), Congress and the EPA commissioned a series of studies aiming to identify and recommend promising hazardous-waste-treatment technologies that could minimize the threats that these substances were posing to both public health and the environment. As a U.S. interagency report bluntly stated in 1980, "The accumulation of uncontrolled, ever-increasing volumes of hazardous wastes" threatened "the public health and the nation's environment" and had made it extremely urgent to invest in safe and environmentally acceptable technologies.[44] Possible alternative methods included such physical processes as sedimentation and filtration, chemical neutralization, and thermal destruction. The most promising of these technological breakthroughs seemed to be the practice at the center of this story: ocean incineration.[45]

At-sea incineration—that is, the destruction of toxic and chemical waste offshore—was first developed and tested in Europe and then adopted and commercialized in the United States—and to a lesser extent in Japan and

Australia—from the first half of the 1970s. The nature of the practice required not only special domestic regulation but also a series of international negotiations. In fact, the designation of oceanic-incineration zones, the definition of incinerable wastes, and the rules concerning both transboundary transportation and port-loading operations overlapped with the ongoing negotiations over the law of the sea and brought ocean incineration to the center of several international debates. Whereas in the United States the task of regulating ocean incineration fell on the EPA, the international discussions and confrontations over it occurred mainly within such intergovernmental settings as the International Maritime Organization, the London Dumping Convention, and the Oslo Commission (OSCOM), which was set up to oversee compliance to the Oslo Dumping Convention.[46]

However, ocean incineration jeopardized entire coastal communities insofar as it took a heavy toll on the quality of ocean waters. The practice entailed the long-term biochemical modification of marine ecosystems and represented therefore a direct threat to the well-being of people relying on sea-related activities, such as fishery and seasonal tourism. For this reason, spontaneous, grassroots protests against ocean incineration proliferated, mirroring to a large extent the rise of a contemporary, broader antitoxics campaign. In those years, people across the United States were denouncing the dangers of several chemical compounds, such as diethylstilbestrol (DES), bisphenol A (BPA), and organochlorines. Above them all, though, were polychlorinated biphenyls, the infamous PCBs—the ubiquitous byproducts not only of the petrochemical, pharmaceutical, and agricultural industries but also of the military.[47] Antitoxics campaigners were using scientific evidence to show the substantial link between chemical pollution and public and environmental health. They advocated for an absolute ban on dangerous chemical derivatives; they did not toy with the mere regulation of their use. In the end, they criticized the very legitimacy and sustainability of modern industrial processes, which could not seem to forgo the use of poisonous chemical compounds.[48] The antitoxics movement's approach was novel. It decried the petrochemical contamination of the biosphere as the most urgent environmental threat. It laid bare the dysfunctional public regulatory agencies. It forced a reconsideration of the idea that a safe threshold for the use of toxic substances existed.[49] Most important, it subverted modern environmentalism's gender and racial dynamics. Women, indeed, inspired and led the antitoxics campaign.[50] They focused on the long-term and intergenerational public-health hazards posed by toxic contamination.[51] Their emphasis on reproductive rights and on the harm that could result from chemical pollution as well as their insistence on the need to safeguard their families' health and on expanding the concept of citizenship to encompass environmental rights allowed women to transform local demands into broader policy goals.[52]

At the same time, the antitoxics campaigners contributed to introducing the idea of environmental justice, blaming the "modern imperatives of technological progress and economic growth" for disproportionately harming the poor and people of color.[53] U.S. antitoxics activists saw that the pattern of environmental degradation simply repeated the deliberate and systematic exclusion of ethnic minorities and the poor from environmental discussions and decision making.[54] Such an antitoxics movement worked to prove the linear relation between the environmental threat and structural racism. Scholars and activists alike characterize the Warren County controversy of 1982 as the starting point of the modern environmental-justice movement.[55] It was in Warren County, North Carolina, that residents—69 percent of whom were African American—filed a complaint against the EPA's authorization to build a landfill site for the disposal of PCBs in the county. Their action became the clarion call for social and racial justice. Civil rights organizations joined forces with local citizens, bringing new protest tactics, funds, expertise, networks, and organizational capabilities to the campaign. Soon, the Warren County protests outgrew the boundaries of the local community and put social, economic, and racial justice at the center of the national environmental debate. A series of cross-sectional studies established a direct link between racial and economic marginalization and environmental exploitation. The well-known report *Toxic Wastes and Race in the United States*, a nationwide analysis compiled by the United Church of Christ in 1987, ultimately found that the race of a community was the decisive factor in where toxins were dumped.

INTRODUCTION

Communities "beset by poverty, unemployment, and problems related to poor housing, education, and health" were thought to be incapable of concerning themselves with the quality of their surrounding environment.[56] As a result, politicians disregarded them as an irrelevant sociopolitical constituency. Forgotten as well by the mainstream (majority-white) environmentalist groups, racial-minority and poor communities saw their localities progressively transformed into gigantic dumping sites. Vulnerable people as diverse as Navajo uranium miners and Latino workers of the Mexican American maquiladoras came to be the new sacrificial victims of industrial capitalism.[57]

The campaign against ocean incineration contributed to broadening the agency of the antitoxics and environmental-justice movement. The women engaged in the struggle against ocean incineration moved beyond such pre- or protofeminist tropes as the archetypal figure of the concerned mother and started criticizing U.S. waste policies as a toxic outcome of male-dominated systems of political and industrial control. Furthermore, the female protagonists of this story contributed to advancing forms of environmental democracy. In fact, they strategically politicized the marine environment as a way to place themselves at the center of environmental decision-making processes and gain control over the management of the complex socioeconomic structures of their own communities.[58] Foregrounding many of the stances of modern hydrofeminism, these women transformed the oceans into a sociopolitical battlefield. On that battlefield, they challenged the U.S. military-industrial complex, which they deemed incapable of conferring a nonmonetary value on the sea and its composite ecosystems.[59] Along the way, these women denounced the shortsightedness of public regulatory agencies and private waste companies and disseminated a holistic approach to environmental policy. At the center of their concerns stood the safeguarding of the entire biosphere.

Similarly, the campaign against ocean incineration questioned the form of justice that many earlier U.S. environmentalists and antitoxics campaigners sought to obtain. The first calls for environmental justice came from farmers and oil and nuclear industry workers, who, effectively organized and mobilized by unions, were able to achieve some important goals,

INTRODUCTION

such as the early drafts of the Radiation Exposure Compensation Act in the late 1970s (although this act wasn't passed until 1990).[60] The lives of these workers were both threatened by and dependent on the industrial processes they denounced. Thus, rather than advocating for the complete abandonment of dangerous practices, these workers often pressured for forms of distributive justice that included reparations, cleanups, and occupational safety.[61] In contrast, the fishermen and seasonal workers who drove the struggle against ocean incineration were scarcely unionized and had no networks of solidarity that could sustain their plea. They had to create their own alliances from scratch to protect their economic interests against the big conglomerates.[62] Moreover, the subsistence of these economically vulnerable groups was not bound to the technology against which they were protesting. Ocean incineration did not promise to spread wealth or strengthen job security. It only threatened. Thus, their struggle could adopt a much more uncompromising tone and more radical demands.

THE TRAJECTORY OF OCEAN INCINERATION

The story that follows, grounded in an interdisciplinary approach and informed by deep archival research, contends that translocal protests represented one of the main constraints on U.S. domestic and international environmental policy making. The book begins with a description of the historical roots of the hazardous-waste crisis that came to haunt the United States—and indeed the West—from the late 1960s onward. Chapter 1 reconstructs the unrestrained production, the difficult management, and the unsafe disposal of organochlorine wastes. It explains how toxic waste and its disposal soon became, as the EPA put it, "everybody's problem."[63] The chapter shows how a series of national regulations and international agreements, driven by a rise in environmental concern, either drastically modified or categorically outlawed common practices such as landfilling and ocean dumping. This trend ironically led to the alternative that emerged as the most promising technological breakthrough: ocean incineration. The

INTRODUCTION

chapter concludes by analyzing how the United States influenced early multilateral discussions around at-sea incineration and how it established a faulty international system of control meant to preserve its own national and private interests and to sideline issues of environmental safety.

Chapter 2 looks at ocean incineration as emblematic of the modern military-industrial complex. U.S. military elites wanted their government to think of at-sea incineration as the safest way to dispose of a strategically untenable and politically embarrassing chemical arsenal. Their participation meant that offshore incineration operations were suffused with secrecy. This, in turn, spread distrust in any U.S. plan and militated against scientific transparency. Notably, wariness of the U.S. government's intentions affected national regulations, hindered multilateral negotiations, and isolated Washington internationally. As with any component of the U.S. military-industrial complex, ocean incineration also gave rise to a damaged relationship between public and private interests. In fact, along with the pressures coming from the military sector, the EPA had to deal with the growing influence and insistence of a series of private companies looking both for cost-effective solutions to the problem of hazardous-waste disposal and for high-yield investments in the promising waste-management business. These companies lobbied the EPA and induced the agency to make a series of rushed and faulty decisions. By the early 1980s, the lure of ocean incineration, with its out-of-sight, out-of-mind character and its promises of incremental profits, had become stronger than ever.

Chapter 3 explains how the environmentalist movement, which in the meantime had gained a global constituency, challenged the status quo concerning ocean incineration. When people raised their voices against the dangers of such a technology, U.S. policy makers found themselves stuck between mounting demands to protect the environment and the pressures applied by the business community. U.S. governmental authorities proved incapable of dismissing people's anxiety out of hand. This chapter argues that early calls for environmental safeguards were most effective at the local level. Later on, community activists, together with the coordinated efforts of transnational NGOs, were able to propel their local demands onto the global stage. Ultimately, this partnership between local and transnational

INTRODUCTION

groups provided greater agency and voice to anti-ocean-incineration activists and boosted their power. The translocal activism mounted by organizations such as Greenpeace and the GCCPH coincided with a series of consultative public hearings on ocean incineration organized by the EPA in late 1983. Those hearings and the unexpected, massive participation they attracted further spotlighted critics of at-sea incineration at the national level, and a public debate ensued.

The clash between people's interests and the government's plans developed locally, nationally, and globally. As chapter 4 describes, ocean incineration became a sociopolitical battleground that intersected with other environmental concerns and mobilized several constituencies in the United States. Women denounced ocean incineration's intergenerational risks and coordinated successful campaigns involving schools, churches, and local political committees. Migrant workers and fishers denounced the broad economic repercussions that ocean incineration had on fragile ecosystems and exposed the racist nature of a practice that endangered ethnic minorities and low-income groups. Soon the concern over incineration outgrew the boundaries of the United States, and coastal communities on both sides of the Atlantic mobilized to safeguard the global marine biota, pointing to its role in the protection of human health. Above all, transnational groups translated bottom-up demands into effective political pressure through their active participation in international and multilateral forums. When U.S. government officials and private entrepreneurs pushed back, their attempts were stymied by increased pressure from the translocal coalition against ocean incineration. The critics of ocean incineration progressively isolated their opponents.

Chapter 5 starts with a description of the infamous accident in Bhopal, India, in December 1984, when a Union Carbide pesticide plant leaked forty tons of methyl isocyanate, exposing half a million people to toxic emissions and sending shockwaves throughout the world. For many, this kind of accident laid bare the urgency of finding adequate methods for the disposal of deadly chemical substances, which included using ocean incineration. For others, environmental safety could not be compromised, not even in the management of hazardous waste. A coalition made up of environmental organizations and citizen groups mounted the Ban the Burn campaign to defend the no-compromise point of view. Within a few months, Ban the Burn succeeded in stopping at-sea incineration in the United States. When the proponents of ocean incineration turned their attention to Europe in the attempt to salvage this high-yield technology and its commercial value, Ban the Burn campaigners dogged their trail, staging a multipronged protest that involved lobbying, international reporting, and direct actions. Ban the Burn centered on the flaws of the technology and vociferously demanded the protection of the global marine environment.

Chapter 6 highlights how some governments and private companies, well into the mid-1980s and supported by commissioned studies, insisted that ocean incineration was a safe method for the disposal of deadly chemical substances. Their insistence only served to invigorate the campaign against the practice. Two forms of protest came to the fore from 1986 onward. On the one hand, the movement, led by Greenpeace and the Oceanic Society, produced independent reports that refuted ocean incineration's environmental sustainability. These studies, in fact, proved once and for all that the practice magnified the environmental disaster of toxic waste and put human health in imminent danger. On the other hand, activists and common people alike started organizing a series of often spectacular and dramatic direct actions with the intent to disrupt and stop offshore operations. The global Ban the Burn campaign thus became immensely popular and in the end proved to be the coup de grâce to ocean incineration.

The book ends by assessing the strengths and weaknesses of the translocal campaign against ocean incineration and by underlining its most important and far-reaching legacies. The offshore burning of toxic waste transformed the oceans into a new frontier where promises of technological progress were tested.[64] Such an optimistic *envirotech* twist, though, did not ease public anxiety. On the contrary, it ignited claims for broader political representation, for more equitable engagement, and for inclusion. The translocal struggle against ocean incineration, situated at the intersection of coastal communities' demands for social equity and the climate fight, paved the way for "ocean justice," a formulation coined by the marine biologist Ayana Elizabeth Johnson.[65] The urgency of such themes persists to

INTRODUCTION

this day. Soon after his inauguration in January 2021, President Joseph Biden of the United States issued an executive order and a presidential memo meant to tackle the climate crisis through actions centered around social justice. His programs acknowledged the fragility of coastal areas and the need for federal investments to benefit traditionally marginalized coastal communities.[66] One could argue that ocean incineration ended up an ephemeral technological gamble. Nevertheless, its trajectory resonates today, warning against the toxicity of the unseen and its unfair toll on humans and the environment.

1

THE DISPOSABLE FRONTIER

The petrochemical industry forged postwar reconstruction. Plastic was the quintessential commodity of the affluent society.[1] In the United States, mass consumption, cheap production, and large exports of petrochemical and allied products drove domestic prosperity. The boom of oil derivatives also helped the U.S. government consolidate its global political and economic dominance.[2] At the same time, though, a "toxicity crisis" crept into the emerging U.S.-led plastics era.[3] Large-scale industrial processes in petrochemicals generated a number of hazardous substances whose management and treatment increasingly became vexed questions.

Throughout the 1950s and 1960s, the main way to get rid of dangerous petrochemical by-products was either to bury them in landfills or to dump them in the sea. But by the early 1970s, because of the emergence of widespread environmental concerns, both methods were considered inadequate and dangerous. Land-based disposal practices were challenged by activists at the local level.[4] A series of accidents and disasters catalyzed water-pollution-control activities, spurring the U.S. federal government to support stricter environmental regulations both at home and abroad. Seminal national legislation and international agreements such as the U.S. Water Quality Act of 1965 and the London Dumping Convention of 1972 set out rules to prevent further toxic degradation of watery ecosystems and substantially curbed the discharge of industrial pollution into the rivers and the seas. By 1972, ocean dumping was outlawed both domestically and internationally.[5]

Such a regulatory approach, however, did not solve the problem of the continuous generation and accumulation of hazardous chemical waste. Quite on the contrary, by limiting the number of options for the disposal of toxic substances, this approach made the hazardous-waste crisis even worse. The greatest challenge became to find an alternative that would simultaneously assuage citizens' anxiety, preserve the interests of the industry, and guarantee U.S. political, military, and economic hegemony.[6] In this context, ocean incineration—at the time a technological breakthrough— seemed the most viable solution for cleaning up toxic waste, and the U.S. government—the EPA in particular—bet heavily on its development, endorsing it almost uncritically.

From the beginning, however, ocean incineration presented a series of technical flaws and diplomatic issues that, in spite of its allure, greatly undermined its sustainability. The practice, indeed, was not fully efficient, and its overall impact on the marine ecosystem could not be adequately measured. At the same time, because ocean-incineration operations were carried out offshore, most of the time in international waters, in a period in which the law of the sea was still being discussed and the international governance of marine environments was being gradually institutionalized both globally and regionally, the regulation of such a practice required careful multilateral negotiations. Washington's endorsement was met with skepticism in western Europe, where a much more cautious approach seemed to prevail. Hence, even though U.S. diplomats succeeded in establishing a rather weak system of international control and in safeguarding U.S. industrial, economic, and military interests, these so-called accomplishments came at the cost of alienating the support of several allies and jeopardizing the health of the oceans.

THE COST OF PROGRESS

Large-scale industry based on hydrocarbons and synthetic chemicals took off in the United States as a result of the research and development coming out of the First World War.[7] Whereas other major powers still relied on coal as the main source for the production of their organic chemicals, many industries in the United States were convinced to switch to oil derivatives by the Great War and the high demand for chemical explosives it generated.[8] The first full-scale petrochemical plant opened in New Jersey in December 1920, operated by Standard Oil. It produced isopropyl alcohol from propylene. From that beginning, the U.S. government progressively consolidated American industry's leadership in the petrochemical sector, channeling heavy investments into the production of carbon black, propylene, methylene, and other fundamental chemical compounds.[9] During the Second World War, the U.S. petrochemical potential increased even further as U.S. industries started producing vast quantities of synthetic rubber. A series of scientific discoveries and the mastery of mass-production processes gave the U.S. petrochemical industry a substantial advantage over other industrial sectors in the United States and over international competitors as well.[10] By 1950, U.S. companies were the undisputed world leaders in the production of such substances as benzene, ethylene, polyethylene, and ethylene oxide.[11]

Considered a sort of "industry's industry" and regarded as "the central industry of modern civilization," the U.S. petrochemical sector improved the quality and durability of many commodities, launched substitutes for a limited number of natural raw materials, and contributed to making manufacturing processes more efficient and affordable than ever.[12] Chemical products rapidly became the major ingredient for such diverse industries as textiles, agriculture, construction, automobiles, and health care. Synthetic products progressively replaced metals, wood, glass, paper, natural fibers, and rubber.[13] The "polymer revolution" heralded the plastic era: cheap, light, sturdy, oil-based materials became ubiquitous.[14] Plastic, in sum, became the very fabric of modernity.[15]

By the early 1950s, driven by U.S. output, the global production of plastics totaled 1.62 million metric tons. A decade later, it topped 6.70 million metric tons.[16] In the same years, the worldwide supply of synthetic fibers grew from 69,000 to 700,000 metric tons.[17] In 1960, the U.S. domestic consumption of synthetic fibers surpassed the combined demand of wool, cotton, and other man-made noncellulosic fibers. Synthetics represented half of the women's and children's clothing market and more than a third of the whole textile industry. By the end of the 1960s, the production of cars, home furnishings, and appliances completely depended on plastic materials.[18] Pushed by an insatiable domestic demand and supported by high capital investment, the U.S. petrochemical industry boomed. It opened, for instance, more than seventy petrochemical plants in Texas alone. In 1965, the U.S. chemical-production index stood at 172.5 points, scoring higher than the index of any other industrial sector. Just five years earlier, the index had stood at 100.[19]

The American chemical industry dominated the world market. In 1966, U.S. chemical exports exceeded $39 billion, and in 1969 they topped $100 billion. U.S. chemical investments abroad increased from $572 million in 1950 to more than $3 billion by 1964; in 1967, they reached $5 billion. Most of the investment—roughly 40 percent—was in western Europe.[20] In 1966, while DuPont was inaugurating the world's largest ethylene plant in Orange, Texas, Dow Chemical was opening the doors of a similar plant in Terneuzen, the Netherlands.[21] At around the same time, ExxonMobil established petrochemical complexes in the United Kingdom, Western Germany, and France. While funding the construction of reprocessing plants, refineries, storage facilities, and infrastructure for the transportation and treatment of chemical compounds, U.S. companies also engaged in the transfer of technology and expertise. Under America's political and industrial aegis, throughout the 1960s the rate of global chemical production grew at an impressive 8.5 percent per year.[22]

The expansion of the petrochemical sector had, however, one major drawback: it generated massive quantities of dangerous industrial waste.[23] The list of toxic by-products included such elements as arsenic, lead, and mercury. There were heavy metals such as nickel, vanadium, cobalt, and molybdenum.[24] Among the most threatening industrial residues were organic liquid substances such as chlorinated hydrocarbons and other organochlorine compounds.[25] Scientists had already largely proven that organochlorines had deleterious effects on both the environment and human health.[26] These compounds are indeed ignitable, corrosive, hyperreactive, and noxious. They are also long-lived, and because of their density they tend to leach into the groundwater if not treated properly.[27] Yet the growth of the petrochemical industry had made organochlorines ubiquitous. The manufacture of such common materials as paints, plastics, pesticides, clothing, fertilizers, and medicines generated enormous amounts of organochlorines. By the early 1970s, organochlorines amounted to roughly two-thirds of the total hazardous waste from chemicals generated in the United States.[28] With an estimated production of 60 million metric tons a year, the organochlorine issue became one of the most urgent problems in the country.[29]

As a matter of fact, the proliferation of chlorinated hydrocarbons was slipping through the fingers of manufacturers and policy makers alike. Such dangerous by-products demanded special handling and extremely careful management. But because "federal, state, and local legislation and regulations dealing with the treatment and disposal" of such hazardous waste were at that time "generally spotty or nonexistent," waste-generating plants were under no pressure to manage these substances adequately.[30] An appropriate method for the safe disposal of hazardous chemical waste was conspicuously absent.[31] Up until the early 1970s, the U.S. chemical industry simply stockpiled their hazardous by-products in pits and landfills or, more often, dumped them directly into the ocean. The land-based disposal methods entailed a series of risks and had considerable downsides: they required extensive monitoring and large infrastructural investments (as much as $60 per metric ton, according to some estimates, which was indeed expensive considering the several million tons of hazardous waste being disposed of annually); the management of storage facilities demanded expertise; seepage into water sources was frequent; and dumping sites could ignite local protests and raise concerns about both the environment and public health.[32]

For all these reasons, ocean dumping became the most common method of disposal of a wide array of toxic substances, including radioactive material, sewage sludge, and, of course, organochlorine compounds.[33] By the end of the 1950s, U.S. chemical, pharmaceutical, and agricultural manufacturing alone had dumped roughly 2.2 million metric tons of toxic waste per year into the sea, which became 4.7 million metric tons per year by the end of the 1960s.[34] Thousands of barrels containing chlorinated hydrocarbons and the residue of ethylene dichloride tar, a dense waste originating from the process of vinyl chloride production, dotted the sea floor. Traces of the infamous PCBs were found in high concentrations along the Hudson River.[35] On top of these industry dumps, the U.S. Department of Defense was dumping into the oceans an unspecified amount of obsolete munitions, including spent rocket fuel, propellants, and radioactive waste. At times, this dumping was done just off the coast of the United States, but at other times it was done in water more than 6,000 feet (1,829 meters) deep.[36] In general, ocean dumping was treated as the panacea for the country's haunting and worsening hazardous-waste problem—obviously, an ephemeral illusion.[37]

REGULATING DUMPING AT HOME AND ABROAD

The publication of Rachel Carson's *Silent Spring* (1962), Ralph Nader's *Unsafe at Any Speed* (1965), and Paul Ehrlich's *The Population Bomb* (1968) heralded the advent of modern environmentalism in exposing the U.S. government's failure to protect public health. To be sure, the emergence of an ecological consciousness had deeper roots and was interwoven with multiple crises that affected U.S.—and Western—society throughout the 1960s.[38] Civil rights protests, women's and students' liberation movements, veterans' campaigns, and transnational peace activism all converged in a wider criticism of U.S. global influence and hegemony and questioned the broader "problem-solving capacity" of its leadership.[39] Environmental concerns, which culminated in the launch of the first Earth Day in April 1970, further exposed the long-term unsustainability of unbounded industrialism and unrestrained capitalism. The military-industrial complex became a main point of contention, and its impactful practices were placed under growing public scrutiny.

This new wave of environmental protests held within it an unprecedented potential for mobilization, which, John McNeill argues, was due to a convergence of interests that cut across political, class, racial, generational, and gender lines.[40] As a consequence, regulatory action became the mantra of politicians as they jumped on the environmental bandwagon. A series of initiatives led to the creation of landmark legislation such as the Clean Air Act of 1970 and the Clean Water Act of 1972 and to the establishment of the new EPA and the White House Council on Environmental Quality (CEQ).[41] In 1970, Congress addressed the issue of hazardous chemical waste by passing the Resource Recovery Act and the Water Quality Improvement Act (WQIA). The former, which amended the Solid Waste Disposal Act of 1965, called for the creation of a national system of sites for the disposal and storage of toxic wastes and officially recognized that hazardous wastes presented a "growing threat to public health."[42] The latter amended the very first piece of national legislation to address water pollution openly and directly, the federal Water Pollution Control Act of 1948. In doing so, the WQIA aligned U.S. legislation with the contemporary international framework that allowed oil discharges at sea only when consistent with the provisions of the International Convention for the Prevention of Pollution of the Sea by Oil of 1954. Moreover, the WQIA authorized the president to determine the quantities of oil and oil derivatives that, if discharged, would be harmful to public health and the environment and provided for federal research and technical assistance to local control programs.[43]

The rise and consolidation of widespread environmental concerns, fostered by a series of shocking accidents such as the Cuyahoga River fire and the Santa Barbara oil spill, turned the spotlight on the degradation and industrial intoxication of America's waters.[44] Curbing the contamination of water resources and ensuring the quality of freshwaters became national priorities.[45] Similarly, finding a way to limit indiscriminate dumping of toxic substances into the oceans rapidly climbed to the top of the U.S. government's environmental agenda. In April 1970, President Richard Nixon authorized the CEQ to study "methods of phasing out ocean dumping of sewage and toxic materials." By October that year, the CEQ had already submitted to the U.S. Congress its first *Ocean Dumping* report.[46] In it, administration experts acknowledged that the oceans were not only "economically valuable" but also "critical to maintaining the world's environment, contributing to the oxygen–carbon dioxide balance in the atmosphere, affecting global climate, and providing the base for the world's hydrologic system."[47] The report pinpointed industrial liquid waste as the largest source of marine pollution and the most urgent threat to the oceans' health. For this reason, it recommended the adoption of legislation to ban the unregulated dumping of hazardous wastes in the ocean. These pressures eventually resulted in Congress passing the Marine Protection, Research, and Sanctuaries Act (MPRSA) in 1972, a law that set up a comprehensive program for the monitoring of the ocean's health and the prevention of further degradation of the seas. The MPRSA for the first time explicitly prohibited the oceanic discharge of high-level radioactive wastes and radiological-warfare agents as well as of certain chemical and biological substances. Though generally laudable, this regulatory approach still gave the EPA ample discretionary power to decide on which toxic materials industries *could* keep discarding into the sea, and it made the agency the focal point for constant pressure and lobbying from the petrochemical industry.[48]

The pollution of the seas informed the environmental debate at the international level, too. Ocean dumping, in particular, was one of the thorniest issues addressed by the UN Conference on the Human Environment in Stockholm in 1972.[49] The consensus among the delegates was that safeguarding the ocean's health was a necessary precondition for the protection of the global environment.[50] Russell Train, the chief U.S. negotiator and head of the CEQ, captured this spirit. To him, the conference represented an opportunity to create "support for the development of a range of conventions, agreements, and other mechanisms to conserve and improve the environment," especially the marine ecosystem.[51] The final document that came out of the Stockholm Conference considered the degradation of the seas as among the most urgent threats to the biosphere and recommended that national governments enter as soon as possible into a more specific instrument of oceanic protection that would directly tackle ocean dumping and pollution in general. Translating this general consensus into shared practices and binding agreements was, however, much more difficult.

On the one hand, Washington's officials were keen to hold out for a comprehensive, multilateral agreement on ocean dumping that would satisfy, first and foremost, U.S. economic and military exigencies and priorities—that is, an agreement that would preserve U.S. national interests and prerogatives. Proof of this self-interest was a draft on ocean dumping that the U.S. government circulated during an intergovernmental meeting held in Reykjavik in April 1972, which provided only a vague and overly broad definition of ocean dumping: simply "any deliberate disposal at sea of matter from vessels or aircraft." The document's text gave each contracting party ample discretion in defining the degree of environmental hazard of the discharged matter. It did not set a common standard for the issuance of diverse national dumping permits. The U.S. draft also purposely avoided any reference to a common system of compliance. According to the U.S. proposal, the enforcement mechanism would simply be each contracting party's reassurance to use "its best endeavors to prevent the pollution of the sea."[52]

On the other hand, many western European governments found a way to moderate their individual national goals and establish a system of collective responsibility. Together, a dozen European countries on the northeastern shores of the Atlantic, on the Arctic, and on the North Sea launched a regional agreement—the Oslo Convention on Dumping of 1972—that gave them a common regulatory framework for the disposal of hazardous waste at sea.[53] The Oslo Convention dealt with the deliberate disposal of nonoperational land-generated wastes from vessels or aircraft. The agreement set common standards for the issuance of specific national dumping permits, banned the dumping of certain substances on an already-formulated blacklist, imposed special handling for the dumping of materials included on a graylist, and called for national approval before the dumping of any compound not on either list. It was the first convention to explicitly deal with dumping at sea and to specify a wide array of hazardous substances. A key element in the convention was the establishment of a supranational authority, the Oslo Commission, or OSCOM, which reviewed the state of the pertinent ocean areas, controlled for effectiveness of antidumping measures adopted at the national level, and promoted best practices among the contracting parties.

Given the distance between the U.S. government position and its main western European allies' position, finding a global, comprehensive agreement on the types and amounts of substances that could be discharged at sea and setting up a broad multilateral regulatory framework that could preserve national interests while guaranteeing effective implementation and control proved to be extremely difficult. Further negotiations and discussions were required.[54] This responsibility fell to the government of the United Kingdom, which called an international conference in London from October 30 to November 13, 1972. The Intergovernmental Conference on Marine Pollution by Dumping of Wastes and Other Matter became the principal forum within which to negotiate a universal ban on ocean dumping. On December 29, 1972, its concluding document, the London Dumping Convention (LDC), was signed by all ninety-one countries that attended the conference, including the Soviet Union, Ukraine, Canada, and all the major coastal countries of the world.

During the LDC negotiations, the U.S. government's stated mission was praiseworthy, yet its underlying attitude had not changed. Washington wanted "to develop and pursue international initiatives directed toward banning unregulated ocean dumping and strictly limiting ocean disposal of materials harmful to the environment."[55] As Henry Kissinger summarized in a memo to President Nixon, however, the U.S. delegation remained fully committed to defending America's room to maneuver. An important goal for the U.S. government was to ensure that the document's final provisions were consistent with U.S. domestic law. In practical terms, this meant the U.S. delegation would not negotiate on certain points, and yet these points were the very ones on which Washington's adhesion to the LDC depended.

Kissinger drew two lines in particular. First, military vessels and aircraft were to be fully exempt from the provisions of the final document. Second, the convention had to include the possibility of future amendments so that the addition of any new substances or criteria would match the changing interests of the U.S. government and industry.[56]

With regard to their concern about military vessels, the U.S. negotiators eventually supported the principle of "sovereign immunity" rather than pushing for full exemption. This decision was based on the fact that at that time the law of the sea was underregulated and still under discussion.[57] Insisting on a military exemption might have jeopardized other concurrent negotiations. As the civilian experts of the U.S. State Department noted, an "injection of the ocean dumping problem into the law of the sea context could not only open an undesirable debate on military vessels and aircraft but also stimulate exhorbitant [sic] claims of jurisdiction by coastal states."[58] Sovereign immunity, however, contrary to military exemption, was a widely accepted international principle, and it was thought an efficient enough shield for U.S. vessels and aircraft from the strict application of the convention.[59] In its final version, article 7 of the LDC stated that the convention did "not apply to those vessels and aircraft entitled to sovereign immunity under international law."[60] To Kissinger, this was a suboptimal compromise, but it was enough to please the Pentagon. The article did not, in fact, explicitly exclude at-sea disposal of military wastes, including decommissioned nuclear submarines and obsolete munitions.[61] With a mind to the possibility of amendments, the LDC provisions eventually mirrored the U.S. government's approach, clearly listing the substances that could not be discharged at sea.[62] The convention outlawed the dumping of high-level radioactive material, biological- and chemical-warfare agents, crude oil, pesticides (i.e., organochlorines), and plastics. Other dangerous substances such as arsenic, lead, copper, and fluorides were allowed to be discharged after national authorities issued special permits.

Russell Train defined the LDC as "a historic step toward the control of global pollution,"[63] and the convention surely reflected a new, more sensitive attitude toward the marine environment. Such a change had been made possible, to a large extent, by the scientific consensus building that, at least since the emergence of the nuclear-fallout debate in the 1950s, had animated much of contemporary environmental regulation.[64] Nevertheless, as Jacob Darwin Hamblin notes, the convention "was less meaningful than it seemed" and not only for its position on radioactive waste. "Many leading scientists, particularly health physicists, fought hard behind the scenes to preserve the essence of existing practices while using language that appeared to make environmental concessions," and it must be admitted that "the rules set forth in the convention itself did not significantly alter the practices of the signatories."[65] The LDC set up a rather weak and substantially arbitrary system of enforcement. Each contracting party maintained ample discretionary control, and national authorities remained responsible for the issuance of dumping permits. Nor did the LDC set up an impartial procedure against infractions.[66] The whole enforcement mechanism was structured around the idea that three actors had to be held accountable for the dumping: the flag state, the port-loading state, and the coastal state. But because the LDC did not specify the extent of coastal states' jurisdiction, and because many flag states were not part of the convention, it was the port-loading state that authorized the dumping and would be responsible for complying with the LDC's provisions. This paradoxical system, where the fox guarded the henhouse, was far from ideal, but it worked to convince most of the contracting parties, including the U.S. government, to ratify the LDC, which officially entered into force at the beginning of 1975.

BURN, BABY, BURN

Both the domestic and the international regulation of ocean dumping worsened the problem of hazardous chemical waste in the United States. Land-based disposal—the only option left after the ban on ocean dumping—was insufficient to cope with the limitless stockpiles of toxic chemical waste.[67] The 225 land-based incinerators active across the country could not even remotely meet the national needs; they were capable of destroying roughly only one percent of all the hazardous waste generated annually by the U.S.

petrochemical industry.[68] Thus, the U.S. government and several U.S. companies showed a growing interest in alternative methods for the disposal of hazardous waste. Among these methods, the most promising ones seemed to be chlorinolysis, wet-air oxidation, decomposition by acids and bases, chemical oxidation, and catalysis. All these methods, however, required further scientific research before they could be implemented and commercialized on a large scale. In addition, only chlorinolysis seemed to guarantee the complete elimination of toxic and hard-to-dispose compounds.[69] In contrast, at-sea incineration seemed to be fit for the purpose. This process promised, through the offshore burning of toxic industrial waste, to get rid of the petrochemical industry's dirt and simultaneously assuage public fears of environmental contamination. In this regard, ocean incineration was considered to be a panacea. It was deemed innocuous because of the buffering capacity of the seas; it held the promise of maintaining high industrial productivity while minimizing private companies' externalities; and it happened far from public view. Given the rampant hazardous-waste crisis, the lure of oceanic incineration was hard to resist.

Studies on the feasibility of at-sea incineration had been conducted at Harvard University at least since 1968.[70] Ocean incineration consisted of the thermal destruction of chemical substances at sea in tanker vessels that were outfitted with specially designed high-temperature combustion chambers. The cost for setting up an incinerator vessel and for running the procedure offshore was high. The types of hazardous wastes that could be burned in shipboard incinerators were limited in scope—they had to be liquid, pumpable, organic compounds. Nevertheless, organochlorine and organohalogen compounds, which were widely used in the manufacture of plastics, herbicides, pesticides, degreasing agents, and medicines, made up a large portion of the substances that *could* be destroyed at sea, which stirred the major industrialized countries of the world to action.[71] Millions of tons of organochlorines were readied for embarkation.

The first country to attempt at-sea incineration was the Federal Republic of Germany. Two large chemical firms, Bayer AG of Leverkusen and Solvay & Cie of Rheinberg, paved the way for large-scale development of the practice. In 1969, these two companies transformed a small ship, the

Matthias I, into an offshore incinerator set to burn chlorinated hydrocarbons generated in the production of benzenes, vinyl, and propylene.[72] The *Matthias I* was supposed to burn roughly 12,000 tons of chemical waste over the course of two years. The positive results of these initial experiments convinced other private companies that the business of at-sea incineration was viable, even a boom. Investment in this sector soared, and several ships were converted for this purpose.[73] The Dutch embarked on this adventure even more enthusiastically. They equipped special vessels with high-capacity incinerators, ready to burn millions of tons of hazardous waste in the North Sea.[74] Rotterdam soon became the home base of the most important company for at-sea incineration, Ocean Combustion Service (OCS), a subsidiary of Royal Dutch Shell. On its main ship, the *Vulcanus I*, OCS burned more than 100,000 metric tons of dangerous chemical waste in the second half of 1969.[75] Between the end of 1969 and 1975, just the waste loaded in the port of Antwerp, another major European hub for ocean-incineration operations, accounted for roughly 400,000 metric tons of hazardous waste burned in the North Sea.[76]

The seemingly successful European experience convinced the governments of Australia and Japan to start incinerating their hazardous chemical waste at sea as well. The U.S. government joined the chorus in 1974. Under the provisions of the MPRSA, the EPA was in charge of testing and development of at-sea incineration in the United States. It was tasked with establishing comprehensive national regulations covering the operations, setting up a plan that would designate specific, safe incineration areas, and formulating clear guidelines for the issuance of incineration permits. In addition, the EPA was responsible for the coordination of the scientific research that was meant to back up the incineration program.[77]

The first U.S. oceanic burns incinerated roughly 4,200 metric tons of a mixture of chlorinated hydrocarbons derived from the production of vinyl chloride and other chemicals. The EPA authorized the destruction of these wastes aboard the Dutch-owned ship the *Vulcanus I* at a site in the Gulf of Mexico, 190 miles (305 kilometers) off the coast of Louisiana.[78] Because several problems arose during the monitoring of the first burn, the EPA decided to grant OCS a second research permit for another shipload. The second burn took place at the same incineration area in December 1974. The generally favorable results of that test led the EPA to grant a special interim permit for the incineration of two more shiploads of waste, which were burned in late December 1974 and early January 1975. The agency's Environmental Impact Statements (EISs) reported that, overall, this set of burns was largely successful. Seawater samples taken from the area of contact between the incinerator plume and the ocean surface were analyzed for the

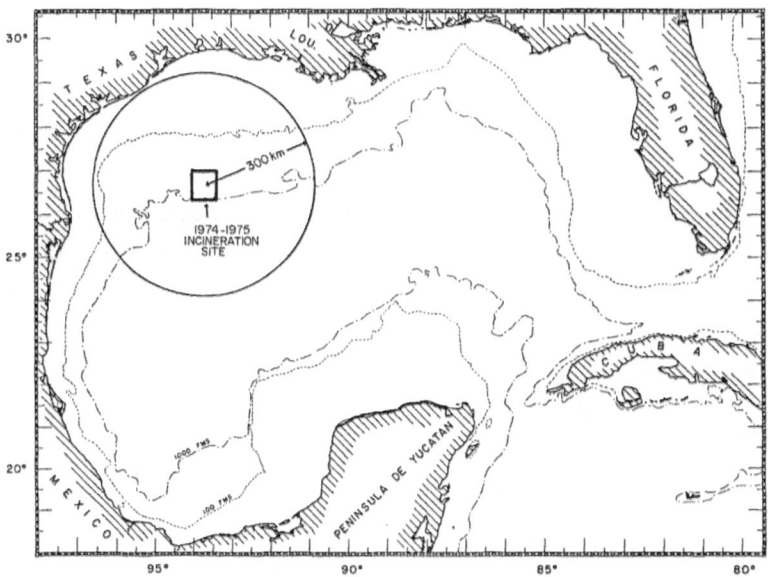

Fig. I-2. Location of 1974-75 incineration site. This site is bounded by 26°20'-27°00'N latitude and 93°20'-94°00'W longitude. From the center of the site to closest land, the distance is 305 km.

FIGURE 1.1 Location of U.S. incineration site in 1974–1975, bounded by 26°20'–27°00'N latitude and 93°20'–94°00'W longitude. From the center of the site to the closest land, the distance was 190 miles (305 kilometers).

Source: U.S. Environmental Protection Agency (EPA), *Designation of a Site in the Gulf of Mexico for Incineration of Chemical Wastes: Final Environmental Impact Statement* (Washington, DC: U.S. Government Printing Office, July 1976), 15, U.S. EPA National Service Center for Environmental Publications.

presence of organochlorines, alkalinity, and trace metals. The EPA experts said that their instruments were unable to detect any relevant change over the ocean's background levels.[79]

The optimism shown by the EPA was understandable but largely unjustified. Ocean incineration suffered from inherent structural problems that would undermine the viability of the program. First, ocean incineration was a complex, risky, and time-consuming procedure. It involved the transportation of hazardous waste from generation sites or storage facilities across the country to specially equipped port-loading facilities. The shipments had to be carefully planned, managed, and executed so as to minimize the risk of accidental contamination en route to the port. Then, the toxic waste had to be loaded aboard ships that were equipped with functioning and fully tested incinerators. Once loaded, the cargo was transported to a designated area lying at least 100 miles (161 kilometers) offshore. Only at this point could incineration start. The whole process required between six and ten workdays for every burn.[80] Meanwhile, just within that time frame, U.S. industries had generated on average roughly 250,000 more metric tons of hazardous waste.[81]

Second, monitoring of at-sea incineration was problematic. Ocean incinerators, unlike land-based ones, were not equipped with air-pollution-control systems.[82] One of the most dangerous effects of the combustion of toxic chemical substances was the emission of hydrochloride. All land-based incinerators had gas scrubs—special air-pollution-control devices that were designed to remove acidic gases and the most hazardous particles resulting from the combustion process.[83] The use of gas scrubbing, however, was not done at sea, and the first-generation incinerator vessels had no emission-control units whatsoever.[84] This meant that the gases produced from the incineration of chlorinated wastes at sea were discharged directly into the atmosphere without treatment under the assumption that the most dangerous substances from these gases would be neutralized by contact with seawater. In other words, the whole process of oceanic incineration relied solely on the ocean's buffering capacity.[85]

A third major problem was the efficiency of ocean incineration. After the first series of burns, the EPA reported that destruction efficiency had averaged 99.955 percent, measured on the basis of total organic carbon. This measurement, however, did not consider the emission of other so-called principal organic hazardous constituents (POHCs) or the more important so-called products of incomplete combustion (PICs). This was not a minor detail. PICs, which were new complex chemicals created by the recombination of unburned chemical waste, were even more toxic than their parent compounds. For example, incomplete combustion generated dioxin, a highly toxic and persistent compound. Given the thousands of metric tons of waste that vessel incinerators burned, even a relatively small percentage of unburned waste generated and emitted a huge volume of destructive substances; a relatively small burn of 1,000 tons of organochlorine destroyed at 99.99 percent efficiency still generated 220 pounds (100 kilograms) of persistent and toxic substances, which were released directly into the marine environment.[86] To guarantee sufficient incineration efficiency, the EPA mandated that incinerators aboard the ships constantly operate at temperatures of roughly 1,200 degrees Celsius. This was the only way ocean incinerators could meet the standards set for land-based incinerators, which had to burn up to 99.99 percent of the waste and up to 99.9999 percent of compounds that were classified as "extremely hazardous," such as dioxin, PCBs, and radioactive matter. Meeting these standards at sea, however, was a gargantuan task and required much more research and evaluation.[87]

Finally, a major problem was that incineration at sea took place in international waters during an era in which the law of the sea was not yet codified. It was therefore imperative to find a way to regulate the process and create common international standards for the issuing of national permits. This meant reaching multilateral agreements on many things: the procedures for the identification of the oceanic-incineration zones, the establishment of shared forms of enforcement and control, methods for coordinating scientific studies, and the sharing of relevant findings and information. The U.S. government, given the interests of its national petrochemical industry, found it crucial that any international mechanism of control be consistent with its own domestic regulation. Just as with ocean dumping, Washington was determined to exert all its power and influence while negotiating ocean incineration at the international level.

INCINERATION AT SEA, THE AMERICAN WAY

The first step the U.S. government took to affect the development of an international regulation of ocean incineration was to use the Committee on the Challenges of Modern Societies (CCMS), a scientific division of the North Atlantic Treaty Organization (NATO) that sponsored and funded a series of environmental pilot studies. Some of these studies were specifically meant to bolster at-sea incineration with scientific data.[88] In most CCMS projects, however, U.S. experts were not the ones taking the lead; this role was usually given to a NATO ally. In the case of ocean incineration, the principal investigators came from West Germany. At the beginning of 1977, the German experts launched a new CCMS project to explore the environmental consequences of offshore burning of biological substances, chemical compounds, and other dangerous materials. The result of these studies was disappointing. The German scientists noted that it was impossible to assess objectively the overall environmental impact of at-sea incineration, just as it was impossible to gauge incineration's overall effects and long-term consequences on human health. As a result of these studies, in 1977 the *Vulcanus I* was barred from the German port of Emden.[89]

Nevertheless, the U.S. government continued to invest time and resources in at-sea incineration. In London in September 1976, Washington seized an opportunity offered at the first intergovernmental consultative meeting of the contracting parties of the LDC to raise the question of at-sea incineration's overall sustainability. The discussion proved difficult. The debate reflected widespread reluctance among the delegates to consider at-sea incineration a viable way to dispose of hazardous chemical waste.[90] The U.S. delegates wanted the LDC to include ocean incineration in its agreements, whereas the negotiators of other countries, such as Spain, Sweden, and Denmark, rejected that idea, stating that at-sea incineration was acceptable only as an interim solution, pending substantial modernization and improvement of land-based alternatives.[91] The final compromise was a call for a new round of consultations among experts and a demand to draft special procedural rules on at-sea incineration before the LDC parties would reconvene again in September 1977.[92]

Western European governments, however, did not wait for another global meeting before attempting to regulate at-sea incineration on their own. Acting within the framework of the Oslo Convention on Dumping, they launched regional consultations in March 1977 in hopes of agreeing without U.S. interference on at least some "technical guidelines on the control of incineration of wastes at sea."[93] Their aim was to arrange an "operational code of practice" that could pave the way for both a regional and a global discussion on the technical and the regulatory aspects of incineration at sea. Against these attempts, the U.S. government circulated a series of special provisions for the control of incineration at sea, all grounded in principles that were far from the ones held by the European countries. The first point of disagreement, for instance, was on the definition of *incineration at sea*, which according to the American diplomats had to be regarded as "the deliberate combustion of wastes or other material on board vessels, platforms or other manmade structures at sea for the purpose of their thermal destruction." This definition was purposely broad. It avoided any reference to either the efficiency of the combustion or the delimitation of the incineration zones, two of the main pillars of the intra-European discussion.[94]

Again, the U.S. government was after an assurance that any system of multilateral control over at-sea incineration would not conflict with its own interests and plans. In this regard, the U.S. experts proposed that any control had to be exerted through two levels of assessment of incinerator performance. First, preliminary investigations had to evaluate the incinerator's ability to completely destroy substances for which only insufficient data on combustion characteristics existed. This held a great advantage for the U.S. authorities because most of the waste they burned came with a set of well-known and mostly U.S.-collected data. Second, more important, the responsibility for the evaluation of the process—including control over its broader environmental impact—was assigned to the vessel's flag state where it was a contracting member of the LDC. Where the flag state was not a contracting part of the LDC—as was the case for the incinerator the EPA used for its testing of the process (the Dutch-owned *Vulcanus I*, sailing under the Singaporean flag)—then another contracting party's authority had to carry out the vessel evaluation, usually the port-loading state. This arrangement left ample room for U.S. authorities to carry out their burns undisturbed and substantially unchecked by third parties.

At the second LDC consultative meeting in September 1977, the U.S. line won. The meeting adopted all of the U.S. recommendations in spite of several delegates' attempts to introduce measures that might have rendered the system of control more impartial. An example of this tragicomedy was when the delegates agreed that an "automatic and continuous recording of liquid waste flow rates" was necessary to guarantee an objective control of incineration at sea but then immediately recognized that the "current flow monitoring technology may not be adequate to accurately measure flow rates because of density variation between wastes and separation of blended wastes in unmixed tanks." The idea was that incinerating vessels should have onboard a series of "suitable" monitoring devices, but such devices were not commercially available. The assessment of the flow, a crucial component to understanding the real hazard of at-sea incineration, was, thus, not included "as a permit condition," and it was decided that controlling the temperature and the level of oxygen was sufficient.[95] This was tantamount to saying, "We do not know if this process is really safe or not, but we assume it is."

Another important goal that the United States achieved during the September 1977 meeting—related to the previous point—was an agreement on temperature control. Scientists and experts alike set the optimal temperature for the process of at-sea incineration between 1,300 and 1,600 degrees Celsius, an enormous challenge in the middle of the ocean. Nevertheless, the final document only noted the *minimum* operating temperature, set at 1,200 degrees Celsius.[96] This omission allowed for a wide deviation in the actual measurement, which relied on the estimated relationship between the heat of the thermocouples and the incinerator's inner temperatures. A more accurate method would have been to allow for a manual/visual measurement of the flame's temperature inside the incinerators, but this method would very likely have revealed a large discrepancy between the actual temperature of the burn and the scientifically optimal one. Once again, expediency in the U.S. position's favor officially made control of the process a practical impossibility.

The U.S. government also managed to hold a free hand over the designation of ocean-incineration sites. Washington wanted the right to determine the exact location, breadth, and number of its own offshore incineration zones. In Europe, at-sea incineration could take place only in the North Sea, within a well-defined area that had a radius of 15 nautical miles and only partly touched the Dutch continental shelf. The closest coast was approximately 70 nautical miles away. An auxiliary area closer to the Dutch coasts could be used, but only in case of extreme inclement weather. Japan incinerated oily sludge in the North Pacific and in its inland waters. Australia burned organochloride and PCB wastes in its territorial waters along the route to Singapore.[97] In the United States, site designation fell, according to the MPRSA, under the EPA's responsibility. In theory, the designation of an oceanic incineration area had to follow formal requirements, which mandated the holding of public hearings. In addition, the EPA was required to prepare an EIS for each site. The urgency of making at-sea incineration fully operational in a relatively short period of time meant that all activities for determining the viability of sites were rushed. The first designated at-sea incineration area was the Gulf of Mexico Incineration Site, which was selected without any public hearing involving the coastal communities and with an EIS that many considered incomplete, inaccurate, and unreliable.[98] For years, the Gulf Site was the only active incineration site in the United States. The area lay in the middle of the gulf, 196 miles (315 kilometers) south of Galveston, Texas, and 217 miles (350 kilometers) south of Cameron, Louisiana. It had an extension of roughly 1,892 square miles (4,900 square kilometers, roughly ten times larger than the site in the North Sea), in waters ranging in depth from 3,280 to 6,562 feet (1,000 to 2,000 meters).[99] But it was not enough. The U.S. authorities, under pressures from private companies, wanted to be free to establish as many incineration sites as they deemed necessary. Thus, the federal government blocked any proposal to regulate internationally the designation of national incineration sites. The LDC meeting explicitly left this responsibility to the discretion of national "licensing authorities."[100] In 1981, the EPA designated another area in the North Atlantic. At the same time, it discussed the possibility of creating new incineration areas off the coasts of California and Florida.[101]

A final, crucial achievement of the U.S. government regarding the LDC was the imposition of its own views on the testing of incineration efficiency. The U.S. delegation convinced their counterparts that data on destruction efficiency were more reliable and accurate than data on combustion efficiency. Destruction efficiency measured the amount of material that incinerators were able to destroy, while combustion efficiency gauged the number of residual compounds such as carbon dioxide that were released through stack gases. The minimum standard for destruction efficiency was set at 99.9 percent, which accounted for normal variations in monitoring equipment. In the end, no measurement on stack gases was required, meaning that nobody would test the interaction between the incinerators' plume and the marine environment, nor could they look at the actual efficiency of the combustion process. This stipulation made it impossible to establish a standard procedure for controlling the atmospheric pollution resulting from ocean incineration.[102]

Many contracting parties of the LDC received the U.S. insistence on and promotion of ocean incineration with skepticism. In particular, the delegations of Norway and Sweden tried to include in the draft resolution of the second LDC consultative meeting a paragraph reflecting the view that incineration at sea should be regarded "as an interim measure." Several contracting parties shared this view. The observer from OSCOM proposed the adoption of a common code of practice on incineration at sea, which the U.S. delegation promptly rejected. Doubts were raised by the Marine Environment Protection Committee of the Inter-Governmental Maritime Consultative Organization (IMCO) about the viability of burning PCBs at sea. But the U.S. diplomats pointed out that offshore incineration of these substances happened under domestic regulation.[103] To a large extent,

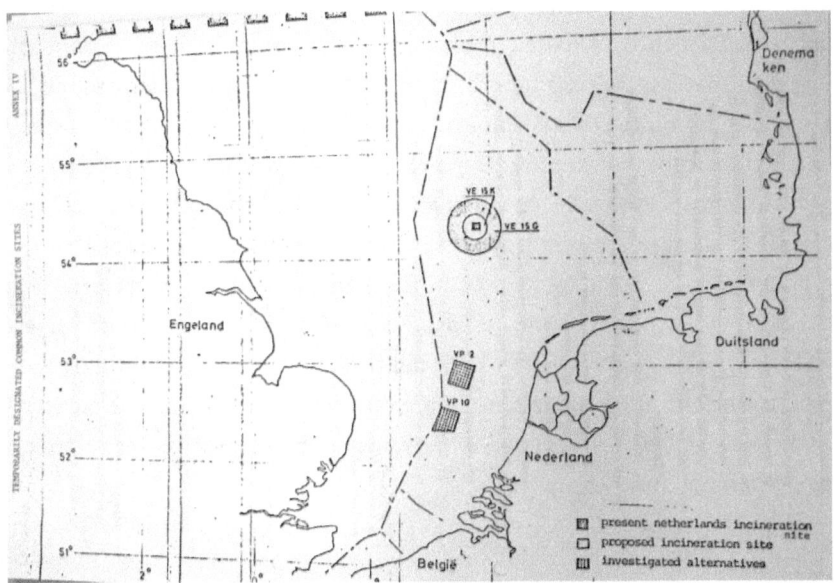

FIGURE 1.2 The main European at-sea incineration site.

Source: Convention for the Prevention of Marine Pollution by Dumping from Ships and Aircraft (Oslo Convention), Fifth Meeting of the Incineration Working Group, October 1, 1979, annex 4, Archief van Rijkswaterstaat, Working Groups Incineration at Sea, 1977–1980, Nationaal Archief, The Hague.

the U.S. government was making sure that the oceans could be its next, unrestrained frontier.

* * *

Since its inception, thus, ocean incineration tested the breadth and the limits of U.S. international leadership, power, and influence. The expansion of the American petrochemical industry had been not only one of the driving forces of U.S. global ascendancy but also one of that ascendancy's most problematic aspects. The main setback, indeed, was that the more the U.S. petrochemical industry grew, the more it generated toxic waste, the disposal of which was dangerous and expensive. The rise of a modern environmental consciousness contributed to exposing such a contradiction and imposed a few dramatic policy changes that limited the actions of American industries both domestically and internationally. This new regulation, in turn, made the disposal of hazardous waste even more difficult and encouraged investments in innovative technological solutions, such as ocean incineration. The need to preserve high productivity rates became a national priority, and, despite the many structural flaws that seemed to characterize the practice, the U.S. government endorsed at-sea incineration almost wholeheartedly. The clash between U.S. political, economic, and military exigencies, on the one hand, and the protection of the global marine environment against the chemical pollution resulting from ocean incineration, on the other, had just begun.

2
THE MILITARY-CHEMICAL-INDUSTRIAL COMPLEX

In his Farewell Address in 1961, President Dwight D. Eisenhower famously warned against the "unwarranted influence" of a growing, ubiquitous, military-industrial complex.[1] This complex could marshal national resources and political support where and when it deemed necessary, and for a while it saw ocean incineration as indispensable.[2] The main pressures came from the military's top brass, who wanted the U.S. government to think of at-sea incineration as the safest way to get rid of part of a chemical military arsenal that by the early 1970s had become untenable and embarrassing. Technical issues and rising environmental concern, in fact, made the inland destruction of certain chemical-warfare agents particularly difficult. For a specific class of chemical weapons, such as the infamous Agent Orange, it was simply impossible. A huge portion of America's chemical arsenal, thus, was set to be burned offshore.

The fact that ocean incineration even while still in an experimental stage found such an important and rather urgent military application further complicated its development and partly changed the U.S. government's attitude. One of the main consequences of such a sudden militarization, indeed, was that it laced the U.S. offshore-incineration program with confidentiality and secrecy. The EPA refused to share all the available data on the oceanic destruction of Agent Orange's leftovers and to clarify some of the most controversial aspects of this operation, which the U.S. Air Force conducted off the coast of a remote atoll in the Pacific Ocean. This secrecy, in turn, further isolated the U.S. government at the international level and irritated its allies.

As with many other defense-driven sectors and industries, the business of ocean incineration flourished. Waste-management companies leveraged the persistent hazardous-waste crisis and capitalized on a series of shocking accidents that turned national attention to it, such as the one that occurred at Love Canal, New York, in 1978. The Reagan administration's wide deregulation and anti-environmentalist approach provided the ocean-incineration business with the ideal conditions to grow. This concurrence of events gutted the EPA's impartial regulatory power and completely transformed the relationship between public and private interests in ocean incineration, intertwining them inextricably and tangling them in corruption.[3] The agency's rushed and faulty decisions favored private companies in search of high-yield investments and sidelined environmental protection. The U.S. government eventually subscribed to the idea, largely crafted by the waste-management business, that the country needed a whole fleet of incinerator vessels, and it started heavily subsidizing this sector.

Given the dangerous effects that ocean incineration had on the marine environment, at that time still largely overlooked or wittingly ignored, by the early 1980s it was making Eisenhower's bleak prophecy upsettingly real: the American people had apparently conceded to "the impulse to live only for today, plundering, for . . . ease and convenience, the precious resources of tomorrow."[4]

BLOWING UP THE OCEAN

By the late 1960s, widespread public criticism had escalated around the U.S. biochemical-warfare program.[5] A series of accidents reinvigorated the discussion on the viability of chemical and bacteriological weapons (CBWs). Incidents such as the dispersion of toxic substances near a U.S. Army proving ground in Utah that resulted in the death of thousands of sheep grazing downwind, the leak of chemical ammunitions at the Chibana depot in Okinawa, and the unrelenting use of herbicides and tear gas in the Vietnam War ignited opposition.[6] Unease about the maintenance of CBWs came from different sectors of U.S. society. Military officers and political scientists questioned the strategic value of the U.S. biochemical arsenal.[7] The *New York Times* wrote wide-ranging and critical articles, which found a broad audience.[8] *Science* published studies on the dangerous characteristics and faulty politics of chemical warfare.[9] Biologists warned of long-term consequences from chemical weapons.[10] Under pressure, the U.S. government addressed the issue both nationally and internationally. In 1972, it signed the trilateral Biological and Toxin Weapons Convention; in 1975, Congress ratified the Geneva protocol for the prohibition of chemical and bacteriological weapons.[11] Domestically, the administration launched a program for the unilateral dismantling and destruction of its biochemical stockpiles.[12]

In November 1969, the U.S. administration launched a comprehensive policy review on the use of CBWs.[13] In February 1970, a public statement by President Nixon and a National Security Decision Memorandum officially committed the U.S. government to abandoning "offensive preparations for and the use of toxins as a method of warfare" and to destroying all existing stocks of toxin agents.[14] According to this plan, the destruction of chemical and biological agents was to occur through on-site elimination. This meant that the bulk of the U.S. biochemical arsenal had to be "sterilized"—that is, made innocuous—at specific military facilities under the supervision of an interdepartmental commission composed of officers from the Department of Defense, the Department of Health, and the Department of Agriculture.[15] The White House CEQ conditioned its final approval of this plan on the completion of an interagency report that would include an EIS.[16]

Disposal started in the first months of 1971, a few months later than planned, and lasted until 1973. At the time, CBW agents were stored at several U.S. Army sites across the country. The Deseret Chemical Depot in Tooele, Utah, hosted various nerve agents (both series G and VX in bombs and shells) and stocks of mustard gas.[17] The Blue Grass Depot in Kentucky and the Rocky Mountain Arsenal in Colorado stored tons of chemical munitions. Pine Bluff in Arkansas, Anniston in Alabama, Umatilla in Oregon, and the Sunny Point Military Ocean Terminal in North Carolina were sites for the manufacturing, reprocessing, and storage of elements of the U.S. chemical arsenal.[18] Ocean Terminal in particular was the largest facility in the country for at-sea disposal of unserviceable CBWs. The U.S. Army had dumped almost 3,000 tons of mustard gas and nerve agents and 450 tons of radioactive waste at Ocean Terminal by the early 1970s.[19]

Faced with such a large and rather dispersed arsenal, the U.S. Army reviewed hundreds of methods that promised to guarantee the safe destruction of America's CBWs.[20] Given the likely ban on ocean dumping in the late 1960s and its eventual institutionalization in 1972, though, only two technologies appeared adequate to deal with the scope of the problem: chemical neutralization and incineration. Whereas the former proved to be expensive, impractical, and unsuitable for those weapons containing mustard gas and other nerve agents, the latter was presented as cost effective, and it was considered environmentally safe if well conducted. In August 1969, the army launched a pilot program at the Rocky Mountain Arsenal for the incineration of mustard gas. The program was code-named Project Eagle. The encouraging results of these burns induced the U.S. Army to incinerate an additional 3,000 tons of toxic agents between August 1972 and February 1974. These initial tests did not produce any significant discharge of dangerous liquid effluent, thus proving that incineration could be conducted in compliance with all the pertinent national and local environmental regulations of the time. As a result, the U.S. Army decided to build the Chemical Agent Munitions Disposal System, a facility that expanded the chemical depot in Tooele, Utah, and was meant to incinerate tons of hazardous substances and unserviceable chemical material.[21]

The problem was, however, that not all the chemical weapons could be safely destroyed inland. Some of the more dangerous and less manageable substances—such as Sarin gas, VX-class nerve agent, and the hallucinogenic BZ agent—endangered the local surroundings when incinerated inland. They had to be stored in either impermeable warehouses or sealed igloos.[22] Similarly, the inland incineration of a certain class of chemical agents was environmentally unsustainable. The incineration of 2,4-D and 2,4,5-T phenoxy herbicide—known as Agent Orange—entailed the risk of releasing high quantities of dioxin in the form of tetrachlorodibenzo-p-dioxin (TCDD), a dangerous compound with immediate and long-term effects on soil, groundwater, and the food chain.[23] Early monitoring reports from a storage facility in Gulfport, Mississippi, showed that a few leaks had released so much dioxin that it was already accumulating "in crayfish, mosquitoes, and fish from the drainage ditch, between seven thousand and nine thousand feet downstream from the storage area."[24] Stockpiling Agent Orange presented problems of its own. Part of the Agent Orange stockpile was in South Vietnam and part in Gulfport, Mississippi. The drums containing the highly volatile and corrosive herbicide deteriorated rapidly.[25] Once they leaked, what was to be done?

The U.S. Air Force, tasked with the disposal of 2.3 million gallons of Agent Orange, tried to develop several alternative scenarios for the destruction of the herbicide, including the commercial release of a purified version of it. None met with success.[26] When President Nixon announced the definitive suspension of Agent Orange's military use in Vietnam and when, shortly thereafter, the secretaries of agriculture, health, and the interior jointly announced the interruption of its agricultural application, the largest stock of the herbicide was sent to a remote offshore storage facility in the middle of the Pacific Ocean.[27] The final destination of 25,000 drums of Agent Orange was Johnston Island, a small atoll a few thousand miles southwest of Hawaii.[28] The atoll, which had been used as a radar station and a base for atmospheric nuclear testing, ended up holding approximately 7 percent of the entire U.S. chemical arsenal.[29]

As the historian Edwin Martini has argued, the remote atoll offered not only its isolated location but also, more important, its "liminal jurisdictional and statutory status."[30] Most of the U.S. environmental regulations, such as the Clean Air Act of 1970 and the Marine Protection Act of 1972, did not apply to the atoll, nor did the EPA have jurisdiction over the island. In other words, the atoll, which Jon Mitchell has described as one of the many "toxic territories" of the U.S. empire, was at the mercy of the U.S. armed forces. It represented an optimal spot for the final destruction of the stores of Agent Orange, which the U.S. Air Force decided to incinerate toward the end of 1972.[31] The plan, however, was not to build an inland incinerator on Johnston Island. Rather, the stocks of Agent Orange were to be incinerated at sea, making use of the brand-new, promising, and still largely unregulated practice of ocean incineration.

On January 9, 1975, while the first U.S. research burns of organochlorines aboard the *Vulcanus I* were coming to a close in the Gulf of Mexico, the U.S. Air Force formally submitted to the EPA a request to incinerate its stockpile of 2.3 million gallons of Agent Orange at sea. A series of public hearings were held between February and April 1975, after which the EPA requested that the air force once again explore the feasibility of reprocessing the herbicide before proceeding with at-sea incineration.[32] An ad hoc air force Scientific Advisory Board studied not only incineration but also deep-well disposal, microbial reduction, soil biodegradation, fractionation, distillation, chlorinolysis, and industrial reprocessing. Yet the experts were unable to find a viable alternative method for reprocessing and safely returning the herbicide to the marketplace.[33] In March 1977, thus, the U.S. Air Force resubmitted its request for ocean incineration, and one month

FIGURE 2.1 Agent Orange barrels stockpiled at Johnston Atoll, 1973.

Source: U.S. government photograph, https://commons.wikimedia.org/wiki/File:Leaking_Agent_Orange_Barrels_at_Johnston_Atoll.jpg.

later the EPA granted the final authorization to destroy a total of 16,520 metric tons of Agent Orange in three separate burns off the coast of Johnston Island.[34] The permit also included the gallons of Agent Orange still stored in Gulfport.[35] The EPA imposed three conditions on ocean incineration. First, the destruction of the herbicide had to be at least 99.9 percent effective and had to be completed by September 1977. Second, the U.S. Air Force was held responsible for the safety of the operation and the protection of all persons living downwind of the burn site. Third, technical monitoring activities had to be carried out directly aboard the incinerator ship throughout the burn series.[36]

Once the EPA issued its permit, the U.S. Air Force began its operation, code-named Pacer HO. Pacer HO started with the transfer of the 4,300 metric tons of Agent Orange stocks located in Gulfport, Mississippi. Then in the second half of July 1977, some 3,520 metric tons were incinerated aboard the Dutch-owned ship *Vulcanus I* at a designated site roughly 120 nautical miles west of Johnston Atoll. A detailed report submitted to the EPA at the end of the burn series earned a green light for the remaining roughly 8,700 metric tons of herbicide, set to be burned in two separate shiploads. The second burn was carried out from August 6 to August 16, 1977, followed by a third one, which began on August 23 and was completed on September 3, 1977.[37]

For all three burns, the EPA certified a destruction-efficiency rate exceeding 99.999 percent. The agency also stressed that none of the dangerous components of the incinerated herbicide had been detected in the stack-gas emissions. A negligible trace of dioxin was found in samples from the second trial, but, according to EPA analysts, it was caused by interference from other substances. Samples of plankton and other living organism collected across the incineration site before and after the first burn showed no relevant alteration or reaction.[38] The final report, published by the EPA in April 1978, stated that the ship combustion chambers had maintained an average temperature of 1,200 degrees Celsius, which granted a combustion efficiency of 99.99 percent. Reported minor issues concerned loose fittings, radio interference, corrosion of steel parts, and several flameouts from the herbicide. Overall, the operation was deemed a success, and at-sea incineration was regarded once again as an environmentally safe method for the disposal of extremely dangerous chemical compounds.[39]

DEFENDING THE INDEFENSIBLE

During Operation Pacer HO, the monitoring programs, including sampling onboard the *Vulcanus I*, were conducted by two U.S. Air Force contractors, Battelle Columbus Laboratories and TRW, Inc. Their data were published in the spring of 1978, seemingly showing no adverse environmental impact on air, water, or soil at either the storage site or the designated burn site. Levels of detected contaminants were below the threshold value. Dioxin—TCDD in particular—was not detected in any air samples.[40] Though reassuring, these data were at best preliminary. Further analyses on the storage facilities and their surroundings, personal recollections, and studies on local biota eventually rendered a far less optimistic picture.

One of the first environmental problems to emerge was soil contamination in the area near the storage sites, both in Gulfport and on Johnston Island. The soil and drainage ditches around the Naval Construction Battalion Center in Gulfport were contaminated by TCDD.[41] Several drums had leaked while stored at the facilities on Johnston. Further studies demonstrated that soil contamination on the island was as high as 449 parts per billion and went as deep as 30 inches (76 centimeters).[42] Even the specialists of Battelle admitted that the large quantity of herbicide spilled during storage at the Johnston Atoll represented a major environmental concern. The sandy island soil and the spill's proximity to the water table posed a considerable danger of long-term contamination in the atoll's groundwater.[43]

Further analyses revealed the limited reliability of monitoring operations onboard the *Vulcanus I*. In this regard, the EPA itself admitted shortly after the Agent Orange burns that "the sampling and analytical instruments employed [had not allowed] measurement" of different destruction efficiencies. The EPA's sources emphasized that "only limited environmental monitoring [had been] conducted" and that this had made it impossible to check the actual level of combustion efficiency. Moreover, the technology employed in monitoring the samples could detect only traces of dioxin that were "unquantifiable"—a significantly different concept from "negligible." This admission cast doubt on the whole operation.[44] After the U.S. tests were carried out, Dutch authorities routinely identified spills on the deck and contamination of other parts of the vessel, such as the burner room, the pump room, and the gangway. Several "impingements of the incinerator plume onto the deck of the vessel were reported." These leaks were attributable mostly to momentary flameouts caused by the accidental presence of water in the chemical waste or by high wind gusts. Importantly, in some cases they resulted in the crew being exposed to dangerous chemical emissions. In addition, the EPA reported that "several small spills of herbicide [had] occurred, caused by accidental breakage of a sampling bottle; sloshing of liquid through a tank hatch, as a result of rough seas; and overfilling of a tank during rinsing." The crew of the *Vulcanus I* reported noticing an orange cloud in the ocean's water. The captain of the ship maintained, however, that the color was caused not by the herbicide but by simple rust.[45]

Subsequent investigations exposed extended environmental contamination due to human mistakes and mismanagement. The EPA reported "serious release of waste . . . caused by the intentional discharge of bilge water, which was apparently contaminated with Agent Orange, into a lagoon at Johnston Atoll."[46] The lagoon's water presented such a high concentration of defoliant—as high as three to five parts per million—that the EPA experts estimated the total release of herbicide at roughly 270 pounds (123 kilograms). Meanwhile, contaminated clothing, rags, and absorbent materials were incinerated without precaution directly on the island, and the ashes buried on-site.[47] Leaks and spills were frequent, especially during the required redrumming of thousands of barrels. The herbicide leached into the soil, reaching and contaminating the island's coral structure.[48] Additional studies revealed that organisms such as algae and fungi in the atoll's coral had absorbed large amounts of TCDD and other dangerous phenols.[49] Dioxin had entered the local biota. A few eyewitness accounts demonstrated that the incineration of Agent Orange took its toll on human health, too. Hans Spoelman, a close friend of Captain Jan Haverda of the *Vulcanus I*, was aboard the ship during two burns off the coast of Johnston Atoll. He recounted that after the second shipload the captain became sick and "took irrational behaviors, such as heavy drinking bouts (not normal for him) and moods ranging from elation to deep depression." In anguish, the captain refused to do a third trip and was fired. Captain Haverda died at age forty-two in 1985. Most of his crew were dead by the age of sixty.[50]

The dubious findings provided by U.S. scientists and the overall lack of transparency shown by the U.S. authorities caused a rift between Washington and some of its Western allies over the future of at-sea incineration. In compliance with the provisions of the LDC, the U.S. government had notified IMCO of its intention to incinerate "organohalogen waste" in the Pacific Ocean. But even as the U.S. government communicated that decision, it refused to release any further information on the trace amount of material it found at the end of its incineration operations. Furthermore, the EPA stated that it had authorized the incineration of "800,000 gallons" of "a 50-50 mixture of 2,4-D and 2,4,5-T defoliant [Agent Orange]" and an additional 1.5 million gallons upon confirmation of the monitoring results. This meant that the U.S. agency had greenlighted the incineration of roughly 9,000 metric tons of defoliant in total, which was significantly less than the 16,000 metric tons the EPA reported in the end.[51] Once the U.S. government sent IMCO a notification of its intended burns of Agent Orange, the news spread rapidly. The reaction was especially harsh in Japan, where people were convinced that the U.S. government was taking advantage of these tests to burn all sorts of toxic substances, from dismissed chemical agents to, possibly, deadly PCBs, dangerously close to Japanese waters. In spite of the EPA's assurances that these burns were substantially harmless, the U.S. Department of State had work to do to convince the Japanese authorities of the soundness of the operation. Foggy Bottom issued an official statement in which it emphasized that several measurements indicated very "little release of potentially toxic residues" and suggested that the environmental impact of the burns was "virtually non-existent."[52]

These rather vague reassurances did not ease mounting international concern. In March 1977, during a meeting of a multilateral working group on ocean incineration, the Dutch delegation asked for stricter regulation of the practice and proposed a series of technical guidelines that included further checks on piping, loading, and the actual offshore burning. The U.S. diplomats rejected all these proposals out of hand.[53] Similarly, during a U.S.–European Commission bilateral meeting in June 1977, Washington ignored a request to provide more information on the nature and the quantities of the substances that it had incinerated in the Pacific.[54] When European governments asked the EPA to share the most updated and detailed information about the results of the burning of Agent Orange, they got no response whatsoever. A few months later, in September 1977, at the second consultative meeting of the LDC contracting parties, the question was brought up again. Once more the U.S. delegation dodged it.[55]

After the test series in the Pacific ended, the U.S. representatives stopped participating in the meetings of the international working group and attended only the general consultative meetings of the LDC contracting parties.[56] The third of these meetings was held in the fall of 1978, and it represented the first opportunity the U.S. government had to disclose the results of its test series.[57] On that occasion, the U.S. delegation showed three different studies confirming that the destruction-efficiency standards set by the LDC had been met and that between 99.95 and 99.99 percent of the hazardous materials had been incinerated.[58] However, especially in the case of the burning of organochlorines in the Gulf of Mexico in 1974–1975, the U.S. experts admitted that there had been "some shortcomings in the monitoring efforts" and that marine pollution had not been fully "detectable."[59] Furthermore, the U.S. studies confirmed that the release of PICs had very likely occurred in most of the burns. As far as the burning of Agent Orange was concerned, the U.S. analysts acknowledged that the testing and sampling of the surrounding waters had been carried out at only a minimal level.[60]

Due to the uncertainty of the scientific data provided by the U.S. government and the apparent impossibility of managing the incineration process in a safe way, the delegates from Scandinavian countries and Mexico asked for an international ban on at-sea incineration. The U.S. negotiators countered by proposing that mandatory control permits be issued that would assess the consequences, limit the downsides, and reduce the risks of incineration involving organohalogen chemicals such as long-lived pesticides and PCBs.[61] A fragile compromise between these positions was reached at the fourth LDC consultative meeting in October 1979, where all the delegates agreed that ocean incineration was dangerous but necessary.[62] The delegates resolved that the convention's overall intention was not to "increase amounts and kinds of wastes or other matter incinerated at sea for which there [were] suitable and practical alternatives."[63] This formula, although allowing the U.S. government to keep incinerating hazardous waste offshore, implicitly defined at-sea incineration as a temporary solution. The showdown between the opponents and the supporters of ocean incineration had just begun. In a series of meetings, the criticism coming from the Nordic countries kept being amplified. The Danish delegation was upfront about its intention to hold out for specific and strict air-quality standards; the representatives of Sweden, Norway, and the Federal Republic of Germany questioned the environmental legitimacy of at-sea incineration, insisting on limits on this practice and delineating just how difficult it was to control. Only the governments of Canada and the United Kingdom followed Washington, refusing to rule out at-sea incineration without any reference to a suitable land-based alternative.[64]

The U.S. administration tried to assuage these rising concerns but was largely unsuccessfully. President Jimmy Carter signed an executive order entitled "Environmental Effects Abroad of Major Federal Actions,"[65] but this did nothing to sort out the contradictions inherent in the U.S. position on at-sea incineration. While establishing "wide procedures for review of environmental effects abroad of major federal actions," the order dealt only with those actions that were "significantly affecting the environment," which did not explicitly include ocean incineration. Although praising the pursuit of "legitimate goals of environmental protection," the order advocated for reconciling such goals with U.S. national security.[66] For many, the creation of a modern fleet of incinerator vessels fell well within the compass of national security.[67] Only marginally mindful of the criticism and still enthusiastic about the promise of ocean incineration, the administration invested heavily in this technology. The EPA and the Department of Commerce launched a program that enhanced the nation's capability to destroy hazardous wastes at sea.[68] Both even drafted plans for new federal subsidies and guaranteed waste contracts. Administrator Douglas Costle of the EPA and Assistant Secretary of Commerce for Maritime Affairs Samuel Nemirow announced these plans with much fanfare and praised high-temperature incineration at sea as the most "effective and environmentally acceptable technology for destroying many combustible hazardous wastes."[69]

IT'S ALL ABOUT THE MONEY

In the early months of 1977, the EPA granted OCS a second special permit for a series of test burns of organochlorine wastes in the Gulf of Mexico. As in the case of the first series, Royal Dutch Shell's subsidiary employed the *Vulcanus I* and destroyed approximately 16,000 metric tons of toxic waste in four different shiploads. EPA scientists were responsible for monitoring the oceanic burns. Their measurements traced the POHCs, the most dangerous organic particles that were also the most difficult to incinerate. POHCs and other dangerous PICs were found in high concentrations in the stack-gas samples. Despite these results, the EPA reported that the destruction efficiency of the total hydrocarbons ranged between 99.991 and 99.997 percent.[70] The unreliability of these data soon surfaced, however, when laboratory tests revealed the adverse environmental and biological impact the burns were having. EPA researchers exposed fish in floating cages to surface water from the area of contact between the incineration plume and the ocean surface. Fish enzyme systems were checked to assess their reaction to specific pollutants generated by incineration. The scientists noted significant physiological stress in the enzymes. Even more interesting, when returned to clean ocean water after days of laboratory analyses, the enzymatic activity of the fish was found to be normal, which proved a direct correlation between the incineration process and alteration in the fish. The EPA interpreted the temporary nature of this effect optimistically. But caution and further research with more constant exposure for longer periods of time would have been more advisable, especially if the goal was to make incineration at sea a routine procedure.[71]

After the completion of the first two series of burns in the Gulf of Mexico and the one off Johnston Island, the EPA was tasked with preparing new, comprehensive national guidelines for ocean incineration. The new criteria were ready in 1979, but the agency initially would not release them. The EPA experts thought it was advisable to keep ocean-incineration regulation under review until further empirical data became available. Such prudence was dictated in part by mounting international pressure and in part by the doubts that circulated within the agency itself. Many EPA scientists questioned whether certain kinds of hazardous waste could ever be incinerated at sea safely and effectively. In particular, they were unsure about such compounds as polychlorinated terphenyls, a class of PCBs that due to their high heat resistance and insolubility in water mandated further study before new incineration permits could be issued.[72]

The solution to these scientific puzzles was given to the U.S. authorities quite indirectly by the Scientific Group on Dumping (SGD), a standing committee of the LDC that supervised the technological breakthroughs in ocean incineration and was responsible for updating technical guidelines to be applied internationally. The SGD drew the LDC parties' attention to any technical problems and recommended the adoption of measures meant to enhance the assessment of ocean incineration's overall environmental impact. The SGD proposed the adoption of common rules for the monitoring of the combustion process, set up procedures for rendering trace contaminants and PICs substantially harmless, identified the chief controversies when divergent opinions emerged (e.g., scheduling of burns or designation and enlargement of the incineration zones), proposed combining measurement of destruction efficiency with that of combustion efficiency, drafted sampling procedures to obtain and analyze stack gases, discussed best practices for the assessment of combustion emissions at sea, and tried to identify what new organic compounds were synthesized during the actual incineration process.⁷³ Although the SGD was attempting to harmonize ocean-incineration practices worldwide, its recommendations yielded ground to the U.S. position for the very simple fact that it did not condemn the practice explicitly.⁷⁴

EPA experts welcomed the outcomes of this international discussion, which did not refute the claim that ocean incineration was a proven technology. On the contrary, the SGD's findings perfectly mirrored the EPA's doubts, a coincidence that the U.S. federal agency interpreted as a greenlight for publishing its own regulations. Once the guidelines were published, the EPA authorized a series of new burns to destroy PCB wastes at a specially designated incineration site in the Gulf of Mexico. They were completed in 1981 and 1982.⁷⁵ To the EPA, the offshore burning of PCBs, criticized both at home and abroad, was innocuous. When the U.S. Senate Subcommittee on Merchant Marine and Tourism interrogated EPA officers, they all reiterated the same, largely positive narrative. Thomas Murphy, the deputy assistant administrator for air, land, and water use in the EPA's Office of Research and Development, testified that all the wastes the agency had incinerated at sea were converted mainly into harmless carbon dioxide and water—though, he admitted in passing, this was true only if the waste had been "burned in the right way."⁷⁶ His colleague, Kenneth Biglane, the director of the EPA's Oil and Special Materials Control Division, explained that after each burn most of the combustion products would disperse as "carbon dioxide, water and slight amounts of hydrogen chloride," all of which were then promptly assimilated in the ocean. Biglane defined the incineration of Agent Orange off the Johnson Atoll as one of his agency's "best success stories."⁷⁷

Despite all the doubts surrounding the practice, the U.S. government, the EPA in particular, went all-in for ocean incineration. The explanation for this enthusiasm is manifold. First, the galloping hazardous-waste crisis laid a foundation for their need to urgently address the issue with innovative methods. Second, there were the exigencies of the armed forces, which needed to dispose of their outdated chemical arsenal. Third, a series of incidents had set the stage by wreaking havoc on U.S. hazardous-waste-management policy. For example, Velsicol Chemical, a plant in Memphis,

Tennessee, had buried dangerous chemical components in the area for years, and polluting agents had started to leak into nearby freshwater reservoirs. In the so-called Iowa Dumpsite Horror, several kinds of toxins had leached into the Cedar River and could be detected in water supplies downstream. In Kentucky, the infamous "Valley of Drums" had made national headlines. The unsupervised site hosted thousands of barrels containing deadly industrial waste. In Lowell, Massachusetts, a million gallons of dangerous liquid chemicals were abandoned in barrels stacked ten feet (three meters) high, rusting and leaking, by a company that had gone bankrupt. Then there was the case in North Carolina where huge amounts of PCBs were illegally dumped along 210 miles (338 kilometers) of road. Several migrant workers became ill after breathing the stench, and local farmers described the situation as nothing less than an "attempted murder."[78] In New Jersey, not far from the New York Giants' stadium, a swamplike industrial site was discovered. Sampling revealed that the site contained a concentration of toxic mercury greater than could usually be found in mercury mines.[79] Finally, in 1978 the illegal dump site for Hooker Chemical at Love Canal in Niagara Falls, New York, attracted nationwide attention. Poorly buried steel drums containing thousands of tons of toxic waste had been leaking there for decades. Contaminated water seeping out of the canal had reached private houses and an elementary school. In August 1978, the State of New York ordered the permanent evacuation of 239 families and advised 100 more to leave.[80]

All these incidents transformed the management of hazardous waste into a national emergency, which ocean incineration was thought to be able to alleviate. In May 1979, Deputy Administrator Barbara Blum of the EPA admitted to President Carter that the breadth of the hazardous-waste problem was alarming.[81] The EPA and the Department of Justice launched a nationwide investigation into the most worrisome waste sites so as to prioritize them.[82] Administrator Douglas Costle of the EPA noted in 1980 that almost 90 percent of U.S. hazardous wastes were disposed of inland through "environmentally unsound methods," which included illegal burial and "midnight dumping." Some estimates spotlighted as many as 4,000 different unsafe sites, 2,000 of which were posing immediate threats to the public health and to the environment due to high concentrations of organochlorine compounds and PCBs.[83] Costle insisted that the federal government had to have innovative solutions, such as ocean incineration, because most of the dumping sites in the United States were already filled to capacity, and local communities were stringently opposed to the creation of new ones.[84]

Finally, pressure from the waste-management industry kept ocean incineration afloat and reinforced the U.S. government's commitment to it. A major breakthrough in this regard occurred in 1980, when one of the largest garbage companies of the United States, Chemical Waste Management (CWM), a subsidiary of the Illinois-based Waste Management, Inc., bought the OCS and its main incinerator vessel, the *Vulcanus I*. Within a few years, Waste Management went from a tiny company to a multinational giant. In 1968, it had operated a dozen garbage trucks in Illinois and had revenues of $68,000; by the early 1980s, it had facilities and offices in forty states in the United States and in half-a-dozen countries abroad, earning net profits of roughly $300 million.[85] The acquisition of OCS catapulted CWM and its parent company into a leading position in the world ocean-incineration market, exponentially increasing its power and influence.[86] CWM obtained permits to refurbish the *Vulcanus I*, which was recommissioned and enlarged. By the end of 1982, CWM inaugurated another incinerator vessel, the *Vulcanus II*, and started conducting burns both off the coasts of the United States and in the North Sea.[87]

The flourishing business of at-sea incineration found Ronald Reagan's newly elected administration to be a perfect incubator. Throughout his campaign, Reagan had been championing a conservative, "counter-environmental" agenda that stigmatized environmental bureaucracy and portrayed it as unnecessarily costly and detrimental to the competitiveness of American companies.[88] He immediately issued an executive order mandating comprehensive review and cost–benefit analysis for any new environmental regulation, which would be enforced by the newly created Office of Information and Regulatory Affairs.[89] Reagan later created the Task Force on Regulatory Relief, headed by Vice President George H. W. Bush, which solicited complaints from industries against any environmental law that imposed a "burden" on businesses, discouraged productivity, or contributed to "economic woes."[90] Such a neoliberal commitment characterized Reagan's pick to head the EPA, too. Anne Gorsuch, the new administrator of the agency, inaugurated a fight against "senseless regulations" that undermined the very functioning of the agency and weakened its reputation and public image.[91] Under the banner of "reorganization," Gorsuch launched plans to drastically reduce the EPA's costs, cutting crucial programs, personnel, and budgets.[92] Perhaps even more disturbingly, the EPA gave up any independent regulatory role by adopting a lenient approach toward industrial polluters and by constantly preferring settlement over sanctions.[93] Business interests, thus, could exert an unprecedented and overwhelming influence over an agency originally established to protect the environment.

CWM and other private companies operating in the field of hazardous-waste management immediately capitalized on such favorable conditions. According to Representative Barbara Boxer (D–CA), the conditions for obtaining an incineration permit for test burns in 1981–1982 were written by an attorney who worked simultaneously for the EPA and CWM.[94] An internal investigation revealed that the *Vulcanus I* had initially been authorized to incinerate only "PCBs in fuel oil," but a wording change at the last minute included "other organic components," too. This change allowed CWM to destroy many other dangerous compounds along with liquid chemical waste and thus to take the pressure off large hazardous-waste landfills.[95] This was the case, for example, with the Emelle facility in Alabama, where CWM had stored hundreds of thousands of tons of hazardous waste, including PCBs.[96] Other private companies rushed to back up the EPA's positive attitude toward at-sea incineration with supportive studies and analysis. TerEco Corp., a Shell subcontractor in Texas and an EPA partner in many of its test burns, produced a series of reports that praised the advantages of oceanic incineration.[97] In a controversial study on PCB burns issued in 1982, TerEco concluded that the oceanic discharge of hazardous substances was simply negligible.[98] CWM went even further and commissioned a series of studies that defined ocean incineration as an "extremely positive experience," a "safe and effective means of destroying liquid organic hazardous waste," and an "environmentally acceptable, safe to handle and cost-effective" method for the destruction of highly toxic industrial waste. Against the argument that alternative methods were to be preferred over at-sea incineration because the latter's real impact was still unknown, the experts on the CWM payroll argued that in the end every scientific process has to be deemed temporary. "Development of more efficient and cost-effective processes leads to the obsolescence of older ones," they maintained. For this reason, ocean incineration had to be considered a valid alternative to "older" land-based incineration practices.[99]

Buttressed by this questionable logic, the EPA and the federal government as a whole supported the expansion of ocean incineration.[100] In December 1982, miscellaneous provisions of Public Law 97-389 amending the Commercial Fisheries Research and Development Act of 1964 lifted the established restrictions on the inspection of incinerator vessels. These changes gave the U.S. Coast Guard and the EPA discretionary powers to conduct drydock and internal examinations of tanks and void spaces of any vessels, including those flying non-U.S. flags, "as would be required by a vessel of the United States." In addition, transportation of hazardous waste from one port to any designated incineration site was considered "transportation by water of merchandise between points in the United States."[101] In other words, ocean incineration and its complex operations were treated as normal, domestic naval transport, which was not subject to any special provision that might be considered too costly by those who designed the rules.

Soon after that, the EPA commissioned its very first market analysis exploring the commercial advantages of incineration of liquid waste at sea. The study, "Assessment of Incineration as a Treatment Method for Liquid Organic Hazardous Waste," was conducted by the military contractor Booz, Allen, Hamilton and was aimed at quantifying the potential size of the domestic ocean-incineration market. The analysis reported a steady growth in the waste supply, noting that the amount of waste to be incinerated increased by 48 percent just between 1983 and 1984. At the same time, the report documented that at-sea incineration capacity of U.S. industries had

FIGURE 2.2 Cover page of a Chemical Waste Management informational brochure illustrating the advantages of ocean incineration, 1986.

Source: Box 5836 (Documentation on Waste Management International [WMI]), International Institute for Social History, Greenpeace International (Amsterdam) Archives.

increased by only 18 percent in roughly the same period. Given this discrepancy between supply and demand, the assessment predicted that the sector would expand enormously and that managing the increase would require at least thirty-three brand-new incinerator ships, each with a minimum burning capacity of 50,000 metric tons a year.[102]

As a consequence, heavily subsidized private investments in ocean incineration skyrocketed. A new company called At-Sea Incineration, Inc., was granted a $55.8 million loan for the construction of two new incinerator ships.[103] Another new company, SeaBurn, Inc., successfully applied for a series of government grants and incineration permits. CWM soon doubled the volume of its operations and asked for a special permit to burn 300,000 metric tons of mixed chlorine waste over a three-year period. These burns were meant to destroy, among other things, thousands of tons of DDT. In April 1982, the U.S. Maritime Administration announced that it guaranteed with public money a multimillion-dollar loan to finance the construction of two new incinerator vessels at Tacoma Boatbuilding Company in Washington state—the *Apollo I* and *Apollo II*.[104] Less than two years later, the *Apollo I*, with a promised burn capacity twice the size of *Vulcanus I*, was christened.[105] The possibilities of burning waste at sea seemed boundless. The profit margins in the newly booming incinerator industry seemed limitless.

BLOWING SMOKE

The EPA's market analysis favored expansion of the at-sea incineration industry. Furthermore, CWM-sponsored studies pointed to the need to increase the overall ocean-incineration capacity of U.S.-based companies, contending that the liquid organic hazardous-waste market, the production of PCBs in particular, was constantly growing.[106] The problem with these studies, however, was that they were based on partial data, false assumptions, and incorrect forecasts. Even the authors of the EPA-backed market analysis openly acknowledged that the statistical reliability of their data was poor and of limited relevance due to the small size of their samples. Survey data were supplemented by confidential information, which had been supplied by unidentified industry sources. These data had been combined with EPA staff members' general and unscientific opinions and had been used to support the EPA's conclusion that a bigger ocean-incinerator capacity was needed. Various environmental organizations opposed the underlying premises of the analysis. They said that assuming a constant flow of hazardous waste was a flawed argument based on speculation, without taking into account pertinent markets' trends. Apparently, no effort was made nationally or internationally to assess the potential reduction in the volume and toxicity of hazardous-waste generation. The studies also lacked a thorough investigation of mobile-incinerator markets and did not contemplate the possible development of alternative inland technologies.[107]

On top of these questions, until the mid-1980s a clear, straightforward, and unequivocal regulatory framework was largely missing. By its own admission, the EPA had failed to address numerous issues, including the impact of an accidental or deliberate release of toxic materials into the sea, the long-term environmental consequences of the practice, and the viability of inland alternatives.[108] Jack E. Ravan, the agency's assistant administrator for water, openly acknowledged that the EPA had yet to fully review the "legal, technical, and operational concerns involving research permits."[109] The agency's licensing policy was grounded in simplistic chemical analyses of exhaust gases that considered only a fraction of the actual emissions and did not account for operational errors and faulty machinery. Any decision to grant incineration permits was usually based on a single test burn, scheduled in advance and carried out under conditions where the incinerator units were operating at peak efficiency.[110] The EPA was criticized for its monitoring standards, too. EPA inspectors usually tested stack-gas samples during the combustion of only a few, well-identified chemicals even as they ignored the release of a broad range of toxins, including dioxins, furans, and polycyclic aromatic hydrocarbons.[111] A report from the U.S. General Accounting Office noted that the EPA, with its inconsistent policy and failure to stop noncompliant operations, had given the impression of going "easy on water polluters" and had abandoned its mission to safeguard the marine environment.[112]

Pamela Zurer's long report in *C&EN News*, the magazine of the American Chemical Society, argued in late 1985 that the main problems with the U.S. ocean-incineration program was the EPA's reliance on inadequate studies and its lack of objectivity. Zurer suggested that it was the hazardous-waste-management industry itself, rather than the EPA, that was dictating the country's hazardous-waste strategy and that had paved the way for ocean incineration. Drawing on the words of Edward W. Kleppinger, an outspoken critic of ocean incineration, Zurer emphasized that the EPA had boosted the idea of a shortage of waste-disposal capacity for the sake of U.S. companies' ocean-incineration plans, thus hindering investment in valid inland alternatives. This tactic, she pointed out, perpetuated rather than solved the nation's hazardous-waste crisis. Furthermore, Zurer noted, the EPA's reluctance to set specific performance standards for ocean incineration created a liability-free market, a paradoxical situation in which hazardous-waste operators could not be held accountable for contaminating the environment.[113] According to Bruce Piasecki, who at that time was a visiting professor at Cornell University's Center for Environmental Research, the agency's insistence on ocean incineration was just "wrong." He contended that no research or development could satisfactorily answer the questions arising from ocean incineration's structural flaws, including storage, handling, and loading of wastes; no safety measures could completely erase the risk of catastrophic spills. The EPA, in other words, was touting ocean incineration as "the panacea for all the hazardous wastes problems" even though it had very little knowledge to back up its claims.[114]

Gorsuch's questionable indulgence toward the waste-management business eventually came under public scrutiny. In 1982, Congress accused the EPA head of mishandling the funds allocated to the Comprehensive Environmental Response, Compensation, and Liability Act, the so-called Superfund, passed in 1980, which was supposed to alleviate the country's daunting hazardous-waste problem. Gorsuch was deemed responsible for withholding disbursements, and when she refused to produce official records, Congress cited her for contempt.[115] The so-called Sewergate scandal cost Gorsuch and twenty-one other EPA employees their jobs and exposed the extent to which private interests were affecting environmental policy.[116] President Reagan was forced to reinstate the EPA's first administrator, William Ruckelshaus, to restore the agency's reputation and proper function. Ruckelshaus effectively improved the enforcement of pollution laws and gave new impetus to the agency's regulatory efforts.[117] As far as ocean incineration was concerned, however, the EPA held its course. In a letter to the head of the Marine Administration, Ruckelshaus pledged his unremitting support to this technology: "I can assure you that I am giving this program high priority in its development and implementation," he wrote, adding that his staff was helping companies to collect and locate the waste needed to launch new test burns.[118] The counterenvironmentalist tide in the end survived Ruckelshaus's reappointment. The assumption that nature was resilient and adaptable was all the military-chemical-industrial complex needed to hear to proceed apace.

* * *

Throughout the early and mid-1970s, the United States was confronted with the necessity of safely disposing not only of an ever-growing amount of hazardous industrial waste but also of a large, outdated, and rather embarrassing chemical-weapons arsenal, which included the remaining stockpiles of Agent Orange, the infamous herbicide that U.S. forces had been deploying in Vietnam. Washington made use of its "extended sovereignty," an exclusive control over large portions of the oceans through the military colonization of several islands scattered all over the world, to incinerate its stocks of Agent Orange in the middle of the Pacific.[119] In spite of the EPA's numerous reassurances, these burns, releasing different kinds of toxic substances, kept taking a heavy toll on the oceans' health. Furthermore, the militarization of ocean incineration made the practice largely unaccountable and stymied forms of international control. The fact that the United States insisted on defending the benefits of ocean incineration solely on the basis of strategic and economic considerations further isolated Washington internationally, irritated its neighbors, and alienated support by some of its European allies. When Ronald Reagan entered office, his administration turned a deaf ear to any kind of environmental concern and rushed to align the development of ocean incineration to its neoliberal agenda. The practice was expanded with the aim to be commercialized as widely as possible. The EPA embarked on an all-out defense of it. Soon, however, the United States would have to reckon with the consequences of such an uncompromising position.

3

TRANSLOCAL ACTIVISM

For a few years, ocean incineration remained an issue for diplomats, experts, and businesspeople, and it largely escaped the limelight. Slowly but inevitably, however, the public started investigating and questioning the overall viability of such a technology. From the early 1980s onward, the greater availability and faster circulation of new scientific data, a more widespread environmental awareness, and mounting anxiety spurred by recurrent accidents made industrial pollution a central theme in U.S.— and Western—public debate.[1] The centrality of the pollution issue increased interest in ocean incineration, too.

In the United States, the EPA kept upholding ocean incineration as a safe method for the disposal of toxic waste, dismissing criticism, and supporting the expansion of the practice. Yet a few independent scientific analyses of the burns that the environmental agency had been carrying out in the Gulf of Mexico were raising doubts about the practice. Inaccuracy in the EPA's measurements, the production and release of toxic by-products of combustion, and the cumulative effective that these substances were having, especially on the richest and most important layers of the oceans, brought several scientists to caution against further developments of and investments in ocean incineration.

For their part, transnational environmental movements and locally driven protests amplified the policy impact of this rising scientific concern. Transnational groups and environmentalist organizations such as the Oceanic Society, the Cousteau Society, and, above all, Greenpeace multiplied their efforts to inform the public about the dire consequences that ocean-incineration operations were having on both marine and coastal environments. Their strategy was threefold: first, they started publicly exposing the dangers of ocean incineration and the contradictions of the EPA's policy; second, they reached out to local communities, especially coastal ones, directly threatened by ocean-incineration operations; and, third, they started promoting a ban on ocean incineration internationally by lobbying the competent international regulatory agencies.

Local groups applied pressure from below. New organizations, such as the GCCPH, were established with the purpose of educating people on the risks of ocean incineration and opposing the EPA's plans to further expand the practice. These groups made use of the protest repertoires that characterized the contemporary antitoxics movement, adding to them specific, local socioeconomic concerns. These groups' campaign against ocean incineration gained national prominence in a few months. A public hearing that the EPA organized in Texas in November 1983 was a watershed in this regard. What was supposed to be an easy meeting to ratify the EPA's decision to authorize new burns in the Gulf of Mexico turned into a massive showcase of criticism and, ultimately, a genuine example of environmental democracy.[2]

Transnational organizations and local groups either directly lobbied policy makers and engaged with government officers or launched and coordinated popular campaigns to create consensus around pro-ecological stances.[3] These efforts resulted in a varied anti-ocean-incineration campaign that put environmental justice at its very center and linked transnational activism and grassroots coalitions in an innovative way. This campaign affected, limited, and at first at least temporarily stalemated the U.S. government's plans to beef up ocean incineration.[4]

TRANSLOCAL ACTIVISM

MURKY WATERS AND LEPER SHIPS

Between late 1981 and early 1982, Chemical Waste Management burned 3,500 metric tons of PCB wastes aboard the *Vulcanus I* in the Gulf of Mexico. Once this test burn series was completed, the EPA accelerated the U.S. ocean-incineration program. The agency approved a plan for the redesignation and enlargement of the Gulf of Mexico Incineration Site. Then it explored the possibility of establishing two additional incineration zones off the northeastern and western coasts of the United States. In August 1982, the EPA granted CWM another research permit for the destruction of several tons of PCBs and closely monitored a test burn of organochlorines aboard the newly built *Vulcanus II* in the North Sea.[5] Finally, in October 1983 the EPA issued permits authorizing CWM to incinerate 300,000 metric tons of mixed chlorine wastes over a period of three years at the Gulf of Mexico Incineration Site. These permits, which allowed CWM to operate over an area of 2,500 square miles (6,475 square kilometers) off the coasts of Texas, Louisiana, and Alabama, explicitly mentioned the disposal of approximately 80 million gallons of PCBs, DDT, and dioxin. To carry out such a complex operation, CWM was given permission to reconfigure logistics centers, transportation routes, and port-loading facilities.[6]

The EPA's decisions were grounded on a rather simple credo: ocean incineration guaranteed a nearly perfect destruction of hazardous waste. The agency's experts believed the release of toxic substances to be negligible and the incineration by-products to be harmless due to the buffering effect of the oceans' water. Russel Wyer, the EPA's representative and cochairman of an interdepartmental task force on ocean incineration, defended the practice, saying it destroyed wastes "away from populated areas" and that it only minimally affected the environment because "acid emissions from the incinerator ships" were "directly dispersed into the ocean without the 'scrubbing' process needed for land-based incinerators" and were mixed "harmlessly with the water."[7] For Wyer, who had been the EPA's project manager for the U.S. Air Force's incineration of Agent Orange off the coast of the Johnston Atoll in 1977, ocean water naturally neutralized most of the acids.[8] In the following years, however, new scientific studies proved that these assumptions were wrong. Between 1977 and 1979, research in West Germany confirmed that the incineration of organohalogen compounds at sea produced and released high amounts of toxic and persistent chemicals. As many as seven different poisonous compounds were detected in the emissions from the German ship *Vesta*.[9] Worried about possible contamination, the Dutch authorities barred the *Vulcanus I* from entering the port of Rotterdam in 1981 because of a leak in the cargo tank. A few months later, German officials found high levels of dioxin in the emissions of another incinerator vessel, the *Matthias II*, and withdrew its license.[10]

Even the EPA's Science Advisory Board (SAB), an independent committee of scientists and engineers established by Congress in 1978 and filled by Reagan with industry-aligned scientists, began to question the safety of ocean incineration and cast doubt on its sustainability.[11] In analyzing several test burns, SAB members noted a series of difficulties that were hindering the progress of the program. Among the most disturbing problems were the detection of vibrations inside the main incinerator, blockages in sampling tubes, and lost samples. While monitoring the burn of organochlorine waste aboard the *Vulcanus II*, the EPA's scientific advisers also found highly toxic dibenzofurans in samples of stack gas.[12] Desmond H. Bond, a chemical engineer on the SAB, published a widely distributed article warning against the multiple risks associated with oceanic incineration. To Bond, the hazards connected to ocean incineration were unjustifiable. He pointed out that even 0.1 percent residue of toxic emissions from a burn amounted to tons of dangerous pollutants because each incineration incident burned thousands of tons of hazardous compounds. He also wrote that "measurements, recorded data and system performance from the sequence of ocean incineration of U.S. wastes" were inaccurate and lacked laboratory verification. Finally, Bond argued that both governmental and industrial support for ocean incineration seemed to be vitiated by commercial purposes and was not grounded on scientific premises.[13]

Another major scientific concern was that at-sea incineration apparently negatively affected the oceans' microlayer. Several members of the scientific community believed that at-sea incineration was modifying the composition of the thin layer of water that constituted the oceans' "surface skin."[14] This stratum of nutrient-rich water supported a wide variety of plant and animal life, "including embryonic forms of commercially important species."[15] Acidic, organic, and metallic emissions were having a detrimental effect on this layer, changing its chemical structure, penetrating it, and reaching the "mixing zone," thus provoking a marked alteration in the water's alkalinity. Taken together, these factors were altering the ecosystem of many vital organisms. Scientific interest in the ocean's microlayer stimulated further research on the bioaccumulative effect of at-sea incineration. The accumulation of toxic materials in marine species and their possible entrance into the human food chain soon became a matter of the utmost concern.[16] The SAB called for new tests to determine the breadth of such a risk.[17] The London Dumping Convention issued new technical guidelines warning against the "undesirable effects" of ocean incineration, by which it meant the possibility that toxic by-products of offshore burns would affect both human health and wildlife.[18] Yet the EPA's experts kept dismissing this criticism and maintaining that the role of the "ocean's surface (the 'microlayer') in capturing and concentrating atmospheric pollutants and providing these materials to the marine ecosystem" was still "unclear" and that further research was needed to clarify this aspect of ocean incineration.[19]

Despites the EPA's attempts to minimize the risks of the practice, once scientific studies began to reveal the potential threat that offshore burning of chemical waste was posing to public health and the marine environment, ocean incineration outgrew the boundaries of public policy and became a sociopolitical concern.[20] Environmental organizations began to expose the fallacies surrounding at-sea incineration and to denounce the process that had removed hazardous-waste disposal from the people's oversight. Ocean incineration was framed within the broader antitoxics campaign. The global environmentalist movement was now demanding a thorough assessment of hazardous-waste production, the enforcement of alternative industrial methods, and the safeguarding of the human ecosystem.[21] Especially in the aftermath of the Love Canal incident, a new sense of urgency arose. Renewed interest in the management of hazardous industrial waste spurred people to action, and they scrutinized governmental decisions.²² "Housewives turned activists" such as Lois Gibbs, Luella Kenny, and Joann Hale, who led the grassroots antitoxics movement, spread mistrust toward unbridled commercial and industrial development and raised compelling questions about the relationship between the local environment and global pollution. The movement put forward the idea that all citizens were entitled to basic environmental rights: the right to clear air and water, the right to environmentally safe neighborhoods and public spaces, and the right to know about private companies' potentially devastating discharges.²³

Scientists, organized groups, and laypeople saw common ground in a serious critique of ocean incineration.²⁴ What a few years earlier had been heralded as the definitive solution to the disposal of hazardous chemical waste was now branded as untenable and irresponsible. Even insiders such as the captain of the *Vulcanus II* raised doubts about the viability of the technology. Quoted in the German magazine *Stern* in an exposé on incineration in the North Sea in 1980, the captain captured the spirit of the time: "I don't blame sailors when they call us leper ships," he told the reporter. "This job stinks and I can't wait for the day when I can leave this ship."²⁵

TRANSNATIONAL WATCHDOGS

Traditional environmentalist groups and newly established ecologist organizations criticized ocean incineration as an example of immoral industrialism and toxic capitalism. The disturbing images of vessels belching great clouds of black smoke over the ocean helped to frame their concerns in ethical terms.²⁶ But empirical studies, data analyses, and scientific evidence that showed a correlation between ocean incineration and environmental hazards gave them even stronger leverage. Environmental NGOs used the data, both domestically and internationally, to mobilize people against offshore burning of chemical waste, influence policy makers, and affect the outcome of multilateral negotiations.²⁷

FIGURE 3.1 Illustration by Gary Viskupic on the cover page of a story by Assistant Director of Media Relations Russel Wild, Greenpeace, 1986.

Source: Box 5309 (Correspondence and Other Related Documents on Ocean Incineration, 1977–1978, 1981–1987, 1989), International Institute for Social History, Greenpeace International (Amsterdam) Archives.

One of the environmental organizations at the forefront of the anti-ocean-incineration campaign was the Oceanic Society.[28] The society was founded in San Francisco in 1969 and was chaired by Christopher du Pont Roosevelt, Franklin Delano Roosevelt's grandson. It sponsored research as a way to stimulate a wider debate on ocean incineration.[29] In doing so, it acted as a clearinghouse for the most up-to-date science that addressed the ecological hazards of the practice.[30] Its main contribution to the anti-ocean-incineration campaign, however, rested in its ability to coordinate different local groups and transform them into an efficient and influential constituency. Under the Oceanic Society's umbrella, several organizations started pushing for the EPA's at-sea incineration program to be reconsidered.[31] The society also supported innovative regulation to take care of the needs and safety of ocean-incineration workers, and it worked to debunk the myth of the profitability of ocean incineration.[32]

Along with the Oceanic Society, another organization, the Cousteau Society, popularized the campaign against ocean incineration. Founded in New York in 1973 by the world-famous French captain Jacques-Yves Cousteau, the Cousteau Society was among the first groups concerned about the impact of the EPA's ocean-incineration program both regionally and globally on the entire marine ecosystem.[33] It sponsored independent studies to collect scientific data on at-sea incineration operations off California's coast. It also collected samples and tested water quality in proximity to incineration sites. With its concurrent interest in ecology, economy, and technological breakthroughs, it established a comprehensive critique of ocean incineration.[34] Cousteau Society activists in particular highlighted the nonsensical idea that one could designate discrete oceanic zones for incineration, calling it a fiction at odds with the actual spread of substances in an ocean. Ocean incineration's toxicity could not be restricted to a region. It was bound to affect the global marine ecosystem. The society thus felt the need to reach out to a global constituency of concerned citizens and to make the anti-ocean-incineration campaign transnational. Its activists regarded the health of the seas as something to be protected "for the generations to come." They thought that the ocean-as-a-dumping-site practice was unjust, unsafe, and immoral, carried out by advanced economies under the principle "out of sight, out of mind."[35] Captain Jacques Cousteau's words in testimony before a U.S. congressional committee in 1983 sounded a bleak alarm against a shortcut such as ocean incineration: "Do not allow fear and emotion to drive you like stampeding cattle to sea," the captain told U.S. policy makers; "there are alternatives available right now and we must go about using them right now."[36]

The Oceanic Society's and Cousteau Society's passionate endorsement of the anti-ocean-incineration campaign exposed the faults of this technology on a global scale. But no group proved to be more active or influential than Greenpeace. Established in Vancouver in 1971, Greenpeace distinguished itself during its initial years by its confrontational, spectacular style of nonviolent, direct actions.[37] Greenpeace's first protests between 1971 and 1977 involved sailing small boats to both French and U.S. nuclear-test zones in the Pacific. Simultaneously, the organization attacked the whaling industries of the Soviet Union and Japan. Animated by the Quaker philosophy according to which the simple act of watching a crime being committed brings with it a degree of responsibility for the crime itself, Greenpeace members soon became famous throughout the world. They confronted local and national authorities, challenged bans, trespassed on private property, and risked arrest. And it was clear to everyone that their actions were in service to social change, mobilization of the public, and protection of the environment.[38]

From the early 1980s onward, Greenpeace targeted at-sea incineration through a mixed strategy that consisted of commissioning scientific study, challenging regulations, spreading awareness, and putting together a transnational consensus. Greenpeace approached the issue as part of a broader toxics campaign that began by criticizing Bayer, the German chemical company that was dumping titanium dioxide in the North Sea. The group moved on to stigmatize waste-disposal policies in Australia, Japan, the United States, the Netherlands, Belgium, France, Spain, and Italy.[39] Greenpeace considered ocean incineration to be a disincentive to investment in alternative, clean technologies. The organization reached out to toxicologists, chemists, and economists in hopes of initiating an independent and comprehensive discussion on the costs and benefits of ocean incineration. Its aim was to strengthen the idea that waste treatment and disposal were but one stage in a complex cycle that included chemical manufacture and product use and that all parts of the cycle needed to be profoundly reformed.[40] Greenpeace produced numerous reports that examined the various alternative methods for the reduction, reprocessing, and destruction of hazardous industrial waste. According to the organization's research, at least thirteen different commercially available technologies and twelve more in the experimental phase could replace at-sea incineration, and twenty-five of the alternatives were cleaner and cheaper.[41]

At the same time, Greenpeace highlighted the "unnecessary" risk of transporting hazardous waste on the sea. In this regard, Greenpeace activists pointed to a paradox: for ocean incineration to work, enormous amounts of dangerous waste had to be transferred from storage facilities to harbors and then to ships, a time- and energy-consuming operation that increased the chances of mismanagement and accidents at every stage, especially considering that each load could weigh as much as 3,500 tons. Once the waste was loaded onto the ships, the trip to a specific offshore incineration zone could expose the vessels to adverse marine conditions and/or human error. Greenpeace reported that the frequency of minor accidents at sea, potentially unleashing catastrophe, was around forty occurrences per year. This rate was, for example, thousands of times higher than the rate of accidents at nuclear power plants.[42] Seen in this way, the rationale for at-sea incineration—the safe disposal of hazardous waste—seemed anything but rational.

Greenpeace openly denounced the conflicts of interest that affected ocean incineration's policies, regulations, and plans—especially in the United States. Its members argued that the U.S. environmental authorities, acting under the assumption that at-sea incineration was an innocuous process, had traded protection of the environment for defense of commercial interests.[43] Greenpeace activists maintained that the EPA was deliberately ignoring environmental risks that were much worse than the hazards of land-based incinerators. The dire consequences of any release of substances such as dioxin, heavy metals, and other toxic chemicals into the sea, which could happen because of human mistake, mismanagement, or equipment failure, were not only long-lasting but also impossible to control. For these reasons, Greenpeace campaigners held that the only alternative was to ban at-sea incineration. Regulation alone was not enough.[44] Greenpeace's vehement crusade against ocean incineration was from the beginning aimed at "changing the mind-sets of most governments and industries" to get them to abandon ocean incineration once and for all.[45]

Greenpeace accused the EPA directly, exposing its conflictual relationship with the waste-management industry and raising doubts about the legitimacy of its permit-issuance policy. Lisa Bunin and Jon Hinck, two of Greenpeace's most outspoken campaigners, sent numerous letters urging the federal agency to reconsider its decision to grant CWM more research permits in 1982–1983. Their concerns were principally environmental, but they also questioned the legality of the permits. In the eyes of Greenpeace activists, the agency lacked a comprehensive program for hazardous-waste management in line with pertinent national legislation. Greenpeace was looking for a plan that would have as its primary components reduction at the source, reuse on-site, and waste exchange. Greenpeace members also noted that numerous EPA reports dismissed environmental contamination from PCBs and other organic pollutants as irrelevant but that scientific evidence proved PCB pollution was high and persistent. Scientists had furthermore concluded that these toxic substances accumulated in living organisms, and their concentration increased as they passed through the food chain. Exposure to these compounds could provoke reproductive failures, depressed growth rates, mutations, and even cancer. With the issuance of these permits, Greenpeace leaders maintained, the EPA was favoring the release of "more PCBs, DDT, other organochlorine pollutants, and their more toxic combustion by-products into the environment."[46] Biomagnification and bioaccumulation amplified the outcomes of such a poor decision and directly threatened public health and marine fauna. Greenpeace believed that by neglecting the transportation risks, the regulatory problems, and the inadequacy of CWM's contingency plans, monitoring, and safety standards, the EPA was giving up its supposedly impartial regulatory role and public mission.[47]

The industry's contrary response to this rising concern was to double down on the technology. CWM even invited a delegation from Greenpeace aboard the *Vulcanus II* during a North Sea test burn that the EPA monitored in February 1983. The company said it wanted to show them the viability of the whole process. On that occasion, Greenpeace's U.S. campaign director, Steve McAllister, took numerous pictures of "clouds of black smoke pouring from the stack intermittently, as toxic compounds were mixed by an engineer pushing buttons at the console."[48] Reportedly, CWM executives approached the Greenpeace leader and offered to exchange information on illegal dumpers in return for Greenpeace's overt support for ocean incineration. McAllister and his colleagues read this offer as

FIGURE 3.2 Picture taken by Greenpeace's Stephen McAllister onboard the *Vulcanus II* on October 1, 1983.

Source: Courtesy of Greenpeace media library.

proof that those operating at-sea incineration were perfectly aware of its impracticality and were concerned with public campaigns such as those Greenpeace organized.

In turn, Greenpeace multiplied its educational efforts. The organization reached out to its 280,000 members and informed dozens of citizens' groups. With an eye to coordinating their actions, it contacted key activists living in the coastal areas potentially affected by ocean incineration.[49] Greenpeace sent out mailings and made phone calls to both environmental supporters and social activists. It circulated relevant information through press releases, public talks, radio announcements, and TV and national press interviews. It wrote and published fact sheets and distributed op-ed pieces. Its members consistently attended rallies, marches, and public hearings on the subject. It also passed out popular petitions and bumper stickers.[50] Throughout its public-education campaign, Greenpeace simplified the nature of the problems associated with ocean incineration. The organization blamed the process for perpetuating the production of dangerous chemical compounds, inhibiting waste reduction, and allowing industry to escape responsibility. It exposed the technology, too, saying it was unsafe because the incinerator stacks emitted an array of toxic, persistent, bioaccumulative chemicals that no equipment could accurately identify or monitor.[51] Described in this way, Greenpeace campaigners believed, ocean incineration could not take root among people in coastal communities, nor was it likely to be favored by anyone living inland either.

Perhaps more importantly, Greenpeace took the lead in promoting an international ban on ocean incineration. It implemented two tactics. On the one hand, Greenpeace engaged directly with governments and private companies, taking part in numerous international negotiations and multilateral discussions over the future of ocean incineration. In 1981, for example, it successfully applied for "observer status" at the meetings of the contracting parties to the LDC at the headquarters of the UN's International Maritime Organization in London.[52] Attendance there gave Greenpeace the ability to be involved and influential. Its representatives could affect the technical discussions and international decision-making processes concerning ocean incineration because they had access to the most up-to-date information about its development. On the other hand, Greenpeace was poised to benefit from its large network of national and regional chapters spread all over the world, with particularly deep roots in western Europe. It could mount an effective transnational campaign against ocean incineration.[53] In Europe, Greenpeace could count on Janus Hillgaard, who worked as its toxics-campaign coordinator and organized multicountry campaigns on shared bodies of water and common environmental threats.[54] Hillgaard also made sure that the anti-ocean-incineration campaign in Europe achieved important political goals. He was responsible for drafting common guidelines that helped Greenpeace activists kick off national anti-ocean-incineration campaigns in those European countries where the public was as yet uninformed about the dangers of such a technology. The guidelines included historical surveys of European countries' involvement in ocean incineration and gave comparative analyses of national companies, industrial processes, waste generation, and pertinent regulations for the different countries. Local activists were instructed to look for information on the "unavailability of land-based alternative methods" in their respective countries.[55] With this information, Hillgaard could effectively lobby national authorities and policy makers, organize regional gatherings, and participate in crucial multilateral organizational meetings such as the Nordic Council and OSCOM.[56]

In sum, Greenpeace—and many other transnational NGOs with it—made sure that ocean incineration was portrayed as a direct threat to people's everyday life and to the environmental security of entire communities and countries. The aim was to convince governments to move toward the progressive abandonment of the practice. Local people soon joined the ambitious call and put on the same kind of pressure from below.

DEMOCRACY IN ACTION

Some of the strongest doubts about and loudest protests against ocean incineration came from those citizens whose communities and vital interests were most directly threatened by this waste-disposal method. Very few residents of areas that were affected by ocean incineration saw sufficient benefits from the technology to warrant the risks connected to it. Many advocated for more research on waste reduction, recycling, and safe transportation. Others stigmatized ocean incineration as a shortcut, an "out-of-sight, out-of-mind" disposal option that did not solve any of the problems associated with the management and disposal of hazardous industrial waste.[57] Among the most concerned groups were farmers and fishers, who worried that ocean incineration's operations might disrupt their commercial activities. Migrant workers and people employed in the tourism industry were anxious about their jobs and looked for support in their communities, reaching out to churches and local environmental groups in an effort to create a broad anti-ocean-incineration front.[58]

Public opposition in local communities shifted people's focus from ocean dumping and land-based incineration to at-sea incineration. Traditional environmental organizations, newly established networks, and ad hoc, single-issue campaigns denounced the long-lasting environmental impact of oceanic burns. More specifically, the anti-ocean-incineration movement exposed the faults in the national incineration programs—their inherent contradictions, their tendency to favor business interests over public ones, and their substantial uselessness. In the United States, well-to-do citizens mobilized, too. They coordinated their efforts autonomously, launched local campaigns with TV and newspapers ads, and made sure that their fellow citizens grasped the EPA's role in using those citizens' oceanic surroundings as a testing ground for a technology that threatened their health and livelihood. These protests, the focus of which was local in nature but global in scope, were genuinely intersectional: they brought together various interests, mobilized people from different religious and educational backgrounds, called ethnic minorities and marginalized groups to action, and saw the cooperation of people across generational, professional, and ideological lines.[59]

In New Jersey, where At-Sea Incineration, Inc., had its headquarters, such grassroots activism gave rise to groups such as the Clean Water Project/New Jersey Environmental Coalition and the Ironbound Committee Against Toxic Wastes. All of them publicly denounced the risks posed by ocean incineration and its satellite industries. They criticized the unsafe transportation of hazardous waste and the largely unregulated port-loading procedures. Ironbound's campaigns, in particular, condemned At-Sea Incineration's plan to transport hazardous waste through densely populated Newark. It mobilized the local community, expanded local networks and alliances, and spread information through its newsletter and local newspapers.[60] In California, the Marin Conservation League remarked how ocean incineration presented a danger for the whole Bay Area because it emitted exhaust into the atmosphere, and the plume from an at-sea burn might be carried by the wind to San Francisco and its coastal area. "If one ship loaded with chlorinated organics were to founder in San Francisco Bay," noted Michele Perrault, Sierra Club's president and the Marin Conservation League's consultant, "the marine ecology, the recreational resource and fishery of the entire bay and much of Northern California could be devastated for years to come."[61] At the same time, the league insisted that at-sea incineration diverted resources from alternative technologies that might dispose of hazardous wastes more cleanly and efficiently.[62] Once Stauffer Chemical Co. announced plans to participate in the ocean-incineration business and burn pesticides, herbicides, solvents, plastics, liquid explosives, and PCBs, people in Indiana protested vehemently. The Northwest Indiana Coalition for the Environment denounced all such plans: "Beneath the glittery surface shown to the public . . . the nation's rapidly, quietly expanding incineration program [has been] built solidly on a foundation of widespread, poorly studied, largely uncontrolled, and virtually undisclosed toxic contamination."[63]

No local group, however, was more influential, better organized, or more vocal against ocean incineration than the Gulf Coast Coalition for Public Health. Concerned women living in the Lower Rio Grande Valley, the area most exposed to the consequences of offshore burns in the Gulf of Mexico, founded the GCCPH. After a meeting at her children's school, Sarah Kulungowski started paying attention to a strange phenomenon that was occurring—quite literally—in her backyard. Kulungowski's family lived close to a canal that flowed directly into the Gulf of Mexico; she noticed a foul odor in the area and dead fish in the pond where her husband and son went fishing. She discovered that they were due to an extremely high level of pesticides and chemicals in the seawater coming from the gulf. "A relative, who has worked for several years in pollution control for a major steel corporation located along Lake Michigan, advised me—and wisely so—to get educated on facts and regulations" about ocean incineration, Kulungowski recalled during a congressional hearing. She surmised that the fish might have been contaminated by poorly conducted and loosely regulated incineration operations taking place somewhere offshore. To assuage her doubt, she sought out information, and she thought that others living in her surroundings should be educated as well.[64]

Similarly, Sue Ann Fruge lived a tranquil, middle-class life in Harlingen, Texas, until ocean incineration encroached upon it. Fruge had never before been involved in environmental issues, but that changed when CWM conducted its test burns in the Gulf of Mexico between 1981 and 1982, some 180 miles (290 kilometers) from Harlingen. The wind carried some of the fumes inland. Ms. Fruge started noticing eye and nose irritation, and her family and friends complained of the same. This was followed by what Fruge described as an "intellectual irritation" when the EPA showed its lack of concern for the health effects of burning toxics at sea. She decided to organize a meeting with other concerned people in the Lower Rio Grande Valley. The strangely outfitted ships that they occasionally saw off the coast of their towns did not leave them indifferent anymore.[65]

Kulungowski and Fruge were soon joined by other committed and passionate women: Joan Brotman, a local social worker and organizer who had experience as a political action coordinator in the National Federation of Temple Sisterhoods, a reformed Jewish organization that advocated for social justice and civic education; Nora Deyaun Boudreaux, a Catholic secondary-education teacher who worked with several schools in South Padre Island and Laguna Vista, two coastal villages most directly threatened by ocean incineration; Gayle Runnels, who had experience in programs for stranded mammals in the gulf area and had been a member of the First United Methodist Church administrative board there; Robin Alexander, a local attorney with a law degree from Columbia University and a master's in physiology with a specialization in occupational safety and health from the Harvard School of Public Affairs, who led local farmworkers' health and safety projects and cooperated with the state's rural legal aid organization; Margaret Wells Diaz, a doctor with degrees from the Universities of London, Guadalajara, and Texas, whose main expertise lay in occupational and preventive medicine.[66] The early organizers spread the workload. Sue Ann Fruge dealt with ocean incineration's potential health hazards and planned strategies to cope with the EPA's commitment to it. Joan Brotman checked flagrant violations in the waste-management industry.[67] Gayle Runnels studied how ocean incineration affected endangered marine species—whales and other mammals in particular. Sarah Kulungowski focused on ocean incineration's inland pollution. Robin Alexander studied ocean incineration in terms of social justice, framing it as another assault on underprivileged and politically impotent racial and economic minorities. When the GCCPH was officially launched in December 1981, it attracted sports enthusiasts, fishers, elected officials, teachers, clergy, environmentalists, developers, homemakers, and agricultural workers.

From its very beginnings, the coalition positioned itself as a genuinely grassroots, volunteer-based, not-for-profit, public-advocacy group. Its board was a cross-section of the valley population, representing a multiethnic, racial, educational, philosophical, religious, and professional point of view. All the people involved in the early activities knew that they were working under particular conditions in an area affected by structural poverty with some of the highest unemployment in the nation. GCCPH's headquarters was hosted by the Harlingen National Bank, which gave local organizers a meeting space, free access to a copier, a telephone, and a gratis Texas Watts line. They started self-financing their activities and studies, relying mostly on solidarity to operate. Small donations and spontaneous local contributions allowed the GCCPH to take off. There was the shared conviction to work in defense of a geographic minority and an isolated region economically rooted in farming, fishing, trade, and tourism and now seriously threatened with the poisoning of its land, air, and waters. A large percentage of the families in the valley lived below the poverty line. Many had very little or no formal education and did not speak English as their first language. In addition, local inhabitants were already facing natural and economic hardship. The Ixtoc oil spill in the Bay of Campeche of the Gulf of Mexico in 1979 had devastated the tourist industry and damaged local fishing. A shrimp-harvesting ground of 5,792 square miles (15,000 square kilometers), for instance, had been irremediably poisoned. Recurrent volcanic eruptions in Mexico blanketed the valley with ash from hundreds of miles away. Severe crop-killing freezes had wiped out the local citrus industry. To harvest, local farmers were bound to an exponential use of herbicides and pesticides, which in turn contaminated the soil and groundwater. Frequent hurricanes also tested the resiliency of the people living in the gulf. Yet GCCPH organizers valued the "spirit of brotherhood" that seemed to animate the locals. Their motto was: "In that those of us who can, do, for those of us who cannot."[68]

GCCPH's most pragmatic mission was to "protect and preserve the Gulf from unnecessary exposure to hazardous waste resulting from ocean incineration."[69] To accomplish this mission, the coalition relied on a wider network throughout the gulf states and other coastal regions. Key members attended national and local conferences and other relevant meetings, traveled to Washington, DC, to meet with EPA officers and SAB experts, and gave talks and speeches at events held by citizens' groups and organizations in the valley. All these efforts later led to the launch of the broad Gulf Initiative in 1986, a project coordinated by the GCCPH in cooperation with the EPA's regional offices. This new organization was supposed to stimulate debate over ocean incineration. GCCPH representatives went to Florida, Mississippi, and Alabama and met with environmental groups to discuss the Gulf Initiative's implementation, goals, and activities. These links generated proposals and ideas ranging from the organization of a Gulf Celebration Day to the drafting of a Gulf of Mexico White Paper. The GCCPH created short promotional videos and filmed a "twenty-six-minute Gulf of Mexico documentary" to be used "for a nationwide television presentation as well as regional educational purposes."[70]

Under GCCPH leadership, the Gulf Initiative garnered support from the Southern Governors Conference in Kentucky, the Southern States Energy Board, and several senators and congressional representatives in the gulf region. The initiative also gained the support of other environmental groups operating in the area, strengthening ties to historical conservationists such as the Sierra Club and the National Wildlife Federation.[71] The coalition obtained grants from the W. Alton Jones Foundation, the Mary Reynolds Babcock Foundation, the William H. Donner Foundation, and the Public Welfare Foundation. It also started funding projects of its own to support the anti-ocean-incineration campaign. For instance, GCCPH coordinators decided to donate $1,000 to the Texas Marine Mammal Stranding Network to study the broader effects of chemical compounds on marine mammals. These findings were crucial to "learning more about the human health effects of toxics on the marine environment" and were used in discussions with local health specialists. The data compiled from public-health records gave fresh insights into the correlation among ocean incineration, birth defects, and cancer.[72]

GCCPH soon became one of the EPA's most attentive watchdogs. Early on, the goal of GCCPH was to collect and study data and to compare official and unofficial sources on EPA regulation and on CWM practices and procedures. The coalition closely followed the agency's permit policy and held meetings with and maintained regular correspondence with EPA officers. On multiple occasions, the GCCPH forced the EPA to address local communities' anxieties. According to Sarah Kulungowski, the EPA led ocean incineration's development simply to please private industry, while it denied local people's needs and demands for "equality."[73] The coalition argued that EPA research was inadequate when it came to health and environmental effects and lacked any true assessment of the risks involved. The GCCPH also stressed that ocean incineration did not meet the necessary requirements of the national environmental-protection laws and that EPA's research permits operated as a disincentive to genuine waste reduction, recycling, and reuse. GCCPH members put the EPA's reports to the test in the larger, independent scientific community, contacting environmental experts and asking them to review the official data on oceanic burns. In this way, the coalition challenged the very linchpins of ocean incineration. According to the activists, ocean incinerators could never be approved for land use due to their low combustion efficiency and lack of scrubbers to trap poisonous metals before their release into the air. The GCCPH mobilizers came across a statement by the U.S. Coast Guard that no technology existed for an efficient cleanup if a spill were to occur on an incineration ship.[74]

The GCCPH's overarching goal was to educate the public on ocean incineration. To this end, the group put together a series of public talks at the local level. Local activists planned informal meetings, all of which were coordinated and conducted by coalition members. They reached out to local television networks and were featured in a three-part news story devoted to ocean incineration. The coalition's activities drew the attention of radio talk shows, national TV shows, and news interviewers. Newspaper coverage was seen as an "excellent" way to raise funds and generate consensus. The GCCPH kept its constituents updated through brochures, pamphlets, and a quarterly newsletter, *Coastwatch*. It also sent out "several hundred packets of information to individuals in government, environmental groups, citizens organization, political entities, and media,"[75] becoming a trusted clearinghouse for information on ocean incineration. A GCCPH steering committee had responsibility for program development and the coordination of task forces, which included "political education, regulatory programs, resource management, and research." Its Data Management Task Force worked "on the problem of data collection, coordination, consolidation and exchange." Its members organized regular public workshops to outline the major environmental problems in the Gulf of Mexico. These workshops identified information needs, defined sociopolitical strategies, and promoted GCCPH campaigns. They made thorny issues accessible, discussing toxics contamination, eutrophication, pathogen contamination, loss of estuarine habitats, changes in living resources, waste disposal, urban/industrial development, fisheries, mineral extraction, recreation, and shipping. GCCPH's anti-ocean-incineration focus was framed within the more general goal to minimize the adverse impact of human activities in the gulf while maximizing the utilization of natural resources in the area. As Joan Brotman remarked, a small group of concerned citizens quickly became a well-respected organization and was able to give thousands of people in the Lower Rio Grande Valley the ability to "see democracy in action."[76]

HITTING THE MAINSTREAM

The pressures coming from both transnational groups and local grassroots movements eventually paid off. In October 1983, on the eve of the authorization of the three-year burn series that would allow CWM to destroy, among other organohalogen compounds, tons of PCBs and DDT in the Gulf of Mexico, the EPA was tied up in a public discussion on ocean incineration. Greenpeace's comments about the issuance of these particular research permits were on point.[77] Local demands were mounting, and pressure was rising. A thorough confrontation with the public had become unavoidable.

For the very first time since the EPA became responsible for the management of the U.S. incineration program, it duly organized—and publicized—a series of consultative hearings on this disposal practice. The first one was held on November 21, 1983, at the Jacob Brown Auditorium in Brownsville, Texas. The next day, another hearing was held at the Mobile

Gas Service Corporation in Mobile, Alabama.[78] The goal was to clarify the extent to which the issuing of the new incineration permits would affect the local communities in the gulf region. According to Ramon de Leon, a dentist who was also a member of the GCCPH, the agency tried its best to keep local communities from participating in the meetings by providing scant information about them. On the public hearing in Brownsville, for instance, de Leon noted how the EPA announced it only in a Houston-based newspaper, a city more than 400 miles (644 kilometers) away from the actual site of the hearing. "And, by the way, this newspaper is not even within the top 10 sources of information for us down in the Lower Rio Grande Valley," he remarked at a congressional hearing the next year.[79] Jon Hinck, Greenpeace's campaign leader, added that people in southern Texas had wanted to participate in public hearings for years, but they never learned in time about the meetings, which in the end "never quite happened." Before the Brownsville hearing, the required announcement was placed in small, classified ads, which went mostly unseen.[80] For de Leon, the EPA's dismissive attitude toward local people's interests—and rights—was directly related to the area's socioeconomic status and demographics: "One of the reasons that I feel, personally, that [this area] was chosen [for ocean incineration] is because we are primarily a very poor [region]—according to the *U.S. News & World Report*, we have the three lowest per capita income areas in the nation. Most of us are very strongly supportive of the Government and we do not question governmental officials. And I feel that that, as a background, is one of the reasons we were chosen as a site to have hearings because we were not going to have a flak [sic]; we were not going to present any arguments against this."[81]

When local communities did receive notification of the hearings, however, they doubled down on their efforts. They multiplied their contacts and distributed information on the meetings' times and places. They also distributed scientific studies. Well before the meetings, local people gained "a whole lot of knowledge on the incineration issue" and were ready to challenge the agency on multiple fronts.[82] The two meetings were ultimately attended by more than 6,400 people: 6,278 persons in Brownsville and 214 people in Mobile. Among the attendees were fishers, public and private employees, residents of coastal communities, migrant workers, church groups, students, and a plethora of local and state officers.[83] It was the largest crowd that had ever attended an EPA public hearing.[84] By the close of the comment period, which the EPA had set for January 23, 1984, the agency had received 2,039 letters and postcards. Most of them came from the gulf region, but the proposed permits had also attracted nationwide attention, with comments coming from forty-one states and the District of Columbia.[85] Citizens proved to be very well informed about the technical aspects of at-sea incineration and eager to testify: 123 citizens testified in Brownsville, and 26 more asked to be heard in Mobile. Their concerns revolved around the many problems connected to ocean incineration: they denounced the lack of adequate information and transparency; they blamed the ways in which the EPA planned the operation and, in particular, how it planned the transportation of toxic materials through local communities; and they challenged the agency's failure to draft strict, overarching regulations before granting the permits.[86] Local people were so motivated and organized that they received the endorsement of Governor Mark White (D) of Texas.[87]

At the hearings, the GCCPH and the Texas Rural Legal Aid Society stood out as mobilizers and coordinators of the local citizenry. Their goodwill forged alliances, ignited activism, and spread local awareness.[88] Perhaps more importantly, the GCCPH followed up on the EPA's activities after the hearings and closely monitored its decision-making process. The coalition wanted the EPA to reconsider the issuing of permits. Sue Ann Fruge, acting as coordinator of the GCCPH's efforts, attended the meeting in Brownsville and then would later go to Washington, DC, to take part in an oversight hearing by the House Subcommittee on Fisheries and Wildlife Conservation and the Environment in July the next year. On that occasion, Fruge again pilloried the EPA's dismissive attitude toward the public and the agency's offhand concern for local and national environmental groups. She said that the EPA's hearings had been planned so that "only one opponent of ocean incineration was originally slated to speak," and she stressed that massive popular participation had induced the agency to change its outlook. Considering this arrogant behavior, after the meetings in November 1983 Fruge convinced her fellow GCCPH activists to sign a petition against ocean incineration. More than 19,000 people signed, and the petition was sent to the EPA's national office. Accompanied by a TV crew, GCCPH members picketed the EPA's headquarters. Within days, the coalition delegation was granted a meeting with Administrator William Ruckelshaus, who shuffled the responsibility down to Assistant Administrator for Water Jack Ravan. Ravan reassured the group that the agency would take into consideration the people's demands and promised the agency's participation in an independent scientific forum slated for Texas at the beginning of 1984.[89]

The GCCPH capitalized on Ravan's offer and organized a scientific meeting in Harlingen, Texas, on January 10, 1984. Moderated by Brent Hunsaker and filmed in collaboration with the local station KGBT-TV, the panel saw EPA officer Marty Allen challenged by Bruce Piasecki, a well-known scientist and outspoken critic of ocean incineration. Steven Safe, a toxicologist from Texas A&M, explained the dangers related to the offshore burning of PCBs and dioxins; George Crozier of the Dauphin Island Sealab defined the EPA's risk assessment as "wholly inadequate"; and Edward Kleppinger spoke not just as a concerned scientist but as a deeply worried citizen. Before the debate was released to the public, however, Alan Rubin, an official in the EPA's Office of Water, asked the local news director not to air it.[90] At the later congressional hearing in July, Fruge denounced this attempt to silence the public, which had left many citizens in the gulf area "doubting even further the credibility and intent" of the agency.[91]

The EPA made one last attempt to salvage the burn permits. In April 1984, Steven Schatzow, the agency's hearing officer, asked the SAB to review the environmental sustainability of both ocean incineration and land-based incineration. His intent was to find in such a comparison a plausible justification for the offshore burns. Terry Yosie, Joe Retzer, and Jean Caufield, three members of the SAB, rejected the request as unfeasible. They noted that Schatzow had formulated the request to generate support for ocean incineration and that a thorough study of the whole incineration program would put the EPA "in a better position to identify specific issues critical to both land and ocean incineration." Furthermore, they said, fulfilling such a request would "indefinitely" postpone the SAB's current review of ocean incineration, a step that was "unwise" and "controversial."[92] Steven Schatzow was left with no other choice than to issue the report on the public hearings' findings, which he finally did on April 23, 1984. The report included a series of recommendations to Ravan, who was ultimately responsible for incineration permits.

Schatzow made four recommendations in his report. First, the special permit for the bulk of the waste had to be denied because any assessment of alternative technologies, a necessary requirement for both national and international regulation, was substantially inadequate. Second, he proposed that any further issuance of research permits be postponed. The State of Alabama had yet to complete its own assessment on burning, which it had delayed to gather more evidence on the viability of at-sea incineration. Without that assessment, in fact, the EPA could not issue any permit. Third, Schatzow pointed out that no special year-round at-sea incineration permit could be justified. Granting CWM these permits, he said, would allow the disposal of the waste without the completion of a preliminary "comparative analysis taking into consideration alternatives," nor would there be the necessary legislation in place.[93]

Finally, Schatzow's report stressed that the EPA could not avoid a full reckoning with public opinion. Many public comments filed with the EPA but not yet fully processed had harshly criticized its optimistic impact assessments and had underlined the inconsistencies between its permits and the National Environmental Policy Act of 1970. Other criticisms revolved around the perception that the EPA was attempting to evade substantive issues and deceive people into thinking that ocean incineration was an innocuous practice. People accused the agency of having abused its authority by trying to convert special permits into research permits. Even special permits required that the public be given an opportunity to comment in advance, so any authorization of special permits was untimely and improper, if not downright illegal.[94] On May 22, 1984, Jack Ravan, aware of the fact that a large part of the public's confidence in the EPA rested on the issuance of these permits, accepted Schatzow's recommendations and officially rejected CWM's application.⁹⁵ He cited "technical, legal and operating deficiencies." He also called for further research to correct for flaws in the information that the EPA had at its disposal. Ravan openly admitted in a press release that his decision was based largely on "the depth and the breadth of the public concern." In his words, the issue of at-sea incineration had drawn "more participation in public hearings . . . than any other subject or hearing that the Agency [had] ever, not just in this subject, but any time, drawn." ⁹⁶ The EPA could not ignore that.

The EPA's decision to deny CWM's application and suspend incineration indefinitely filled a procedural gap but did not entirely resolve the issue. For the very first time, the public had been involved in the agency's decision-making process regarding ocean incineration. But as Representative Barbara Boxer (D–CA) pointed out, it was only "the tip of the iceberg with respect to the deficiencies shown by EPA in the past in regulating ocean incineration." Ravan's momentous decision was no more than an ex post recognition "of the past inadequacies of the permitting process."⁹⁷ Numerous questions remained about whether ocean incineration was safe or even effective. Lisa Bunin of Greenpeace noted that critics were still awaiting the time when the EPA could "produce some evidence that burning toxic waste at sea and putting all our vital fisheries at peril will actually do something to help us with the present waste crisis."⁹⁸ To be sure, Greenpeace celebrated the EPA hearings' outcome as a victory. It was especially pleased with the consolidation of a network of activists. Jon Hinck stressed that in coming to its deliberations, the EPA's Office of Water had been "confronted with formidable pressure from Gulf region grassroots movements and Greenpeace, with significant additional pressure from other national environmental organizations, a small coterie of technical experts, some tenacious competing firms (and notable consultants), a scant few Congressional types, and enough people in two states' governments to tip the balance against the burns in the Gulf." Hinck warned, however, that "all we know for sure is that the decision is temporary, and the announcement was carefully worded not to discourage those people who believe in the future of ocean incineration."⁹⁹

The meetings in Brownsville and Mobile in November 1983 did not stop ocean incineration but did force the EPA to reconsider its permit-issuance policy and to opt for a moratorium on the granting of new special and research permits. The whole U.S. ocean-incineration program was at a stalemate. Those meetings were also crucial in raising the level of national awareness around the issue of ocean incineration. The mainstream press started focusing on the risks of ocean incineration, and people throughout the country were finally informed about the environmental and health hazards of the process. As a result of the meetings, the national press blamed the EPA for being too close to the ocean-incineration business and reproached it for insufficient safety procedures, a general lack of transparency, a nonserious attitude to science, and scarce scientific monitoring of its test burns.

A series of articles in the *Washington Post* and the *Wall Street Journal* pointed to the flaws in the EPA's management of the ocean-incineration program.[100] Philip Shabecoff stressed in the pages of the *New York Times* the nationwide repercussions of the meetings in Texas and Alabama. He noted how the grassroots mobilization for those meetings served as a working model for other communities across the country. In particular, Shabecoff reported, resistance was "growing in Delaware, New Jersey and Maryland because of plans . . . to burn hazardous chemicals off their shores." People feared "the dangers of accidents in transit as well as pollution generated by burning."[101] An editorial in the *New York Times* warned against the damage that ocean incineration was doing to the EPA's reputation—and, by extension, to the federal government's. Alan Rubin of the EPA Office of Water, for instance, had earned the nickname "Captain Meteorite" for saying during the hearings in Brownsville, "You have as much a chance of stopping this [ocean burning] as I have of getting hit by a meteorite." On another occasion, Rubin was reported to have said, "The chances of [an incinerator] ship splitting open in the middle of the ocean and releasing its cargo are like the chances of me going out and getting hit by a meteorite." His uncritical defense of ocean incineration was so dismissive of local concerns that even he had to admit that "in New Jersey, everybody spits when they hear my name."[102] *Time* magazine reported on the rising concern among physicists. National experts criticized the impossibility of maintaining a required minimum heat under seagoing conditions. According to them, a suboptimal temperature could allow "the escape of dangerous emissions like dioxins." In turn, these substances could taint seafood and eventually end up in the human food chain.[103] Larry Stammer of the *Los Angeles Times* later recounted the many blind spots of at-sea incineration. Spills in the ports, collisions at sea, air pollution, and degradation of the marine habitat were risks that neither the EPA nor any private company had adequately addressed. The difficulty of protecting the marine environment and its fauna was an unsolved issue. In sum, at-sea incineration was a growing industrial sector and an attractive disposal method mostly because of its liability-free character: "After an accident at sea," Stammer commented lucidly, "a cleanup is impossible and it's almost impossible to determine the origin of toxic waste." These factors made the process appealing to industry and appalling to communities at the same time.[104]

These criticisms convinced a large portion of the public that at-sea incineration was unsafe. As Representative John B. Breaux (D–LA) commented at a hearing of the House Subcommittee on Fisheries and Wildlife Conservation and the Environment in December 1983, the meetings in Texas and Alabama a month earlier had publicly exposed the extent to which the disposal of hazardous wastes at sea was confronting the nation "with human tragedies" because of toxic contamination. Even more disturbing was that the meetings had revealed that the whole U.S. hazardous-waste-management policy had, in Breaux's own words, "serious deficiencies." "If we took a public opinion poll of the people in our country," Breaux commented, "we would probably find the overwhelming majority would be opposed to putting hazardous chemicals and toxic wastes in surface impoundments, landfills, or injection wells in their backyard." He added that the momentum from the hearings in Alabama and Texas had made it so that "incinerating such wastes . . . in urban areas or at sea" generated fierce and wide opposition.[105] When polls were taken a few years later, some 69 percent of the American people still

FIGURE 3.3 People protesting against ocean incineration in Brownsville, Texas, 1983.

Source: From the *Valley Morning Star*, Harlingen, Texas, November 22, 1983, Box 5766 (Correspondence and Documentation Concerning Ocean Incineration in Europe, 1986), International Institute for Social History, Greenpeace International (Amsterdam) Archives.

"worried a great deal" about water contamination resulting from incineration of toxic waste at sea.[106]

* * *

The early 1980s changed the landscape and in part the fate, too, of ocean incineration. The first scientific studies denouncing the overall environmental risks of the practice and its dire impact on the oceans' microlayer captured the attention of a few transnational environmentalist organizations. Groups such as the Oceanic Society, the Cousteau Society, and Greenpeace openly challenged the EPA, criticizing its intention to expand the practice and designate new incineration zones in U.S. waters. More generally, however, these organizations were denouncing the shadowy relationship between U.S. policy makers and the waste-management business. The credibility of U.S. environmental regulatory bodies and by extension of U.S. environmental policy as a whole was further undermined by the emergence of a wave of local dissent, which stigmatized ocean incineration as a dangerous drift toward the commodification of natural resources at the expense of public health. Such a discourse gained traction and convinced large portions of U.S. society, well beyond those coastal communities that were most directly exposed to the dangers of the practice, to act. From the periphery to the center, the U.S. government was being challenged by rising demands for environmental justice that could not be ignored. Afraid of losing its own influence, the waste-management industry reacted.

4

RELENTLESS COMMITMENT

The controversy over ocean incineration did not end with the EPA's decision in May 1984 to deny further operational permits to Chemical Waste Management. On the contrary, it flourished on local, national, and international levels through the rest of that year and into the next. The supporters and opponents of the practice held to antithetical and irreconcilable scientific claims.[1]

In the United States, the EPA experts produced a series of studies that, although acknowledging the risks of ocean incineration, considered the process a sustainable and necessary method for the disposal of hazardous waste. According to the agency's assessments, further research could help clarify the breadth of ocean incineration's environmental impact, but the country's need for such a technology was undisputable. These assessments brought the EPA to propose new burns and support the commercial expansion of the ocean-incineration business at the same time. By the mid-1980s, dozens of incinerator vessels were about to be built in the United States.

The EPA's renewed and rather contradictory activism in favor of at-sea incineration triggered Congress to investigate the agency's management of the national ocean-incineration policy. What emerged from several hearings that both the House and the Senate held in 1984 and 1985 was a highly polarized situation. On the one hand, EPA officers and the representatives of the waste-management business who spoke at the hearings deemed the technology safe and essential. On the other hand, concerned national and local policy makers, environmentalists, independent scientists, and common citizens asked for its immediate dismissal and questioned the EPA's impartiality and credibility on the matter.

The EPA's commitment to ocean incineration was met with stark criticism abroad, too. Mexican authorities complained about the contamination of the Gulf of Mexico and the infringement of different multilateral and bilateral treaties. Several U.S. allies in western Europe subscribed to the idea that ocean incineration was too dangerous and pushed either for stricter international regulation of the practice or for its ban. The distance between these positions and the U.S. government one made any progress in setting up a common regulatory framework substantially impossible.

To break the stalemate, environmental groups resorted to a many-sided strategy that mobilized different constituencies and transformed ocean incineration into a sociopolitical battleground.[2] Anti-ocean-incineration campaigners denounced at-sea incineration's wider ecological repercussions and exposed its discriminatory nature: it disproportionally endangered economically fragile and disadvantaged communities.[3] While framing ocean incineration in terms of environmental injustice, transnational and local advocacy groups amplified people's demands in public hearings and international discussions through lobbying, educational campaigns, and direct actions.[4] The EPA and those private companies that had benefited from its policies tried to push back but were unsuccessful, while the critics of ocean incineration gained the upper hand.[5] Ocean incineration's house of cards was about to fall.

TECHNOLOGY FIRST

"To me, ocean incineration is simply another option to dispose of wastes. It should be weighed based on the scientific evidence. . . . I must quickly add that there is much controversy about the possibility of incineration at sea as a means of disposal. We need to do a substantial amount of research to determine as much about the truth of that situation as we can."[6] Just a few months after having brought the nation's ocean-incineration program to a standstill, Assistant Administrator for Water Jack Ravan reopened the door to further burns. In the aftermath of the public hearings that the EPA had held in Brownsville and Mobile in November 1983, which saw thousands of people mobilized against ocean incineration, Ravan had said his office would not authorize further burns without first issuing comprehensive regulation based on new and clear "research criteria to be incorporated into a research strategy."[7] But now, in a sudden twist in the late summer of 1984, Ravan was defending the necessity of issuing immediate research permits and authorizing new oceanic burns even before the EPA could craft adequate guidelines and a wide-ranging policy plan.

It is interesting and telling to note that the waste-management industry had already prepared for the new ocean-incineration frenzy, months ahead of Ravan's new decision. In Tacoma, Washington, and in Newark, New Jersey, Tacoma Boatbuilding and its subsidiary At-Sea Incineration, backed by $70 million in federally guaranteed loans, launched two new incinerator vessels, the *Apollo I* and *Apollo II*, in April 1984. Together, the *Apollos* promised to increase the U.S. ocean-incineration capacity to 60 million gallons of hazardous waste per year.[8] Along with OCS's *Vulcanus I* and *II*, there was now a small fleet of incinerator ships on which U.S. chemical industries could finally rely. The news of Ravan's about-face, however, soon reached coastal communities in Texas and Alabama that were already on the alert. The *Mobile Press Register* reported that the EPA was about to authorize new research burns in the Gulf of Mexico and that the agency was planning to establish new incineration zones in the North Atlantic and off the coast of California.[9] Ocean incineration was ramping up, but so was the struggle against it.

Greenpeace "toxics campaign" coordinator, Jon Hinck, wrote to Ravan in September 1984 asking for clarification. Hinck interpreted Ravan's words as a breach of faith. After all, germane research on ocean incineration was still pending, and the need for at-sea disposal of organochlorine wastes was

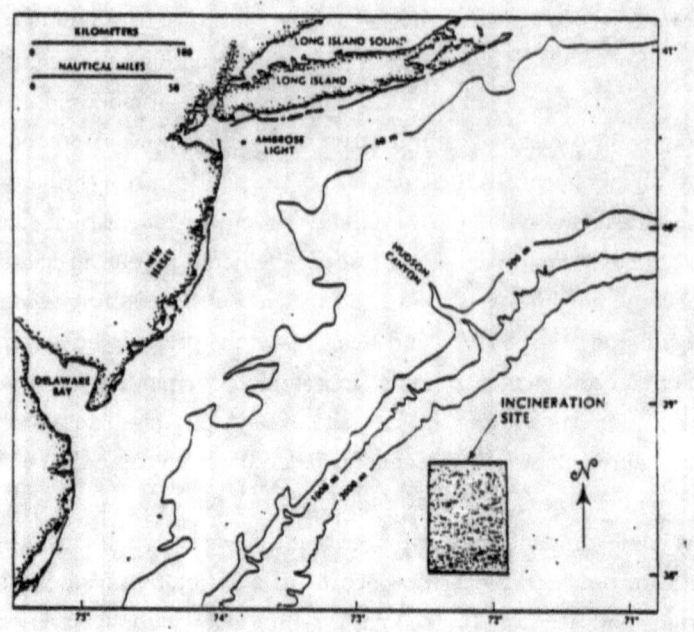

FIGURE 4.1 Location of proposed North Atlantic incineration site, 1981.

Source: U.S. EPA, Office of Water Regulations and Standards, Criteria and Standards Division, "Environmental Impact Statement (EIS) for North Atlantic Incineration Site Designation: Final," December 1981, 5, U.S. EPA National Service Center for Environmental Publications.

not yet explicitly established. Furthermore, as Hinck pointed out, the EPA had not solved the issue of accountability in ocean incineration. The technology remained largely liability free. "Last spring you asked for and received a degree of public trust by promising a careful review of ocean incineration, the impacts and implications of the technology, *before* decisions would be made on whether ocean burning in U.S. coastal waters would proceed," remarked Hinck, quite piqued. It was unacceptable, he continued, that a few months after that public promise, the EPA officer was subverting the terms of the equation.[10] Ravan replied to Hinck on November 8, 1984, writing that additional research was indeed needed to test the environmental efficacy of the whole process. "On May 25, 1984, I affirmed the need for additional ocean incineration research," Ravan stressed, highlighting that part of this decision entailed the preparation of a comprehensive research strategy that could address the legal, technical, and operational concerns involving research permits. Ravan reassured Hinck that no actual decision on new research burns had yet been made and invited him to participate in an open, public, consultative meeting on November 13. "Prior to finalizing the research strategy the agency will consider the comments emanating from the November 13 meeting," confirmed Ravan. He added that the agency was also waiting for the recommendations coming from its own Science Advisory Board, which were expected by the end of that year.[11]

At the meeting on November 13, EPA officials pushed back against public concerns by simply reiterating that they needed to wait for the SAB's final review. The board eventually released its findings in April 1985. "Report on the Incineration of Liquid Hazardous Wastes by the Environmental Effects, Transport, and Fate Committee," as the SAB's report was officially titled, provided a comprehensive examination of the "public health and environmental impacts" of at-sea incineration and compared the environmental and human risks associated with both land-based and ocean incineration. The study also expounded on the safety of hazardous wastes' transportation, the efficiency of the combustion process, and the difficulties in plume and stack sampling. The report highlighted several blind spots. The SAB identified where data were incomplete or insufficient. In particular, the board lamented the impossibility of reliably monitoring incinerator emissions and calculating their actual toxicity. This meant that, at least theoretically, an adverse impact on human health and on the environment could not be excluded—nor could it be scientifically assessed. In so stating, the study challenged the EPA's measurement of destruction efficiency, which addressed only selected compounds, as a basis for evaluating the total performance of incinerators. The study also emphasized the hazardous nature of PICs, which had never been quantified or exhaustively analyzed. SAB experts maintained that due to the "considerable uncertainty" of the data on ocean incineration and the necessity to better identify and characterize emissions, effluents, and overall operating conditions, it was impossible to exclude "the possibility of short-term and long-term public health and environmental effects." Yet, even despite these doubts, the SAB still considered ocean incineration "a valuable and potentially safe means for disposing of hazardous chemicals" compared to land-based incineration methods. It recommended strengthening the EPA's existing programs rather than discontinuing them. The panel stressed that any identified uncertainties applied equally to land-based and oceanic incineration and, in many cases, to other common combustion processes as well. For this reason, the scientists on the board would not settle on a negative assessment of ocean incineration's impact.[12]

Presenting the results of the report to Lee Thomas, the EPA's new administrator, Norton Nelson and Rolf Hartung explained that ocean incineration, in spite of the shortcomings, was largely advisable.[13] The two experts framed the incineration of hazardous waste at sea as "a very important part of the Agency's strategy to properly manage and dispose of hazardous chemicals." In the end, they stressed, ocean incineration had produced "no adverse consequences to the public health or the environment." The "considerable uncertainty" that existed, including the assessment of emissions' overall toxicity, meant that further testing and research had to be carried out, mostly through the granting of new at-sea incineration permits. Hence, it was recommended that the agency enhance its overall incineration capability by pursuing the ocean-incineration program and to increase the awareness of "the public to realize the benefits of this waste disposal technology."[14]

Almost simultaneously, the EPA's Office of Policy, Planning, and Evaluation (OPPE) published another study in March 1985. Titled "Assessment of Incineration as a Treatment Method for Liquid Organic Hazardous Wastes," it reviewed ocean incineration's technology, regulation, commercial potential, environmental and health risks, and public concerns.[15] Assistant Administrator Milton Russell at the OPPE outlined this study to James Barnes, the EPA's acting deputy administrator, using rather cautious tones. Russell emphasized that the OPPE's market analysis rested on volatile data, that the risk assessment included "extensive sensitivity analysis," and that essentially the study needed additional information. Russell recognized the existence of "little adverse health or environmental impact" and agreed, in general terms, "with many citizens who are concerned about protecting our country's marine environment." Russell also argued that the agency's position was objectively complicated because the regulation occurred "in three different programs under three different statutes," which made it difficult to collect and organize up-to-date information on which to ground a policy plan. According to the OPPE's findings, however, Russell felt that at-sea incineration could be considered "an environmentally sound treatment technology," which offered "advantages over current disposal options for liquid organic hazardous wastes under some circumstances." Thus, he tried to belittle citizens' opposition to ocean incineration. To him, people along the Gulf of Mexico were concerned about ocean incineration because they held the incorrect assumption that the practice would negatively affect the marine and coastal environment.[16] Russell believed that all these communities needed was reassurance, "given the current evidence indicating little adverse health or environmental impact from incineration, the safeguards provided by existing and proposed regulations, the existence of risks of some degree from other alternatives, and the need for sound methods of treatment and disposal for liquid organic hazardous wastes," as stated in the OPPE's report. The report concluded that it was "imperative for the nation to maintain the option of carefully controlled and monitored incineration activities on land and at sea."[17]

The OPPE's study substantially upheld the SAB's report. The EPA essentially regarded at-sea incineration as a safe method for the disposal of hazardous waste. Both reviews indicated "no clear preference for ocean or land incineration in terms of risks to human health and the environment," and both panels deemed land-based and oceanic incinerators "valuable and environmentally sound."[18] Perhaps even more interestingly, both reports recommended that the EPA favor the expansion of the country's broader incineration capacity and assumed a constant rise in the production of hazardous waste. Thus, the EPA's Office of Water, going on preliminary drafts of both the SAB and OPPE studies, published a comprehensive review of the whole U.S. ocean-incineration program in February 1985. Titled "Incineration-at-Sea: Research Strategy," the document called for more research burns so as to gather new data on incineration performance, the toxicity of gas emissions, and the broader environmental effects of the technology. The plan dismissed scientists' concerns about bioaccumulation on the oceanic microlayer. The EPA's research strategy stated that "the dimensions and composition of the surface microlayer" had not been thoroughly defined yet and that "the ecological significance of the living portion of the microlayer" was still "poorly understood."[19] The oceans' microlayer played only an "apparently" vital role; according to a later report by the U.S. Congress Office of Technology Assessment (OTA), the layer's "ability to become enriched in toxic organic compounds and metals," though raising "legitimate concerns," was unfortunately impossible to verify without "the development of an adequate methodology to sample and monitor" it.[20]

Based on these findings and given the earlier congressional amendments to the Resource Conservation and Recovery Act of 1984, the agency recommended the launch of as many as thirty-three new incineration vessels operating full-time.[21] In spite of the scientific impossibility of determining the extent to which ocean incineration was actually affecting the oceans' health or endangering humans and other life forms, the EPA decided to boost the technology. Thus, even before the SAB and OPPE studies were released, the EPA publicly released new guidelines on February 28, 1985, and included an open call for incinerator-ship companies to submit proposals to conduct extensive research burns. According to the EPA, the purpose of these burns was to identify specific chemicals in the stack emissions, determine the fate of emissions once they left the stack, and assess the risk of exposure and resultant adverse effects on human health and marine ecosystems.[22] New research permits were immediately issued for a nineteen-day oceanic burn, during which the agency experts were to conduct wide-ranging sampling and monitoring. In these burns, of course, CWM would incinerate tons of toxic waste, including PCBs, in a newly designed incineration zone in the Atlantic Ocean.[23] The EPA's relentless commitment to ocean incineration triggered reactions at home and abroad.[24]

THE PEOPLE'S OVERSIGHT

The EPA pursued its goals seemingly unaffected by external opposition and scientific criticism. Congress meanwhile had already started to closely scrutinize ocean incineration.[25] The lead was taken by Representative Barbara Boxer (D–CA), and both the House and the Senate had put forward a series of actions aimed at reviewing, reassessing, and possibly modifying U.S. ocean-incineration policy. Beginning in July 1984, Congress held a series of public hearings on the matter; the EPA's dismissive attitude toward the public was seen as harmful to the government's credibility. The agency's lack of transparency, its shadowy relations with the waste-management business, and, as Boxer noted, President Reagan's decision to appoint former EPA administrator Anne Gorsuch as chair of the National Advisory Committee on Oceans and Atmosphere further aggravated the overall crisis of legitimacy.[26] Moreover, the congressional hearings were particularly urgent given the environmental agency's decision to proceed with new research permits, even without, stated Boxer, "the information necessary to evaluate and comment intelligently on the proposed regulations."[27]

The first public hearings took place in July 1984 before the House Subcommittee on Environment, Energy, and Natural Resources, with Boxer as acting chair. In her opening statement, Boxer said the relevance of the hearing revolved around the "environmental health of our people." She recalled her shock that the EPA was planning a test burn off the coast of California. But what disappointed her most was the EPA's indifferent attitude toward the public: "These plans had proceeded . . . without any apparent notification to citizens who might be affected or opportunity for public comment." Boxer called for a congressional investigation because it had become "too apparent that the secretiveness of the Pacific site designation process was not unique, but typical of EPA's mode of action with respect to ocean incineration." The EPA kept public involvement at a minimum. The permits for the burns in the Gulf of Mexico were issued without the (mandatory) publication of an EIS; when the public was notified, relevant information was omitted, and opportunities for comments were few. "At each step," Boxer commented heatedly, "the public was brought into the process only at the final stage, long after most details had been worked out between the EPA and the applicant."[28]

Most of the invited speakers confirmed the lack of transparency that characterized the EPA's approach. Jack O'Connell, vice chairman of the State of California's Education Committee, provided evidence that showed how the EPA's procedures had failed to efficiently handle toxic-waste management. To him, ocean incineration presented "potential for environmental damage and disaster" but that the EPA had hidden this potential from U.S. citizens. Furthermore, the EPA had underestimated the impact that at-sea incineration would have on the health of the citizens of California: a series of burns in San Francisco Bay, for example, would bring about a spike in hydrochloric acid in the atmosphere, resulting in the "formation of acid rain and acid fog" that could move on the wind across the state. The EPA at best had ignored this risk and at worst had deliberately kept it from the public.[29]

Jean-Michel Cousteau, who spoke at the congressional hearing on behalf of the Cousteau Society, said the EPA's public hearings were organized to deceive people into thinking that they could affect the agency's decision making when "decisions to incinerate at sea [had] already been made." Cousteau declared that public hearings and studies were nothing more than "public appeasements" and were not meant to foster "a serious scientific inquiry of the problem." In 1983, for instance, the agency had issued permits without a thorough risk assessment or an objective evaluation of all the possible alternatives, in contravention to both the LDC and the MPRSA. Cousteau criticized the shaky scientific grounds on which the EPA established its defense of ocean incineration: inadequate and insufficient study, wrong assumptions, misrepresentations, and the constant downplaying of the environmental consequences. "We also note that baseline studies have not been conducted, nor was there a scientifically valid monitoring plan in place," Cousteau added. Finally, he stressed that such a technology maximized environmental hazards, including those from waste transport, accidental release, and unmonitored contamination. "From our extensive experience on ships and at sea," said Cousteau, "we can assure you that docks, harbors, and the open ocean are not" fit for the destruction of toxic substances. "We can think of no worse place to transport and destroy such wastes," he announced; if sufficiently informed, people would reach the same conclusion.[30]

The Oceanic Society raised the same kind of criticism. In his testimony to Congress, Michael Herz, the society's senior vice president, stressed three main points: first, "the need for sound, scientific and technical information as a basis for the regulatory policies"; second, "the inadequacies of the process"; and third, "the concerns about the preferred approaches" adopted by the EPA. Herz was particularly harsh on what he called the EPA's double-cross: EPA officers reassured environmental groups that the agency would draft new, environmentally sound regulation, even while document leaks and official statements confirmed that the EPA had already drafted legislation dismissive of environmental concerns. The EPA, in sum, was not credible.[31]

The widespread mistrust of the EPA's practices launched Greenpeace's testimony as well. Cathy Ryan and Elizabeth Otto spoke on behalf of that organization and got straight to the point. To them, the EPA had deceived people into thinking that their opinions counted. After the hearing in Brownsville in November 1983, the EPA had arranged public meetings with selected citizens, environmental groups, and incineration companies in an apparent attempt to incorporate people's concerns into any future regulation. During the second such meeting on June 26, 1984, however, attendees discovered that the EPA had already drafted comprehensive ocean-incineration regulations before the meeting had even started. Greenpeace activists argued that the EPA, contrary to its stated mission, was promoting the interests of private companies. "Incredibly," the Greenpeace representatives maintained, "it has not even been determined that this technology is needed, and, if even developed and adopted, would alleviate our toxic waste problem." The problem, in this regard, rested with the EPA's own "needs assessment," which was regarded as a "comparative assessment of the environmental and human health risks associated with ocean incineration as compared to feasible land-based alternatives." Given this definition, ocean incineration was considered needed and viable because it posed "no greater risk" than land-based incineration. In this assessment, however, the EPA was complying with neither domestic nor international regulations that demanded proof if a claim were made that there was no better alternative to ocean incineration. "Chemical dechlorination of PCB's, closed-loop systems, and reduction of hazardous waste output" were just a few of the possible alternatives, "all feasible land-based techniques" that the EPA should have taken into consideration. "To our knowledge, EPA has not even looked at these new technologies," Ryan and Otto remarked. The agency was instead "actively promoting yet another, what we call, 'out of sight, out of mind' technology."[32]

The EPA was grilled throughout the hearings. But no exchange was more emblematic, surreal, and tragic than the one between Representative Tom Lantos (D–CA) and the two EPA officers who had managed the Brownsville hearings, Jack Ravan and Steven Schatzow. In it, Lantos directly challenged these EPA representatives on the scientific viability of the U.S. at-sea incineration program. He exposed the intimate contradictions of the decision-making process and ultimately the whole system, which, he emphasized, rested on uncertainty, doubt, and untold truths:

> *Mr. Lantos:* Do you believe incineration at sea is a viable alternative?
> *Mr. Schatzow:* I believe it's every bit as viable as land. That's my personal opinion.
> *Mr. Lantos:* Mr. Ravan, do you believe, at this point with what you know, that incineration at sea is a viable alternative?
> *Mr. Ravan:* I don't reach that conclusion, Mr. Lantos. It is not that I disagree, speaking with as much precision as I can. I have not made up my mind.
> *Mr. Lantos:* You are not speaking with precision at all. You are not answering the questions. You are the responsible EPA official in this field. You cannot take a Chaucer-like stand here, sitting on the

fence, watching the passing parade go by. You are a governmental decisionmaker. You don't have the luxury of not giving answers to this committee. You have no idea whether incineration at sea is viable or not, is that your testimony?

Mr. Ravan: At this point in time, sir, I have not made up my mind as to what . . .[33]

After the House hearings, Greenpeace, the Oceanic Society, and other environmental groups sought congressional backup "to facilitate the proper decision-making" on ocean incineration. The organizations prepared draft legislation to be introduced as an amendment to the MPRSA and then helped draft the Ocean Incineration Research Bill. That bill called for a moratorium on at-sea incineration, more research into its environmental viability, study of other, less exploitative technologies, and the development of a national, long-term hazardous-waste reduction and management plan.[34] Twenty-nine representatives cosponsored the bill, which Barbara Boxer introduced at a press conference organized by Greenpeace in February 1985. Senator Alan Cranston (D–CA) introduced a companion bill that called for a three-year moratorium on the EPA's oceanic-incineration program.[35] The newly proposed legislation asked to prohibit, at least temporarily, the issuance of further permits for incineration of hazardous waste at sea.[36]

The bills never became a law, but ocean incineration remained on Congress's agenda. In fact, the Senate held a new round of public hearings on ocean incineration in June 1985 before the Subcommittee on Environmental Pollution of the Committee on Environment and Public Works.[37] They were chaired by Senator John Chafee (R–RI). The House committee had focused on the EPA's responsibilities; the hearings in the Senate investigated the views of multiple local authorities. The hearings aimed to collect the opinions and experiences of civil society writ large and included state governors, environmental activists, citizen groups, and representatives of industry, among others. The purpose was to obtain a comprehensive overview of all the pros and cons of ocean incineration. As Senator Chafee lucidly summarized, the hearings were meant to provide satisfying answers to some critical questions: First, "is ocean incineration needed? Second, has adequate research been done on the effects of this technology on marine life? Third, are appropriate steps being taken to prevent a catastrophic spill? Fourth, is it as safe or safer than incineration on land?"[38]

Governor Mark White (D) of Texas testified early in the hearings. He had gained firsthand experience with ocean incineration during the EPA's public hearings in Brownsville in late 1983. After stating that his concerns were shared by the National Governors Association and by the Coastal States Organization, he stressed "the lack of any logical sequence in the way the Environmental Protection Agency has handled questions about the viability of ocean incineration as being a safe and efficient disposal method." White highlighted the many flaws in the EPA's new regulation, and, in particular, he pointed to the liability question. "In the event of a mishap or disaster, who is going to pay?" he asked. "The proposed regulations only require that the applicant demonstrate evidence of insurance coverage within a range of $50 to $500 million. . . . The EPA's vague proposal on insurance did not adequately deal with our concern about the protection of the interest of third parties. And second, any limitation of liability related to ocean incineration operations is unacceptable."[39]

Local authorities' remarks revealed widespread dissatisfaction with the EPA's centralized and opaque management of ocean incineration. Richard Gimello, the executive director of the New Jersey Hazardous Waste Facilities Siting Commission, accused the EPA of having ignored his state's hazardous-waste policy, which included in order of preferred action: source reduction, waste recycling, recovery, treatment, secure disposal, and only then incineration. Gimello said that the EPA forced New Jersey to accept plans for both land-based and at-sea incineration that were inconsistent with the state's priorities and needs. He noted that most of New Jersey's hazardous waste comprised sludges and solids, which could not be incinerated on marine vessels. To Gimello, the agency had "failed to demonstrate the need for ocean incineration" and thus was openly violating the terms of the LDC. To further aggravate the situation, the EPA was making false claims about the commercial viability of at-sea incineration. In fact, the EPA had grounded this judgment on a market study that used data "interpreted beyond statistically valid limits" and that suggested only one possible outcome. For all these reasons, Gimello concluded, New Jersey and twenty-four other states had created the Consortium of State Hazardous Waste Siting Authorities, Inc., which had completed its own analysis and had evaluated the market needs of ocean incineration much more accurately. These data showed unequivocally that "no one state, and in most areas of the U.S., no one region will generate the volumes of liquid waste necessary to support an ocean incineration operation."[40]

A long list of speakers went on the offensive, representing the interests of civil society and environmental groups. The senators invited Sue Ann Fruge and Joan Brotman of the GCCPH, Sharon Stewart from the Texas Environmental Coalition, Kenneth Kamlet of the Pollution and Toxic Division of the National Wildlife Federation, Sally Ann Lentz of the Oceanic Society, Neal Shapiro from the Cousteau Society, and Deryl Bennett of the American Littoral Society. All agreed on the same points: ocean incineration was dangerous, expensive, and unaccountable. It did not solve the problem of the disposal of hazardous waste; quite on the contrary, it posed serious threats to the environment and to the health of millions of U.S. citizens residing in coastal areas. Zeke Grader, the executive director of the Pacific Coast Federation of Fishermen's Associations, brought to the fore the concerns of the small businesses that completely relied on the ocean's water quality. To him, the main problems were incineration's impact on fisheries "either in direct fish kills or in harm to that resource, in a sense of lowered resistance to disease, lowered fecundity," as well as the chronic poisoning of the ecosystem. The second concern was also a public-health hazard because incineration rendered seafood resources not only unmarketable but also dangerous for human health. In sum, ocean incineration was a technology that, in Bennett's words, seemed attractive "but for all the wrong reasons."[41]

The Senate's subcommittee also called representatives of the waste-management business to testify. First was Howard Canter, in charge of the governmental affairs department of At-Sea Incineration, Inc. He defended ocean incineration, referring back to the EPA, which had deemed the technology to not have "any significant impact on human health." Furthermore, according to Canter, ocean incineration provided a realistic solution to the necessity of disposing of hazardous waste. Each year, Canter remarked, U.S. industry produced 350 to 400 million metric tons of hazardous waste. Each year, the EPA updated the national priority list for the cleanup of hundreds of sites. "How much longer can we fool the public into believing that strides are being made to protect their water supplies, their environment, their health, and the health of our children?" he asked rhetorically. Pragmatism and the preservation of the American way of life demanded, in his view, the continuation of the ocean-incineration program.[42]

Then it was the turn of William Brown, the CWM's marine affairs director. Accompanied by George Vander Velde, a biophysicist on CWM's payroll, Brown completely upended the environmentalist narrative about ocean incineration: "Ocean incineration destroys pollution," he said. "It is an alternative to the dumping that used to occur routinely in the Gulf and in the Atlantic. Ocean incineration is a way to prevent the cancer that toxic chemicals may cause if they are not destroyed." To Brown, incineration was "an operationally proven state-of-the-art technology." The U.S. government must use it "to meet the enormous, accelerating need for alternatives to landfilling that will permanently eliminate toxic waste and better protect human health and the environment." Brown even used apocalyptic terms: "Enormous amounts of PCB's and other hazardous wastes," he said, would keep contaminating air, water, and land. That contamination would reach the surface microlayer of all ecological systems, not just the oceanic one. No human being could be safe. "Just three incineration ships . . . would double the existing commercial capacity for incineration of liquid organic hazardous waste [and] dramatically increase the rate at which these chemicals [could] be removed from our environment forever." To abandon ocean incineration, according to Brown, was to condemn the world to a "huge and rapidly growing reservoir of toxic chemicals on land."[43]

The Senate subcommittee's hearings demonstrated that when it came to ocean incineration, there was no middle ground. Its opponents argued against its scientific validity, its efficacy, and its environmental soundness. Its supporters counterattacked, talking about the lack of better alternatives and the urgency of the hazardous-waste problem. Thus, because the debate was open—and polarized—the House decided to hold another series of hearings. This time, they were held before the Subcommittee on Oceanography of the Committee on Merchant Marine and Fisheries. And this time the consensus shifted: ocean incineration was not a viable or an environmentally sound practice.

On November 11, 1985, Representative Barbara Mikulski (D–MD), chair of the subcommittee, opened the sessions and set the goal of the hearings: "First, to consider how adequate is current research on ocean incineration; and second, whether additional research is necessary before EPA should issue regulations that permit commercial ocean incineration activity." Mikulski's real goal, however, was to reassess the EPA's behavior and practices regarding the issuance of permits. In fact, the chairwoman believed that the EPA's proposal to resume oceanic burns was misguided and ultimately illegal because it lacked a thorough EIS. Furthermore, the EPA had done no risk assessment on the transportation phase, the port-loading activities, and the actual incineration. As Mikulski put it, she was "not convinced EPA [had] a clear picture of how ocean incineration [fit] into the overall issue of waste management and disposal."[44] Mikulski's criticism received bipartisan support. Representatives Jim Saxton (R–NJ) and Claudine Schneider (R–RI) agreed with Representatives Roy Dyson (D–MD), Solomon Ortiz (D–TX), Thomas Carpenter (D–DE), and Barbara Boxer (D–CA): ocean incineration was dangerous and had to be more strictly regulated, if not stopped.[45]

Barbara Boxer in particular highlighted ocean incineration as "one of the greatest existing threats to the health of our marine environment." All the technical aspects of incineration entailed incontrollable risks. "With the enormous amount of scientific uncertainty about the technology and potential adverse impacts of ocean incineration," Boxer argued, "I believe that we must seek to clearly separate the research stage from the actual granting of permits." In other words, she understood that the EPA needed more research to evaluate the environmental hazards, but operating under the general principle of precaution, dictated by common sense and the breadth of the potential implications, she advised against any further burns.[46]

Once again Greenpeace's criticism during the hearings was forthright. Speaking on behalf of its more than half a million members, Peg Stevenson openly denounced ocean incineration and the EPA's new regulation by citing a statement prepared by Lisa Bunin, Jon Hinck, and Elizabeth Otto a few months earlier.[47] In it, Greenpeace organizers hammered on the contention that ocean incineration was risk free. They said that any promise of liability-free waste disposal served as a disincentive for waste reduction. Greenpeace especially warned against the risks in routine operations, accidents, and profit-motivated illegal dumping. The catalog of human health and environmental damage resulting from the release of organochlorines at sea represented a truly unacceptable risk, but all the new regulations ignored it. Greenpeace leaders emphasized that the chemical compounds released into the atmosphere did not tidily degrade but remained toxic and accumulated in animal tissue, ending up in the human food chain. What ultimately worried Greenpeace the most was that the EPA's insistence on ocean incineration exacerbated hazardous-waste production, waylaid efforts to reduce waste at the source, and made it impossible to find other viable disposal methods for hazardous chemical waste.[48]

Joan Brotman, who spoke on behalf of the GCCPH, lamented that ocean incineration was not a total-destruction technology, that it had no backup devices for safety in case of malfunctions, and that it relied on inadequate research. "We ask ourselves just how bad do the results of this research have to be before Congress tells EPA to halt the program?" Brotman argued that the EPA had "deviated from its primary responsibility as an impartial regulatory agency and [had] become a promoter of ocean incineration technology."[49] In the end, Brotman echoed the same criticism that Senator Joseph Biden (D–DE) had been using to stigmatize the EPA's paradoxical and untrustworthy policy. After failing to get the agency to respond to his questions concerning ocean incineration's complex procedures and their overall environmental viability, Biden had stated in despair in the earlier Senate hearings: "We have environmental impact statements on the siting of post offices in this nation. I hope to hell, we develop environmental impact statements on the siting of loading docks."[50] EPA officers did not reply to any of these criticisms. Their silence was both revealing and embarrassing at the same time.

INTERNATIONAL POLARIZATION

When the EPA published its tentative determination to issue a new research permit to CWM in December 1985, it did so in spite of the criticism raised at the congressional hearings in June and December.[51] The agency was also green-lighting new oceanic burns in the midst of mounting international pressure, too.

In particular, the EPA's plans to restart incineration in the Gulf of Mexico had ignited fierce protests by Mexican authorities, who considered U.S. ocean incineration a direct threat to their country's natural environment and vital commercial interests. A series of articles appeared in Mexican newspapers denouncing the incineration operations in the gulf, saying they could irremediably compromise shrimp fishing. The Mexican press accused the U.S. government of treating Latin America like a giant dump site. Ramon Álvarez Larrauri, a Mexican ecologist specializing in marine biology, said that ocean incineration not only was in line with "the traditional colonialist politics of [the] U.S.A" but was also putting at risk the economy of all the countries on the Caribbean Sea.[52] Jorge Mora Pérez, the director of the Mexican Agency for the Protection of the Sea Environment, and Javier Flores, a professor of environmental law, argued that Mexico should appeal to the Stockholm Declaration of 1972, which mandated the international safeguarding of the marine environment. Another option to stop the EPA, they suggested, was to bring a case under the bilateral treaty of 1980 that mandated mutual assistance between the U.S. Coast Guard and the Mexican navy in case of ocean dumping.[53] José Lizarraga, the regional director for Latin America and Caribbean Countries in the UN Program for the Environment made even harsher comments. He said that the EPA was not only violating a treaty on the protection of the sea that had been signed in 1983 by all the countries on the Gulf of Mexico, including the United States, but also flouting the basic moral obligations of international aid. Lizarraga also emphasized that the burning of more than 300,000 tons of PCBs some 200 miles (322 kilometers) away from the coast of Texas would generate "incalculable damages" to the "ecology of the entire continent."[54] Finally, the Mexican Agency for Urban and Ecologic Development, the Mexican Ecological Alliance, and even the Mexican Parliamentary Committee on the Environment publicly protested against the EPA's proposal and asked it to stop any plan for incineration of hazardous waste in the Gulf of Mexico.[55]

Critical voices from Mexico did not stand alone. Doubts and uncertainties shaped the broader international debate on ocean incineration—now more polarized than ever. At a special session of the LDC Scientific Group on Dumping that convened in March 1985, supporters and opponents of ocean incineration clashed repeatedly. The SGD was composed of experts from forty different countries.[56] Most of them, including those from countries deeply invested in ocean incineration, agreed that the technical drawbacks could be improved and perfected. More specifically, the experts pointed to the performance of shipboard incinerators, the lack of reliable measurements, and the absence of a common protocol for the monitoring of the burns.[57] Aside from this consensus on improving incineration standards, however, the delegates were deeply divided. Positions coalesced around two antithetical studies that had been circulated to the members in advance. Written by two independent researchers, Edward Kleppinger and Desmond Bond, the first oppositional report was titled *Ocean Incineration of Hazardous Waste: A Critique*. The second was authored by CWM's consultant David Ackerman and his team and was emphatically titled *The Capability of Ocean Incineration—a Critical Review and Rebuttal of the Kleppinger Report*.[58]

The Kleppinger report argued that complete destruction of liquid wastes containing refractory organochlorines—such as PCBs—could not be carried out safely aboard incinerator ships. It stated that the equipment on the vessels did not allow for valid measurements because the liquid waste, the resulting plume, and oceanic sediments could not be evaluated. The technology, therefore, was totally unverifiable, and the report warned against the "catastrophic hazardous consequences" that ocean incineration entailed.[59] The Ackerman report presented contrasting conclusions. To Ackerman and his colleagues, Kleppinger and Bond's argument was based on false premises. The second group of scientists noted that the Kleppinger report incorrectly interpreted the combustion efficiency of incinerator vessels. Kleppinger and Bond considered incinerator ships to be inefficient because they could not keep a temperature of 1,200 degrees Celsius inside the combustion chambers for an average of two seconds throughout the operations—a threshold required in land-based incineration. The Ackerman report stressed that because a two-second residence time was not required for ocean incinerators, it made no sense to deem them inefficient and unverifiable. To Ackerman and his colleagues, in the end there was a good chance—though hypothetical—that efficiency at sea could exceed the 99.9 percent level in a much shorter residence time than two seconds.[60]

Delegates from Finland, the Netherlands, Sweden, and West Germany, along with Greenpeace observers, strongly defended the Kleppinger report. Although the U.S. delegation relied on the EPA's SAB report, a study that in part agreed with Kleppinger and Bond's findings but in the end approved of ocean incineration, they decided to back Ackerman's conclusions. The American experts acknowledged that the PICs were one of the most dangerous drawbacks of ocean incineration. Nonetheless, the U.S. delegation, headed by Tudor Davies of the EPA, embargoed the SAB report, which never made it to the LDC scientific panel. The United States and the European Council of Chemical Manufacturers' Federation openly supported further development and testing of ocean incineration. Swiss delegates endorsed ocean incineration to safeguard the interests of important multinational chemical industries located in the Alpine country. The U.K. delegation aligned with the Americans and promoted a series of collateral studies in support of Ackerman's findings.[61] Belgium, too, had a vested interest in defending the practice inasmuch as the harbor of Antwerp was the main waste-collection and distribution center and the hub for ocean incineration in Europe.[62] The meeting ended in a stalemate, and the scientists decided to adjourn their discussion until further studies became available.

A POLYCENTRIC OPPOSITION

To break the deadlock, activists diversified their strategy and attacked the supporters of ocean incineration. In the end, they not only affected policy makers but also put the whole ocean-incineration business into a deep, irreversible crisis of liquidity and legitimacy.

Environmental groups developed stable working relationships with regional and multilateral organizations. Even if groups such as Greenpeace and the Oceanic Society were only observers at the LDC, they still were able to affect international discussions. Their most effective contribution was the production of scientific reports and studies focused on the bioaccumulative nature of the toxic compounds emitted by ocean incineration.[63] In cooperation with a broad coalition of environmental and citizen groups, the Oceanic Society raised several legal, scientific, and technical concerns about ocean incineration that, above all, highlighted the lack of "adequate information on the effect of the various stages of the incineration process on the marine environment and human health." In the widely circulated "Briefing Report," the society's criticism pointed out that national authorities often granted incineration permits in violation of the terms of the LDC, showing an utter "disregard for domestic and international legal imperatives."[64]

For its part, Greenpeace strengthened its ties with the Oslo and Paris Commissions, which monitored polluting activities, respectively, on the North Sea and on the Northeast Atlantic.[65] In March 1985, Greenpeace representatives addressed the Standing Advisory Committee for Scientific Advice (SACSA) of OSCOM, which gathered in Hamburg a few days after the LDC SGD discussed the Kleppinger and Ackerman reports.[66] In Hamburg, Greenpeace representatives presented a detailed paper that addressed the technical flaws of ocean incineration. In a fifteen-minute talk, they explained their position and urged both the scientific committee and the general commission to seriously consider December 31, 1987, as the deadline to ban ocean incineration in the North Sea. SACSA delegates unanimously agreed that Greenpeace's report was a state-of-the-art assessment on ocean incineration.[67] Soon after addressing the SACSA, Greenpeace prepared a comprehensive independent review of ocean incineration's theoretical foundations and practical developments and forwarded it to the LDC scientific working group.[68] Greenpeace's report was meant to overtake the Kleppinger/Ackerman controversy. OSCOM and LDC delegates decided to consider Greenpeace's report as the foundation for a Joint LDC/OSCOM Group of Experts Meeting on Incineration at Sea, which they planned for the spring of the following year.[69]

For the rest of 1985, Greenpeace focused its antitoxics campaign solely on ocean incineration. The organization worked with the press to publicize and educate, especially in those coastal areas directly exposed to the hazards of ocean incineration. At the SACSA meeting, for instance, when OCS organized a press conference to announce that the newly built *Vulcanus II* was going to be berthed in Hamburg, the local Greenpeace chapter circulated to all the journalists an information folder containing hundreds of documents demystifying ocean incineration. The impression among Greenpeace activists was that the journalists did not buy OCS's position and were inclined to see the issue as the environmentalists did.[70]

Greenpeace activists thought that their main responsibility was to help people grasp the broader implications of the issue. To this end, they clarified which interests were at stake and explained the overall hazards of ocean incineration. They wanted people to understand that ocean-incineration operations had a long-lasting impact on both human and the oceans' health. In the United States, they got this across by distributing clear-cut fact sheets that described in simple terms what was wrong with at sea incineration:

> Fact 1: Under a proposed plan promoted by industry and subsidized by the federal government, ships loaded with industrial toxic waste would be allowed to burn thousands of gallons of PCBs, chlorine and other toxic chemicals off the East, West, and Gulf coasts.

Fact 2: Burning toxic waste in shipboards incinerators releases an array of toxic chemicals into the marine environment. Unburned chemical waste and deadly dioxins pose dangers to human health and the marine environment.

Fact 3: According to the U.S. Coast Guard, if a chemical spill from an incinerator ship occurred, the toxic chemicals spilled at sea would be impossible to retrieve or isolate from the marine environment.[71]

This no less than shocking information was instrumental in stirring up the people, a strategy that Greenpeace adopted in several countries. The Dutch chapter of Greenpeace, for instance, distributed an analysis that disclosed the names of hundreds of multinational companies that produced the organochlorine wastes that were destined to be incinerated in the ocean.[72] A Greenpeace USA report denounced the U.S. delegation at the LDC for taking a position in support of ocean incineration, saying the delegation did so only because the U.S. Maritime Administration had given a multimillion-dollar loan guarantee for the construction of more incinerator ships.[73] Greenpeace slowly "developed a reputation for being the opposition leaders on ocean incineration."[74] The organization was called upon more and more to address any breaking news on ocean incineration and on other issues related to toxic wastes.

A crucial element in making Greenpeace a central player was its use of nonviolent, direct action. As one Greenpeace leader noted, "Going to the scene of the environmental crime to interfere non-violently" was what distinguished Greenpeace from other environmental groups. Spectacular actions magnified the popularity of the anti-ocean-incineration campaign and expanded the network that supported it.[75] Greenpeace activists started tracking the hazardous waste being collected for subsequent ocean burns, a tactic that proved "to be fairly explosive in itself," as one campaigner recalled. It required huge resources and coordination but ultimately raised awareness of the problem even in areas not directly threatened by offshore operations.[76] As one observer noted, Greenpeace actions "restore[d] faith in a new generation" as young people in such different places as the United States, West Germany, England, and Denmark were on the front line against the exploitative forces in favor of ocean incineration.[77] In March 1985, Greenpeace launched a new boat, the *Beluga*, from the port of Hamburg with the specific aim of organizing offshore actions against incinerator vessels.[78] Greenpeace leaders claimed to be ready to coordinate "a flotilla of boats to blockade an incinerator ship and prevent it from leaving its harbor." They promised to pair the blockades with land-based rallies and unceasing lobbying, all developed "in conjunction with local environmental groups."[79]

Greenpeace local networks were another point of strength in its anti-ocean-incineration campaign. When the EPA decided to authorize CWM to burn hazardous waste in the North Atlantic, for instance, Greenpeace hired two marine biologists, Ada Sanchez and Lyn Davidson, as members of its wildlife team. The organization asked them, along with local activists and experts, to identify the species, their habitats, and their feeding and nesting grounds that were being jeopardized by incineration operations.[80] The organization also reached out to state governors and local authorities to help them redraft bills to favor legislation that could ban ocean incineration once and for all.[81] While endorsing Barbara Boxer's bill, Greenpeace leaders in the United States invited their fellow activists to "phone, write, visit, send a telegram [to]" their local and national representatives. A Greenpeace leaflet urged, "Alert your friends to the hazards of ocean incineration and spark activism in your community by writing a letter to the editor of your local newspaper. Ask your City Council and State government to pass a resolution in support of H.R. 1295. Such resolutions are already in the works in California and Texas. Together we can make a difference."[82]

In Texas, these pressures paid off. Local lawmakers there faulted the EPA's policies, using words that mirrored exactly Greenpeace's points of contention. Representative Don Lee from Harlingen, for instance, introduced a resolution that urged the U.S. Congress to impose a moratorium on permits to burn toxic wastes at sea until more research could take place. Representative Al Price from Beaumont voiced concern about official scientific data and pointed to Greenpeace's reports instead as a source of valid information. "The EPA thought we were a little sleepy community and coast and that we paid very little attention to what was going on. They thought they'd go out there and run around with those ships and burn it, and we'd never realize what they were doing," Lee stated.[83] But Texans had shown that they would no longer tolerate any kind of toxic burns in the gulf.

In this regard, the GCCPH's activities proved crucial in linking ocean incineration's environmental repercussions to its deeply uneven exploitation. If the EPA's spokesman, Tudor Davies, thought ocean incineration was mainly a policy issue, GCCPH organizers thought of it as a "demographic and geographic" question—indeed, a question of environmental justice.[84] "Our concerns are local, national, and due to our proximity to Mexico, international" as well, GCCPH leaders maintained.[85] To them, care of the marine environment made sense at a socioeconomic level. Opposing ocean incineration meant ensuring the health and prosperity of the gulf and its multinational socioeconomic structure "for this and future generations." GCCPH organizers framed their dissent in terms of proper management of natural marine resources. They pointed to such successful environmental programs as the ones that federal authorities had implemented in the Chesapeake Bay and the Puget Sound.[86] In those instances, the GCCPH coordinators believed, the EPA had shown a more sensitive attitude than it did toward the disadvantaged communities living along the gulf coast. Ocean incineration not only threatened the valuable industries of tourism and fisheries but also replicated institutional racism toward people on the margins of the public agenda.[87] This deep sense of injustice spread anti-ocean-incineration sentiments at the local level.

The polycentric opposition to ocean incineration was succeeding. It was informing and mobilizing people and gathering political consensus to limit the growth of the ocean-incineration business. "Five years ago no one thought much about ocean incineration," a Greenpeace internal memo recounted in 1985, but by this time citizen groups and environmental organizations could influence national governments and lobby for the banning of ocean incineration.[88] In the United States, the campaign that Greenpeace, the Oceanic Society, and the GCCPH mounted was endorsed by state and federal senators and representatives, governors, and public officers.[89] Even though this pressure did not lead to the introduction of formal legislation outlawing ocean incineration, it was able to put pressure on businesses, who counterpunched to salvage their reputations—and the marketability of the technology. Geert Heinemann, the head of OCS, fearing that the growing anti-ocean-incineration campaign would negatively affect national and international regulation, released interviews in which he framed ocean incineration as innocuous "as putting salt back in the sea."[90] Freddy Gielen, Solvay & Cie's director of organochlorinated products, maintained that companies had to ensure that governments continued to regard ocean incineration as an "appropriate recycling-and-recovery technology." With revenues of $4.5 billion, Solvay, at that time one of Europe's largest chemical conglomerates, depended on both land-based and ocean incineration to dispose of chemical by-products. "We as an industry eventually can reduce the quantities of wastes generated, but it will be a long time before they're completely eliminated," remarked Gielen. "That means there must be burning on land or at sea . . . for a long time to come, at least another 50 years." Elke Jordan, a top manager at OCS, said that if ocean incineration were to be eliminated, "there would be a grinding down of economic activity in Europe, not only within the chemical industry, but in general."[91]

Greenpeace and other environmental groups and coalitions scoffed at these hyperbolic claims, seeing them as signs of the twilight of ocean incineration. Peter Montague, for instance, an active environmentalist and coeditor of the *New Jersey Hazardous Waste News*, denounced At-Sea Incineration, saying it was trying to gain political clout through "representatives lurking in the hallways of power throughout New Jersey and Washington," who misrepresented facts and even "claim[ed] to have secured permits that they had not." Montague also condemned CWM's "pattern of dishonesty," which was confirmed in a *New York Times* story that told of former employees who covered up the company's many illegal practices. To Montague, CWM was "ruthless and predatory," while the EPA had proven to be a "joke."[92] Donald Carruth, the president of the American Eagle Foundation, a private company that had served as an external environmental adviser for the EPA's ocean-incineration program, emphasized that the agency had never established a fully transparent, competitive, and coordinated certification system. This omission allowed the agency, he continued, to award incineration permits almost exclusively to CWM and undermined a truly competitive and financially solid market. The EPA had a "very poor track record" in its relations with the private sector, and its insistence on building a vast fleet of incineration ships was, in Carruth's words, not only misleading but "a blot on the agency."[93]

These criticisms were sharply on point. They exposed a general lack of transparency and reliability that in turn cut off private investors' trust. In the first two quarters of 1985, for example, Tacoma Boatbuilding reported losses of $52.5 million. In the third quarter of that year, the company declared another loss of more than $41 million and disclosed that its main subsidiary, At-Sea Incineration, would cease operations. At-Sea Incineration was supposed to build new incinerator ships for the destruction of chemical waste in newly designated zones off the coasts of New Jersey and Texas. But the company was unable to attract private investments, nor could it obtain further operating funds after the parent corporation filed for bankruptcy in September 1984. At-Sea Incineration, which owned $63.7 million in government-backed bonds, defaulted in November 1985 despite an additional, last-minute $4.1 million bond payment guaranteed by the U.S. Maritime Administration. The Maritime Administration paid off the bonds and moved to seize At-Sea Incineration's remaining ships. The total loss for the American taxpayers amounted to roughly $70 million.[94] This economic collapse gave the anti-ocean-incineration campaign further leverage and arguments for its fight.

* * *

In the mid-1980s, the EPA kept looking at ocean incineration as a safe method for the disposal of hazardous waste, pushing for further commercial expansion of the practice. But the mood in the country and abroad had changed. Congress launched a series of investigations into the practice and, perhaps even more important, encouraged a thorough exchange of ideas and opinions about the environmental viability of it. Along with congressional oversight, a stronger feeling of discontent started emerging from those countries whose coastal areas were directly affected by U.S. ocean-incineration operations, such as Mexico. In reaction, the U.S. administration tried to garner support in defense of the practice from those allies that shared a vested economic and industrial interest in it, a move that further polarized the international discussions and deliberations. In the meantime, both local and transnational environmentalist groups kept promoting the idea that ocean incineration was untenable and mounted a polycentric opposition that further limited the U.S. government's options. The stage for an escalation of this socioecological struggle was set. The last push against ocean incineration had begun.

5

BAN THE BURN

In December 1984, a Union Carbide pesticide plant in Bhopal, India, leaked 40 tons of methyl isocyanate, exposing half a million people to toxic emissions and sending shockwaves around the world.[1] The nightmare of hazardous waste, which had seized the United States since at least the Love Canal incident in 1978, came back to haunt the country in a more hideous form. During a period of forty-eight hours in August 1985, another Union Carbide plant in West Virginia leaked a toxic cloud affecting 135 people; a chemical train exploded in Valentine, Arizona, sending residents to evacuation centers; a chemical-waste truck crashed on the Washington Beltway, stranding 7,000 motorists and forcing 300 families to flee; and residents in Camden, New Jersey, had to be evacuated when a chemical storage tank ruptured due to careless handling.[2] For many, these accidents heralded the urgency of finding adequate methods for the disposal of deadly chemical substances, including a reconsideration of ocean incineration. For others, the management of hazardous waste simply could not wait on an evaluation of environmental safety.

When toward the end of 1985 EPA managers decided to authorize further offshore burns and expand the ocean-incineration zones in U.S.

territorial waters, a massive wave of protest emerged. A large coalition made up of environmentalist organizations and citizen groups mounted a campaign—Ban the Burn—to defend the point of view that wanted action against ocean incineration right away. National policy makers and local administrators endorsed Ban the Burn, too. Coordinated by Greenpeace, Ban the Burn campaigners flocked to the EPA's public hearings and blamed the agency for putting the health of both U.S. citizens and the marine environment at risk. As had happened in Texas and Alabama in late 1983, once again this kind of pressure and mobilization convinced the EPA officers to block the issuance of new incineration permits. Within a few months, Ban the Burn activists succeeded in stopping the development of at-sea incineration in the United States.[3]

But the struggle was not over. The proponents of incineration, in fact, turned their attention to Europe to salvage this high-yield, commercially valuable technology. Ban the Burn campaigners, then, pursued them, staging multipronged protests that involved lobbying, international reporting, and, above all, direct actions. These protests, which had at their center both opposition to the ocean-incineration technology and protection of the global marine environment, slowly moved away from the sole objective of affecting policy and progressively aimed at changing people's mind. The popularization of concerns over the fate and the health of the oceans through the organization of spectacular and exemplary actions, in other words, became the main pillar upon which Ban the Burn was secured.[4]

NOT IN MY OCEAN

On November 26, 1985, the U.S. Environmental Protection Agency announced that it was about to issue a new permit for the incineration of 700,000 gallons of PCB-laden waste at sea.[5] A series of oceanic burns were set to take place in a newly designated zone in the North Atlantic, off the coasts of New York, New Jersey, Maryland, Pennsylvania, and Delaware. The beneficiary of the draft permit, which appeared in the *Federal Register* in mid-December, was Chemical Waste Management, the company that owned the biggest incinerator vessel in the world, the *Vulcanus II*.[6] The EPA also announced that people living in the coastal areas near the designated incineration site would be given the chance to comment and discuss the burns in a series of public hearings planned for Philadelphia, Redbank, Wilmington, and Ocean City in the second half of January 1986.[7] The EPA's decision to issue a new permit came in the wake of mounting congressional criticism and gave the anti-ocean-incineration forces fresh impetus. It was the beginning of a two-year struggle led by proponents and members of Ban the Burn.

Lisa Bunin, Greenpeace's campaign coordinator, coined the name "Ban the Burn," and with that she was just getting started. She wrote and circulated fact sheets and packets, prepared informational material for the press, spoke to local community groups, presented testimony, and participated in local meetings and town halls.[8] She organized a tricoastal movement that mobilized people across the country. The EPA's new permit, indeed, implied the creation of a vast incineration zone that impinged on five states and brought with it the prospect of establishing even more offshore sites. There were already sites in the Gulf of Mexico, the Atlantic and Pacific Oceans, and off the coast of northern California. The anti-ocean-incineration struggle acquired a truly national character, and the coalition that coalesced around Ban the Burn—like what was happening in the concurrent anti-toxics campaign and environmental-justice movement—cut across political, racial, and class lines.[9] Conservatives and liberals, workers and students, local authorities and church groups participated in the campaign. The widening of the constituency was instrumental in maximizing the chances of legislative reform.[10] Greenpeace leaders believed that the actions of traditional environmental groups such as the Sierra Club were politically ineffective, whereas grassroots mobilization and single-issue campaigns did comparatively better in bringing about change.[11] The main consequence of this strategic shift was that the anti-ocean-incineration campaigners compromised on a number of issues. For instance, they pushed for a moratorium on ocean siting and on permit issuance rather than demanding the immediate prohibition of the practice. But this approach in turn allowed the coalition to grow in both size and influence. With greater financing available, the alliance could sponsor independent research and studies. A larger membership enabled the coalition to demand a better and more transparent public engagement in the policy-making process. The idea was to empower those communities that were exposed to the hazardous-waste cycle so that they could be involved in all stages of the regulatory process, negotiating directly with industry and the pertinent local and federal authorities. This population covered a wide swath of people, including those living next to chemical-production facilities and storage sites as well as those living along transportation routes or near disposal sites.

What kept the alliance unified was the harsh criticism of the EPA's ocean-incineration strategy. Supported by Robin Alexander from the GCCPH and Susan Silver and Sally Ann Lentz from the Oceanic Society, and with the endorsement of other environmental organizations, such as Friends of the Earth, Lisa Bunin publicly denounced the EPA's decision to issue a new permit in November 1985 "as an attempt to justify permanent ocean incineration plans." She sent reports, articles, and studies on the dangerous effects of ocean incineration to 550 congressional representatives.[12] The Ban the Burn coalition denounced the EPA's plan to ship highly toxic chemical waste from Philadelphia to New Jersey and on to the North Atlantic, saying it would jeopardize tourism, fisheries, public health, and the safety of the oceans.[13] At the same time, Greenpeace blamed the EPA for ignoring the scientific criticism that had been raised. Ban the Burn organizers thought that the agency's real intention was to launch full-scale commercialization of ocean incineration. They maintained, of course, that the expansion of at-sea incineration would not contribute to solving the problem of hazardous-waste disposal. Rather, it would allow the destruction of only a small fraction of the waste that U.S. industries generated and certainly would not eliminate the problem of what to do with solid wastes, sludges, and contaminated residues.[14]

Most of Bunin's and her fellow campaigners' work consisted in coordinating local efforts and organizing a common response to prepare for the scheduled public hearings. Their idea was to replicate the successful experience of Brownsville and Mobile, where massive popular participation had effectively stopped the EPA's program. "We can do the same on the East Coast," a Greenpeace leaflet maintained.[15] Hence, the Ban the Burn activists spent a great deal of time and resources to prepare the local communities for the hearings' showdown. A few days before the first meeting in Philadelphia—which had been designated a loading zone for toxic waste—Greenpeace released a statement addressed to the inhabitants of that city. Ocean incineration was presented as "an enormous threat to the oceans, to the health of the residents, and to a tourism industry dependent on clean beaches and edible seafood."[16] While keeping the local communities informed, Lisa Bunin also tried to buy time. On January 9, 1986, less than a week before the first meeting, she sent a letter to Lawrence Jensen, the EPA's acting administrator, asking for a "30-day extension of the comment period," which the EPA had set to end six weeks after the hearings. Bunin wanted local residents to have more time to digest the relevant and complex information, review the draft permit, and formulate pertinent comments on the permit application. The Greenpeace leader said that the comment period stretched over public holidays, which made it more difficult to obtain information on the proposed permits. She thought that six weeks was insufficient for people working full-time.[17]

Greenpeace and its allies employed a series of tactics to raise public awareness on ocean incineration at the local level. The group circulated easily accessible fact sheets that summarized in layman's terms the main dangers of ocean incineration.[18] It drafted short radio announcements on the objectives and relevance of the meetings.[19] The campaigners set up phone trees, drafted issue papers, circulated petitions, arranged town halls, and distributed bumper stickers.[20] They even proposed the proclamation of symbolic ocean celebration days. In preparation for the hearings, the Ban the Burn organizers sent out mailings and informative materials to local unions, especially the local associations of dockworkers and deckhands; to the local chapters of the National Association for the Advancement of Colored People; and to dozens of churches and synagogues, the editorial boards of local newspapers, chambers of commerce, and local and state legislators.[21] The most time-consuming activity, however, was their organization of demonstrations. Initially, local activists organized these events, but

Greenpeace soon took up managing the logistics. The Ban the Burn organizers visited local businesses, such as boat and bike rental shops, restaurants, hotels, and motels, soliciting their participation. Greenpeace asked radio stations to air public-service announcements and give time to feature stories on ocean incineration. Greenpeace leaders applied to authorities for permission to hold their demonstrations near beaches, a tactic meant to maximize press attention and attract new activists.[22] Lisa Bunin was usually behind the organizational effort. She met with local officers, activists, community leaders, and organizers, attended their meetings, encouraged them, and explained the broader environmental, societal, and economic risks of the oceanic burns. She put anti-ocean-incineration protesters in contact with local and national media outlets and helped organize local fundraising campaigns. For many local activists, Greenpeace became, as an observer noted, a "source of aid and comfort, an ally."[23]

But Greenpeace did not fight on its own. One of its most important allies in the Ban the Burn coalition was the Oceanic Society. It helped Greenpeace inform and mobilize people and systematically worked to dismantle the idea of ocean incineration's environmental viability. Sally Ann Lentz, the society's staff attorney, criticized the concept of "destruction efficiency," on which the EPA had grounded its defense. Lentz quoted research produced by the EPA's SAB. According to Lentz, destruction efficiency was a deceptive indicator that did not "completely address the problem of what is emitted from the incinerator stacks," nor did it constitute "a reliable basis for developing exposure assessment."[24] The EPA had failed to prove that ocean incineration was a safe process. The Oceanic Society was committed to making sure that people understood that failure. Right before the EPA's hearings, it submitted a fifty-five-page report that included specific comments on the EPA's proposed research permits. It maintained that the permits did not satisfy the requirements of either domestic or international regulation. It accused the federal agency of not complying with the LDC or with the Ocean Dumping Act, MPRSA. It also pointed out that the EPA had not accurately determined the toxicity and the long-term accumulative impacts of oceanic burns, including effects on the ocean's microlayer. Finally, the Oceanic Society denounced the inadequate

FIGURE 5.1 Greenpeace's Ban the Burn leaflet, 1986.

Source: Box 5320 (Documentation Office Concerning Ocean Incineration, 1985–1987), International Institute for Social History, Greenpeace International (Amsterdam) Archives.

monitoring systems, data analyses, and operating conditions of the EPA's proposed burns.[25]

Another point of contention was the dubious use of taxpayers' money.[26] The EPA was about to grant new permits to CWM, a company that, according to both Greenpeace and the Oceanic Society, had a poor record on transparency and compliance with environmental regulations. Greenpeace questioned CWM's lack of financial accountability. Greenpeace researchers underlined that CWM had paid $17 million in fines "in the past 19 months alone" for breaking federal laws, and the company had never solved "well-documented technical problems" concerning its incineration methods, nor had it effectively reduced "the danger of a spill and transportation hazards."[27] A study prepared by Greenpeace members David Rapaport and Jon Lax drew attention to CWM's inadequate insurance coverage. Nobody would insure the company to a degree sufficient to cover potential environmental damages resulting from ocean-incineration operations. This was a serious shortcoming in light of the extensive claims that would likely be filed in the event of a major accident. "The cost of cleaning up a spill should not be larger than 10 million [dollars], but the potential cost of restoring the environment and/or compensating third parties may be greater," the Greenpeace researchers stressed. A spill in Philadelphia, for example, would affect a large number of third parties, including the fishing industry, property owners, and people whose drinking water was susceptible to contamination. The possibility that the claims could exceed CWM's maximum insurance coverage put the local, state, and federal governments at risk. Moreover, Greenpeace's study continued, no claim could be made against the *Vulcanus* in the event of spills or accidents occurring outside the "designated area," even though the EPA had no clear definition of such an area. In short, Greenpeace wrote, CWM could not possibly have sufficient insurance for the burns that the EPA was authorizing—a conflict with the EPA's own regulations.[28] In addition, while scrutinizing the relations between the EPA and CWM, Lisa Bunin and David Rapaport discovered that in spite of the EPA's repeated injunctions ordering CWM to dispose of the dangerous industrial waste stored in Emelle, Alabama, CWM had avoided paying a $321,000 fine and had settled the issue with the federal agency, agreeing to a $100,000 civil penalty that would be refunded once CWM removed the waste. Ironically, most of that waste was supposed to be incinerated in the Atlantic. Greenpeace condemned the settlement as wrong, as did the State of Alabama, which considered it excessively favorable to the company. Alabama proposed instead a $1.05 million penalty. All these problems notwithstanding, the EPA continued to grant CWM incineration permits, and it never questioned the company's licenses.[29]

CWM's financial unreliability hit a nerve with federal and state officials.[30] After Greenpeace's revelations, Congresswoman Barbara Boxer sent a letter to Administrator Lee Thomas urging him to deny the research permit to CWM because of the company's multiple violations of state and federal environmental regulations. Boxer remarked that CWM's parent company, Waste Management Inc., had been fined $4 million for federal hazardous-waste violations at its Kettleman Hills facility near Los Angeles. A settlement was reached, and Waste Management paid $2.5 million for illegally diluting PCBs with liquid waste and selling 6 million gallons of it as reclaimed oil. The company had also paid $600,000 in fines for improper storage of waste, and it had to reimburse $10 million to the State of Ohio for improper waste management. The firm was under investigation by as many as six states for its disposal practices, and Boxer reminded Thomas that even the EPA had put Waste Management under investigation for a series of accidents.[31] Representatives Roy Dyson (D–MD), William Hughes (D–NJ), James Howard (D–NJ), and Tom Foglietta (D–PA) joined in Boxer's criticism. Several Republican and Democratic representatives from California (including the Republican Norman Shumway and the Democrat Tony Coelho), New York, Kentucky, Michigan, and Minnesota formally endorsed Boxer's opposition and threw their support behind the Ban the Burn campaign.[32]

Local authorities followed suit. The waste to be incinerated aboard the *Vulcanus* had to be transported by train from Emelle, Alabama, to Philadelphia, thus crossing eight states.[33] Then it had to be loaded aboard ship in an operation that took several days. Once ready, the incinerator ship would sail through the Delaware Bay out to sea, where it would finally burn its load in the North Atlantic. Depending on weather and atmospheric conditions, some 20 million U.S. citizens in at least three coastal states—Delaware, New Jersey, and Pennsylvania—were directly at risk. According to the Coastal Zone Management Act of 1972, the states affected had the right to review the federal plans. In technical terms, this type of oversight was called "determination of coastal zone management (CZM) consistency."[34] The State of Pennsylvania granted approval without conditions. Delaware granted transit limited to daylight hours and required prior notification of movement of the ship. Furthermore, Delaware asked the EPA to prepare a separate EIS on the transit route. New Jersey's determination of CZM consistency, however, was much more exacting: that state prohibited transit during the summer, extended the moving safety zone, and insisted on verifying the composition of the waste.[35]

Maryland, too, claimed the right to make a determination of CZM consistency, arguing that the proposed burn would affect its coastal areas. The National Oceanic and Atmospheric Administration ruled in favor of Maryland, which was granted a period of six months to conduct its review. Tired of waiting, CWM filed a lawsuit against the Atmospheric Administration and the EPA, contending that Maryland was not entitled to conduct a consistency review and that New Jersey's conditions hindered the whole process. The State of Maryland and CWM reached a settlement, with Maryland agreeing to withdraw its CZM consistency review request; New Jersey softened its positions as well.[36] Once these legal issues were cleared, the EPA thought that its plan could go forward. Its last formal duty was to hold public hearings to inform local people about the forthcoming burns.

EPA's officers could hardly have forecast that these meetings would spell the end of ocean incineration in the United States.[37] The first hearing was held in Philadelphia on January 13, 1986. Even though it was a workday, people filled the thousand-seat auditorium well beyond capacity. When the EPA's officers presented their plans, people started chanting, "Ban the burn." When an EPA representative argued that the burns would help researchers make ocean incineration safer, more affordable, and more efficient, people booed him off the stage. The people who gathered in

Philadelphia shouted down most of the EPA's speakers. When City Manager James White, representing Mayor Wilson Goode and the Philadelphia City Council, took the floor to condemn the EPA's plans, the public gave him a standing ovation.[38] All subsequent hearings were similarly well attended and displayed the same attitude toward the EPA's plans. At the January 16 meeting in Redbank, New Jersey, Mayor Ralph J. Gorga of Lavallette, a shore town, spoke on behalf of several local coastal communities, which depended "upon a clean ocean and healthy fish for their very existence." He said that a large spill of hazardous chemicals would de facto destroy the tourist industry and property values in ocean-front communities.[39] These same points were reiterated by some 200 Cape May County residents, who demanded that the responsibility for disposing of hazardous wastes be given to the companies that produced them. A few days later, at the meeting in Ocean City, Maryland, Mayor Frank McCall of Wildwood Crest said that the EPA's proposal was a fairy tale without a happy ending. The only possible outcome, he said, was that the EPA deny permits for offshore burns. President Edward Herman of the Wildwood Crest City Council suggested that the EPA officials take some bumper stickers with "Ban the Burn" on them. "There are a few of these stickers around, if you change your mind," Herman said. "It might help you get out of town a little easier."[40] Mayor Rolando Powell of Ocean City spoke out so vehemently against the EPA's program that he became a rising star among the protesters. During the hearing, he said: "This is not a threat, it's a vow: I'll fight you." He then presented Greenpeace with the keys to the city.[41]

In total, 2,845 people attended the hearings, most of them in Philadelphia, though around 800 people participated in Ocean City; a total of 267 statements were released.[42] The EPA records show that the hearing officer received an additional 1,644 submissions, including forty-two petitions with 15,713 signatures.[43] Greenpeace sources mention that more than 23,000 signatures were collected in all.[44] The campaigners convinced congressional representatives from all the states directly involved in the EPA's plans to speak out against ocean incineration. The issue remained in the press for more than five months. Some local officials even publicly threatened to blockade the ship if the permit were issued. As reported by the *New York Times*, Ban the Burn was a success.⁴⁵ The campaign had attracted the interest of different organizations and had effectively informed and mobilized people. "Representatives of such environmental and civic groups as Greenpeace, Clean Ocean Action, the Marine Mammal Stranding Center, Clean Water Action, the Save Our Ocean Committee and the Women's Environmental Coalition" had come together to denounce the EPA's plans as "dangerous and risky." Many opposing at-sea incineration were well aware that the highly carcinogenic PCBs "could contaminate the ocean and would be a threat to fish, ocean mammals and, eventually, people." Ken Brown, a spokesman for Clean Water Action, reportedly said that the EPA was continuing "to relentlessly push ocean incineration" with an irresponsible "out of sight, out of mind" attitude. "We must do everything we can to insure [sic] that our oceans cease to serve as the dumping grounds for all sorts of human and industrial wastes." Brown succinctly summarized the prevalent sentiment that had emerged from the public meetings.⁴⁶

GRAVE MISGIVINGS

As had happened in 1983, the public outcry over ocean incineration induced the EPA to reconsider its plans. On May 1, 1986, Patrick Tobin, the EPA's hearing officer, submitted the *Hearing Officer's Report on the Tentative Determination to Issue the Incineration-at-Sea Research Permit* to Assistant Administrator for Water Lawrence Jensen.⁴⁷ This report acknowledged the many concerns that the public had raised during the hearings. Tobin recommended that the permits not be issued before solving the scientific, technical, and legal problems. To him, the EPA had first to integrate "the planning for hazardous waste management programs and [include] ocean incineration as part of the Agency's comparative evaluation of hazardous waste disposal options." Then, it should conduct and make publicly available "a qualitative assessment of the risks associated with the transporting of PCBs or other potentially incinerable hazardous waste down the

Delaware river and through Delaware Bay to the Site." Only after all these steps had been taken would the EPA be able to make an objective assessment of the viability of another oceanic burn. Tobin admitted that the conclusion was very likely to be negative.[48] Based on these recommendations, Jensen decided to deny any new research permits. In the context of that May 28 decision, Jensen announced that the EPA would be deferring any further ocean incineration until special regulations could be promulgated.[49]

In his decision to deny CWM's application, Jensen raised two pragmatic points. First, he acknowledged that the oceans were a vital resource for every U.S. citizen and that the EPA had a responsibility to avoid the degradation of the marine environment. Second, he reiterated the urgency and seriousness of the nation's hazardous-waste-management problem, saying that U.S. industries generated 250 million tons of hazardous waste a year—more than a ton for every U.S. citizen—thus forcing the hand of the EPA to explore options, including ocean incineration. At the same time, Jensen admitted that further research was needed to verify the risks of ocean incineration, and, above all, new, comprehensive guidelines had to be drawn up to regulate such research. Jensen was flashing a caution light. Rather than outlawing ocean incineration tout court, the EPA administrator called for further assessment in the hope that new regulation could "minimize the real and perceived risks, including possibly using less hazardous chemicals."[50]

The constituent organizations in Ban the Burn considered the EPA's decision a major success. They called it "a great victory for environmental and citizen groups who participated in the public hearings on the proposed permits" because it denied CWM's application for further burns. In addition, the EPA had again been forced to reckon with citizens' regulatory influence and interests.[51] Nevertheless, Greenpeace and Oceanic Society leaders warned the Ban the Burn coalition to remain vigilant.[52] Indeed, CWM was both offering technical help to "assist" the EPA in drafting any new regulations and challenging the EPA in court, claiming that the permit denial cost the company roughly $6 million. Shrewdly, CWM did not seek reimbursement. Rather, it tried to obtain an order to countermand the EPA's decision and allow for new research and commercial permits without reform of the regulations.[53] The Federal District Court for the District of Columbia ruled in favor of the EPA, finding that there was good reason to deny all research permits until new regulations were announced.[54]

The battlefield thus became the content of the EPA's new regulations. The report *Ocean Incineration: Its Role in Managing Hazardous Waste*, prepared by Congress's Office of Technology Assessment in August 1986, described incineration technology, its premise and promise, and its contradictions.[55] According to Lisa Bunin, the report paradoxically advocated for ocean incineration as an "interim" method to dispose of toxic waste while also praising waste reduction as the best solution to the hazardous-waste crisis. "There is no need for any interim method of waste disposal," Bunin noted. "A safe solution to the toxic waste crisis—waste reduction—is available right now. While the development of an ocean incineration program has already taken 12 years, waste reduction technology is currently being used by companies around the world."[56]

Representative William Hughes of New Jersey said that the OTA's report was "unrealistic." It provided no solution to hazardous-waste management and threatened the health of the oceans. "There's no such a thing as an interim solution when it comes to the ocean. The risks are very high," said Hughes, who defined the EPA's new ocean-incineration plans as a "Band-Aid approach."[57] Ten ranking members of the House Committee on Merchant Marine and Fisheries sent a critical letter to Administrator Lee Thomas on August 20, 1986. "To protect human health and the environment, hazardous wastes must be safely managed through treatment, storage, destruction or disposal," they wrote, lamenting that the EPA's plans did not meet minimum safety standards. According to the representatives, the EPA's approach had been "erratic," and its frequent change in direction had a "chilling effect" on the development of alternative waste-disposal technologies.[58]

In July 1986, Jon Hinck, Greenpeace's toxics campaign coordinator, commented on the OTA's final draft and on the EPA's impending regulations. Hinck served as a member of the EPA's advisory panel on waste in the marine environment. He found that the OTA's work was vitiated by "grave misgivings," especially concerning the data on ocean incineration's overall environmental sustainability. He stressed that the OTA's draft "reflected [a] grievously illogical analysis of available data" and that, if published as a draft, it would be "a discredit to the Office of Technology Assessment." The report, in Hinck's opinion, "perpetuated misconceptions regarding the nature of the problem [of hazardous waste] in a time in which synthetic toxic substances posed a serious and growing threat to human health and the environment." Many of these problems stemmed from "inaccurate assessment of the properties of the wastes in question." The report categorized the wastes eligible for ocean incineration as liquid, pumpable, and chlorinated hydrocarbons, but it did not identify the origins of these wastes, thus making it impossible to push for reduction of the waste. To Hinck, the greatest failure in the report was its inadequate assessment of the effects of ocean incineration on human health and the marine environment. References to the physical and toxicological properties of the chemicals involved were "glaringly absent," and the report's conclusions therefore lacked credibility. "What is most baffling to me as a reviewer," Hinck wrote, "is that major information gaps did not prevent the authors from reaching sweeping conclusions." With its largely positive tone, the report was dismissive of the extreme toxicity, persistence, and bioaccumulative nature of the wastes that ocean incineration was supposed to destroy. Finally, Hinck thought that the report seemed to indicate that the only difference between ocean incineration and land-based incineration was human exposure versus marine contamination. To Hinck, that was reductionist logic because there was no assurance that "an incinerator pitching and rolling at sea will operate as effectively as one firmly anchored on land." Furthermore, this faulty logic did not contemplate the "bioconcentration of pollutants in marine biota of the highly lipophilic chlorinated hydrocarbons," which meant that toxic by-products of ocean incineration were destined to enter the human food chain.[59]

Lisa Bunin thought Hinck's comments were too soft. She decried the faulty logic of U.S. hazardous-waste policy to the international community, which had grown and become more skeptical of ocean incineration. The OTA's report, to Bunin, crystallized the rift between the United States and Europe. In Europe, a few governments and the most important regional and multilateral organizations were moving toward outright dismissal of the technology. In the United States, the government seemed intent to salvage it at any cost.[60] The inherent contradictions in the OTA's report gave Bunin the opportunity to reiterate Greenpeace's categorical opposition to the practice.[61] Bunin circulated a report that she had drafted in March 1986 in the form of a Greenpeace "global ocean incineration campaign issue paper." The document exposed the risks and technical faults of ocean incineration, the hazards it posed for the global environment, and its threat to the oceans and the people in coastal communities who worked with or consumed seafood. The campaign paper had six points of opposition to ocean incineration: (1) ocean incineration perpetuated the production of organohalogen compounds and inhibited waste reduction; (2) the technology allowed industry to escape responsibility because environmental damage could not be linked to the source that generated the waste; (3) the ships' incinerator stacks emitted an array of toxic substances that were persistent and bioaccumulative, damaging the marine ecosystem; (4) the emissions could not be accurately measured, identified, or monitored; (5) ocean incineration increased the risk of spills and accidents; and (6) there was no consensus on which chemicals could be safely incinerated at sea.[62]

Greenpeace's issue paper was sent to governments and the national press in Europe, Asia, Oceania, and the United States. It stressed sound international regulations and demanded a ban on ocean incineration and on the global trade of incinerable material, with particular emphasis on the export of hazardous waste from the United States. The report marked an abandonment of the gradualist approach. It challenged ocean incineration both domestically and internationally, locally and transnationally. According to Greenpeace, it was time to outlaw ocean incineration and make it economically disadvantageous once and for all.[63] The private companies that had invested heavily in this sector reacted to the Greenpeace report with renewed vigor. Now that grassroots mobilization had made it difficult to incinerate off the coasts of the United States, they had started looking at Europe as the most promising frontier. So, for the environmental activists in turn Europe became the new front line of struggle.

BAN THE BURN

BATTLEGROUND EUROPE

In July 1985, the European Economic Community (EEC) proposed regulation to progressively phase out ocean incineration.[64] The EEC discussed a directive that would ban ocean incineration from 1990 onward and prevent countries outside the EEC from carrying out incineration operations in waters within the jurisdiction of EEC member states. If approved, the provision would de facto forbid OCS, a subsidiary of the U.S.-based company CWM, to burn hazardous wastes off the coasts of the Netherlands in the North Sea. The EEC proposal followed the general principle of caution. Quoting the final declaration of an international conference on the protection of the North Sea, it stated that incineration of wastes at sea was to be avoided and outlawed for the protection of the whole marine environment. The proposal also attempted to prevent disparities in national legislation, harmonize existing national laws, and avoid competition. Finally, it stated that offshore burns were plausible only if no safer and more sustainable alternative could be found.[65]

The EEC proposal opened debate in Europe on ocean incineration and its future. OCS publicized a favorable image of the technology in a variety of informational materials complete with illustrated technical details, attractive pictures, and catchy graphs. OCS brochures described how harmless and convenient ocean incineration was. At times, the wording was purposely vague. For instance, OCS had to concede that "no clear connection" existed "between incineration and destruction" and that there was no instrument that could guarantee "the continuous measurement of destruction efficiency during the incineration of organochlorine waste." It defined hydrochloric acid, a highly toxic and carcinogenic by-product of waste incineration that was released through the gas plume, simply as a "not entirely harmless substance."[66] Throughout most of the material it produced, however, OCS was keen on reiterating the claim that pollutants in the ocean as a result of at-sea incineration were insignificant. The company said that severe biological effects on the marine ecosystem could be ruled out with absolute certitude.[67]

To further substantiate these claims, OCS sponsored an international scientific conference in Antwerp on February 27, 1986. Its goal was to prove that incineration operations in the North Sea had a largely negligible impact. H. Compaan, an expert from the Netherlands Organization for Applied Scientific Research who had authored the Dutch government's report that stated ocean incineration did not have "harmful effects on the marine environment," presented a paper. To Compaan, there simply were not enough available data to establish a correlation between ocean incineration and pollution in the North Sea. He augmented his point by saying that enough was known about marine pollution to exonerate incinerator ships.[68] J. D. Bletchly, a consultant on environmental affairs for the Organization for Economic Cooperation and Development, expounded on PCBs and their persistence in the marine environment. He thought the North Sea did not present worrying levels of PCBs and that ocean incineration would substantially reduce the threat that PCBs posed across Europe.[69]

OCS also directly lobbied. On April 16, 1986, the company reached out to Carole Tongue, a U.K. member of the European Parliament, to discuss the EEC draft directive on ocean incineration. OCS representatives pointed out that "scientific evidence from such bodies as the American Environmental Protection Agency, and from research carried out in the Netherlands" suggested that at-sea incineration was "probably the safest and most efficient method of disposal, particularly of chlorine-based substances," and furthermore was the only effective method for the disposal of "some 20 years' supply of highly dangerous PCBs" stored in European facilities. Ocean incineration, to OCS, was the easiest way to dispose of these stocks, so the EEC should not ban the practice.[70] OCS lawyers contacted Kenneth D. Collins, another British member of the European Parliament and vice chairman of the Committee on the Environment, Public Health, and Consumer Protection. Collins's committee was in the middle of discussing the EEC draft directive on at-sea incineration and had made several amendments to it, including one that suggested examining a proposal to ban the practice. In light of these developments, the committee members were asked to collect information and engage in briefings in preparation for a debate in September 1986. In August, OCS gave all committee members original

OCS informational material supporting ocean incineration and its scientific, economic, and environmental viability.[71] These efforts paid off in part. While examining the proposed EEC legislation, the British House of Lords rejected the ban on ocean incineration and deemed the technology safe, effectively stalemating the EEC legislative process.[72]

The OCS counteroffensive continued. The company circulated fact sheets defining ocean incineration as safe and praising the Gulf of Mexico research burns.[73] An OCS booklet titled *Facts About Ocean Incineration* remarked succinctly: "Ocean incineration is not an environmental problem, it is a solution to an environmental problem."[74] Pamphlets, leaflets, and brochures in defense of ocean incineration's efficiency multiplied. Taking a long perspective, the pamphlets talked of the "fifteen years of waste incineration at sea" and praised the commercial advantages of the technology.[75] Moreover, in October 1986 OCS sponsored the establishment of the transnational Association of Maritime Incinerators (AMI).[76] Located in Rotterdam and chaired by Executive Director Gert Heinemann of OCS, the AMI was to make sure that ocean incineration could be "properly regulated both in the United States and in Europe." In its first press release, it acknowledged that at-sea incineration had instigated a "wide-ranging and controversial" debate, but it also maintained that "the most up-to-date scientific evidence" supported the technology's environmental safety and economic attractiveness. Ocean incineration, according to the AMI, was harmless, cheap, highly sophisticated, and well regulated, and it had a capacity "sufficiently high to meet the needs of a modern industrial society." Above all, the AMI touted ocean incineration's safety, saying it took "place well away from centers of population."[77]

The Ban the Burn campaign rebutted pro-ocean-incineration propaganda point for point. For instance, while OCS gathered a number of scientists in Antwerp, Greenpeace organized an international meeting on at-sea incineration in Amsterdam, attended by delegates from a dozen European countries and the United States.[78] The meeting was called "Ban the Burn," and it had a broad geographical and strategic scope. The attendees assessed the ongoing negotiations within such multilateral fora as the LDC and OSCOM, drafted common positions, and discussed tactics and proposals that were meant to enhance the campaign's visibility and political efficacy. The shared feeling was that Europe represented a better springboard than the United States for a global campaign to ban ocean incineration because most of the European governments had always regarded the practice as a temporary solution. In addition, activists in Europe did not have to fight multinational giants such as CWM because only two companies, OCS, the owner of the *Vulcanus I* and *II*, and Lehnkering, the owner of the *Vesta* sailing out of Antwerp, were authorized to operate in the North Sea. European issuance of incineration permits was more dispersed than U.S. issuance, which was handled only by the EPA, because permits had to be obtained from the country where the waste originated and from the country where the waste would be incinerated (the Netherlands). In addition, the Rijkswaterstaat in the Netherlands was responsible for controlling the performance of incinerators, while the companies were obliged to report to both OSCOM and the LDC. As complex as this system was, it nevertheless gave the anti-ocean-incineration activists a better chance to monitor permit issuance. At the Amsterdam conference, Greenpeace decided to coordinate among national offices and send a delegation to the pertinent multilateral regulatory bodies. Lisa Bunin was designated the delegation's chair.[79]

Compared to what was happening in the United States, the public in Europe was generally unaware of the risks and implications of ocean incineration. Ban the Burn leaders needed to double down on their educational efforts there. They began presenting papers, writing op-eds, displaying banners, organizing rallies, participating in media interviews, signing petitions, and passing out bumper stickers. They replicated the protest repertoire that had worked so well in the United States. In addition, Greenpeace lobbied both OSCOM and the LDC directly, steering the international discussion toward phasing out the technology. In the spring of 1986, Bunin submitted to the ninth meeting of the LDC/International Maritime Organization Scientific Group on Dumping in London Greenpeace's official position on ocean incineration. The SGD meeting was timely and relevant. It helped the LDC contracting parties overcome the Kleppinger–Ackerman controversy by providing updated information on the safety, management, and control of marine incineration, including a full revision of mandatory regulations and technical guidelines. Greenpeace's presentation and the submission of its terms of reference were of crucial importance to the Ban the Burn campaign in Europe.

Greenpeace's paper was based on the thirty-eight-page report that Edward Kleppinger and Desmond Bond had published in 1985 under the title *Ocean Incineration of Hazardous Waste: A Revisit to the Controversy*.[80] It summarized the main frictions between Kleppinger's and D. J. Ackerman's studies, which revolved around the adequacy of testing and the design of the incinerators.[81] Lisa Bunin decided to avoid any specific reference to ocean incineration's phase-out in the Greenpeace report, trying not to alienate support from certain participants and delegations. Rather, she insisted that the burden of proof of ocean incineration's safety rested with its proponents.[82] In its initial draft version, Greenpeace's paper generated a vibrant discussion within the anti-ocean-incineration forces. Oceanic Society campaigners in particular were dissatisfied with it. According to Sally Ann Lentz, the society's coordinator and staff attorney, the report blurred the assessment of destruction efficiency and referred only vaguely to the environmental consequences of the practice. Lentz said Greenpeace's text did not make explicit the problems associated with destruction efficiency. She thought that the inability to determine gas flow and composition had to be the centerpiece of the international discussion. For Lentz, any consideration of the environmental impact of incineration emissions should not be limited to a "review" of effects but should entail a detailed assessment. In substance, the Oceanic Society was urging Greenpeace to stress the adverse impacts of ocean incineration on the microlayer. Up to then, Greenpeace was more interested in highlighting other drawbacks of the technology, such as the disincentive to invest in cleaner alternatives, the impossibility of linking environmental damage to the waste generator, and the resultant liability-free character of the incineration industry.[83]

Bunin took the Oceanic Society's input seriously and decided to give more prominence to the collection of further scientific evidence on the environmental impact of ocean incineration. In the final version of its report, thus, Greenpeace proposed a series of independent studies to solve the

Kleppinger–Ackerman controversy and to account for the composition of stack gases, the hazardous nature and persistence of the emissions, and the amounts of PICs released during the burning process. These new studies would have information on what effect emissions had on the microlayer and the microorganisms dependent on that layer, the frequency of fish disease, and what impact ocean incineration would have on the food chain. All these points were considered key and had been left largely untouched by both Kleppinger and Ackerman.[84] As Lisa Bunin put it, if Greenpeace were to commission a report on the role of the marine microlayer in transporting and reconcentrating toxic chemicals, "I think it would be a feather in our cap." Greenpeace knew that such a study would also affect the international debate. This new approach would allow Greenpeace to counter private companies' arguments and would help the organization secure more public support on both sides of the Atlantic.[85]

Greenpeace's international board endorsed Bunin's adjusted line and agreed to refocus Ban the Burn on the oceans' microlayer and on the overall biological effects of at-sea incineration.[86] In Bunin's view, this strategic shift was crucial to convincing the LDC to move forward with a joint LDC/OSCOM meeting of experts.[87] The U.S. delegation at the LDC, however, opposed the idea. According to the EPA's representatives to the LDC, it was "prudent to defer a joint LDC/OSCOM meeting until new information" was available. Greenpeace countered that the U.S. government had already delayed the gathering for more than a year, reportedly to obtain more data.[88] The delegates from Denmark and Germany backed Greenpeace and said that the information available at the time was enough to hold a workshop, but the ones from the United Kingdom and Canada deemed such a meeting worthless. Given these contrasts, the LDC secretariat decided to allow the submission of independent studies in preparation for the joint LDC/OSCOM meeting. The Oceanic Society and Greenpeace started working on a report immediately.[89] Then, acceding to the environmental groups' line, the secretariat called a general meeting of the LDC contracting parties for the fall of 1986 and a joint LDC/OSCOM meeting for the spring of 1987.[90]

RAISING THE STAKES

Ban the Burn inflamed the battle against ocean incineration in Europe. Greenpeace and its allies were busy on all fronts, from researching to presenting at international conferences and multilateral meetings. They even sought to gain observer status at the Helsinki Convention, which had been organized in 1974 to curb marine pollution in the Baltic Sea.[91] But what distinguished Greenpeace was its signature protest style: the spectacular, direct-action approach that had characterized it from the very beginning.

In the United States, Greenpeace's grassroots strategy—coalition building and networking—had worked so well that it had not found a serious need to employ confrontational tactics. But in Europe the situation was different. Local mobilizations were scarce, and stirring people to action required enormous coordination among different national offices. Bunin and the Greenpeace international board decided that direct-action operations would be the best way to break through and generate the attention that Ban the Burn needed to succeed.[92]

The first action was organized in the summer of 1986, and the target was the *Vulcanus II*. Greenpeace tracked the vessel when it was harbored in Rotterdam. The main antitoxics campaigners, Lisa Bunin, Jon Hinck, and David Rapaport, remained on the sidelines, overseeing the operation from their U.S. headquarters. Kirsten Hansen worked from Denmark to coordinate communications and develop briefings and press releases for Greenpeace national offices in Europe. Monika Griefahn monitored from Germany.[93] On September 9, 1986, Greenpeace campaigners in Europe received a Ban the Burn info pack that contained relevant information about the proposed action and its background. The material explained that the *Vulcanus II* left Antwerp every three weeks loaded with some 3,000 tons of highly toxic chemical waste to be burned in the North Sea. This practice—the Greenpeace leaflet emphasized—posed a severe threat to the marine environment, but the national and international regulatory bodies, including the EPA in the United States and OSCOM in Europe, were either denying permits for further burns or moving toward ending ocean incineration altogether. The informational packet explained that the *Vulcanus II* was operated by OCS, a subsidiary of the giant U.S. firm Waste Management, Inc. The ship's agent was German, and the flag was Liberian. Another ship, the *Vesta*, was owned by a German company. To motivate its members, Greenpeace presented ocean incineration as "another method of dumping waste at sea hidden by the slick image of high technology," promoted by "an international ring of waste dumpers" whose unscrupulous, profit-oriented design had to be stopped.[94]

In the early evening of September 14, 1986, eight Greenpeace activists from Germany, Ireland, the United Kingdom, Sweden, and Belgium intercepted the *Vulcanus II* in the Antwerp harbor, while the ship docked at the loading pier. The activists were aboard two dinghies, the *Zodiac* and the *Iver*, which they put between the *Vulcanus II* and the quay side when the incinerator ship was only thirty-three feet (ten meters) off the pier.[95] The crew onboard the *Vulcanus II* responded with water hoses, pushing and crushing the *Zodiac* to the quay side. One *Zodiac* crew member was injured, and the dinghy's engine was damaged. The harbor police ultimately intervened at midnight, ordering the people aboard the Greenpeace boat out of the water. The police confiscated any photographic equipment and film and charged the boat's crew with hindering port operations by sailing "pleasure yachts" in the harbor, by swimming, and by filming harbor facilities. Sixteen people were arrested and released at 4:00 a.m. after being interrogated.[96]

Shocked by what the people involved in the action defined as the "brutality of the *Vulcanus II* crew," Greenpeace coordinators organized a press conference at the harbor on September 15. They sent a press release to national and international press services and invited the local unions and the mayor of Antwerp to attend. Greenpeace pilloried the Belgian police for arresting its activists and criticized the confiscation of its video material as an attack against the freedom of expression.[97] The video shot during the action had been commissioned by the Greenpeace film division in London and had been filmed by Pino Gorin, a freelance professional filmmaker from Amsterdam. Greenpeace had planned to circulate the film within hours after the action to maximize public attention, but this

FIGURE 5.2 Greenpeace activists in actions against the *Vulcanus II*, 1986.

Source: Box 5836 (Documentation on Waste Management International [WMI]), International Institute for Social History, Greenpeace International (Amsterdam) Archives.

strategy was halted by the confiscation. The film was exculpatory, showing, for instance, that chemical detergents had been added to the water cannons that had been used against the activists, that the Greenpeace inflatables had been damaged, and that its activists had been placed in a life-threatening situation. Greenpeace contacted the Belgian and Dutch federations of professional journalists and asked for a public expression of solidarity. They also filed an official complaint against the Belgian police. The film had been confiscated under a law that prohibited filming in the port for amateur purposes. But Greenpeace maintained that it had operated with professional journalists and film technicians.[98]

The action attracted harsh criticism from the proponents of ocean incineration. The AMI replied that Greenpeace's propaganda was misleading and based on unscientific notions.[99] The British and the Irish governments officially commented on the action, requested that the LDC secretariat review the action at its meetings of environmental NGOs, including Greenpeace, and lamented that Greenpeace talked with the press too much and was interested only in sensational actions.[100] By contrast, Greenpeace leaders thought the direct action was a success. In spite of the film confiscation, Greenpeace's action was widely covered. Newspapers throughout Europe featured the story in terms that were largely sympathetic to Greenpeace's goals.[101] This coverage convinced the organization of the value of similar protests. The campaign organizers considered actions on the high sea, at burning sites, or onboard the ships, including chimney climbing and chaining. Greenpeace figured out ways to intercept and blockade incinerator ships at the estuary of the Scheldt, near the Dutch city of Vlissingen. It also envisioned replicating the blockade in Antwerp with inflatables and support ships to hinder loading operations or prevent incinerator vessels from berthing.[102] All in all, Greenpeace was convinced that only a manifold strategy consisting of grassroots mobilization, transnational advocacy, scientific reporting, lobbying, and direct actions could bring about an end to ocean incineration.

* * *

Given the industry's and the EPA's relentless commitment to defend ocean incineration, in 1986 the many opponents of the practice decided to coalesce their efforts into a common campaign, Ban the Burn, which was coordinated simultaneously locally and transnationally. The campaigners attacked ocean incineration on many fronts, denouncing its high environmental risks, the consequences it had on human health, its financial unviability, and the inconsistency in both domestic and international regulation. The EPA reacted by unsuccessfully proposing new legislation and, more interestingly, by supporting the progressive delocalization of the practice to Europe. This response betrayed a structural weakness of the U.S. government, which was boxed in by its own environmental rules and the requirement to foster people's involvement and democratic participation. The waste-management industry understood that the battle over ocean incineration had moved away from government to public opinion and tried to promote a positive narrative of the practice, though unsuccessfully. The Ban the Burn campaigners, indeed, reacted to this attempt by debunking the false myths surrounding the technology and by doubling down not only on their lobbying but also on their attention-grabbing strategy. All of it worked out well, and the end of ocean incineration was in sight.

6

QUITTING SMOKING

Until the mid-1980s, the U.S. chemical industry on its own produced more than 250 million tons of poisonous waste per year. Only a fraction of it could be destroyed at sea.[1] Ocean incineration was, in other words, completely unable to solve the rampant hazardous-waste crisis. Yet a few governments and private companies still tried to restore the technology's reputation and justify its use. The anti-ocean-incineration campaigners challenged those who supported the practice, opening up several fronts against them.

First, the opponents of ocean incineration grounded their criticism on a series of scientific studies that disproved the actual need for the technology and pointed to better and safer alternatives. The campaigners also sponsored new independent research, aiming to counter the overly positive image of ocean incineration provided by the waste-management industry and to bring together a scientific consensus about the risks involved in offshore burns. Second, they kept lobbying both national and international institutions in the attempt to erode ocean incineration's political support and commercial appeal. Third, they organized direct actions to give further visibility and public prominence to the dangers of the practice.

The governments that wanted to keep incinerating hazardous waste at sea funded and disseminated further studies and scientific reports that assessed ocean incineration positively in an attempt to dismiss environmentalists' concerns as irrational and naive. The companies managing ocean incineration reacted to the protests by framing the campaigners as terrorists and thus trying to undermine their international legitimacy and overall credibility. Neither strategy, however, worked. The opponents of ocean incineration, indeed, succeeded in proving a causal relationship between the technology and the release of persistent substances toxic to both the marine biota and human health.[2] Their success in revealing this truth, which was eventually accepted both by the U.S. authorities and by the competent international regulatory agencies, represented the final blow to ocean incineration.

THE CLASH OF REPORTS

In the first half of 1986, local protests that made up the Ban the Burn campaign brought plans for ocean incineration in the United States to a standstill. But the overall fate of the technology remained under discussion. By the early months of 1987, a series of international scientific meetings were supposed to say whether the technology was environmentally viable and to decide on its future development. The debate among experts turned the Ban the Burn campaign into an "ecomodernist" movement. The anti-ocean-incineration advocates developed "an inclusive and scientifically engaged response" to the environmental threat of incineration at sea.[3] They commissioned a series of independent studies that questioned ocean incineration's environmental sustainability. In the end, they wanted to create a scientifically grounded consensus in support of phasing out and eventually banning ocean incineration.

The tenth consultative meeting of the LDC was held at the headquarters of the International Maritime Organization in London on October 13–17, 1986. Here the anti-ocean-incineration campaigners had an opportunity to challenge the scientific foundations of the technology and expose its contradictions and flaws.[4] The meeting opened up a year-long battle that engaged Greenpeace and its allies. The starting point for the international discussion was the recommendations of the LDC SGD, issued in May 1986. The SGD suggested that any reassessment of ocean incineration had to pay attention to its environmental repercussions. The panel of experts highlighted the "chemical and biological effects" of the gases emitted by ocean incineration and compared them to emissions from alternative methods for the disposal of hazardous waste.[5] For Greenpeace, the SGD was implying not only that ocean incineration was an environmental hazard but also that its existence curbed investment in cleaner, alternative technologies.[6] The Oceanic Society supported this view, claiming that ocean incineration was an unproven technology with unquantifiable and unacceptable ecological consequences.[7]

The U.S. delegation to the LDC, however, took a completely different approach. It defended the viability of the practice and said the safety of ocean incineration should be left up to national authorities. The draft resolution circulated by the U.S. representatives gave national regulatory bodies discretionary power over site designation and the classification of incinerable materials. It also recommended a loose mechanism of international control and proposed a set of voluntary technical guidelines that private ocean-incineration operators could follow or not.[8] Oceanic Society representative Sally Ann Lentz censured the U.S. proposal and urged the other delegates to support mandatory international surveillance of tank cleaning and stack emissions. She wanted to minimize any discretionary application of environmental standards.[9] Once again, the negotiations reached a stalemate, complicating any hope of reaching a common agreement. To break the deadlock, the LDC secretariat called a meeting of experts and asked them to settle the issue with a universally acceptable summary of the environmental viability of the technology. The meeting, jointly organized by the LDC and OSCOM, was scheduled for May 1987.

The six months that preceded the LDC/OSCOM meeting were characterized by a whirl of activity. Greenpeace's campaign coordinator, Lisa Bunin, channeled resources to support and oversee the development of rigorous and innovative scientific work on ocean incineration. She entrusted two experienced activists, Alan Pickaver and Paul Johnston, with preparing position papers that Greenpeace would present at the LDC/OSCOM meeting. Alan Pickaver was director of ocean ecology for Greenpeace International. At the time, he was studying microlayer fish diseases to find ways to minimize the impact of hazardous waste on the marine environment.[10] Paul Johnston was a Greenpeace chief scientist with substantial international experience studying marine reserves.[11] Pickaver and Johnston were joined by Ruth Stringer, a graduate in chemistry and biochemistry from the University of London. She was hired to research the effects of organochlorines on the marine environment.[12] The final document compiled by this team was titled "Comparative Assessment of Available Alternatives to Incineration at Sea: Hazardous Waste Reduction—the Best Approach to Hazardous Waste Management." Greenpeace thought that this thoroughgoing report would finally debunk the myth of the need for ocean incineration and definitively discredit any claim that ocean incineration was a sound method for the disposal of hazardous industrial waste.[13]

While the Greenpeace paper was being researched and written, Lisa Bunin involved Greenpeace in a broader "political game." The goals that Bunin aimed to achieve through the LDC/OSCOM meeting were not only scientific ones. She wanted the meeting to lead to an internationally binding agreement that would ban incineration at sea or, at a minimum, set up a timeline for its progressive phaseout. She wanted the meeting to outlaw the export of the technology in order to erase its commercial appeal.[14] To this end, Bunin asked Henk Kersten, the head of Greenpeace in the Netherlands, to coordinate the lobbying efforts of the various Greenpeace national offices in Europe. Kersten was to ensure that Greenpeace activists had updated information on ocean incineration so they could maximize their national influence and pressure. He also worked to identify the specific concerns of each national delegation to the LDC/OSCOM meeting so that Greenpeace could more effectively tailor its lobbying.[15] Several information packets and policy questionnaires were written to guide the national delegations. They were to go armed with Greenpeace's key agenda:

outlaw the export of ocean incineration, prevent the establishment of new incineration zones, and limit the commercialization of the technology.[16]

Once the LDC/OSCOM meeting started in May 1987, the delegates were split into three working groups.[17] The first dealt with the environmental effects of emissions. It focused on the ocean's microlayer, the stratum of water that provides habitat for many different bacteria, neuston, and invertebrate larvae at the foundation of the marine ecosystem and food chain. The delegates in this group noted that because plankton migrated to and from the surface microlayer, toxic pollutants could easily be transported by them to other parts of the ocean. Several studies submitted to this panel indicated that acid emissions from incineration rapidly and substantially affected the microlayer.[18] The second working group tackled the technological characteristics of ocean incineration. The panel discussed the parameters used to assess combustion and destruction efficiency, the release of PICs, and the potential pollutants such as dioxin that could enter the marine environment and atmosphere. Although acknowledging that the temperature in the incinerator ships' combustion chambers was adequate and stable—though the heat flow was very turbulent—this group emphasized that the release of organic by-products was unavoidable.[19] The third working group was tasked with studying suitable alternatives to ocean incineration. This panel classified different treatment methods according to the chlorine content of the waste. For highly chlorinated wastes, they recommended the use of chlorinolysis, oxychlorination, chlorination, and catalytic dichlorination, all of which were commercially available technologies. For medium chlorinated waste, the group suggested the use of closed systems with chlorinated solvents instead of a water-based approach. For low-chlorinated wastes, the panel pointed to catalytic dichlorination and wet oxidation as the best alternatives to ocean incineration.[20] In sum, ocean incineration was not needed for a single category of organic, chlorinated waste. The consensus was that investment needed to be made at the source of the problem—in the prevention and reduction of hazardous waste in the manufacturing process.

The pro-incineration AMI took part in the LDC/OSCOM meeting as an international observer. It wanted to influence the scientific discussion.

The AMI defended both the environmental soundness and the commercial prospects of ocean incineration. It presented a series of topical responses to Greenpeace and other environmental organizations.[21] To support its views, it referred to the OTA study issued in August 1986. Perhaps unsurprisingly, that study defined the technology as safe and reliable. Moreover, the AMI maintained that all the phases that led to actual offshore incineration were rigorously controlled and held to national and international regulation standards.[22] Sally Ann Lentz, who spoke on behalf of the Oceanic Society and Friends of the Earth, easily rebutted the AMI's position. With the help of prominent scientists and environmental advocates such as Barry Commoner, George Crozier, and Joseph Goldman, and with support from Richard Denisen, the principal author of the OTA's report, Lentz exposed the many fallacies of the AMI's arguments. The reassurances provided by the private association were misleading, she said, and did not address the environmental concerns raised by ocean incineration. To Lentz, the supporters of the practice, unabashedly the U.S. delegation, ignored ocean incineration's poor performance standards, overlooked its environmental liability, and left largely unclear its financial accountability.[23] The risk of long-term and irreversible consequences and the threat posed by this "unneeded" technology were, as Lisa Bunin and Ruth Stringer put it, simply "unacceptable."[24] The idea of shipboard incinerators able to destroy chemical substances was based on theory rather than on actual measurements. According to the Greenpeace activists, "A single complete analysis of the full range of chemicals emitted from incinerator stacks has not been conducted and cannot be conducted." For this reason, Bunin maintained, no conclusion could be drawn "about the environmental acceptability of the technology."[25]

The environmentalists' tone had become one of alarm, yet some governments still pursued ocean incineration without pause. Confronted by the necessity to get rid of a huge stockpile of PCBs, the Dutch government authorized a new series of burns in the North Sea right after the LDC/OSCOM meeting. The request for a permit for the proposed burns was submitted to OSCOM in early June 1987 by Chemical Waste Cleaning, a Dutch company. The proposed burn was to take place in the fall.[26] The

Dutch Ministry of Economic Affairs and Ministry of the Environment green-lighted the burns and renewed the *Vulcanus I* license, extending it until September 1989.[27]

The Dutch government's activity caused a cascade of events. The prospect of new burns in the North Sea convinced both the LDC and OSCOM to postpone another joint meeting. In the United States, the EPA and the multinational corporate leaders of the global ocean-incineration business tried to capitalize on the opportunity offered by the Dutch burns to circumvent domestic pressure and outsource the destruction of PCB-laden waste abroad.[28] Following in The Hague's footsteps, the Spanish government, too, considered designating its own incineration site off the coast of Cantabria.[29] The idea was to burn some 10,000 metric tons of toxic wastes over a one-year period on ships operated by OCS. The Cantabrian Sea was an area where the Galician and Cantabrian fishing fleets plied the waters.[30]

These developments transformed the June 1987 OSCOM meeting in Cardiff into a showdown between the proponents and opponents of ocean incineration in Europe. The Dutch government defended its position by highlighting the interim nature of ocean incineration, even as it acknowledged that the most promising means for the disposal of organochlorine wastes were all land based. Safer and more efficient land-based incinerators were already operative in Belgium, Denmark, and France. The Dutch delegation maintained, however, that these alternative methods notwithstanding, 85,000 tons of PCB waste a year still needed to be incinerated at sea. A drastic reduction in waste could not be expected until 1995. Before that, ocean incineration was simply unavoidable.[31] This argument was so strong that when the delegations of the Nordic countries submitted a proposal calling for an end to ocean incineration by December 1991, the Dutch, British, and Spanish representatives blocked it immediately.[32]

Once again, the burden of proving that ocean incineration was unsound fell on environmentalist organizations. Lisa Bunin highlighted the statement in annex 8 to the final report of the joint LDC/OSCOM experts' meeting, repeating the argument that valid alternatives existed for every chlorinated waste stream that was incinerated at sea. Bunin also noted that the technology had been born only as an interim solution. The first agreement to end it was signed in 1981. At the sixth annual OSCOM meeting, the member countries had already designated January 1990 as "a final date for the termination of incineration at sea."[33] Finally, Bunin remarked that "the quantities of waste going to incineration at sea would decline, leading to doubt over the continued viability of marine incineration as a commercial preposition." The latter comment disproved one of the leading arguments made by supporters of the technology.[34] In the end, Bunin repeated the environmentalists' anthem: ocean incineration had to be terminated, the designation of new incineration zones and new port-side storage facilities had to be prohibited, and the development and use of hazardous-waste-reduction techniques had to be promoted.[35] Only by fulfilling all these conditions could the OSCOM countries and all the major industrial powers live up to the declaration that 1990 would be the "Year of the Environment."[36]

The final resolution voted on by the delegates in Cardiff did not outlaw ocean incineration. It included, however, a decisive clause, annex 4. This important clause mandated the termination of the practice by the beginning of 1990.[37] Greenpeace's and other organizations' unceasing scientific reporting and coordinated transnational lobbying had opened a crucial breach in the pro-ocean-incineration front.[38]

NAVAL SKIRMISHES

Through scientific reporting, the anti-ocean-incineration campaigners had influenced the international debate. And through their symbolic demonstrations and direct actions (known as "mind bombing"), Greenpeace and its allies had popularized the fight against ocean incineration.[39] Small, committed groups of trained activists began to track incinerator vessels with a plan to interfere in every stage of the incineration process. They boarded the vessels, hung banners from their masts, and staged protests at harbors to interrupt port-loading operations. Aside from the coordination skills and financial resources necessary for such operations, there were also legal

FIGURE 6.1 Greenpeace activists climbing the stack of the *Vulcanus II*, 1987.

Source: From *The Times* (London), August 24, 1987, Box 5860 (Press Clippings Concerning the Action Against the Ocean Incinerators Vesta and Vulcanus, August 1987), International Institute for Social History, Greenpeace International (Amsterdam) Archives.

expenses to consider because the actions usually involved confrontations with local authorities and private companies. All these efforts eventually paid off, though.

Greenpeace organized one of its first direct actions against ocean incineration in Europe on the outskirts of Mannheim, an industrial city along the Rhine River in Western Germany, in May 1987. A dozen Greenpeace activists symbolically blockaded a tank motorship, the *Wedau*, while it was berthed in port. The vessel was being loaded with PCB waste destined for incineration at sea. The activists blocked the harbor exit with a rope and twelve buoys. On the buoys they hung a banner reading "Stop the Poison-Tanker Wedau." When the ship sailed to Antwerp, Greenpeace members accompanied it with two inflatables. Their intention was to make the toxic transport visible to the public and to make sure that the almost 20 million people who got their drinking water from the Rhine would know that "the tanker Wedau transported about every two weeks a dangerous cocktail of chemicals from Mannheim to Antwerp, to be loaded on Vulcanus there."[40] The blockade did not engage in interfering with the *Wedau*'s navigation. They were not trying to stop the tanker. Rather, they followed it closely, generating as much publicity as possible with noise and chanted slogans and constant interviews with the local press.

Greenpeace carried out these attention-grabbing activities throughout the summer of 1987. In mid-August, one of Greenpeace's boats, the *Sirius*, was berthed in Middelburg, the capital of the Dutch province of Zeeland.[41] The mayors of the main municipalities of the area, including the seaside town of Vlissingen, visited the group onboard the *Sirius*. This coastal area was particularly exposed to hazards because the incinerator vessels transited from Antwerp through the Scheldt River and out to the North Sea. After discussion with the activists, the mayors released a joint press statement expressing grave concern about the burns that the Dutch government was about to authorize.[42] To follow up, Greenpeace organized a press conference on the *Sirius* on August 15. There, the organization presented the independent study it had commissioned to Aviv, a company based in Enschede, the Netherlands. The Aviv report, titled "Incineration at Sea of Waste: The Risk of Transport in the Western Scheldt," modeled the consequences of an accident involving an ocean-incineration vessel in the Scheldt delta. According to the study, this type of calamity would result in the ignition of part of the hazardous cargo and the subsequent release into the atmosphere of poisonous gases such as phosgene, dioxin, chlorine, and hydrochloric acid. In the event of such an accident, those living close to Vlissingen's seafront would suffer immediate damage to their health. Chlorine and hydrochloric acid would cause irritation of the eyes and tightness in the bronchial tubes and lungs; the release of phosgene, dioxin, and dibenzofurans would result in even more severe effects over a longer time frame. An accident of this sort, the report warned, would result in the release of 1,000 tons of hazardous waste that would contaminate the whole delta.[43]

Meanwhile, as Greenpeace was holding its press conference, the incinerator ship *Vulcanus II* was on its way to Antwerp. It arrived on August 17. Another incineration ship, the *Vesta*, was approaching the area, too. The crew of the *Sirius*, which counted twenty members from nine different countries, including two veteran campaigners and five members of the press, got ready for action.[44] On August 19, the *Sirius* got wind that the *Vulcanus II* was about to leave Antwerp carrying some 100,000 tons of poisonous waste.[45] At the last minute, however, the departure was postponed due to weather conditions. The attention of the *Sirius* crew then turned to the *Vesta*, which was crossing the Scheldt. Greenpeace activists boarded the *Vesta* near Vlissingen and hung their banner from the ship's deck.[46] The Dutch police intervened, boarded the *Vesta*, and started negotiations between the action team and the *Vesta*'s crew.[47] Hours later, the *Vesta* returned to port with six Greenpeace protesters chained to the incineration stack. When the *Vesta* reached Vlissingen, the police took the activists into custody and interrogated them.[48] Later in the evening, they all were released. The *Vesta* resumed its route and set sail for the burn site. In the meantime, the *Vulcanus II* asked for a police escort. The ship had set sail from Antwerp, but the *Sirius* was racing after it to interfere with its passage in international waters.[49]

It took the *Sirius* several hours to intercept the *Vulcanus II*. At around 10:00 p.m. on August 23, in thick sea fog the *Sirius* finally located the largest ocean-incineration vessel in the world. Several Greenpeace activists from the *Sirius* attempted to board the *Vulcanus II* but were beaten back by high-pressure water hoses. The small dinghy that the Greenpeace activists used to approach the vessel was surrounded by a wall of water. The campaigners kept trying to board the *Vulcanus II*, but finally at 2:30 a.m. they gave up. The group made one last peaceful display alongside the incinerator vessel, demanding that the ship return to shore. After three exhausting days, the *Sirius* set sail for the Dutch port of Den Helder. Greenpeace's main coordinator onboard, Andy Booth, deemed it "only wise and safe to return to shore."[50] The action had only modest success in that it didn't stop the burn, but press coverage of all the action events was wide. Greenpeace made headlines in Norway, Sweden, Germany, the United Kingdom, Belgium, and the Netherlands. Largely sympathetic front-page stories stressed the courage and bravery of Greenpeace protesters, risking life and limb on the high seas to challenge polluters and protect the health of the environment and the people.[51]

The action infuriated OCS, the owner of *Vulcanus II*, and the company reacted vehemently against Greenpeace. An August 24, an OCS press statement defined Greenpeace's action as an "illegal harassment" and a "murderous threat." According to the company spokespersons, Greenpeace had ignored the regulations concerning ocean incineration and the law of the sea, and Greenpeace activists had deliberately endangered the life of the *Vulcanus II* crew. "In seeking to obstruct and ultimately abolish the practice of ocean incineration," OCS maintained, Greenpeace was "endangering human health and the environment they claim to protect." The company portrayed the use of fire hoses against the activists as simply guarding the security of those onboard.[52] OCS's narrative praised the cool-headed decisions of the *Vulcanus II* crew. In another press release dated August 27, OCS denied that there had been any skirmishes between the *Vulcanus II* and the *Sirius* crews and stressed that the captain of the incinerator vessel had done everything to avoid direct confrontation with the activists. To OCS, Greenpeace had talked to the press about skirmishes only "to drag the good name of OCS through the mud."[53]

OCS's words did not curb Greenpeace. On the contrary, the organization multiplied its efforts and planned spectacular actions, the most consequential of which would occur in October 1987. On that occasion, Greenpeace would try to prevent the burning of some 2,000 metric tons of chemical waste off the northern coast of Spain. This action was part of a broader campaign against establishing an incineration zone in the Cantabrian Sea. Greenpeace's Spanish chapter contacted trade unions, mobilized fisher associations, and reached out to the city councils along the Galician and Cantabrian coasts, asking these groups to condemn their government's plan and demand a revocation of the incineration permit. Greenpeace received support from the two most important labor unions in Spain, the General Union of Workers and the Workers' Commissions. Approximately fifty villages officially endorsed Greenpeace's position on ocean incineration, and fisher associations sent critical notes to the government in Madrid.[54] On September 25, 1987, largely as a result of this massive local response, the Spanish government revoked the incineration permit. According to the Spanish minister for transport, tourism, and communication, the permit was withdrawn because of "the special sensitivity shown by the public in relation to this issue, and because of the wish of the government to protect the marine environment."[55] It wasn't long before Greenpeace discovered, however, that the Spanish government had only changed the incineration permit to authorize the *Vulcanus II* to incinerate its load in another area rather than off the coast of Cantabria. On October 6, the *Vulcanus II* arrived in Santander to complete loading. At 2:30 a.m. on October 7, two Greenpeace volunteers chained themselves to the mooring lines and remained there until 8:00 a.m. Greenpeace's action exposed the presence of the incinerator vessel in Spain, which had arrived unannounced under cover of darkness.[56]

The Spanish port authorities released the *Vulcanus II*, and the ship sailed to the United Kingdom, where it had gotten permission to burn its toxic load at a newly designated site roughly 100 miles (160 kilometers) east of the Yorkshire coastal resort of Scarborough. The *Sirius*, however, intercepted the *Vulcanus II* on the open sea, and forced it to head to Antwerp.[57] Andy Booth saw this maneuver as a victory for Greenpeace because the organization wanted the U.K. government to forbid incineration operations off its national coast. In Antwerp, the *Vulcanus II* was supposed to load more waste before heading first to Rotterdam and then to the Dutch incineration zone in the North Sea. The Belgian authorities, however, prompted by Greenpeace's legal office, blocked the vessel before it could enter the harbor, charging it with violating a decree from 1987 that regulated toxic waste. According to that decree, waste that was not loaded in Belgium and that was merely going through a Belgian port was subject to special rules. OCS had failed to provide the Belgian Ministry of the Environment with the appropriate documentation concerning the waste on the *Vulcanus II* that had been collected in France and Spain. The *Vulcanus II* remained anchored off the coast of Belgium, waiting for OCS managers to sort out the paperwork.[58] On October 14, when the OCS cleared all the formalities, the *Vulcanus II* refueled in Antwerp and headed off to its final destination in the North Sea. Greenpeace, determined to stop the burn at any cost, sent one of its ships, the *Beluga*, to prevent the *Vulcanus II* from leaving the port of Antwerp. The *Beluga* then clashed with the Belgian port authorities in a scuffle that caused damage to the Greenpeace ship. The Belgian police arrested several demonstrators, and the Belgian Coast Guard escorted the *Vulcanus II* to the Dutch border; from there, the Dutch police took over and safely conducted OCS's ship to Rotterdam en route to the North Sea.[59]

The Belgian authorities filed a claim for damages against Greenpeace even though, according to Lisa Bunin, the *Vulcanus II* had caused damage to both the *Beluga* and the police boats. Greenpeace's leaders put the "moral responsibility" for the damages on OCS but did not make any formal complaint against the company.[60] They hired a marine surveyor and a consultant to estimate the damages on the *Beluga* and on the three police boats. The surveyor argued with the police that the owner of the *Vulcanus II* was the party responsible for the damages. Greenpeace's consultant explained that the captain of the *Vulcanus II* had not followed the rules of good seamanship and had jeopardized the safety of the personnel on the boats. The police agreed and dropped the charge against Greenpeace.[61]

In the meantime, the *Vulcanus II* had reached Rotterdam. There, after a few attempts, three Greenpeace activists boarded the ship. Two protesters handcuffed themselves to a chimney, while the third one climbed a mast to unfurl a banner proclaiming "Ban the Burn." Reportedly, the *Vulcanus II* crew "reacted very violently," hurting one activist when cutting off the handcuffs. Eugene Stuik, a Greenpeace spokesperson, said that the crew pulled the activists by the hair and twisted their arms while using high-pressure hoses to prevent other people from coming onboard.[62] The police took the activists into custody. A local court issued an injunction barring Greenpeace from interfering with the *Vulcanus II*. It ordered that Greenpeace keep its members at least 300 feet (91 meters) from the incinerator ship and leveed a fine of 25,000 Dutch guilders (roughly U.S.$14,000) for each day the order was violated. The court enjoined Greenpeace to terminate actions against the free passage of the *Vulcanus II* and to refrain from future actions. The penalty for noncompliance in this case was set at 50,000 guilders for each infringement.[63]

But, again, Greenpeace was unbowed. On October 18, something akin to a battle began 80 miles (129 kilometers) north-northwest of the Dutch port of Den Helder near the designated incineration site. In the early morning, a fleet of Danish fishing boats intercepted the *Vulcanus II* and, in support of Greenpeace's protests, sprayed fire hoses at the ship. Peter Willcox, the captain of the *Sirius*, steered his boat closer to the action. He arrived just as the *Vulcanus II* was firing high-pressure hoses at the roughly thirty Danish fishing vessels that surrounded it.[64] The situation grew tense, and the Danish fishers warned the *Vulcanus II* crew that they were going to drop their nets to "keep fishing" in the area. They threw the nets close to the incinerator vessel, fouling its main propellers. The ship drifted out of control and was forced to put down anchor.[65]

The *Vulcanus II* had to cancel its operation and was escorted back to the port of Rotterdam. The ship's owner, OCS, immediately announced legal action against Greenpeace, accusing it of having coordinated and arranged the demonstration. OCS claimed that two Greenpeace ships had broken the court order and had come within 328 feet (100 meters) of the *Vulcanus II*. On October 22, the legal owner of the *Vulcanus II*—"a somewhat obscure company called the Vulcanus II Shipping Company, registered in Monrovia, Liberia, believed to be owned by an American Company called

FIGURE 6.2 Danish fishing vessels and Greenpeace boats surrounding the *Vesta*, 1987.

Source: From *The Independent*, October 19, 1987, Box 5861 (Press Clippings Concerning the Action of Danish Fishers and Greenpeace Against Vulcanus II, October 1987), International Institute for Social History, Greenpeace International (Amsterdam) Archives.

International Waste Inc., which also formally owned OCS"—registered a claim for damages amounting to 1.4 million Dutch guilders (approximately U.S. $784,000).[66] Formally, the claim was against three of the Danish fishers.[67] OCS hoped that a sanction would make its point and that a huge financial loss would discourage further action against its high-seas operations. It entirely underestimated the translocal movement against ocean incineration. The Danish Sea Fishery Association underwrote the requested 1.4 million Dutch guilders. Greenpeace celebrated the fishermen as heroes and told their story in the headlines of major newspapers across Europe and beyond.[68]

TERRORISM VERSUS ACTIVISM

In its description of the August 1987 action, OCS blamed Greenpeace for "resorting to acts of terrorism" and pledged that the company would "resist this strenuously."[69] On October 19, right after the clash with the Danish fishers, OCS issued a stinging statement titled "Greenpeace Terrorism Disables Vulcanus." The company repeated the same accusation: Greenpeace had endangered the safety of the crew, damaged the ship, and hurt the very environment it claimed to protect. To OCS, Greenpeace was tantamount to a "guerrilla-like organization," and its members were "environmental terrorists."[70] A few days later, the AMI sent an official note to the secretariat of the International Maritime Organization stigmatizing the "acts of terrorism committed by Greenpeace and its supporters against the incinerator vessel," *Vulcanus II*. Greenpeace was accused of sabotage, scorned for inciting "mindless violence," and denounced for its blatant disregard of court rulings. Its actions were seen as an escalation of violence "calculated to endanger the lives of crewmen and cause a chemical spill in the North Sea." Greenpeace's behavior was "gross irresponsibility."[71]

The incinerator companies followed up on these accusations. On November 6, 1987, for instance, the Antwerp Commercial Court, at OCS's request, issued an injunction against both the captain of the *Beluga* and Greenpeace Belgium, forbidding them to hinder or take any action against incinerator vessels, nor could they board them or navigate around them "in a manner contrary to good seamanship and to national and international regulations." They also had to keep their allies in check and could not incite "supporters, sympathizers, sister organizations and all persons in their service to undertake any action" against the company's operations. A fine of one million Belgian francs (roughly U.S.$30,000 at the time) would be levied on any infringement of this sanction. In the Netherlands, OCS laid a claim for 3.5 million Dutch guilders (U.S.$1,842,000) due to the losses resulting from the clash with the Danish fishers.[72] Most worrisome to Greenpeace was the AMI's petition to eject Greenpeace from the LDC and from other international fora because of its "terroristic" strategy.[73]

The accusation of terrorism impinged on Greenpeace's freedom of expression. The allegation undermined its ability to coordinate actions with allies, hit its international reputation, and undermined its trustworthiness. As Lisa Bunin noted, Greenpeace had previously been accused of terrorism in Norway due to its actions against whaling. The case against that characterization, however, had been won in a national court. The organization was advised against going to court again. Rather, Greenpeace campaign leaders decided to deal with the accusation publicly at an international level. They drafted an open letter in response to the AMI that emphasized the repercussions of such a serious allegation.[74] Lisa Bunin and her fellow activists also sent a note to OCS in which they condemned the use of expressions such as "terrorism," "sabotage," "calculated violence," and "guerrilla-like" as defamatory and libelous. Greenpeace's letters invited both the AMI and OCS to retract their statements.[75]

OCS's parent company, the U.S.-based Chemical Waste Management (as noted earlier, a subsidiary of Waste Management, Inc.), countered with its enormous resources and launched a campaign against Greenpeace's credibility. At the end of November 1987, CWM spokespersons circulated a commentary denouncing Greenpeace's campaign as nothing more than an attempt to manipulate public opinion. Greenpeace was accused of distorting the truth and riding on popular discontent to advance its own political agenda. It was charged with editing photos and videos for sensationalist purposes. CWM representatives said that Greenpeace was famous for distributing "pictures of smoke coming from the stacks of *Vulcanus II*," but they maintained that the smoke in the photos was merely the emissions from fuel for the ship. In fact, according to CWM's version of the story, a chemical additive was burned with the waste to create a transparent plume in accordance with the pertinent regulation.[76] Once the CWM report was circulated, an OCS press conference denounced Greenpeace for fostering unjustified "hysteria." The environmental group was faulted for diverting attention from the real problems of the North Sea and accused of aggravating the hazardous-waste crisis. Bert de Boer from OCS Rotterdam put the issue in simple terms: contrary to what Greenpeace believed, his company was the solution not the problem.

Anyone who thought otherwise was a victim of Greenpeace's irresponsible propaganda.[77]

The confrontation between Greenpeace and the waste business was in essence a conflict between environmentalists and industrialists. It highlighted the antithetical nature of industrial growth and environmental protection.[78] For Greenpeace, the waste industry's violent, coarse, even irrational behavior was dictated by its exigency to preserve investments and profits. The biological balance of the marine ecosystem simply could not enter into its consideration. Jim Vallette, a coordinator of Greenpeace USA, exposed the ecological contradictions in CWM's criticism. He said the company's rebuttal of Greenpeace's anti-ocean-incineration campaign was "deliberately distanced from CWM." There was no identifying cover page, author, or date, and it was filled with scientifically unproven claims. Greenpeace reports, by contrast, listed fully disclosed governmental facts or findings disseminated by local agencies and establishment media or private companies' own documents. Before publishing on ocean incineration, Greenpeace cross-referenced its documents and submitted them to peer review. Its reports were grounded on more than 220 reliable sources.[79]

Studies backed by Greenpeace, according to Vallette, had clear, incontrovertible, and scientifically proven evidence that ocean incineration provoked "acute mortality of organisms over tens of square kilometers," released "high level of persistent chemicals" into the marine environment, and left high concentrations of waste residue "in an area ranging from 25 square km [to] 300 square km."[80] To Vallette, incineration companies were defaming Greenpeace because they could not convincingly reply to its scientific claims, nor could they justify the need and viability of their business model. Their only defense rested on vague technological investment and improvement. CWM and OCS maintained that their ships were equipped with "highly sophisticated computer systems" that kept the overall impact of ocean incineration under control. According to Vallette, however, this equipment did not automatically guarantee environmental controls; the systems were accident detectors rather than pollution-prevention mechanisms. Devices such as scrubbers, electrostatic precipitators, and other pollutant reducers did not exist onboard incinerator ships, nor had private companies ever invested in them. Vallette concluded that if this absence of preparation was not "ecocide," it was at least proof that the incinerator operators lacked any interest in environmental safeguards.[81]

In November 1987, the standoff between Greenpeace and the ocean-incinerator business was tested on both sides of the Atlantic. In the United States, the Oceanography, Fisheries, and Wildlife Conservation Subcommittee and the Environment Subcommittee of the House Merchant Marine and Fisheries Committee held a series of hearings. Seven of the eight representatives at the meetings were critical of ocean incineration. They were joined by representatives of the state legislatures of Washington, New Jersey, Maryland, Pennsylvania, Texas, and Rhode Island.[82] In Europe, an intergovernmental meeting on the protection of the North Sea saw ministers from Belgium, Denmark, the Federal Republic of Germany, France, the Netherlands, Norway, Sweden, and the United Kingdom reach a decision to "phase out" ocean incineration by December 31, 1994. In addition, it was agreed that by January 1991 the amount of waste to be burned at sea would be reduced by not less than 65 percent.[83] The ministers further agreed to prohibit the export of waste for ocean incineration outside of the North Sea area. This was an implicit rebuke of the OCS representative, who had floated the idea of incinerator ships in the Irish Sea.[84]

It took CWM a few months to digest the news. By January 1988, the company understood the battle was over, at least in the United States. CWM announced its decision to abandon its ocean-incineration efforts in U.S. territorial waters and not to pursue any more permits for ocean incineration in the United States.[85] The aggressive way it had gone up against Greenpeace and the movement had not paid off. The public outcry that led to politicians pulling their support had ended offshore burns.

THE END OF OCEAN INCINERATION

By the end of 1987, OSCOM and some sixty-five contracting parties of the LDC agreed on a worldwide ban on ocean incineration to come into force in 1995. Shortly after the OSCOM decision, ocean incineration was completely abandoned in the United States. An issue of *Inside EPA* published on January 8, 1988, revealed that the U.S. agency had "begun reassessing its proposed hazardous waste ocean incineration program—pointing to possible elimination of the program." The publication referred to "recent developments" that were "forcing the agency" to decide whether there was a need for ocean disposal of hazardous waste. Without explicitly mentioning it, the EPA acknowledged that popular pressure had been a main reason for ending the practice.[86] A few weeks later, in mid-February 1988, the EPA officially announced its intention to abandon its ocean-incineration plans, which would include no longer developing pertinent regulation or evaluating potential incineration sites.[87]

Greenpeace and its allies welcomed the news but warned that a true and widely held consensus was yet to be found. The risk remained that companies and governments alike would keep the door open to outsourcing burns to developing countries. Lisa Bunin raised the alarm in the *International Union for the Protection of Nature Bulletin* in December 1987. Bunin stated that an end to ocean-incineration operations in the Atlantic and the North Sea was imminent. But, she cautioned, the industry already had plans to reestablish the technology elsewhere in the world. OCS was exploring possibilities in the Caribbean, the Mediterranean, and the South Pacific. Bunin stressed that by all scientific standards available at that time, incineration was environmentally unsafe and inefficient, again highlighting the production of persistent poisonous elements. She quoted recent studies on killifish and plankton, explaining the biological structure and behavior of overexposed marine species. In addition, Bunin remarked, the toxic chemicals emitted by incineration were impossible to measure or control and were an outsize burden on the global ecosystem.[88]

In complete contravention to Bunin's appeal, in April 1988 the LDC SGD came out with a document stating that it was still possible to sustain "the environmental acceptability and safety of incineration at sea."[89] Leo Spaans, the chair of the SGD Technology Workgroup, authored this idea in a paper titled "Incineration of Chlorinated Waste at Sea: Process and Emissions."[90] Greenpeace saw Spaans's argument, which was largely accepted by the LDC, as the last pro-ocean-incineration gasp. While governments welcomed the paper as an unexpected chance to reopen the debate, Greenpeace, Friends of the Earth, and the delegations of the Danish and German governments fiercely disagreed.[91]

In this same period, the government of Spain was in the process of authorizing a new series of offshore burns to rid itself of its rising stocks of chlorinated waste. Madrid was not a signatory to OSCOM's amendment that phased out ocean incineration. On April 12, 1988, the Spanish government sought OSCOM's help to designate a new incineration site 600 miles (966 kilometers) off Spain's north coast and only 300 miles (483 kilometers) southwest of the Irish coast. OSCOM's response was negative, and on April 26 the Irish Fishermen Association asked the Irish government to stop these plans.[92] When the Spanish authorities tried to switch to another site closer to Spanish territorial waters, protests mushroomed all over Europe.[93] Greenpeace activists led a huge demonstration in Santander in May, and in early June there were protests in front of the Spanish embassies in Sweden, Denmark, Norway, and Belgium.[94] In Copenhagen, demonstrators chained themselves to the door of the Spanish embassy and hung a banner in Spanish reading, "Denmark Says No to Ocean Incineration." The action led to the arrest of eight people.[95] On June 17, 1988, two Greenpeace volunteers and members of the Association for the Defense of Natural Resources of Cantabria chained themselves to a toxic-waste container docked in Santander and unfolded a banner reading "Stop *Vulcanus II*."[96]

The Spanish attempt reinvigorated the anti-ocean-incineration front. Government representatives and ministers in Germany, Ireland, Norway, and Sweden publicly criticized Madrid's choice and supported a ban on ocean incineration.[97] At an informal EEC Council meeting on the environment, the Danish minister for the environment and minister for fisheries insisted on more information from the Spanish authorities and threatened to protest "on a technical-scientific basis" against Spain.[98] The Danish governmental delegation rejected Spaans's views and stated that the time had "come to make full use of the best available technology and thus, in turn, to bring incineration of wastes at sea to an end."[99] After two years of discussion, the Dutch government, too, decided to abandon the technology.

While granting exemptions to those burns that had already been planned, it pledged an end to new permits after 1988. As for the waste produced abroad that was to be incinerated off the coast of the Netherlands in the North Sea, The Hague mandated that incineration operations take place in the country where the waste originated. The government decided that incineration at sea of PCB-laden waste had to be banned by January 1990 and that all ocean incineration in the Dutch zone had to be "completely terminated" by January 1994.[100] In Belgium, where the government had reduced the volume of at-sea incineration out of Antwerp, citizens then protested the inland facilities and targeted storage sites where waste was stockpiled. When OCS applied for a permit to build a storage facility in Ghent in December 1987, the mayor rejected the request, saying that the risk to the population was unacceptable. Similarly, the community of Hemiksem, near Antwerp, successfully stopped a local company, Panocean, from renting its storage facilities to OCS.[101]

Greenpeace capitalized on this convergence of interests and launched its final attack against ocean incineration's residual reputation. It wanted to rebut Spaans's argument once and for all and to affirm the technology's danger to the environment. The SGD gave permission to Greenpeace to submit a reply to Spaans that would show irrefutably the impact that ocean incineration had on the environment and human health.[102] Studsvik Energiteknik, an independent research institute in Stockholm, carried out the study for Greenpeace. The institute's experts explored the theoretical and technological linchpins of ocean incineration and compiled two reports: "A Discussion of Ocean Incineration for Chlorinated Waste" and "Chlorinated Environmental Pollutants Emitted from Ocean Incineration Stacks." The two papers provided incontrovertible evidence of the soundness of the anti-incineration position. They proved that the burns discharged unburned organic waste and therefore produced new toxic chemical compounds; that is, the destruction of chlorinated waste at sea led to the unavoidable emission of a large number of chlorinated substances, including polychlorinated dibenzo-p-dioxine, polychlorinated dibenzofurane, and PCBs. The reports also found that the monitoring systems on incineration vessels were incapable, either by accident or due to their structural design, of tracking combustion residues. Finally, they showed that the documentation supposedly proving claims of ocean incineration's efficacy was full of errors and omissions.[103] The University of Hamburg also weighed in on behalf of Greenpeace, revealing a "hot spot" of hexachlorobenzene found in sediments collected near the North Sea ocean-incineration site. There was no possible explanation for the high concentration of this compound in that area other than the ocean burns.[104]

Greenpeace leaders submitted the findings of the Studsvik study to the International Maritime Organization and to the LDC parties. They asked the LDC's SGD to take these reports extremely seriously when reviewing the most recent international guidelines for ocean incineration. Lisa Bunin and Janus Hillgaard presented the reports—translated into six languages—and emphasized that they scientifically demonstrated the technical flaws in Spaans's work.[105] The Swedish researchers had indeed established that gas samples taken at the opening of the incinerator funnel were not reliable. They suggested instead that it was "highly probable" that the formation of hazardous chlorinated hydrocarbons occurred "*after* combustion gases [had] left the combustion zone, i.e., in the plume away from the stack." Because Spaans had been employing measurements taken near the funnel, his study was of limited or no value.[106] The Studsvik reports stated that it was useless to gauge the toxicity of the emissions of chlorinated compounds, which debunked the persistent myth that destruction efficiency was the main way to assess incinerator vessels' performance. A more reliable method was to measure combustion efficiency. But the Studsvik experts noted that even combustion efficiency had its limits; it could not calculate the exact amount of hydrocarbons emitted in the flue gas. A Studsvik researcher, Lars Strömberg, added that the "temperature inside the incinerator was never constant," and for this reason offshore incinerators could not be "regarded as a completely, stirred, tank reactor;" their overall efficiency could not be calculated the same as that of land-based incinerators—which was exactly what Spaans had been doing.[107]

Greenpeace's scientism, despite its accuracy, attracted wide criticism from neoliberal pro-incineration actors. On May 21, 1988, *The Economist* featured a story suggesting that the organization did not "appreciate how nasty some of these wastes are to have around" on land and was naive about ocean incineration.[108] The AMI accused Greenpeace of prejudice, propaganda, and an "abject lack of scientific objectivity," blaming the environmentalist organization, not without irony, for having drawn a "smoke-screen" around ocean incineration. It called the Studsvik reports "tendentious and deceptive."[109] Greenpeace's reply to the editors of *The Economist* repeated the organization's goal of solving the hazardous-waste crisis and said that it favored investments in alternative methods, including source reduction. The organization championed its "precautionary approach" to the risk of releasing dioxin, "the deadliest substance known."[110] Greenpeace campaigners also reacted to AMI's criticism, penning a point-by-point denunciation of the idea that incineration technology was viable.[111] Building on the Studsvik reports, Greenpeace commissioned another independent study on the ocean's microlayer. This time the research was done at the University of Lund in Sweden. The final report was released at a press conference on September 30, just before the LDC was set to meet on October 3–7, 1988.[112] This study found that ocean incineration saturated the microlayer with products of incomplete combustion and PCBs, which inevitably accumulated in fish. This finding established that a causal relationship existed between the concentration of organochlorine residues in the air and those in the ocean's water and microlayer.[113] And because the microlayer hosts primary organisms at the very base of the marine food chain, its contamination with persistent compounds represented a threat to all aquatic life. Studies on the subject proliferated. The *Marine Pollution Bulletin* published several reports on sea disposal, waste dilution, and the sediments left by ocean incineration. Slowly but inexorably, scientific truth surfaced. It became common knowledge that at-sea incineration produced elevated pollution levels of products of incomplete combustion, and high concentrations of PCB and organochlorine pesticides.[114]

Greenpeace and its many allies ultimately triumphed. The twelfth consultative meeting of the LDC contracting parties in August 1989 officially endorsed Greenpeace's views on ocean incineration. The meeting proposed the dismissal of the practice by 1992 or, at the very latest, by January 1994.[115] The thirteenth LDC consultative meeting in September 1990 reiterated this timetable for a comprehensive ban.[116] From that moment, the term *ocean incineration* disappeared from the vocabulary of the major industrialized countries. By the end of 1990, Greenpeace had closed down its Ban the Burn campaign.[117] In 1997, the International Maritime Organization complemented the International Convention for the Prevention of Pollution from Ships (MARPOL) with an appendix titled "Prevention of Air Pollution from Ships." This document formally prohibited toxic emissions of ozone-depleting substances and greenhouse gases from any ship. The regulation, entered into force in 2005 and amended in 2013, explicitly prohibited at-sea incineration of any PCBs and exhaust-gas cleaning-system residues.[118] After four intense decades, ocean incineration faded into oblivion.

* * *

During a couple of topical international meetings held in the second half of the 1980s, the translocal opponents of ocean incineration presented and defended their stances against the last attempts by the U.S. government and a few of its western European allies to salvage the practice. Environmentalist organizations were able to prove once and for all that ocean incineration was dangerous and toxic. But given the industry's resistance, overall denialism, and counterinformation campaign, some of them abandoned an approach purely grounded on science and opted for a much more radical and confrontational one. The main consequence of this confrontation was the further erosion of both political and public support for the practice. U.S. policy makers did not find it politically convenient to endorse ocean incineration anymore. The translocal outcry against it had undermined its original appeal, and wider socioecological concerns had eventually prevailed over economic and industrial interests. The victory was small but substantial and consequential, testifying to the limits of U.S. political and economic power both at home and abroad.

CONCLUSION

When asked why she got involved in the struggle against ocean incineration, Sue Ann Fruge replied that she was motivated by anger. Fruge and her friends thought national authorities were arrogant and disrespectful toward their community. They also wanted to put an end to the exploitative private waste companies that, in their eyes, systematically and disproportionately targeted citizens in the Lower Rio Grande Valley. After having suffered from natural disasters and accidents ranging from hurricanes to massive oil spills, after years of structural unemployment and erosion of their buying power due to the devaluation of the Mexican peso and the U.S. dollar, people like Sue Ann Fruge living in a remote corner of southern Texas were, as she put it, "fed up" with being ignored and sidelined.[1]

Anger and frustration were essential for mobilizing local constituencies. Personal "skin in the game" proved to be fundamental to the success of the Ban the Burn campaign.[2] Yet Sue Ann Fruge's radical-homemaker advocacy and the grassroots demands connected to it tell only half the story.[3] The activities of the more structured and organized environmental organizations were equally important to affect and limit the actions of the U.S.

government and its allies. This was where relevant information and guidance, new channels of communication, and coordinated protest strategies came from. The established groups supported, promoted, financed, and distributed relevant studies. They confronted political authorities in public hearings and the media, and they were primed to participate at both the national and the international level. It was the combined pressure of citizen groups and environmentalist organizations—acting locally and transnationally—that paved the way for substantial and effective policy change. Structured environmentalist organizations and environmentally fragile communities: the dynamism of thinking globally and acting locally paved the way for the abandonment of ocean incineration. The translocal dimension of the campaign against at-sea incineration is perhaps the legacy that stands out the most among the many left by Ban the Burn.

The campaign against ocean incineration was an act of responsible citizenship. Organochlorine and other toxic compounds such as dioxin and PCBs, much like the residue of nuclear processes, posed a threat to communities dependent on a symbiotic relationship with the natural environment. When the oceans became the new wasteland, low-income coastal communities, which relied on fishery and seasonal tourism, realized they were the new victims of unbounded industrialism.[4] The risk of toxic contamination spurred them, especially women, to action. Fighting against ocean incineration gave large groups of women the opportunity to be active and speak with a voice that brought them prominence and respect within their own communities. Sue Ann Fruge maintained that the anti-ocean-incineration campaign proved that women could be "free and independent" and most definitely that they could "make a difference."[5]

By bringing to the fore and empowering the voices of usually underrepresented environmental interests, constituencies, and communities, the campaign against ocean incineration signaled a transformative moment for U.S. environmental politics and entanglements with the exploitation of the natural world. The heyday of this controversial technology, indeed, coincided with the U.S. government's turn toward a hyperconservative and committedly antiregulatory environmental policy making. In the early 1980s, the EPA's supposedly impartial role was sidelined by the

CONCLUSION

administration's defense of military, industrial, and economic priorities. A strict application of cost–benefit analyses imprinted a neoliberal mark on the agency and, in general, on America's environmental agenda, which at times industrial interests seemed to dictate fully. Such an approach ended up compromising the EPA's reputation and undermining the effectiveness of its actions. The simultaneous erosion of the EPA's expertise and credibility weakened its role as protector of the environment and triggered a long-lasting partisan confrontation over its broader mission. Moreover, as the story of ocean incineration shows, such a dynamic had multiple reverberations at the international level, too. On a global scale, indeed, the EPA's attitude and commitment toward controversial practices such as ocean incineration contributed to spreading mistrust toward U.S. environmental practices and Washington's ability to lead the world in this field. The almost absolute alignment between industrial and governmental interests was in due course received with skepticism by several U.S. allies and worked against the U.S. government's authoritativeness within the main international fora where environmental regulations were discussed and approved. The scant regard for the safety of the oceans and for the complaints of coastal communities eventually isolated American negotiators and exposed the limits of an environmental policy constructed almost entirely around the defense of economic interests.[6] This evolution was in stark contrast with the U.S. early regulatory approach, which throughout the 1970s had helped to export a vision of modernity that tried at least to alleviate its impact on the environment. The embracement of neoliberalism in international environmental policy making, which ocean incineration to a large extent embodied, gave growing prominence to criticism of U.S. leadership worldwide.

These critical voices, as the campaign against ocean incineration shows, converged into a current for environmental justice, a varied movement that put at its center women, Native communities, ethnic minorities, and other disadvantaged groups who bore the brunt of environmental risk.[7] Such a convergence spearheaded the creation of a broader coalition that criticized increasing globalization, neoliberalism, and an unjust world. From the 1990s onward, consumer, worker, and ecologist groups established strategic alliances and organized numerous joint campaigns.[8] This wide, cross-sectional constituency resulted in transnational calls to liberate marginalized communities around the world from toxic pollution and long-standing disparities. Environmental-justice activists built global networks and connections, reinforcing their legitimacy at both the domestic and the international levels. And these efforts had results. The final declaration of the Rio Global Summit of 1992 and President Bill Clinton's Executive Order 12898 of 1994, addressing ecological equity among ethnic minorities and low-income groups, are two outstanding examples of environmental principles that were turned into policy.[9] At the same time, the EPA progressively tried to free itself from the most radical neoliberal tendencies and turned to a much more committed protection of those communities threatened by industrial degradation and socioecological marginalization. The agency even established its Office of Environmental Justice, which started to monitor closely the needs of vulnerable people, decrease their environmental burdens, and build sustainable communities.[10]

The experience of ocean incineration exposed the complexity of hazardous-waste management and how deeply intertwined this problem was—and still is—with ever-changing socioenvirotech systems. In this field, industrial innovation, governmental regulation, scientific debate, and translocal activism coexist and influence each other.[11] Phasing out at-sea incineration was in fact a victory for some and a lost opportunity for others. The campaign against this practice empowered a few underprivileged groups and communities but undermined U.S. policy makers' legitimacy. The rise and fall of ocean incineration showed that governments and international organizations alike could be at the mercy of the rather volatile demands of public opinion as it swung from apathy to opposition and ultimately be unable to objectively assess new technologies' full potential to preserve high standards of living based on continuous industrial growth. In the end, the public's attitude to ocean incineration had vetoed what seemed to be a groundbreaking technology but one that really could not provide a solution to the ever-present hazardous-waste crisis and that even multiplied it.[12] Preventing ships from incinerating toxic compounds offshore did not and could not stop the production of hazardous chemical waste, nor could it facilitate the finding of new methods for safe disposal. After the practice

CONCLUSION

was outlawed, the largest industries kept generating an astounding amount of dangerous waste. In 1985, the U.S. OTA estimated a domestic production of 569 million tons of toxic waste a year.[13] In 1987, the U.S. Chemical Manufacturers Association calculated that the U.S. petrochemical sector alone generated 212 million tons of toxic wastes per year.[14] The U.S. National Intelligence Council and the DCI Environmental Center estimated that throughout the 1980s and 1990s the annual production of toxic waste in the United States ranged, on average, between 198 and 306 million tons per year.[15] Things did not go any better in Europe. Throughout the 1990s and well into the early 2000s, the most industrialized countries still relied on inadequate disposal methods such as landfilling and land-based incineration. Perhaps even more worryingly, the demise of ocean incineration boosted unsafe methods for the disposal of hazardous waste, including land dumping, which polluted both surface water and groundwater while simultaneously magnifying the greenhouse effect through emissions of methane. Dumping on land also meant the loss of both agricultural and natural land. Similarly, the abandonment of ocean incineration increased the productivity of land-based incineration, which since the late 1980s has been responsible for the release of roughly one-third of all the dioxins and furans present on earth, not to mention the release of other toxic elements such as mercury, chromium, and cadmium.[16]

In addition to the rising awareness of and opposition to these adverse developments, the struggle against ocean incineration imposed an overall reconsideration of the U.S. government's attitude toward toxic waste and pollution. It convinced environmental advocates, who deemed U.S. companies largely responsible for the global spread of toxic waste, to double down on their efforts against the uneven spread of contaminants throughout the world. It also exposed a close relationship between hazardous waste and (neo)colonial exploitation.[17] Incinerator vessels and their toxic plumes represented, indeed, an example of the industrialization of marine and coastal landscapes and an instance of toxic colonialism. Ocean incineration meant the transboundary movement of hazardous wastes from richer to poorer, more vulnerable communities.[18] These challenges expanded the environmentalists' agendas and protest repertoires. Some organizations adopted new technocratic approaches that relied on the role of scientific research to find solutions to contemporary environmental problems.[19] Others focused on the precautionary principle, placing emphasis on the perception of risk as the main agent of environmental change.[20] Still others favored legislative efforts to stymie toxic pollution through sanctions of polluters and the empowerment of local communities.[21] After the ocean-incineration battle ended, the antitoxics movement built a wide coalition to ignite activism across national borders. The coalition addressed several threats, from the depletion of the ozone layer to desertification and deforestation, from plastic pollution to climate change.[22]

Furthermore, the battle over ocean incineration contributed to giving a new sense of political urgency to the issue of toxic contamination at both the domestic and the international levels. U.S. governmental agencies and policy makers reacted to this pressure by investing time and energy in finding new ways to put toxic pollution under control. At times, these efforts were successful, as in the case of the Montreal Protocol of 1987, which banned those substances depleting the ozone layer and represented the main international initiative to address the effects of dangerous chemicals on the earth's upper atmosphere. Other times, such efforts did not gain the necessary political support at home to be translated into effective international regulatory frameworks, as in the case of the Basel Convention on the transboundary movement of hazardous waste. Nevertheless, the experience of ocean incineration induced the EPA to keep the proliferation, distribution, storage, and disposal of dangerous chemical compounds under stricter control. In 1992, the agency released a comprehensive inventory of toxic substances that made completely public the environmental risks and health hazards of hundreds of chemical compounds; with such a move, the playing field was made much more level.[23] Since then, the unbounded release of toxic chemicals into the environment has dropped drastically. As a matter of fact, according to some of the most recent EPA models, the overall environmental risk to populations in the United States has been reduced by 43 percent in the past three decades.[24]

The campaign to ban ocean incineration was also a powerful reminder of the seemingly unstoppable anthropogenic deterioration of the world's fragile and complex oceans. Oceanic bioaccumulation and biomagnification of toxic substances leads to eutrophication, a biological process where dissolved nutrients cause the proliferation of oxygen-depleting bacteria and plants that kill other forms of aquatic life. Anti-ocean-incineration campaigners were among the first ones to point fingers at the toxic degradation of the oceans as a direct consequence of unbounded industrialization. That serious threat remains ever present. In fact, from the early 2000s onward, the industrialization of previously underdeveloped economies beyond Europe and the United States, the lack of international control and enforcement of safe protocols, and the rapid diffusion of the by-products of the electronics industry, or so-called e-wastes, have cast a dark shadow over the future of the oceans' health.[25] Today, the global production of toxic wastes amounts to more than 400 million tons annually.[26] Even if only a minor portion of such toxic waste enters the oceans, the overproduction and overconsumption of plastics still pose a major threat to marine ecosystems and represent a hazardous-waste crisis. Of the 350 million tons of plastic produced globally every year, more than 90 percent is not recycled, and roughly 10 percent end up in the seas. Almost 8 million metric tons of plastics and microplastics enter the world's oceans every year, accounting for 85 percent of all marine pollution.[27] The relevance of the fight against ocean incineration, thus, goes well beyond its own historical trajectory. It invites all of us to stem the tide of toxic practices in the future and to confront and modify the envirotech systems that endanger the interdependent health of the oceans and human beings.

The Ban the Burn campaign was also an emblem of early environmental democracy at work. It was, indeed, an example of "polysemic social transformation"—a sociopolitical struggle in which (self-)organized social movements bring about a desired change in environmental policy through the inclusion of their counternarrative in the official decision-making process. Polysemic transformations like the one induced by those who opposed ocean incineration exert the influence of communities and their networks against corporations and government; such a dynamic consolidates the population's role as a legitimate and trustworthy political subject.[28] Specifically, the campaign against ocean incineration fostered environmental democracy through a series of consequential innovations. The campaign insisted on transparency in hazardous-waste-management policies and business; it denounced the arbitrary interpretation and application of national and international norms; and it stigmatized the dubious legality of industrial practices impinging on the marine environment. Most important, the campaign exposed the shadowy overlap between governmental and industrial interests, an alignment that by its very existence worsened the toxic-waste crisis.

One of the main legacies of the anti-ocean-incineration campaign was that it increased citizens' environmental awareness. Both local groups and transnational organizations grounded their campaigns on disseminating correct information to the public, which they saw as crucial to managing hazardous wastes in an environmentally sound and sustainable way.[29] The media's ability to grab attention was highly instrumental in achieving concrete goals in environmental policy. In fact, the anti-incineration experience illustrated a dynamic found in modern democracies: governing elites' responsiveness is a variable dependent on public pressure. Arguably, public authorities and agencies may be interested in developing reasonable frameworks for the implementation of sound environmental policies. A society lacking adequate public and media attention, however, allows for disengagement at the top and the subsequent adoption of inappropriate policies with little room for revision and innovation.[30] The Ban the Burn campaigners, thanks to their unceasing promotion of their counternarrative, exposed the multiple risks of at-sea incineration to human and environmental health and subverted this trend. They were successful in stimulating policy responses, and they convinced international regulatory bodies, national governments, local authorities, and the mainstream press that it was necessary to outlaw the practice.

In the end, the campaign against ocean incineration empowered the global environmental movement and transformed it into a diverse and influential constituency. Anti-ocean-incineration campaigners swelled the ranks of those demanding that industry produce and use fewer toxic materials, and they joined with those advocating the prohibition of waste-disposal methods that threaten the planet.[31] Ocean incineration was a

CONCLUSION

testing ground for developing a broad critique and effective strategy against technologies and consumption patterns that degraded public health. The success of the Ban the Burn campaign propelled environmentalists worldwide to seek an industrial transition from toxic-based processes to eco-compatible substitutes.[32] Waste reduction and toxic avoidance became their signature slogans—two goals that push the movement forward to this day.[33]

All in all, the Ban the Burn campaign embodied a long-term struggle for increased civic engagement in political, industrial, and economic decisions with relevant socioecological repercussions. The origins of the campaign grew out of what made sense to a few endangered communities, which started deploying previously inert democratic institutions to their own advantage. Once the people took the reins, they altered the terms of discussion and drove socially inclusive change. The campaign won long-term popular support and ultimately gained political efficacy. The fate of the oceans, threatened by offshore incineration, came to represent a shared environmental concern and a new sociopolitical battleground. Free and inclusive communication on the environment among organized movements operating at multiple levels paved the way for effective action and policy change nationally and internationally. The campaign against ocean incineration opened the door of environmental governance to citizens previously unaware of, uninterested in, or simply excluded from policy making.

If environmental democracy sets the standard for the involvement of aware citizens in ecological decisions, then the trajectory of ocean incineration sets the standard for the governance of environmental information and collective action rising out of the family's backyard to the depths of the ocean. In a world where both democracy and the environment are under threat, the story of ocean incineration offers a beacon of hope for the future.

ACKNOWLEDGMENTS

This book is the result of a long intellectual journey that started a few years ago at the Roosevelt Institute for American Studies (RIAS) in Middelburg, the Netherlands, and was made possible—and extremely pleasant—by all the people I met along the way.

One of the oldest and most well-established traditions at the RIAS is to have long chats during incredibly generative coffee breaks. We all like to hold them especially when we host visiting scholars. It was during one of these informal gatherings that the idea about this book came to be. Anne Foster, who was spending some time with us in Middelburg, was among the first to encourage me to move forward with this research. All my RIAS colleagues, present and past, have remained incredibly supportive throughout its stages, listening for years to my talks about strangely designed ships and frightening chemical compounds. Special thanks go to the Executive Director Damian Pargas and former academic director Giles Scott-Smith, its indefatigable office manager Leontien Joosse, the amazing coterie of PhD students and postdoctoral researchers who have animated and keep reinvigorating the RIAS, and the many scholars whose paths crossed with

ACKNOWLEDGMENTS

that of the institute, including Alessandro Brogi, Petra Goedde, Justin Hart, Charles Postel, and Maarten Zwiers.

I was lucky enough to get all my primary research done by the onset of the global COVID-19 pandemic. The archivists at the International Institute for Social History in Amsterdam provided me with all the support I needed to collect the most relevant materials from their incredibly rich archives. And so did the people working at all the other repositories I visited, from the National Archives and Records Administration in College Park, Maryland, to the Jimmy Carter Presidential Library in Atlanta. The only place where I could not go because of public-health restrictions was the Indiana University–Purdue University Library in Indianapolis (IUPUI), where the Ruth Lilly Special Collections and Archives are located and where some crucial papers for this story are preserved. But nice people do exist and clearly abound at the IUPUI. I am extremely grateful to the IUPUI staff for scanning and sending all the files I needed; their work has been simply priceless.

By the time I got my hands on these papers, the pandemic had already changed our way of life and affected our mobility. Teaching online and fathering a child of three who was forced to stay home became all I could do during the day. But at night I could focus on the writing I needed to do. Furthermore, the pandemic gave me the rather unexpected opportunity to take part in several mushrooming online activities, which proved to be crucial to the strengthening of my project. Paul Kramer put together a group discussion with world-class scholars interested in investigating the broader outreach of the U.S. military empire. He was kind enough to invite me to join the conversation, letting me present my findings to old and new friends such as François Doppler-Speranza, Rebecca Herman, Lauren Hirshberg, Jana Lippman, Dan Margolies, Harvey Neptune, and Holly Wilson, all of whom gave me indispensable feedback. Similarly, the online Writing Support Program sponsored by the European Society for Environmental History and coordinated by Andrea Gaynor was fundamental to putting my first writings to the test of a growing community of young environmental historians, while the Cold War Research Network in Utrecht connected me with fellow historians of the United States here in the Netherlands.

ACKNOWLEDGMENTS

I benefited a great deal from the interdisciplinary exchanges I had online, and I want to acknowledge all the people I have been meeting virtually in the past few years.

Mostly thanks to vaccines and collective immunization, we slowly went back to real-world events, which enabled me to present this research, now in a much more definite shape, to colleagues at the Institute for History in Leiden through the meetings organized by the Politics, Culture, and National Identities research cluster coordinated by Maartje Janse and through the many chats I had with Michiel van Groesen, Anne Heyer, Kenan van de Mieroop, Herman Paul, Eric Storm, and Henk te Velde. At the same time, it was nice to attend the conferences organized by the Netherlands Association of American Studies, the Center for American Studies in Rome, and the European Association for American Studies. But the turning point was surely my participation in the annual meeting of the Society for the Historians of American Foreign Relations (SHAFR) in New Orleans in 2022, for many reasons.

First, SHAFR conferences are always a great opportunity to meet friends and learn from brilliant colleagues' new research. Second, in New Orleans many diplomatic historians of the United States seemed to share an interest in U.S.-driven anthropogenic transformations of the planet and in analyses combining U.S. foreign relations with environmental policies and dynamics. The panels organized and the discussions led by such outstanding scholars as Megan Black, Kristin Hoganson, and Julia Irwin were absolutely revealing in this regard, and the possibility to present my research in that context contributed to making it more solid and effective. Third, because life is also made of fortunate encounters, it was at the SHAFR conference in New Orleans that I met Jay Sexton and Sarah Snyder, the editors of the Global America series for Columbia University Press. Sarah handed me a flyer for it and asked me if I was working on a manuscript that could fit its general purposes. I could not believe my eyes. Global America was exactly the series I was looking for. I saved the flyer, and back in Europe I made use of it to approach Columbia University Press editor Stephen Wesley. In all honesty, I could not have hoped for a better reception of and support for my study. Stephen's help has in fact been essential

ACKNOWLEDGMENTS

to getting my manuscript submitted, accepted, and published, and I am truly grateful to him. Similarly, I must thank Annie Barva for her incredibly helpful and masterly copyediting.

Once the book was almost ready, I experienced two more crucial twists in my life that made it possible for me to finalize it. The first one was that Gaetano Di Tommaso joined us at the RIAS. Gaetano has been an old and trusted friend since grad school, but, perhaps even more important, he is one of the most brilliant and intellectually honest colleagues I have ever met. He challenged me to rethink the whole project almost word by word, opening my mind through sharp criticism and pointing me in the right direction with punctual suggestions on a daily basis. I am enormously indebted to him for the time and energy he has devoted to this project, and I feel privileged to work with him. The second twist was that, together with Gaetano, I had the opportunity to organize an international conference on environmental justice history at the RIAS, which put in me in touch with such giants of this field as Martin Melosi and Ellen Griffith Spears. Their help with drafts of this project has been invaluable. At the same time, this conference put me in touch with scholars and colleagues such as Amy Hay, who lives and works right where much of this story happened, and her positive comments further convinced me of the relevance of my work.

Throughout the writing of this book, friends, colleagues, and activists have helped, encouraged, and challenged me. I am sure that I am forgetting some of them, and I apologize for this in advance, but I cannot avoid mentioning at least Valeria Benko, George Blaustein, Albertine Bloemendal, Mario Del Pero, Thomas Doherty, Sue Ann Fruge, Katy Hull, Tim Jelfs, Oran Kennedy, Marco Mariano, Frank Mehring, Jessie Morgan-Owens, Nancy Mykoff, Davide Orsini, Sara Polak, Kathryn Roberts, and Mike Schmidli.

I am grateful for the extremely useful reports I got from the three anonymous reviewers who read my manuscript. But I have no words to express my gratitude to my friend Michael Strange, who has helped me to write the whole of it. Michael is just a blessing. She is competent, knowledgeable, and incredibly elegant and punctual in her remarks, so her editorial assistance is pretty much like the work of the masters of the Italian

ACKNOWLEDGMENTS

Renaissance. She can transform with just a stroke of her pen a rough idea into a masterpiece, and she has done it so many times with my writings that I cannot genuinely thank her enough for it.

Writing at night may seem a solitary experience, but it actually requires a complex organization, especially within the family. Parenting is by far one of the hardest yet most rewarding jobs in the world. I have had the pleasure to share it with my wife, Laura, who constantly sustains me with patience, care, and love. If I had any energy left to write this book at night, it was just because of her unceasing support during the day. Our son, Leonardo, was just a toddler when I embarked on this project. Now that you are reading it as a book, he teaches me words and idiomatic expressions in Dutch, shows me how to swim properly, and makes me a proud and happy father all the time. When I started writing, he asked me what this book was all about, and I told him it was about weird ships doing bad stuff in the oceans. This description stuck and convinced him that what I was doing was somehow important to protect the sea, which he absolutely loves. I am infinitely grateful for his unconditional trust and tender-hearted nature.

NOTES

INTRODUCTION

1. Author's interview with Sue Ann Fruge, January 2022.
2. *Incineration of Hazardous Waste at Sea, Hearing Before the Subcommittee on Fisheries and Wildlife Conservation and the Environment and the Subcommittee on Oceanography of the Committee on Merchant Marine and Fisheries, House of Representatives, Ninety-Eighth Congress, First Session, on an Oversight Regarding the Incineration of Hazardous Waste at Sea as Part of the Overall Efforts of Congress to Confront the Problem of Managing Hazardous Waste, December 7, 1983*, Serial no. 98-31 (Washington, DC: U.S. Government Printing Office, 1984), statements of Sue Ann Fruge, Gulf Coast Coalition for Public Health (GCCPH), 79.
3. GCCPH, history, September 24, 1985, Box 149, Folder 9 "Organizations: Gulf Coast Coalition for Public Health, 1985–1987," Grant Records, 1950–2007, Public Welfare Foundation Records, Ruth Lilly Special Collections and Archives, Philanthropic Studies Archives, University Library, Indiana University–Purdue University, Indianapolis, (hereafter GCCPH Records), 75; author's interview with Sue Ann Fruge, January 2022.
4. Gary Gerstle, *The Rise and Fall of the Neoliberal Order: America and the World in the Free Market Era* (New York: Oxford University Press, 2022).
5. Matt K. Matsuda, *Pacific Worlds: A History of Seas, Peoples, and Cultures* (New York: Cambridge University Press, 2012), 5–6; Sujit Sivasundaram, Alison Bashford, and David Armitage, "Introduction: Writing World Oceanic Histories," in *Oceanic Histories*, ed. David Armitage, Alison Bashford, and Sujit Sivasundaram (New York: Cambridge University Press, 2017), 4; David Naguib Pellow, *Resisting Global Toxics: Transnational*

INTRODUCTION

Movements for Environmental Justice (Cambridge, MA: MIT Press, 2007); Brian Doherty and Timothy Doyle, "Beyond Borders: Transnational Politics, Social Movements, and Modern Environmentalism," *Environmental Politics* 15, no. 5 (2006): 697–712.

6. Mark Atwood Lawrence, David Kinkela, and Erika Marie Bsumek, introduction to *Nation-States and the Global Environment: New Approaches to International Environmental History*, ed. Erika Marie Bsumek, David Kinkela, and Mark A. Lawrence (New York: Oxford University Press, 2013), 5–10.

7. On international environmental history, see Robert Boardman, *International Organization and the Conservation of Nature* (Bloomington: Indiana University Press, 1981); John McCormick, *Reclaiming Paradise: The Global Environmental Movement* (Bloomington: Indiana University Press, 1989); John E. Carroll, ed., *International Environmental Diplomacy: The Management and Resolution of Transfrontier Environmental Problems* (New York: Cambridge University Press, 1988); Richard Elliot Benedict, *Ozone Diplomacy: New Directions in Safeguarding the Planet* (Cambridge, MA: Harvard University Press, 1991); Lawrence E. Susskind, *Environmental Diplomacy: Negotiating More Effective Global Agreements* (New York: Oxford University Press, 1994); and Robert G. Darst, *Smokestack Diplomacy: Cooperation and Conflict in East–West Politics* (Cambridge, MA: MIT Press, 2001). On global ecology, see John McNeil, "Historical Perspectives on Global Ecology," *Journal of New Paradigm Research* 59, nos. 3–4 (2003): 263–74; Kurk Dorsey, "Dealing with the Dinosaur (and Its Swamp): Putting the Environment in Diplomatic History," *Diplomatic History* 29, no. 3 (2005): 573–87; Akira Iriye, "Environmental History and International History," *Diplomatic History* 32, no. 4 (2008): 643–46; and Andrew T. Price-Smith, *Contagion and Chaos: Disease, Ecology, and National Security in the Era of Globalization* (Cambridge, MA: MIT Press, 2009). On transnational and global approaches, see Ian R. Tyrrell, *True Gardens of the Gods: Californian–Australian Environmental Reform, 1860–1930* (Berkeley: University of California Press, 1999); Richard P. Tucker, *Insatiable Appetite: The United States and the Ecological Degradation of the Tropical World* (Berkeley: University of California Press, 2000); Ramachandra Guha, *Environmentalism: A Global History* (New York: Longman, 2000); Paul Sutter, "Reflections: What Can U.S. Historians Learn from Non-U.S. Environmental Historiography?," *Environmental History* 8, no. 1 (2003): 109–29; William Beinart and Lotte Hughes, *Environment and Empire* (New York: Oxford University Press, 2007); I. G. Simmons, *Global Environmental History* (Chicago: University of Chicago Press, 2008); Donald Hughes, *An Environmental History of the World: Humankind's Changing Role in the Community of Life* (London: Routledge, 2009); Thomas G. Andrews, *Killing for Coal: America's Deadliest Labor War* (Cambridge, MA: Harvard University Press, 2008); Anthony Penna, *The Human Footprint: A Global Environmental History* (Malden, MA: Wiley-Blackwell, 2009); Jessica B. Teisch, *Engineering Nature: Water, Development, and the Global Spread of American Environmental Expertise* (Chapel Hill: University of North Carolina Press, 2011); and Paul S. Sutter, "The World with Us: The State of American Environmental History," *Journal of American History* 100, no. 1 (2013): 94–119.

INTRODUCTION

8. The literature on ocean incineration has so far dealt mostly with either its technical aspects or its national and international regulation. On offshore-incineration policy, see S. Daryl Ditz, "Interpretation of Need in US Ocean Incineration Policy," *Marine Policy* 13, no. 1 (1989): 43–55; Arnold W. Reitze and Andrew N. Davis, "Reconsidering Ocean Incineration as Part of a U.S. Hazardous Waste Management Program: Separating the Rhetoric from the Reality," *Environmental Affairs Law Review* 17, no. 4 (1990): 688–798; and Navarro Ferronato and Vincenzo Torretta, "Waste Mismanagement in Developing Countries: A Review of Global Issues," *International Journal of Environmental Research and Public Health* 16, no. 6 (2019): 1–28. On ocean incineration's technical aspects, see Kenneth S. Kamlet, "Ocean Disposal of Organochlorine Wastes by at-Sea Incineration," in *Ocean Dumping of Industrial Wastes*, ed. Bostwick H. Ketchum, Dana R. Kester, and P. Kilho Park (Dordrecht, Netherlands: Springer, 1981), 295–314; H. Compaan, "Waste Incineration at Sea," in *Pollution of the North Sea: An Assessment*, ed. Wim Salomons, Brian L. Bayne, Egbert Klaas Duursma, and Ulrich Förstner (Heidelberg, Germany: Springer, 1988), 258–74; and George Vander Velde, Edward Glod, and George P. Nassos, "Ocean Incineration: The European Experience," *Waste Management & Research* 6, no. 1 (1988): 70–79.

9. Jason W. Moore, "The Modern World-System as Environmental History? Ecology and the Rise of Capitalism," *Theory and Society* 32, no. 3 (2003): 307–77; Teisch, *Engineering Nature*; David Kinkela, *DDT and the American Century: Global Health, Environmental Politics, and the Pesticide That Changed the World* (Chapel Hill: University of North Carolina Press, 2011); Thomas Robertson, *The Malthusian Moment: Global Population Growth and the Birth of American Environmentalism* (New Brunswick, NJ: Rutgers University Press, 2012); Jacob Darwin Hamblin, *Arming Mother Nature: The Birth of Catastrophic Environmentalism* (New York: Oxford University Press, 2013); Bsumek, Kinkela, and Lawrence, *Nation-States and the Global Environment*; Kurkpatrick Dorsey, *Whales and Nations: Environmental Diplomacy on the High Seas* (Seattle: University of Washington Press, 2013); Ian Tyrrell, *Crisis of the Wasteful Nation: Conservation and Empire in Teddy Roosevelt's America* (Chicago: University of Chicago Press, 2015); Stephen Macekura, *Of Limits and Growth: The Rise of Global Sustainable Development in the Twentieth Century* (New York: Cambridge University Press, 2015); Donald Worster, *Shrinking the Earth: The Rise and Decline of American Abundance* (New York: Oxford University Press, 2015); John R. McNeill and Peter Engelke, *The Great Acceleration: An Environmental History of the Anthropocene Since 1945* (Cambridge, MA: Harvard University Press, 2015). For a synthesis on the global turn in (U.S.) environmental history, see Sutter, "The World with Us."

10. Chalmers Johnson, *The Sorrows of Empire: Militarism, Secrecy, and the End of the Republic* (New York: Metropolitan, 2005), 13.

11. Paul G. Harris, "International Environmental Affairs and U.S. Foreign Policy," in *The Environment, International Relations, and U.S. Foreign Policy*, ed. Paul G. Harris (Washington, DC: Georgetown University Press, 2001), 18.

INTRODUCTION

12. Thomas Robertson, "'This Is the American Earth': American Empire, the Cold War, and American Environmentalism," *Diplomatic History* 32, no. 4 (2008): 561–84; Jeffrey Santa Ana, Heidi Amin-Hong, Rina Garcia Chua, and Zhou Xiaojing, eds., *Empire and Environment: Ecological Ruin in the Transpacific* (Ann Arbor: University of Michigan Press, 2022).
13. Stefano B. Longo, Rebecca Clausen, and Brett Clark, *The Tragedy of the Commodity: Oceans, Fisheries, and Aquaculture* (New Brunswick, NJ: Rutgers University Press, 2015); Laura A. Pratt, "Decreasing Dirty Dumping? A Re-evaluation of Toxic Waste Colonialism and the Global Management of Transboundary Hazardous Waste," *William & Mary Environmental Law and Policy Review* 35, no. 2 (2011): 619–20; John R. McNeil, *Something New Under the Sun: An Environmental History of the Twentieth-Century World* (New York: Norton, 2001).
14. Helen M. Rozwadowski, "The Promise of Ocean History for Environmental History," *Journal of American History* 100, no. 1 (2013): 136–39.
15. Megan Black, *The Global Interior: Mineral Frontiers and American Power* (Cambridge, MA: Harvard University Press, 2018).
16. Paul A. Kramer, "Power and Connection: Imperial Histories of the United States in the World," *American Historical Review* 116, no. 5 (2011): 1349.
17. Jenifer Van Vleck, *Empire of the Air: Aviation and the American Ascendancy* (Cambridge, MA: Harvard University Press, 2013); Marc-William Palen, "Empire by Imitation? US Economic Imperialism Within a British World System," in *The Oxford Handbook of the Ends of Empire*, ed. Martin Thomas and Andrew S. Thompson (New York: Oxford University Press, 2018), 195–211; G. John Ikenberry, *Liberal Leviathan: The Origins, Crisis, and Transformation of the American World Order* (Princeton, NJ: Princeton University Press, 2011).
18. Charles S. Maier, "'Malaise': The Crisis of Capitalism in the 1970s," in *The Shock of the Global: The 1970s in Perspective*, ed. Niall Ferguson, Charles S. Maier, Erez Manela, and Daniel J. Sargent (Cambridge, MA: Harvard University Press, 2010), 25–48; Daniel J. Sargent, "The United States and Globalization in the 1970s," in *The Shock of the Global*, ed. Ferguson et al., 49–64.
19. Edith Brown Weiss, "The Evolution of International Environmental Law," *Japanese Yearbook of International Law* 54 (2011): 1–27.
20. Jon Birger Skjaerseth, "Toward the End of Dumping in the North Sea: The Case of the Oslo Commission," in *Environmental Regime Effectiveness: Confronting Theory with Evidence*, ed. Edward L. Miles, Steinar Andresen, Elaine M. Carlin, Jon Birger Skjaerseth, and Arild Underdal (Cambridge, MA: MIT Press, 2002), 65–86.
21. Thomas Risse-Kappen, "Public Opinion, Domestic Structure, and Foreign Policy in Liberal Democracies," *World Politics* 43, no. 4 (1991): 479–512; Paul Burstein, "The Impact of Public Opinion on Public Policy: A Review and an Agenda," *Political Research Quarterly* 56, no. 1 (2003): 29–40; Jon Agnone, "Amplifying Public Opinion: The Policy Impact of the U.S. Environmental Movement," *Social Forces* 85, no. 4 (2007): 1593–620; Robert Y.

INTRODUCTION

Shapiro, "Public Opinion and American Democracy," *Public Opinion Quarterly* 75, no. 5 (2011): 982–1017.

22. *The Rising Significance of World Opinion* (1977), 2, Reel 17, 0405, S-5-77, Part 1: Cold War Era Special Reports, Series B, 1964–1982, Records of the U.S. Information Agency, Roosevelt Institute for American Studies (RIAS), Middleburg, Netherlands.
23. *The Importance of Foreign Public Opinion to U.S. Foreign Policy* (1978), 1, Reel 18, 0717 S-10-78, Part 1: Cold War Era Special Reports, Series B, 1964–1982, Records of the U.S. Information Agency, RIAS.
24. *Corporate Priorities in Europe* (1979), 5, Reel 20, 0070, S-11-79, Part 1: Cold War Era Special Reports, Series B, 1964–1982, Records of the U.S. Information Agency, RIAS.
25. Hajo Eicken, Finn Danielsen, Josephine-Mary Sam, Maryann Fidel, Noor Johnson, Michael K Poulsen, Olivia A. Lee, et al., "Connecting Top-Down and Bottom-Up Approaches in Environmental Observing," *BioScience* 7, no. 5 (2021): 467–83; Gregory Rosenthal, "Workers of the World's Oceans: A Bottom-Up Environmental History of the Pacific," *Resilience: A Journal of the Environmental Humanities* 3, no. 1 (2016): 290–310.
26. Jackie Smith, "Global Politics and Transnational Social Movement Strategies: The Transnational Campaign Against International Trade in Toxic Wastes," in *Social Movements in a Globalizing World*, ed. Donatella della Porta, Hanspeter Kriesi, and Dieter Rucht (London: Palgrave, 1999), 170–88.
27. Sarah A. Vogel, *Is It Safe? BPA and the Struggle to Define the Safety of Chemicals* (Berkeley: University of California Press, 2012), 126.
28. Andrew Szasz, *Ecopopulism: Toxic Waste and the Movement for Environmental Justice* (Minneapolis: University of Minnesota Press, 1994), 38–102.
29. U.S. Environmental Protection Agency (EPA), "Hazardous Waste Disposal Damage Reports," 1975, 1–12, U.S. EPA National Service Center for Environmental Publications (EPA-NSCEP).
30. Thomas H. Fletcher, *From Love Canal to Environmental Justice: The Politics of Hazardous Waste on the Canada-U.S. Border* (Toronto: University of Toronto Press, 2003).
31. J. Brooks Flippen, *Nixon and the Environment* (Albuquerque: University of New Mexico Press, 2000); Melvin Small, *The Presidency of Richard Nixon* (Lawrence: University Press of Kansas, 1999); Stephen Macekura, "Environment, Climate, and Global Disorder," in *The Cambridge History of America and the World*, vol. 2, ed. David C. Engerman, Max Paul Friedman, and Melani McAlister (New York: Cambridge University Press, 2022), 488–511.
32. Lisa M. Brady, "War from the Ground Up: Integrating Military and Environmental Histories," in *A Field on Fire: The Future of Environmental History*, ed. Mark D. Hersey and Ted Steinberg (Tuscaloosa: University of Alabama Press, 2019), 250–62; Alvin Lee Young, *The History, Use, Disposition, and Environmental Fate of Agent Orange* (New York: Springer, 2009); Katherine C. Epstein, *Torpedo: Inventing the Military-Industrial Complex in the United States and Great Britain* (Cambridge, MA: Harvard University Press, 2014); Edwin A. Martini, "'This is Really Bad Stuff Buried Here': Agent Orange,

INTRODUCTION

Johnston Atoll, and the Rise of Military Environmentalism," in *Proving Grounds: Militarized Landscapes, Weapons Testing, and the Environmental Impact of U.S. Bases*, ed. Edwin A. Martini (Seattle: University of Washington Press, 2015), 111–42; Simone M. Müller, "'Cut Holes and Sink 'Em': Chemical Weapons Disposal and Cold War History as a History of Risk," *Historical Social Research* 41, no. 1 (2016): 263–84; Jon Mitchell, *Poisoning the Pacific: The US Military's Secret Dumping of Plutonium, Chemical Weapons, and Agent Orange* (Lanham, MD: Rowman & Littlefield, 2020); Alex Roland, *Delta of Power: The Military-Industrial Complex* (Baltimore, MD: Johns Hopkins University Press, 2021).

33. Martin V. Melosi, *Effluent America: Cities, Industry, Energy, and the Environment* (Pittsburgh: University of Pittsburgh Press, 2001).

34. Alfred Chandler Jr., *Shaping the Industrial Century: The Remarkable Story of the Evolution of the Modern Chemical and Pharmaceutical Industries* (Cambridge, MA: Harvard University Press, 2005), 16.

35. U.S. EPA, "Resource Conservation and Recovery Act (RCRA) Overview," updated June 29, 2022, https://www.epa.gov/rcra/resource-conservation-and-recovery-act-rcra-overview; Marquita Kill, *Understanding Environmental Pollution*, 4th ed. (New York: Cambridge University Press, 2020), 268; U.S. EPA, "Report of the Interagency ad Hoc Work Group for the Chemical Waste Incinerator Ship Program, September 1980," v, U.S. Department of Commerce—Maritime Administration, U.S. Department of Transportation—Coast Guard, U.S. Department of Commerce—National Bureau of Standards, EPA-NSCEP. See also U.S. EPA, "Assessment of Industrial Hazardous Waste Practices, Inorganic Chemicals Industry," 1975, 1–5, EPA-NSCEP; and Halina Szejnwald Brown, Brian J. Cook, Robert Krueger, and Jo Anne Shatkin, "Reassessing the History of U.S. Hazardous Waste Disposal Policy—Problem Definition, Expert Knowledge, and Agenda-Setting," *RISK: Health, Safety, & Environment* 8, no. 3 (1997): 249–72.

36. U.S. EPA, "Ocean Dumping: A Briefing Document for the President's Water Pollution Control Advisory Board," September 1972, 3–15, EPA-NSCEP. See also "Ocean Waste Disposal in Selected Geographic Areas," prepared by the Interstate Electronics Corporation, subsidiary of A-T-O Inc., for the U.S. EPA, Ocean Disposal Program, July 1973, 1–28, EPA-NSCEP.

37. U.S. EPA, *Environmental News*, press release, October 29, 1980, Box 121 (Hazardous Waste, 2/1980), Douglas M. Costle Papers, Jimmy Carter Presidential Library, Atlanta, GA.

38. Iris Borowy, "Hazardous Waste: The Beginning of International Organizations Addressing a Growing Global Challenge in the 1970s," *Worldwide Waste: Journal of Interdisciplinary Studies* 2, no. 1 (2019): 1–10.

39. Emily Brownell, "Negotiating the New Economic Order of Waste," *Environmental History* 16, no. 2 (2011): 262–89; Helen M. Rozwadowski, *Vast Expanses: A History of the Oceans* (Chicago: University of Chicago Press, 2019), 210–11.

40. "Program for the Management of Hazardous Wastes," final report, prepared for the U.S. EPA, Office of Solid Waste Management, July 1973, 5–11, EPA-NSCEP. On the

INTRODUCTION

deterioration of U.S. landfills, see Donald Farb and S. Daniel Warb, "Information About Hazardous Waste Management Facilities: A Solid Waste Management Inventory Prepared for the US Environmental Protection Agency," February 1975, 2–6, EPA-NSCEP. On the overall inadequacy of land-based disposal methods, see U.S. EPA, "Hazardous Waste Disposal Damage Reports," Document no. 2, 1975, iii, EPA-NSCEP; on Love Canal, see Elizabeth D. Blum, *Love Canal Revisited: Race, Class, and Gender in Environmental Activism* (Lawrence: University Press of Kansas, 2008).

41. U.S. EPA, "Report of the Interagency ad Hoc Work Group," v. See also Travis Wagner, "Hazardous Waste: Evolution of a National Environmental Problem," *Journal of Policy History* 16, no. 4 (2004): 306–31.
42. U.S. Department of Commerce, National Technical Information Service, "Assessment of Hazardous Waste Practices in the Petroleum Refining Industry," PB-259 097, Jacobs Engineering Co., prepared for U.S. EPA, June 1976, 22, EPA-NSCEP.
43. U.S. EPA, "Report to Congress on Hazardous Waste Disposal," June 30, 1973, v, EPA-NSCEP; U.S. EPA, Office of Solid Waste Management Program, "Report to Congress: Disposal of Hazardous Wastes," 1974, 1, EPA-NSCEP.
44. U.S. EPA, "Report of the Interagency Ad Hoc Work Group," v.
45. U.S. EPA, "Report to Congress on Hazardous Waste Disposal," 93.
46. Rémi Parmentier, "Greenpeace and the Dumping of Waste at Sea: A Case of Non-state Actors' Intervention in International Affairs," *International Negotiations* 4, no. 3 (1999): 435–57.
47. Nicholas Freudenberg and Carol Steinsapir, "Not in Our Backyards: The Grassroots Environmental Movement," *Society & Natural Resources: An International Journal* 4, no. 3 (1991): 235–45.
48. Liam Leonard, *The Environmental Movement in Ireland* (Dordrecht, Netherlands: Springer, 2008), 119–29; Luke W. Cole and Sheila R. Foster, *From the Ground Up: Environmental Racism and the Rise of the Environmental Justice Movement* (New York: New York University Press, 2001), 22. On the supposed unsustainability of modern industrialism, see Ulrich Beck, *Risk Society: Towards a New Modernity* (London: Sage, 1992); and Kenneth Alan Gould, David N. Pellow, and Allan Schnaiberg, *The Treadmill of Production: Injustice and Unsustainability in the Global Economy* (London: Routledge, 2008).
49. Etienne S. Benson, *Surroundings: A History of Environments and Environmentalisms* (Chicago: University of Chicago Press, 2020), 135–63.
50. Blum, *Love Canal Revisited*; Nancy C. Unger, *Beyond Nature's Housekeepers: American Women in Environmental History* (New York: Oxford University Press, 2012); Jennifer Thomson, *The Wild and the Toxic: American Environmentalism and the Politics of Health* (Chapel Hill: University of North Carolina Press, 2019).
51. Ellen Griffith Spears, *Rethinking the American Environmental Movement Post-1945* (London: Routledge, 2019), 120.
52. Cole and Foster, *From the Ground Up*, 22.
53. Vivien Hamilton and Brinda Sarathy, "Introduction: Toxicity, Uncertainty, and Expertise," in *Inevitably Toxic: Historical Perspectives on Contamination, Exposure, and Expertise,*

ed. Brinda Sarathy, Janet Brodie, and Vivien Hamilton (Pittsburgh: University of Pittsburgh Press, 2019), 21.

54. Robert D. Bullard and Beverly H. Wright, "Environmental Justice for All: Community Perspectives on Health and Research," *Toxicology and Industrial Health* 9, no. 5 (1993): 821–41; Eileen Maura McGurty, "From Nimby to Civil Rights: The Origins of the Environmental Justice Movement," *Environmental History* 2, no. 3 (1997): 301–23; Jennifer Frost, *An Interracial Movement of the Poor: Community Organizing and the New Left in the 1960s* (New York: New York University Press, 2005).

55. Eileen McGurty, *Transforming Environmentalism: Warren County, PCBs, and the Origins of Environmental Justice* (New Brunswick, NJ: Rutgers University Press, 2007); Dorceta E. Taylor, *Toxic Communities: Environmental Racism, Industrial Pollution, and Residential Mobility* (New York: New York University Press, 2014); Ellen Griffith Spears, *Baptized in PCBs: Race, Pollution, and Justice in an All-American Town* (Chapel Hill: University of North Carolina Press, 2014).

56. Commission for Racial Justice, United Church of Christ, *Toxic Wastes and Race in the United States: A National Report on the Racial and Socio-economic Characteristics of Communities with Hazardous Waste Sites* (1987), xii, https://www.nrc.gov/docs/ML1310/ML13109A339.pdf.

57. Traci Brynne Voyles, *Wastelanding: Legacies of Uranium Mining in Navajo Country* (Minneapolis: University of Minnesota Press, 2015); Phaedra Pezzullo, *Toxic Tourism: Rhetoric of Pollution, Travel, and Environmental Justice* (Tuscaloosa: University of Alabama Press, 2007); Martin V. Melosi, *Water in North American Environmental History* (London: Routledge, 2022).

58. Joni Seager, *Earth Follies: Feminism, Politics, and the Environment* (London: Routledge, 1993), 253–79.

59. Kuntala Lahiri-Dutt, "Introduction: Reflections on Gender and Water," in *Fluid Bonds: Views on Gender and Water*, ed. Kuntala Lahiri-Dutt (Kolkata, India: Bhatkal and Sen, 2006), 22–50; Cara Daggett, "Petro-masculinity: Fossil Fuels and Authoritarian Desire," *Millennium: Journal of International Studies* 47, no. 1 (2018): 25–44; Steve Mentz, "Is Compassion an Oceanic Feeling?," *Emotions: History, Culture, Society* 4, no. 1 (2020): 109–27.

60. Sarah Alisabeth Fox, *Downwind: A People's History of the Nuclear West* (Lincoln: University of Nebraska Press, 2014).

61. Luke W. Cole, "Empowerment as the Key to Environmental Protection: The Need for Environmental Poverty Law," *Ecology Law Quarterly* 19, no. 4 (1992): 619–83; Seth M. Holmes, *Fresh Fruit, Broken Bodies: Migrant Farmworkers in the United States* (Berkeley: University of California Press, 2013); Joshua Kahn, Stephen D'Arcy, Tony Weis, and Toban Black, eds., *A Line in the Tar Sands: Struggles for Environmental Justice* (Oakland, CA: PM Press, 2014); Stefania Barca, "Laboring the Earth: Transnational Reflections on the Environmental History of Work," *Environmental History* 19, no. 1 (2014): 3–27; Voyles, *Wastelanding*; Dina Gilio-Whitaker, *As Long as Grass Grows: The Indigenous Fight for Environmental Justice, from Colonization to Standing Rock* (Boston: Beacon Press, 2020), 15–19.

1. THE DISPOSABLE FRONTIER

62. Cole and Foster, *From the Ground Up*, 27. See also Michael Dreiling, "From Margin to Center: Environmental Justice and Social Unionism as Sites for Intermovement Solidarity," *Race, Gender, & Class* 6, no. 1 (1998): 51–69; Dimitris Stevis, "Labour Unions and Environmental Justice: The Trajectory and Politics of Just Transition," in *Environmental Justice: Key Issues*, ed. Brendan Coolsaet (London: Routledge, 2020), 249–65.
63. U.S. EPA, Office of Water and Waste Management, *Everybody's Problem: Hazardous Waste* (May 1980), 14, Box 121 (Hazardous Waste, 2/1980), Costle Papers, Carter Library.
64. Rozwadowski, *Vast Expanses*; Gary Kroll, *America's Ocean Wilderness: A Cultural History of Twentieth-Century Exploration* (Lawrence: University of Kansas Press, 2008).
65. Ayana Elizabeth Johnson, interview by Beth Gardiner, "Ocean Justice: Where Social Equity and the Climate Fight Intersect," *Yale Environment 360*, July 16, 2020, https://e360.yale.edu/features/ocean-justice-where-social-equity-and-the-climate-fight-intersect,m.
66. White House, "Executive Order on Tackling the Climate Crisis at Home and Abroad," January 27, 2021, https://www.whitehouse.gov/briefing-room/presidential-actions/2021/01/27/executive-order-on-tackling-the-climate-crisis-at-home-and-abroad/; White House, "Memorandum on Restoring Trust in Government Through Scientific Integrity and Evidence-Based Policymaking," January 27, 2021, https://www.whitehouse.gov/briefing-room/presidential-actions/2021/01/27/memorandum-on-restoring-trust-in-government-through-scientific-integrity-and-evidence-based-policymaking/.

1. THE DISPOSABLE FRONTIER

1. Brian C. Black, "Oil for Living: Petroleum and American Conspicuous Consumption," *Journal of American History* 99, no. 1 (2012): 40–50; Tyler Priest, "The Dilemmas of Oil Empire," *Journal of American History* 99, no. 1 (2012): 236–51; Robert J. Gordon, *The Rise and Fall of American Growth: The U.S Standard of Living Since the Civil War* (Princeton, NJ: Princeton University Press, 2017), 339.
2. Daniel Yergin, *The Prize: The Epic Quest for Oil, Money, and Power* (New York: New Press, 1992), 328–88.
3. Sarah A. Vogel, *Is It Safe? BPA and the Struggle to Define the Safety of Chemicals* (Berkeley: University of California Press, 2012), 110–34.
4. Eileen McGurty, *Transforming Environmentalism: Warren County, PCBs, and the Origins of Environmental Justice* (New Brunswick, NJ: Rutgers University Press, 2007), 50–81.
5. U.S. Environmental Protection Agency (EPA), Office of Public Awareness, *Hazardous Waste Information* (May 1980), 1, Box 121 (Hazardous Waste, 2/1980), Douglas M. Costle Papers, Jimmy Carter Presidential Library, Atlanta, GA.
6. Louis Blumberg and Robert Gottlieb, *War on Waste: Can America Win Its Battle with Garbage?* (Washington, DC: Island Press, 1989), 218–20.

1. THE DISPOSABLE FRONTIER

7. Brian C. Black, "How World War I Ushered in the Century of Oil," *The Conversation*, April 4, 2017, https://theconversation.com/how-world-war-i-ushered-in-the-century-of-oil-74585.
8. As Fred Aftalion details, organic derivatives, in particular dyes, phenol, and benzene, were needed to support the explosives industry and meet strong Allied demand. Although there was no shortage of synthetic dyes at first, in 1916 the U.S. federal government established a five-year tariff barrier that allowed such companies as Du Pont, Calco, and Dow to start petrochemical-based dye production. See Fred Aftalion, *A History of the International Chemical Industry: From the "Early Days" to 2000* (Philadelphia: Chemical Heritage Press, 2001), 123–24.
9. Aftalion, *A History of the International Chemical Industry*, 130, 214–15.
10. John Kenly Smith Jr., "Patents, Public Policy, and Petrochemical Processes in the Post–World War II Era," *Business and Economic History* 27, no. 2 (1998): 413–19.
11. Aftalion, *A History of the International Chemical Industry*, 216. See also Earnest F. Gloyna and Davis L. Ford, *The Characteristics and Pollutional Problems Associated with Petrochemical Wastes*, summary report prepared for the Federal Water Pollution Control Administration of the U.S. Department of Interior (February 1970), 6, U.S. EPA National Service Center for Environmental Publications (EPA-NSCEP).
12. Daniel J. Brennan, *Process Industry Economics: An International Perspective* (Rugby, U.K.: IChemE, 1998), 39; Elkhan Asanov and Mübariz Hasanov, "Analysing the Relationship Between Oil Prices and Basic Petrochemical Feedstocks," in *Energy Economy, Finance, and Geostrategy*, ed. André B. Dorsman, Volkan Ş. Ediger, and Mehmet Baha Karan (Cham, Switzerland: Springer, 2018), 115.
13. John Kenly Smith Jr., "The American Chemical Industry Since the Petrochemical Revolution," in *The Global Chemical Industry in the Age of the Petrochemical Revolution*, ed. Louis Galambos, Takashi Hikino, and Vera Zamagni (New York: Cambridge University Press, 2007), 168–92.
14. Mark Peplow, "The Plastics Revolution: How Chemists Are Pushing Polymers to New Limits," *Nature* 536, no. 7616 (2016): 266–68.
15. Jeffrey L. Meikle, *American Plastic: A Cultural History* (New Brunswick, NJ: Rutgers University Press, 1995), 63–90.
16. Roland Geyer, Jenna R. Jambeck, and Kara Lavender Law, "Production, Use, and Fate of All Plastics Ever Made," *Science Advances* 3, no. 17 (2017), https://advances.sciencemag.org/content/3/7/e1700782.
17. Mourad Krifa and Sara Stewart Stevens, "Cotton Utilization in Conventional and Nonconventional Textiles—a Statistical Review," *Agricultural Science* 7, no. 10 (2016), https://m.scirp.org/papers/71537.
18. European Petrochemical Association, "The European Petrochemical Association, Petrochemicals, and EPCA: A Passionate Journey," n.d., 16–17, https://epca.eu/ebooks/history/files/assets/common/downloads/publication.pdf.
19. U.S. Department of Commerce, Business and Defense Service Administration, "Industry Trends" and "Economic Trends in the Chemical and Allied Products Industries," *Chemicals* 13, no. 2 (June 1966): 3 and 11, https://bit.ly/2I5J7DQ.

1. THE DISPOSABLE FRONTIER

20. U.S. Department of Commerce, Business and Defense Service Administration, "Industry Trends" and "The Chemical Industry Abroad," *Chemicals* 15, no. 3 (September 1968): 3 and 15.
21. Peter H. Spitz, *Petrochemicals: The Rise of an Industry* (New York: Wiley, 1988), 350.
22. Takashi Hikino, Louis Galambos, and Vera Zamagni, introduction to *The Global Chemical Industry in the Age of the Petrochemical Revolution*, ed. Galambos, Hikino, and Zamagni, 1–20.
23. The EPA's definition of industrial hazardous waste included "toxic, chemical, biological, radioactive, flammable, and explosive wastes." See Robert E. Landreth and Charles J. Rogers, *Promising Technologies for Treatment of Hazardous Wastes*, National Environmental Research Center, Office of Research and Development, U.S. EPA (November 1974), 8, EPA-NSCEP. See also Paul E. Rosenfeld and Lydia Feng, *Risks of Hazardous Wastes* (Amsterdam: Elsevier, 2011), 1–4.
24. Paul B. Tchounwou, Clement G. Yedjou, Anita K. Patlolla, and Dwayne J. Sutton, "Heavy Metal Toxicity and the Environment," *Experientia Supplementum* 101 (2012): 133–64.
25. James Edward Huff and John S. Wassom, "Hazardous Contaminants: Chlorinated Dibenzodioxins and Chlorinated Dibenzofurans," in *Environmental Chemicals: Human and Animal Health*, Proceedings of 2nd Annual "Environmental Chemicals: Human and Animal Health" Conference, organized by the U.S. EPA, Office of Pesticides Programs, Colorado State University, Fort Collins, July 25–29, 1974, ed. Eldon P. Savage, 175–98, EPA-NSCEP.
26. See "Collaborative Study in the EEC Framework of the Determination of Organochlorine Residues in Biological Materials," March 1974, Box 5540 (EEC Study on Organochlorine Residuals), Rijksinstituut voor de Volksgezondheid (RIV), 1934–1983, Nationaal Archief, The Hague.
27. Joe Thornton, *Pandora's Poison: Chlorine, Health, and a New Environmental Strategy* (Cambridge, MA: MIT Press, 2000), 277. See also U.S. EPA, Office of Water Programs, *Industrial Liquid Wastes Surveys*, training manual (January 1973), 1–4, EPA-NSCEP.
28. Alexander E. Farrell, "Overview of the Superfund Program," in *Reclaiming the Land: Rethinking Superfund Institutions, Methods, and Practices*, ed. Gregg P. Macey and Jonathan Z. Cannon (Cham, Switzerland: Springer, 2007), 25.
29. U.S. EPA, Office of Water and Waste Management, *Everybody's Problem: Hazardous Waste* (May 1980), 14, Box 121, Costle Papers, Carter Library.
30. U.S. EPA, "Report to Congress on Hazardous Waste Disposal," June 30, 1973, v, EPA-NSCEP.
31. Bruce Piasecki and Hans Sutter, *The Origins and Decline of Ocean Incineration in Europe: The German Example* (Berlin: Umweltbundesamt [Federal Environmental Agency], Federal Republic of Germany, 1988), 2, Box 5762 (General Correspondence on Land and Ocean Incineration with Other Related Documents, 1988–1990), International Institute for Social History (IISH), Greenpeace International (Amsterdam) Archives (GIAA).
32. Program for the Management of Hazardous Wastes, Office of Solid Waste Management, "Final Report," prepared for the U.S. EPA, July 1973, 5–11, EPA-NSCEP. On the

1. THE DISPOSABLE FRONTIER

deterioration of U.S. landfills, see Donald Farb and S. Daniel Warb, *Information About Hazardous Waste Management Facilities: A Solid Waste Management Inventory Prepared for the US Environmental Protection Agency* (February 1975), 2–6, EPA-NSCEP. On the overall inadequacy of land-based disposal methods, see U.S. EPA, "Hazardous Waste Disposal Damage Reports," Document no. 2, 1975, iii, EPA-NSCEP. In 1980, the EPA revealed that more than 27,000 waste sites across the United States were unsafe and that most of them required immediate remedial action because of their dangerous conditions. Further studies confirmed that the cleanup of dangerous chemicals disposed of or abandoned in uncontrolled sites across the country could cost as much as $44 billion. See U.S. EPA, *Environmental News*, press release, October 29, 1980, Box 121, Costle Papers, Carter Library.

33. James A. Rogers, "Ocean Dumping," *Environmental Law* 7, no. 1 (1976): 1–23; Marc A. Zeppetello, "National and International Regulation of Ocean Dumping: The Mandate to Terminate Marine Disposal of Contaminated Sewage Sludge," *Ecology Law Quarterly* 12, no. 3 (1985): 619–64.
34. Thaddeus A. Wastler, "Ocean Dumping Permit Program Under the London Dumping Convention in the United States," *Chemosphere* 10, no. 6 (1981): 660.
35. Piasecki and Sutter, *The Origins and Decline of Ocean Incineration in Europe*, 2–5. See also Thomas E. Kopp, "PCB Disposal, Reclaiming, and Treatment," U.S. EPA, National Conference on Polychlorinated Biphenyls, November 1975, Chicago, Conference Proceedings, 108–24, EPA-NSCEP. PCBs were so dangerous that the U.S. federal government even created an interdepartmental task force to manage their environmental impact, which concluded that PCBs had to be restricted to "essential or nonreplaceable uses" so as to minimize "the likelihood of human exposure or leakage to the environment." See "Polychlorinated Biphenyls and the Environment: Interdepartmental Task Force on PCBs," May 1972, 1, EPA-NSCEP.
36. "Ocean Waste Disposal in Selected Geographic Areas," prepared by the Interstate Electronics Corporation, subsidiary of A-T-O Inc., for the U.S. EPA, Ocean Disposal Program, July 1973, 1–28, EPA-NSCEP.
37. Ocean dumping had become the most common method in the United States for the disposal of hazardous waste. In 1970, a report to the U.S. president presented ocean-dumping practices as the most common disposal method for six materials: dredge spoil, sewage sludge, solid waste, industrial wastes, construction and demolition debris, and radioactive wastes. See U.S. EPA, *Ocean Dumping: A Briefing Document for the President's Water Pollution Control Advisory Board* (September 1972), 3–15, EPA-NSCEP.
38. Jason W. Moore, "'The Modern World-System' as Environmental History? Ecology and the Rise of Capitalism," *Theory and Society* 32, no. 3 (2003): 307–77.
39. Thomas Robertson, *The Malthusian Moment: Global Population Growth and the Birth of American Environmentalism* (New Brunswick, NJ: Rutgers University Press, 2012), 138–39.
40. John R. McNeill, "Observations on the Nature and Culture of Environmental History," *History and Theory* 42, no. 4 (2003): 5–43. Other authors place the origins of

1. THE DISPOSABLE FRONTIER

environmentalism within the context of the Progressive Era. See, for instance, Ian Tyrrell, *True Gardens of the Gods: Californian-Australian Environmental Reform, 1860–1930* (Berkeley: University of California Press, 1999); and Tyrrell, *Crisis of the Wasteful Nation: Empire and Conservation in Theodore Roosevelt's America* (Chicago: University of Chicago Press, 2015). According to Thomas Raymond Wellocks, however, urban environmentalism stemmed first from the transformation of conservationism into preservationism and then from the evolution of the latter into a modern, ecological approach. See Thomas Raymond Wellocks, *Preserving the Nation: The Conservation and Environmental Movements 1870–2000* (Wheeling, IL: Harlan Davidson, 2007). In this regard, see also Charles C. Chester, "Environmentalism," in *The Palgrave Dictionary of Transnational History*, ed. Akira Iriye and Pierre-Yves Saunier (New York: Palgrave, 2009), 339.

41. White House, "Chronological List of President Richard M. Nixon's Record on the Environment from 1/11/69 to 8/6/71," August 6, 1971, U.S. Declassified Documents Online, https://bit.ly/2UsZHQY.
42. Program for the Management of Hazardous Wastes, "Final Report," 8–9. See also Robin R. Jenkins, Elizabeth Kopits, and David Simpson, "Policy Monitor—the Evolution of Solid and Hazardous Waste Regulation in the United States," *Review of Environmental Economics and Policy* 3, no. 1 (2009): 104–20.
43. On both U.S. and international regulation of dangerous chemical pollutants, see David Kinkela, "The Paradox of US Pesticide Policy During the Age of Ecology," in *Nation-States and the Global Environment: New Approaches to International Environmental History*, ed. Erika Marie Bsumek, David Kinkela, and Mark A. Lawrence (New York: Oxford University Press, 2013), 115–30. See also "Federal Water Pollution Control Act (Clean Water Act)," in *Digest of Federal Resource Laws of Interest to the U.S. Fish and Wildlife Service* (2022), https://bit.ly/41rRzkK.
44. Sarah Praskievicz, "From Hetch Hetchy to the Cuyahoga: How Rivers Shaped the American Environmental Movement," *The Professional Geographer* 73, no. 1 (2021): 26–37.
45. Paul Charles Milazzo, *Unlikely Environmentalists: Congress and Clean Water, 1945–1972* (Lawrence: University Press of Kansas, 2006).
46. White House, "Chronological list of President Richard M. Nixon's Record on the Environment from 1/11/69 to 8/6/71."
47. Council on Environmental Quality, *Ocean Dumping: A National Policy*, a report to the president (Washington, DC: U.S. Government Printing Office, October 1970), 4, https://files.eric.ed.gov/fulltext/ED055891.pdf.
48. Margarete S. Steinhauer and Christine E. Werme, *Ocean Incineration: Background and Status*, prepared for David P. Redford, U.S. EPA, Office of Marine and Estuaries Protection, September 4, 1987, 12, EPA-NSCEP. See also U.S. EPA, *EPA and the Environmental Aspects of Dredged-Material Disposal* (December 7, 1990), 1–10, https://www.govinfo.gov/content/pkg/CZIC-td195-d72-e63-1990/html/CZIC-td195-d72-e63-1990.htm; and Jacob Darwin Hamblin, "Gods and Devils in the Details: Marine Pollution,

1. THE DISPOSABLE FRONTIER

Radioactive Waste, and an Environmental Regime circa 1972," *Diplomatic History* 32, no. 4 (2008): 539–60.

49. John McCormick states that the Stockholm Conference "was without doubt the landmark event in the growth of international environmentalism" (*Reclaiming Paradise: The Global Environmental Movement* [Bloomington: Indiana University Press, 1989], 88). According to Paul Harris, "The Stockholm Conference and its final declaration were crucial to setting up some principles that would later be codified by the UN Environment Program and that paved the way for the 1992 Rio Declaration on Environment and Development" ("International Norms of Responsibility and U.S. Climate Change Policy," in *Climate Change and American Foreign Policy*, ed. Paul G. Harris [New York: Palgrave, 2000], 227). But according to J. Brooks Flippen, the conference also served the purpose to assuage domestic environmental pressures and win back the voters who criticized President Nixon's conduct of the Vietnam War (*Nixon and the Environment* [Albuquerque: University of New Mexico Press, 2000], 260).

50. Hamblin, "Gods and Devils in the Details," 541–42; Daniel S. Margolies, "Introduction—Oceans Forum," *Diplomatic History* 44, no. 3 (2020): 409–12.

51. Train considered the conference to be a great success because the U.S. government not only had played a strong role in it but had also achieved practically all its goals. For the quote, see Russell E. Train, "Memorandum from the Chairman of the Council on Environmental Quality (Train) to President Nixon," Washington, DC, June 1, 1972, in *Foreign Relations of the United States, 1969–1976*, vol. E-1: *Documents on Global Issues, 1969–1972*, ed. Susan K. Holly and William B. McAllister (Washington, DC: U.S. Government Printing Office, 2005), Document 323, https://history.state.gov/historicaldocuments/frus1969-76ve01/d323. See also Russell E. Train, "Memorandum from the Chairman of the Council on Environmental Quality (Train) to President Nixon," Washington, DC, June 19, 1972, in *Foreign Relations of the United States, 1969–1976*, vol. E-1: *Documents on Global Issues, 1969–1972*, ed. Holly and McAllister, Document 324, https://history.state.gov/historicaldocuments/frus1969-76ve01/d324; Maxwell Bruce, "The London Dumping Convention, 1972: First Decade and Future," *Ocean Yearbook* 6, no. 1 (1986): 298–318; and John McCormick, "The Origins of the World Conservation Strategy," *Environmental Review* 10, no. 3 (1986): 177–87.

52. "Text of Draft Articles of a Convention for the Prevention of Marine Pollution by Dumping. Adopted at Reykjavik, Iceland, on 14 April 1972," 4, 2–3, Box 5245, Folder 150, Ministerie van Verkeer en Waterstaat. Directie Nordzee, 1971–1989, Nationaal Archief, The Hague. The text described vessels and aircrafts as "waterborne and airborne craft of any type whatsoever."

53. The Convention for the Prevention of Marine Pollution by Dumping from Ships and Aircraft (Oslo Convention) was a regional instrument regulating the dumping of toxic substances into the Northeast Atlantic, the Arctic Oceans, and the North Sea and was opened for signature in Oslo on February 15, 1972. The convention entered into force on April 6, 1974. It was ratified by Belgium, Denmark, Finland, France, the Federal Republic of Germany, Iceland, Ireland, Netherlands, Norway, Portugal, Spain, Sweden, and

1. THE DISPOSABLE FRONTIER

the United Kingdom. The framework established by the Oslo Convention was successfully expanded by the Convention for the Prevention of Marine Pollution from Land-Based Sources (Paris Convention), which was opened for signature in Paris on June 4, 1974. The Paris Convention entered into force on May 6, 1978, and was ratified by Belgium, Denmark, the European Economic Community, France, the Federal Republic of Germany, Iceland, Ireland, Luxembourg, Netherlands, Norway, Portugal, Spain, Sweden, and the United Kingdom. See Bruce P. Kilho Park and Thomas P. O'Connor, "Ocean Dumping Research: Historical and International Development," in *Ocean Dumping of Industrial Wastes*, ed. Bostwick H. Ketchum, Dana R. Kester, and P. Kilho Park (New York: Plenum Press, 1981), 3–5; Zhiguo Gao, *Environmental Regulation of Oil and Gas* (London: Kluwer Law, 1998), 59, 149; and Veronica Frank, *The European Community and Marine Environmental Protection in the International Law of the Sea: Implementing Global Obligations at the Regional Level* (Leiden, Netherlands: Martinus Nijhoff, 2007), 299–300. At around the same time, the UN sponsored the International Convention for the Prevention of Pollution from Ships (MARPOL) and favored the adoption of the Convention on the Law of the Sea in 1982, which designated the 200-nautical-mile exclusive economic zones that gave coastal states ownership and sovereignty of the vast majority of natural resources within each zone. See John Barkdull, "Nixon and the Marine Environment," *Presidential Studies Quarterly* 28, no. 3 (1998): 587–605; and Paul G. Harris, "International Environmental Affairs and U.S. Foreign Policy," in *The Environment, International Relations, and U.S. Foreign Policy*, ed. Paul G. Harris (Washington, DC: Georgetown University Press, 2001), 11.

54. See "Verslag van de Nederlandse delegatie naar de Intergovernmentele Bijnkomst inzake 'Ocean Dumping' te Rijkiavik, IJland, 10–15 April 1972," 3, Box 5245, Folder 150, Ministerie van Verkeer en Waterstaat, Directie Nordzee, 1971–1989, Nationaal Archief.

55. John N. Irwin, "Memorandum from the Chairman of the Under Secretaries Committee (Irwin) to President Nixon," Washington, DC, May 29, 1972, in *Foreign Relations of the United States, 1969–1976*, vol. E-1: *Documents on Global Issues, 1969–1972*, ed. Holly and McAllister, Document 321, https://history.state.gov/historicaldocuments/frus1969-76ve01/d321.

56. Henry H. Kissinger, "National Security Decision Memorandum 169," May 29, 1972, 1–2, National Security Decision Memoranda, Richard Nixon Presidential Library, Yorba Linda, CA, https://www.nixonlibrary.gov/sites/default/files/virtuallibrary/documents/nsdm/nsdm_169.pdf.

57. Ann L. Hollick, *U.S. Foreign Policy and the Law of the Sea* (Princeton, NJ: Princeton University Press, 1981), 196–239; and for an interpretation that stresses the "imperial" aims of the U.S. government's involvement in the negotiations on the law of the sea, see Daniel S. Margolies, "Imperial Reorderings in US Zones and Regulatory Regimes, 1934–50," in *The Extraterritoriality of Law: History, Theory, Politics*, ed. Daniel S. Margolies, Umut Özsu, Maïa Pal, and Ntina Tzouvala (London: Routledge, 2019), 151–81.

58. Irwin, "Memorandum from the Chairman of the Under Secretaries Committee (Irwin) to President Nixon."

1. THE DISPOSABLE FRONTIER

59. John Irwin noted how U.S. military commanders insisted that "disposal of matter incident to or derived from the operation of vessels or aircraft . . . shall not constitute dumping." The Pentagon, indeed, kept reiterating the necessity of achieving full military exemption, though unsuccessfully. To the U.S. commanders, according to Irwin, "although military vessels and aircraft adhere to more stringent pollution standards than contained in various conventions, deviations [were] required due to operational necessity" (Irwin, "Memorandum from the Chairman of the Under Secretaries Committee [Irwin] to President Nixon").
60. International Maritime Organization, Convention on the Prevention of Marine Pollution by Dumping of Wastes and Other Matter, 1972, ix, https://www.imo.org/en/OurWork/Environment/Pages/London-Convention-Protocol.aspx.
61. Bruce, "The London Dumping Convention, 1972," 316. Besides puzzling out the breadth of the convention, U.S. negotiators had to deal with another issue that emerged during the LDC discussion—namely, the definition of coastal zones. The most industrialized countries, indeed, were sticking to a traditional definition of territorial seas, whereas developing countries wanted to adopt a definition of coastal zones based purely on jurisdiction. The first option would have outlawed ocean dumping just within a 50-mile (80-kilometer) range; the second one would have extended it beyond 200 miles (322 kilometers). Given the impossibility of reaching any agreement on this definition, the delegates decided to shelve the issue and let the UN Conference on the Law of the Sea tackle it. See "Verslag van de Nederlandse delegatie op de 'Intergovernmental Conference on the Convention on the Dumping of Wastes at Sea' te Londen van 30 oktober tot 13 november 1972," 4, Box 5245, Folder 150, Ministerie van Verkeer en Waterstaat. Directie Nordzee, 1971–1989, Nationaal Archief.
62. Zeppetello, "National and International Regulation of Ocean Dumping," 630.
63. "Statement by Mr. Train," *Department of State Bulletin* 67, no. 1747 (December 18, 1972): 710. See also "29 Countries Sign Pact on Sea Dumping," *Los Angeles Times*, November 14, 1972.
64. Peter M. Haas, "Do Regimes Matter? Epistemic Communities and Mediterranean Pollution Control," *International Organization* 43, no. 3 (1989): 377–403; Haas, *Saving the Mediterranean: The Politics of International Environmental Cooperation* (New York: Columbia University Press, 1990), 263; Haas, "Introduction: Epistemic Communities and International Policy Coordination," *International Organization* 46, no. 1 (1992): 1–35; Haas, "Banning Chlorofluorocarbons: Epistemic Community Efforts to Protect Stratospheric Ozone," *International Organization* 46, no. 1 (1992): 187–224; Emanuel Adler, "The Emergence of Cooperation: National Epistemic Communities and the International Evolution of the Idea of Nuclear Arms Control," *International Organization* 46, no. 1 (1992): 101–45; Benjamin W. Goossen, "A Benchmark for the Environment: Big Science and 'Artificial' Geophysics in the Global 1950s," *Journal of Global History* 15, no. 1 (2020): 149–68.
65. Jacob Darwin Hamblin, *Poison in the Well: Radioactive Waste in the Oceans at the Dawn of the Nuclear Age* (New Brunswick, NJ: Rutgers University Press, 2008), 8–9.

1. THE DISPOSABLE FRONTIER

66. Jules Arbose, "91 Nations Agree on Convention to Control Dumping in Oceans," *New York Times*, November 14, 1972. On the LCD's weaknesses, see Bruce, "The London Dumping Convention, 1972," 304–6. The LDC in particular avoided a face-off on the question of the jurisdiction of a contracting party to enforce the convention (save when it was a flag state or a port-loading state) by failing to specify the area of enforcement. This lacuna was then filled by the UN Convention on the Law of the Sea, Article 216 (1-a), which enabled the coastal state to prohibit dumping within its Territorial Sea and Exclusive Economic Zone or onto its continental shelf without its prior approval. At the same time, the UN Convention on the Law of the Sea imposed the obligation to establish national laws and regulations for the control of pollution by dumping.
67. Versar, Inc., *Assessment of Industrial Hazardous Waste Practices, Storage, and Primary Batteries Industries*, prepared for the U.S. EPA (January 1975), 150, EPA-NSCEP.
68. Steinhauer and Werme, *Ocean Incineration*, 3.
69. In 1973, deep-well disposal, land burial, landfill disposal, and ocean dumping were still considered "ultimate disposal processes," though studies on possible alternatives, such as incineration and pyrolysis proliferated. See TRW System Group, *Recommended Methods of Reduction, Neutralization, Recovery, or Disposal of Hazardous Waste*, vol. 3, prepared for the U.S. EPA (August 1973), v, EPA-NCEP; and Robert E. Landreth and Charles J. Rogers, *Promising Technologies for Treatment of Hazardous Wastes*, National Environmental Research Center, Office of Research and Development, U.S. EPA, Cincinnati, OH (November 1974), 4, EPA-NSCEP.
70. "Proceedings of Congress and General Congressional Publications," *Congressional Record*, 90th Cong., 2nd sess., 114, pt. 5 (March 6, 1968–March 15, 1968): 6554.
71. "Greenpeace Submission on Ocean Incineration to the 10th Consultative Meeting of the Contracting Parties London Dumping Convention, London," October 10–17, 1985, introduction, 2, Box 5309 (Correspondence and Other Related Documents on Ocean Incineration, 1977–1978, 1981–1987, 1989), Folder "Correspondence Concerning Ocean Incineration, 1984–1986," IISH, GIAA.
72. Piasecki and Sutter, *The Origins and Decline of Ocean Incineration in Europe*, 3.
73. Between 1969 and the late 1970s, several incinerator vessels were built. Along with the *Matthias I*, there were the *Matthias II* and *III*, the *Vesta*, and the *Vulcanus I* and *Vulcanus II*. See Greenpeace USA, "Ocean Incineration of Toxic Waste—Chronology," 1985, 1, Box 5320 (Documentation Office Concerning Ocean Incineration, 1985–1987), Folder "Chronology and Clippings," IISH, GIAA.
74. George Vander Velde, Edward Glod, and George P. Nassos, "Ocean Incineration: The European Experience," *Waste Management & Research* 6, no. 1 (1988): 70–79.
75. Stichting Natuur en Mileu, *Verbranding Op Zee*, Studierapport (1987), Folder "Behandeling in Raad en Commissie," Archieven van de Raad van de Waterstaat en zijn taakvoorgangers, 1892–1992, Nationaal Archief.
76. Piasecki and Sutter, *The Origins and Decline of Ocean Incineration in Europe*, 4.
77. Steinhauer and Werme, *Ocean Incineration*, viii.

1. THE DISPOSABLE FRONTIER

78. The EPA leased the *Vulcanus I* from OCS to burn four shiploads of liquid organochlorine wastes in the Gulf of Mexico. See Greenpeace USA, "Ocean Incineration of Toxic Waste—Chronology," 1.
79. U.S. Congress, Office of Technology Assessment (OTA), *Ocean Incineration: Its Role in Managing Hazardous Waste*, OTA-O-313 (Washington, DC: U.S. Government Printing Office, 1986), 179, https://www.princeton.edu/~ota/disk2/1986/8616/8616.PDF.
80. Steinhauer and Werme, *Ocean Incineration*, 3.
81. U.S. EPA, *Disposal of Hazardous Waste*, Report to Congress (1974), 4, EPA-NSCEP.
82. U.S. EPA, Office of Water and Hazardous Materials, *Disposal of Organochlorine Wastes by Incineration at Sea* (July 1975), 4–5, EPA-NSCEP.
83. U.S. Department of Commerce, National Technical Information Service, "Survey of Methods Used to Control Wastes Containing Hexachlorobenzene," prepared for the U.S. EPA, 1976, 64–65, EPA-NSCEP.
84. Piasecki and Sutter, *The Origins and Decline of Ocean Incineration in Europe*, 3.
85. E. Timothy Oppelt, "Incineration of Hazardous Waste," *JAPCA: Journal of the Air & Waste Management Association* 37, no. 5 (2012): 566; Vander Velde, Glod, and Nassos, "Ocean Incineration," 75.
86. "Greenpeace Submission on Ocean Incineration to the 10th Consultative Meeting of the Contracting Parties London Dumping Convention, London," introduction, 4.
87. Steinhauer and Werme, *Ocean Incineration*, 4.
88. Linda Risso, "NATO and the Environment: The Committee on the Challenges of Modern Society," *Contemporary European History* 25, no. 3 (2016): 505–35; Evanthis Hatzivassiliou, *The NATO Committee on the Challenges of Modern Society, 1969–1975: Transatlantic Relations, the Cold War, and the Environment* (New York: Palgrave, 2017), 119–20.
89. See Greenpeace USA, "Ocean Incineration of Toxic Waste—Chronology," 1. See also U.S. Mission to NATO to Secretary of State, Washington, DC, telegram, February 12, 1977, Electronic Telegrams, 1977, Central Foreign Policy Files, Created 7/1/1973–12/31/1979, Documenting the Period ca. 1973–12/31/1979, Record Group (RG) 59, Access to Archival Databases (AAD), U.S. National Archives and Records Administration (NARA), Washington, DC, https://aad.archives.gov/aad/createpdf?rid=21563&dt=2532&dl=1629.
90. Secretary of State, Washington, DC, to U.S. Embassy London, telegram, December 19, 1975, Electronic Telegrams, 1975, Central Foreign Policy Files, Created 7/1/1973–12/31/1979, RG 59, AAD, NARA, https://aad.archives.gov/aad/createpdf?rid=251836&dt=2476&dl=1345; U.S. Embassy London to Secretary of State, Washington, DC, telegram, September 22, 1976, Electronic Telegrams, 1976, Central Foreign Policy Files, Created 7/1/1973–12/31/1979, RG 59, AAD, NARA, https://aad.archives.gov/aad/createpdf?rid=320993&dt=2082&dl=1345.
91. Secretary of State, Washington, DC, to U.S. Embassy Brussels, telegram, "Subject: EC-US Environmental Consultations," June 27–28, 1977, Electronic Telegrams, 1977, Central Foreign Policy Files, Created 7/1/1973–12/31/1979, RG 59, AAD, NARA, https://aad.archives.gov/aad/createpdf?rid=160316&dt=2532&dl=1629.

1. THE DISPOSABLE FRONTIER

92. U.S. Embassy London to Secretary of State, Washington, DC, telegram, September 27, 1976, Electronic Telegrams, 1976, Central Foreign Policy Files, Created 7/1/1973–12/31/1979, RG 59, AAD, NARA, https://aad.archives.gov/aad/createpdf?rid=320993&dt=2082&dl=1345.
93. Convention for the Prevention of Marine Pollution by Dumping from Ships and Aircraft, Third Meeting of a Working Group on Incineration at Sea, Paris, March 14–15, 1977, 1, Box 5245, Folder 140, Ministerie van Verkeer en Waterstaat, Directie Nordzee, 1971–1989, Nationaal Archief.
94. "Report on the Consultation of Incineration at Sea," March 21–25, 1977, 3–10, Box 5245, Folder 140, Ministerie van Verkeer en Waterstaat, Directie Nordzee, 1971–1989, Nationaal Archief.
95. "Report on the Consultation of Incineration at Sea," 11–14. See also U.S. Embassy London to Secretary of State, Washington, DC, telegram, October 3, 1977, Electronic Telegrams, 1977, Central Foreign Policy Files, Created 7/1/1973–12/31/1979, RG 59, AAD, NARA, https://aad.archives.gov/aad/createpdf?rid=253281&dt=2532&dl=1629.
96. "Report on the Consultation of Incineration at Sea," 7.
97. European Council of Chemical Manufacturers' Federations, "Incineration at Sea: History, State of the Art, and Outlook," report submitted to the Scientific Group on Dumping (of the LDC), Eighth Meeting, March 11–15, 1985, 4, Agenda Item 7, LDC/SG.8/INF.7, quoted in U.S. Congress, OTA, *Ocean Incineration*, 198–202.
98. Only the Sierra Club, the National Wildlife Federation, and the American Eagle Foundation were consulted, very briefly. No trace of their comments is available in the official EIS. See U.S. EPA, "Final Environmental Impact Statement, Designation of a Site in the Gulf of Mexico for Incineration of Chemical Wastes," prepared by the Division of Oil and Special Materials Control, Office of Water and Hazardous Materials with Contractual Assistance from Texas A&M University, EPA-EIS-WA 76x-054, July 8, 1976, 13–14, EPA-NSCEP; *Hearings Before the Subcommittee on Environmental Pollution of the Committee on Environment and Public Works, United States Senate, Ninety-Ninth Congress, First Session, June 19 and July 17, 1985* (Washington, DC: U.S. Government Printing Office, 1985), 235–36.
99. See U.S. EPA, "Final Environmental Impact Statement, Designation of a Site in the Gulf of Mexico for Incineration of Chemical Wastes," 15–18.
100. Intergovernmental Maritime Consultative Organization, Second Consultative Meeting of the Contracting Parties to the Convention on the Prevention of Marine Pollution by Dumping of Wastes and Other Matter, "Report of the Second Consultative Meeting," October 6, 1977, annex II, 7, https://www.imo.org/en/KnowledgeCentre/ReferencesAndArchives/IMO_Conferences_and_Meetings/London_Convention/LCandLDCReports/Documents/Report%20of%20LDC%202%20September%201977.pdf.
101. The EPA released a final EIS for the North Atlantic Incineration Site in 1981. The site, about 140 miles (225 kilometers) east of the coasts of Delaware and Maryland and covering 1,640 square miles (4,248 square kilometers), however, was never formally designated. See U.S. Congress, OTA, *Ocean Incineration*, 185.

1. THE DISPOSABLE FRONTIER

102. The meeting's final document stated that the substances released into the marine environment had to be rendered "harmless." An operative definition of "harmlessness," however, was never provided. Moreover, the meeting noted that "insufficient information existed on the interaction between the plume of an incinerator vessel and the marine environment to determine a standardized procedure for the definition of acceptable concentrations" of dangerous substances released by combustion gases. Thus, the combustion check was sidelined. See "Report on the Consultation of Incineration at Sea," 8–9.
103. Intergovernmental Maritime Consultative Organization, Second Consultative Meeting of the Contracting Parties to the Convention on the Prevention of Marine Pollution by Dumping of Wastes and Other Matter, "Report of the Second Consultative Meeting," annex II, 6.

2. THE MILITARY-CHEMICAL-INDUSTRIAL COMPLEX

1. President Dwight D. Eisenhower, Farewell Address, January 17, 1961, transcript, https://www.ourdocuments.gov/doc.php?flash=false&doc=90&page=transcript.
2. Ben Baack and Edward Ray, "The Political Economy of the Origins of the Military-Industrial Complex in the United States," *Journal of Economic History* 45, no. 2 (1985): 369–75; Chalmers Johnson, *Dismantling the Empire: America's Last Best Hope* (New York: Metropolitan Books, 2010), 141; Pierre Guerlain, "The Social and Economic Consequences of US Militarism," *LISA E-Journal*, 2013, https://journals.openedition.org/lisa/5371?lang=en#quotation.
3. Ron Smith and Dan Smith, *The Economics of Militarism* (London: Pluto Press, 1983); Rebecca U. Thorpe, *The American Warfare State: The Domestic Politics of Military Spending* (Chicago: University of Chicago Press, 2014); Linda Weiss, *America Inc.? Innovation and Enterprise in the National Security State* (Ithaca, NY: Cornell University Press, 2014).
4. Eisenhower, Farewell Address, January 17, 1961.
5. Jonathan B. Tucker, "A Farewell to Germs: The U.S. Renunciation of Biological and Toxin Warfare, 1969–70," *International Security* 27, no. 1 (2002): 107–48.
6. For contemporary analyses on the U.S. biochemical arsenal, see J. B. Neilands, "Vietnam: Progress of the Chemical War," *Asian Survey* 10, no. 3 (1970): 209–29; "CBW Agents: Ban on Toxins," *C&EN News* 48, no. 8 (February 23, 1970): 16; and Amoretta M. Hoeber and Joseph D. Douglass Jr., "The Neglected Threat of Chemical Warfare," *International Security* 3, no. 1 (1978): 55–82. For historical works on the subject, see Victor A. Utgoff, *The Challenge of Chemical Weapons: An American Perspective* (New York: Palgrave, 1991), 101–4; Albert J. Mauroni, *America's Struggle with Chemical-Biological Warfare* (Westport, CT: Praeger, 2000), 31–32; Judith Miller, Stephen Engelberg, and William Broad, *Germs: Biological Weapons and America's Secret War* (New York: Simon & Schuster, 2001), 47, 81; Jonathan B. Tucker and Erin R. Mahan, *President Nixon's Decision to Renounce the U.S. Offensive Biological Weapons Program* (Washington, DC: National Defense University Press, 2009); Jon Mitchell, "US Military Defoliants on

2. THE MILITARY-CHEMICAL-INDUSTRIAL COMPLEX

Okinawa: Agent Orange," *Asia-Pacific Journal* 9, no. 37 (2011): 1–13; Roger Eardley-Pryor, "Better to Cry Than Die: The Paradoxes of Tear Gases in the Vietnam Era," in *Toxic Airs: Body, Place, Planet in Historical Perspective*, ed. James Rodger Fleming and Ann Johnson (Pittsburgh: Pittsburgh University Press, 2014), 50–76; and Jon Mitchell, *Poisoning the Pacific: The US Military's Secret Dumping of Plutonium, Chemical Weapons, and Agent Orange* (New York: Rowman & Littlefield, 2020), 106–9.

7. Frederic J. Brown, *Chemical Warfare: A Study in Restraints* (Princeton, NJ: Princeton University Press, 1968); John Cookson and Judith Nottingham, *The Control of Chemical and Biological Weapons: A Survey of Chemical and Biological Warfare* (New York: Monthly Review Press, 1969); Steven Rose, ed., *CBW: Chemical and Biological Warfare* (Boston: Beacon Press, 1969); Carnegie Endowment for International Peace, *The Control of Chemical and Biological Weapons* (New York: Carnegie Endowment for International Peace, 1971); J. B. Neilands, Gordon H. Orians, E. W. Pfeiffer, Alje Vennema, and Arthur H. Westing, *Harvest of Death: Chemical Warfare in Vietnam and Cambodia* (New York: Free Press, 1972); Julian Perry Robinson, *The Problem of Chemical and Biological Warfare: A Study of the Historical, Technical, Military, Legal, and Political Aspects of CBW, and Possible Disarmament Measures*, vol. 2 (Stockholm: Almqvist & Wiksell, 1973).

8. For example, Jack Raymond, "Decision on Gas Not President's, White House Says: Area Commanders Control Weapon, Reedy Asserts—Chemicals Called Mild," *New York Times*, March 24, 1965; Robert M. Smith, "Germ War: What Nixon Gave Up; Forsworn Weapons Called Probably Unusable," *New York Times*, November 26, 1969; Robert M. Smith, "Two Agencies Clash Over Toxins," *New York Times*, December 16, 1969. In 2017, the *New York Times* published an overview of the deployment of chemical weapons in Vietnam, uncovering the newspaper's role in denouncing it: see David Biggs, "Vietnam: The Chemical War," *New York Times*, November 24, 2017.

9. Elinor Langer, "Chemical and Biological Warfare (II): The Weapons and the Policies," *Science* 155, no. 3760 (January 20, 1967): 299–303.

10. Jozef Goldblat, "Are Tear Gas and Herbicides Permitted Weapons?," *Bulletin of the Atomic Scientists* 26, no. 4 (1970): 13–16; Matthew Meselson, "Chemical Weapons and Chemical Arms Control," *Bulletin of the American Academy of Arts and Sciences* 32, no. 1 (1978): 14–21. On scientists' role, see David Zierler's excellent essay "Going Global After Vietnam: The End of Agent Orange and the Rise of an International Environmental Regime," in *Nation-States and the Global Environment: New Approaches to International Environmental History*, ed. Erika Marie Bsumek, David Kinkela, and Mark A. Lawrence (New York: Oxford University Press, 2013), 97–114.

11. Convention on the Prohibition of the Development, Production, and Stockpiling of Bacteriological (Biological) and Toxin Weapons and on Their Destruction, signed at Washington, DC, London, and Moscow, April 10, 1972, https://fas.org/nuke/control/bwc/text/bwc.htm; "Ratification of the 1925 Geneva Protocol for the Prohibition of the Use in War of Asphyxiating, Poisonous or Other Gases, and of Bacteriological Methods of Warfare," *International Legal Materials* 14, no. 1 (1975): 49–50.

2. THE MILITARY-CHEMICAL-INDUSTRIAL COMPLEX

12. Robert A. Wampler, "The September 11th Sourcebooks: The Nixon Administration's Decision to End U.S. Biological Warfare Programs," in *National Security Archive Electronic Briefing Book No. 58*, October 25, 2001, https://nsarchive2.gwu.edu/NSAEBB/NSAEBB58/#doc10. The U.S. history professor Vincent Ferrario has collected and digitized a substantial number of primary sources concerning Nixon's decision to abandon CBW programs; see https://www.mtholyoke.edu/acad/intrel/chemical.htm.
13. Utgoff, *The Challenge of Chemical Weapons*, 100–102.
14. Tucker and Mahan, *President Nixon's Decision to Renounce the U.S. Offensive Biological Weapons Program*, 16. See also White House, press release, Washington, DC, February 14, 1970, in *Foreign Relations of the United States, 1969–1976*, vol. E-2: *Documents on Arms Control and Nonproliferation, 1969–1972*, ed. David I. Goldman and David C. Humphrey (Washington, DC: U.S. Government Printing Office, 2007), Document 189, https://history.state.gov/historicaldocuments/frus1969-76ve02/d189%20.
15. Tucker, "A Farewell to Germs," 117–18.
16. Jeffrey K. Smart, "History of Chemical and Biological Warfare: An American Perspective," in *Medical Aspects of Chemical and Biological Warfare*, ed. Russ Zajtchuk and Ronald Bellamey (Washington, DC: TMM Publications, 1997), 72. See also National Security Council Report, "Annual Review of the United States Chemical Warfare and Biological Research Programs as of 1 November 1970," November 1, 1970, 23, Weapons of Mass Destruction, Brill Primary Sources Collections, https://bit.ly/3mVwod1.
17. Robert Harris and Jeremy Paxman, *A Higher Form of Killing: The Secret History of Chemical and Biological Warfare* (New York: Random House, 1982), 196.
18. U.S. Army, "Chemical Stockpile Disposal Program: Final Programmatic Environmental Impact Statement," report, January 1988, 16, Weapons of Mass Destruction, Brill Primary Sources Collections, https://bit.ly/3KNZhOS.
19. *Ocean Disposal of Unserviceable Chemical Munitions: Hearings Before the Subcommittee on Oceanography of the Committee on Merchant Marine and Fisheries, Ninety-First Congress* (Washington, DC: U.S. Government Printing Office, 1970), statement of General Becker, U.S. Army–Resumed, 294. See also Mitchell, *Poisoning the Pacific*, 106.
20. National Research Council, *Review of the Army Non-stockpile Chemical Materiel Disposal Program: Disposal of Chemical Agent Identification Sets* (Washington, DC: National Academies Press, 1999), 31–37.
21. National Research Council, Committee on Review and Evaluation of the Army Chemical Stockpile Disposal Program, *Occupational Health and Workplace Monitoring at Chemical Agent Disposal Facilities* (Washington, DC: National Academies Press, 2001), https://www.ncbi.nlm.nih.gov/books/NBK207465/. See also U.S. Congress, Office of Technology Assessment (OTA), *Disposal of Chemical Weapons: Alternative Technologies* (Washington DC: U.S. Government Printing Office, June 1992), appendix A: "Selected Chemical Weapon Destruction Techniques," 31–34, https://www.princeton.edu/~ota/disk1/1992/9210/921006.PDF.

2. THE MILITARY-CHEMICAL-INDUSTRIAL COMPLEX

22. Steve Gaither, *Looking Between Trinity and the Wall: Army Materiel Command Cold War Material Culture Within the Continental United States, 1945–1989* (Plano, TX: Geo-Marine, 1997), 87–88.
23. National Academy of Sciences, National Research Council, Assembly of Life Sciences, *The Effects of Herbicides in South Vietnam: Part A—Summary and Conclusions* (Washington, DC: National Academy of Sciences, 1974), 33–40, https://www.nal.usda.gov/exhibits/speccoll/files/original/a60451fccdcede2554597d92fb5961b5.pdf. See also Institute of Medicine, Committee to Review the Health Effects in Vietnam Veterans of Exposure to Herbicides, *Veterans and Agent Orange: Health Effects of Herbicides Used in Vietnam* (Washington, DC: National Academies Press, 1994), https://www.ncbi.nlm.nih.gov/books/NBK236351/.
24. Edwin A. Martini, "'This Is Really Bad Stuff Buried Here': Agent Orange, Johnston Atoll, and the Rise of Military Environmentalism," in *Proving Grounds: Militarized Landscapes, Weapons Testing, and the Environmental Impact of U.S. Bases*, ed. Edwin A. Martini (Seattle: University of Washington Press, 2017), 134–35 (citing but not quoting the documentary record of Pacer HO). See also Air Force Logistic Command, "Programming Plan 75-19 for the Disposal of Orange Herbicide," April 1977, 8-2, Notes, Memoranda, Reports: Johnston Island Studies, Special Collections, U.S. Department of Agriculture (USDA) National Agricultural Library, Beltsville, MD, http://www.nal.usda.gov/exhibits/speccoll/items/show/5259; and T. J. Thomas et al., "Land Based Environmental Monitoring at Johnston Island: Disposal of Herbicide Orange: Final Report for Period 11 May 1977–30 September 1978," 2, Special Collections, USDA National Agricultural Library, http://www.nal.usda.gov/exhibits/speccoll/items/show/4940.
25. U.S. General Accounting Office, *The Army's Program to Assure the Security and Safety of the Chemical Munitions Stockpile Is Comprehensive and Effective*, report to the chairman, Subcommittee on Investigations, Committee on Armed Services, House of Representatives (Washington, DC: U.S. General Accounting Office, July 1, 1983), 10–12, https://www.gao.gov/assets/150/140327.pdf.
26. See Kenneth S. Kamlet, "Ocean Disposal of Organochlorine Wastes by at-Sea Incineration," in *Ocean Dumping of Industrial Wastes*, ed. Bostwick H. Ketchum, Dana R. Kester, and P. Kilho Park (New York: Plenum Press, 1981), 306–8. See also Mitchell, *Poisoning the Pacific*, 106; and Alvin L. Young, *The History, Use, Disposition, and Environmental Fate of Agent Orange* (New York: Springer, 2009), 142.
27. President Richard Nixon overruled his military commanders, ordering them to phase out all herbicide operations in Vietnam by the end of 1970. See Martini, "'This Is Really Bad Stuff Buried Here,'" 111. See also "Press Release: Home Use of 2,4,5-T Suspended," Series VIII, Subseries 1, Document no. 05170, Alvin L. Young (ALY) Collection on Agent Orange, USDA National Agricultural Library; and U.S. Department of Air Force, "Final Environmental Statement: Disposition of Orange Herbicide by Incineration," November 1974, Series II, Box 3, Document no. 0094, ALY Collection, USDA National Agricultural Library.

2. THE MILITARY-CHEMICAL-INDUSTRIAL COMPLEX

28. See Mitchell, *Poisoning the Pacific*, 196–97; and William A. Buckingham Jr., *Operation Ranch Hand: The Air Force and Herbicides in Southeast Asia, 1961–1971* (Washington, DC: Office of U.S. Air Force History, 1982), 189.
29. See U.S. Environmental Protection Agency (EPA), Region 9: Waste Programs, *Johnston Atoll Chemical Agent Disposal System (JACADS)* (2003), https://archive.epa.gov/region9/features/jacads/web/html/index.html.
30. Martini, "'This Is Really Bad Stuff Buried Here,'" 124. In this regard, see also Daniel Immerwahr, *How to Hide an Empire: A History of the Greater United States* (New York: Farrar, Straus and Giroux, 2019), 661.
31. Mitchell, *Poisoning the Pacific*, 196–97; Martini, "'This Is Really Bad Stuff Buried Here,'" 121.
32. Bruce F. Meyers, "Soldier of Orange: The Administrative, Diplomatic, Legislative and Litigatory Impact of Herbicide Agent Orange in South Vietnam," *Boston College Environmental Affairs Law Review* 8, no. 2 (1979): 170. See also "Telegram: Regarding Herbicide Orange—Ocean Burning Permit and EPA Hearing," 1975, Special Collections, USDA National Agricultural Library, http://www.nal.usda.gov/exhibits/speccoll/items/show/4849.
33. Young, *The History, Use, Disposition, and Environmental Fate of Agent Orange*, 144–45.
34. Margarete S. Steinhauer and Christine E. Werme, *Ocean Incineration: Background and Status*, prepared for David P. Redford, U.S. EPA, Office of Marine and Estuaries Protection, September 4, 1987, 5, U.S. EPA National Service Center for Environmental Publications (EPA-NSCEP). See also "Message from Commander Johnston Atoll/Pacer HO Director to Several Recipients, with Subject CLN Project Pacer HO Schedule," July 20, 1977, Special Collections, USDA National Agricultural Library, http://www.nal.usda.gov/exhibits/speccoll/items/show/4901.
35. CRS, *Chemical and Biological Warfare: Issues and Developments During 1976 and January 1–June 30, 1977* (July 1, 1977), 7, Weapons of Mass Destruction, Brill Primary Sources Collections, https://bit.ly/3KVSbrt.
36. Secretary of State Vance to High Commissioner Trust Territory, Pacific Islands, Saipan, telegram, June 8, 1977, Electronic Telegrams, 1977, Central Foreign Policy Files, Created 7/1/1973–12/31/1979, Documenting the Period ca. 1973–12/31/1979, Record Group (RG) 59, Access to Archival Databases (AAD), U.S. National Archives and Records Administration (NARA), https://aad.archives.gov/aad/createpdf?rid=131100&dt=2532&dl=1629.
37. Thomas et al., "Land Based Environmental Monitoring at Johnston Island," 2.
38. U.S. Congress, OTA, *Ocean Incineration: Its Role in Managing Hazardous Waste*, OTA-O-313 (Washington, DC: U.S. Government Printing Office, 1986), 179–81, https://www.princeton.edu/~ota/disk2/1986/8616/8616.PDF. See also Greenpeace USA, "Ocean Incineration of Toxic Waste—Chronology," 1985, 1, Box 5320 (Documentation Office Concerning Ocean Incineration, 1985–1987), Folder "Chronology and Clippings, 1985," International Institute for Social History (IISH), Greenpeace International Archives (GIAA), Amsterdam.

2. THE MILITARY-CHEMICAL-INDUSTRIAL COMPLEX

39. Kamlet, "Ocean Disposal of Organochlorine Wastes by at-Sea Incineration," 306–8. U.S. Air Force sources and EPA documents reported that all three burns went smoothly without any significant environmental effect. According to the U.S. Air Force experts, concentrations of 2,4-D and 2,4,5-T found in the ambient air and in water samples were minimal. No TCDD was detected, nor was any change noted in indigenous plants or bird populations. Results of quality-control sampling revealed that the required level of drum cleaning was achieved, too. See Thomas et al., "Land Based Environmental Monitoring at Johnston Island," abstract.
40. Young, *The History, Use, Disposition, and Environmental Fate of Agent Orange*, 143–44, 157.
41. Young, *The History, Use, Disposition, and Environmental Fate of Agent Orange*, 150, 269.
42. U.S. Department of the Interior, Fish and Wildlife Service, National Wildlife Refuge System, Johnston Atoll National Wildlife Refuge, Johnston Atoll, Central Pacific Ocean, "Annual Narrative Report Calendar Year 1994," 20, Environmental Impact Statement Files, 1977–1998, Records of the Environmental Protection Agency, RG 412, NARA. See also Young, *The History, Use, Disposition, and Environmental Fate of Agent Orange*, 294.
43. Young, *The History, Use, Disposition, and Environmental Fate of Agent Orange*, 276.
44. U.S. Congress, OTA, *Ocean Incineration*, 181. See also Martini, "'This Is Really Bad Stuff Buried Here,'" 131; and U.S. Department of the Army, "Hearing of March 20, 1990 in Honolulu, Hawaii Regarding the Draft Second Supplemental Environmental Impact Statement for the Storage and Ultimate Disposal of the European Chemical Munition Stockpile (February 1990)," testimony of Jon M. Van Dyke, in Johnston Atoll Chemical Agent Disposal System, *Final Second Supplemental Environmental Impact Statement*, vol. 2: *Comments Received from the Public and Agencies on the Draft Second Supplemental Environmental Impact Statement* (Washington, DC: U.S. Department of Energy, Office of Scientific and Technical Information, June 1990), 6.
45. U.S. Congress, OTA, *Ocean Incineration*, 184.
46. U.S. Congress, OTA, *Ocean Incineration*, 184–85.
47. Young, *The History, Use, Disposition, and Environmental Fate of Agent Orange*, 158.
48. Young, *The History, Use, Disposition, and Environmental Fate of Agent Orange*, 273.
49. Young, *The History, Use, Disposition, and Environmental Fate of Agent Orange*, 293.
50. Hans Spoelman's account given in Greenpeace QMC to Lisa Bunin, letter, August 6, 1990, Box 5771 (Correspondence Concerning the Vulcanus I and II, 1987–1989), IISH, GIAA.
51. Secretary of State Vance to U.S. Embassy London, telegram, June 6, 1977, Electronic Telegrams, 1977, Central Foreign Policy Files, Created 7/1/1973–12/31/1979, RG 59, AAD, NARA, https://aad.archives.gov/aad/createpdf?rid=127261&dt=2532&dl=1629.
52. Secretary of State Vance to U.S. Embassy Tokyo, telegram, June 25, 1977, Electronic Telegrams, 1977, Central Foreign Policy Files, Created 7/1/1973–12/31/1979, RG 59, AAD, NARA, https://aad.archives.gov/aad/createpdf?rid=146696&dt=2532&dl=1629.
53. Convention for the Prevention of Marine Pollution by Dumping from Ships and Aircraft, Third Meeting of a Working Group on Incineration at Sea, Paris, March 14–15, 1977, 1, Box 5245, Folder 140, Ministerie van Verkeer en Waterstaat. Directie Nordzee,

2. THE MILITARY-CHEMICAL-INDUSTRIAL COMPLEX

1971–1989, Nationaal Archief, The Hague; "Report on the Consultation of Incineration at Sea," 11–13, Box 5245, Folder 140, Ministerie van Verkeer en Waterstaat. Directie Nordzee, 1971–1989, Nationaal Archief.

54. Secretary of State Vance to U.S. Embassy Brussels, telegram, July 13, 1977, Electronic Telegrams, 1977, Central Foreign Policy Files, Created 7/1/1973–12/31/1979, RG 59, AAD, NARA, https://aad.archives.gov/aad/createpdf?rid=160316&dt=2532&dl=1629.

55. U.S. Embassy London to Secretary of State, telegram, October 3, 1977, Electronic Telegrams, 1977, Central Foreign Policy Files, Created 7/1/1973–12/31/1979, RG 59, AAD, NARA, https://aad.archives.gov/aad/createpdf?rid=253281&dt=2532&dl=1629; Intergovernmental Maritime Consultative Organization (IMCO), Second Consultative Meeting of the Contracting Parties to the Convention on the Prevention of Marine Pollution by Dumping of Wastes and Other Matter, "Report of the Second Consultative Meeting," October 6, 1977, annex II, 6, https://www.imo.org/en/KnowledgeCentre/ReferencesAndArchives/IMO_Conferences_and_Meetings/London_Convention/LCandLDCReports/Documents/Report%20of%20LDC%202%20September%201977.pdf.

56. Convention for the Prevention of Marine Pollution by Dumping from Ships and Aircraft, Fourth Meeting of the Working Group on Incineration at Sea, London, June 20, 1978, Box 5245, Folder 140, Ministerie van Verkeer en Waterstaat. Directie Nordzee, 1971–1989, Nationaal Archief. This meeting was attended by representatives from France, the Federal Republic of Germany, the Netherlands, Sweden, and the United Kingdom, with the addition of one observer from the IMCO.

57. IMCO, Third Consultative Meeting of the Contracting Parties to the Convention on the Prevention of Marine Pollution by Dumping of Wastes and Other Matter, "Report of the Third Consultative Meeting," October 9–13, 1978, https://www.imo.org/en/KnowledgeCentre/ConferencesMeetings/Pages/LDC-LC-Reports-of-Consultative-Meetings.aspx. See also U.S. Embassy in London to Secretary of State Vance, telegram, October 1, 1978, AAD, NARA, https://aad.archives.gov/aad/createpdf?rid=253611&dt=2694&dl=2009.

58. Steinhauer and Werme, *Ocean Incineration*, 7.

59. T. A. Wastler, Carolyn K. Offutt, Charles K. Fitzsimmons, and Paul E. Des Rosiers, *Disposal of Organochlorine Wastes by Incineration at Sea* (Washington, DC: Division of Oil and Special Materials Control, Office of Water and Hazardous Materials, U.S. EPA, July 1975), 2.

60. T. A. Wastler, "Draft Environmental Impact Statement (EIS) for Proposed North Atlantic Incineration Site Designation," October 1980, U.S. EPA, 1–16.

61. IMCO, Third Consultative Meeting, "Report of the Third Consultative Meeting," 12.1–12.10.

62. IMCO, Fourth Consultative Meeting of the Contracting Parties to the Convention on the Prevention of Marine Pollution by Dumping of Wastes and Other Matter, "Report of the Fourth Consultative Meeting," October 22–26, 1979, https://www.imo.org/en/KnowledgeCentre/ConferencesMeetings/Pages/LDC-LC-Reports-of-Consultative

2. THE MILITARY-CHEMICAL-INDUSTRIAL COMPLEX

-Meetings.aspx. See also Convention for the Prevention of Marine Pollution by Dumping from Ships and Aircraft, Fifth Meeting of a Working Group on Incineration at Sea, Hamburg, October 1, 1979, 2, Box 5245, Folder 140, Ministerie van Verkeer en Waterstaat. Directie Nordzee, 1971–1989, Nationaal Archief.

63. U.S. Embassy London to Secretary of State, telegram, October 6, 1978, Electronic Telegrams, 1978, Central Foreign Policy Files, Created 7/1/1973–12/31/1979, RG 59, AAD, NARA, https://aad.archives.gov/aad/createpdf?rid=253611&dt=2694&dl=2009.
64. U.S. Embassy London to Secretary of State, telegram, October 29, 1979, Electronic Telegrams, 1979, Central Foreign Policy Files, Created 7/1/1973–12/31/1979, RG 59, AAD, NARA, https://aad.archives.gov/aad/createpdf?rid=289447&dt=2776&dl=2169.
65. "Executive Order 12114: Environmental Effects Abroad of Major Federal Actions," January 4, 1979, 1–6, https://www.energy.gov/sites/prod/files/2020/08/f77/EO%2012114_0.pdf.
66. Council on Environmental Quality, "Environmental Effect Abroad of Major Federal Actions, Executive Order 12144: Implementing and Explanatory Documents," *Federal Register* 4, no. 62 (1979): 18722–724, https://www.energy.gov/sites/prod/files/nepapub/nepa_documents/RedDont/G-CEQ-EffectsAbroad.pdf.
67. U.S. EPA, U.S. Department of Commerce—Maritime Administration, U.S. Department of Transportation—Coast Guard, U.S. Department of Commerce—National Bureau of Standards, *Report of the Interagency ad Hoc Work Group for the Chemical Waste Incinerator Ship* (September 1980), Executive Summary, v, EPA-NSCEP, https://nepis.epa.gov/Exe/ZyPDF.cgi/94004ICM.PDF?Dockey=94004ICM.PDF.
68. The EPA's overall underestimation of the risk and open favoritism to business in designing this plan is also at the center of the analysis in Daryl W. Ditz, "Hazardous Waste Incineration at Sea: EPA Decision Making on Risk," *Risk Analysis* 8, no. 4 (1988): 499–50.
69. U.S. EPA, *Environmental News*, press release, October 29, 1980, Box 121 (Hazardous Waste, 2/1980), Douglas M. Costle Papers, Jimmy Carter Presidential Library, Atlanta, GA.
70. Steinhauer and Werme, *Ocean Incineration*, 5–8.
71. U.S. Congress, OTA, *Ocean Incineration*, 179.
72. "Joint Comments of Environmental and Other Citizen Organizations in Response to the Environmental Protection Agency's Draft Regulations on Ocean Incineration," February 15, 1986, 3–6, Box 5321 (Research of the Oceanic Society Concerning the Draft Regulations of the EPA Regarding Ocean Incineration, 1985–1987), IISH, GIAA.
73. Maxwell Bruce, "The London Dumping Convention, 1972: First Decade and Future," *Ocean Yearbook* 6, no. 1 (1986): 298–318.
74. See "Briefing Report, Preliminary Analysis of EPA's Draft Ocean Incineration Regulations, Prepared by the Oceanic Society, April 18, 1985," 4–5, Box 5321, IISH, GIAA.
75. Steinhauer and Werme, *Ocean Incineration*, 6.
76. *Hearings Before the Subcommittee on Merchant Marine and Tourism of the Committee on Commerce, Science, and Transportation, United States Senate, Ninety-Sixth Congress, First*

2. THE MILITARY-CHEMICAL-INDUSTRIAL COMPLEX

Session, Serial No. 96-77 (Washington, DC: U.S. Government Printing Office, 1979), statement of Dr. Thomas A. Murphy, deputy assistant administrator for air, land, and water use, Office of Research and Development, U.S. EPA, accompanied by Kenneth E. Biglane, director of the Oil and Special Materials Control Division, Office of Water and Waste Management, U.S. EPA, 30.

77. *Hearings Before the Subcommittee on Merchant Marine and Tourism of the Committee on Commerce, Science, and Transportation*, statement of Kenneth E. Biglane, 34.
78. U.S. EPA, "Hazardous Waste Outline—Better Living Through Chemical Control," *Environmental News*, November 14, 1980, Box 121, Costle Papers, Carter Library. See also "Recent Toxic Waste Accidents," *National Journal* 4, no. 14 (April 14, 1979): 605.
79. Boyce Rensberger, "Unusual Clusters of Cancer Place Medical Spotlight on Rutherford," *New York Times*, May 2, 1978; Robert Hanley, "Mercury Is Polluting the Meadowlands and Scientists Are Uncertain on Impact," *New York Times*, May 19, 1978.
80. Richard S. Newman, *Love Canal: A Toxic History from Colonial Times to the Present* (New York: Oxford University Press, 2016), 100–105; Michael Stewart Foley, *Front Porch Politics: The Forgotten Heyday of American Activism in the 1970s and 1980s* (New York: Hill & Wang, 2013), 153–55.
81. Barbara Blum, "Weekly Report to the President," May 4, 1979, Box 64 (Weekly Reports to the President, 1979), Costle Papers, Carter Library.
82. U.S. EPA, "Hazardous Waste Outline—Better Living Through Chemical Control."
83. U.S. EPA, "Hazardous Waste Information," May 1980, 2, Box 121, Costle Papers, Carter Library. See also U.S. EPA, "Siting of Hazardous Waste Management Facilities and Public Opposition," November 1979, iv, Box 121, Costle Papers, Carter Library, and EPA-NSCEP, https://nepis.epa.gov/Exe/ZyPDF.cgi/10003J1L.PDF?Dockey=10003 J1L.PDF.
84. Douglas M. Costle, "Report to the President," February 29, 1980, and "Report to the President," May 9, 1980, Box 121, Costle Papers, Carter Presidential Library.
85. Environmental Research Foundation, "Waste Management Gains Pipeline to Grass Roots Movement's Plans," *Hazardous Waste News* 72 (April 11, 1988), Folder 5780 (Correspondence of Waste Management Companies Ocean Combustion Service [OCS] and Waste Management New Zealand [WMN] Concerning Ocean Incineration, 1987, 1989–1990), IISH, GIIA.
86. Michael Spears, "Companies Turn to the Ocean for Alternative Disposal Site," *Environmental Management News*, January–February 1987, 7–8, Box 5766 (Correspondence and Documentation Concerning Ocean Incineration in Europe, 1986), IISH, GIIA.
87. D. J. Ackerman, J. F. Metzger, and L. L. Seinto, *History of Environmental Testing of the Chemical Waste Incinerator Ships M/T Vulcanus and I/V Vulcanus II* (Redondo Beach, CA: TRW, 1983), 72.
88. Judith A. Layzer, *Open for Business: Conservatives' Opposition to Environmental Regulation* (Cambridge, MA: MIT Press, 2012), 83–84.
89. Curtis Copeland, *Federal Rulemaking: The Role of the Office of Information and Regulatory Affairs* (Washington, DC: Congressional Research Service, 2009), 5–7.

2. THE MILITARY-CHEMICAL-INDUSTRIAL COMPLEX

90. Herbert Needleman, "The Removal of Lead from Gasoline: Historical and Personal Reflections," *Environmental Research* 84, no. 1 (2000): 30–35. See also "Remarks Announcing the Establishment of the Presidential Task Force on Regulatory Relief," January 22, 1981, Ronald Reagan Presidential Library, Yorba Linda, CA, https://www.reaganlibrary.gov/archives/speech/remarks-announcing-establishment-presidential-task-force-regulatory-relief.
91. Robert Ginsburg, "Once Burned . . . Twice Shy? Incinerating Hazardous Wastes," *Environmental News*, November–December 1981, 6–7.
92. David Sheridan, Jonathan Lash, and Katherine Gillman, *A Season of Spoils: The Reagan Administration's Attack on the Environment* (New York: Pantheon, 1984), 36–40, 54–56; Doug Rossinow, *The Reagan Era: A History of the 1980s* (New York: Columbia University Press, 2015), 44.
93. Leif Fredrickson, Christopher Sellers, Lindsey Dillon, Jennifer Liss Ohayon, Nicholas Shapiro, Marianne Sullivan, Stephen Bocking, et al., "History of US Presidential Assaults on Modern Environmental Health Protection," *American Journal of Public Health* 108, no. 2 (2018): S95–S103.
94. Representative Boxer stated, "Between March 23, 1981, and June 4, 1982, the same period during which the improper permit changes were made . . . the EPA employed as a consultant James Sanderson, an attorney whose firm represented Chemical Waste Management on EPA matters. Sanderson was also nominated but never confirmed as an Assistant Administrator at EPA. He was one of the individuals included in the Department of Justice's investigation of alleged improprieties during the tenure of former Administrator, soon to be confirmed commissioner, Anne Gorsuch Burford" (*Hearings Before a Subcommittee of the Committee on Government Operations House of Representatives, Ninety-Eighth Congress, Second Session, July 12, 1984* [Washington, DC: U.S. Government Printing Office, 1985], statement of Representative Barbara Boxer, 70).
95. Ralph Blumenthal, "A Waste Hauler Under the Gun," *New York Times*, November 25, 1984. See also Elsa M. Bruton, *Banning the Burn: The Fight Against Ocean Incineration*, report prepared for Dr. Ken Geiser, January 1989, Box 5180 (Correspondence on Viewpoints and Background Information on Ocean Incineration, from the Archives of Lisa Bunin, 1989), IISH, GIAA.
96. Blue Ridge Environmental Defense League, "WMI's Record: Environmental and Contract Crimes," October 2002, https://www.bredl.org/pdf/WMI_trackrecord2002.PDF; "Alabama Waste Company Fined $1 Million," *The Lantern*, November 1, 1984; "Waste Concern Is Said to Agree to Pay Fines," *New York Times*, November 1, 1984; Bill Boyce, "$2.5 Million Fine Settles Waste Suit," *Chicago Tribune*, April 6, 1985; David Beers and Catherine Capellaro, "Greenwash!," *Mother Jones*, March–April 1991.
97. Wastler et al., *Disposal of Organochlorine Wastes by Incineration at Sea*, 62.
98. TerEco Corp., *Biological Monitoring of PCB Incineration in the Gulf of Mexico* (Washington, DC: U.S. EPA, Office of Water, 1982).
99. For the quotes, see George Vander Velde, Edward Glod, and George P. Nassos, "Ocean Incineration: The European Experience," *Waste Management & Research* 6, no. 1

2. THE MILITARY-CHEMICAL-INDUSTRIAL COMPLEX

(1988): 70–79, passim. See also Wileen E. Sweet, Richard D. Ross, and George Vander Velde, "Hazardous Waste Incineration: A Progress Report," *Journal of the Air Pollution Control Association* 35, no. 2 (1985): 138–43; and George P. Nassos, "The Problems of Ocean Incineration: A Case of Modern Mythology," *Marine Pollution Bulletin* 18, no. 5 (1987): 211–16.

100. Michael R. Greenberg, *Siting Noxious Facilities: Integrating Location Economics and Risk Analysis to Protect Environmental Health and Investments* (London: Routledge, 2020), 36, 188–212.
101. An Act to Amend the Commercial Fisheries Research and Development Act of 1964, Public Law 97-389, December 29, 1982, https://www.govinfo.gov/content/pkg/STATUTE-96/pdf/STATUTE-96-Pg1949.pdf.
102. U.S. Congress, OTA, *Ocean Incineration*, 75, 78 n. 25 (citing "Assessment of Incineration").
103. Sweet, Ross, and Vander Velde, "Hazardous Waste Incineration," 142.
104. Greenpeace USA, "Ocean Incineration of Toxic Waste—Chronology," 1.
105. Lisa Bunin to Greenpeace Offices, telegram, "Return of OI Vessels in USA—Apollo I and Apollo II," October 6, 1989, Box 5794 (Correspondence Concerning the Ocean Incinerators Apollo I and Apollo II, 1989–1990), IISH, GIAA. See also Philip Shabecoff, "Gaps Seen in Data on Burning Toxic Wastes," *New York Times*, January 17, 1985.
106. Nassos, "The Problems of Ocean Incineration," 212.
107. Greenpeace, "EPA Promotes Incineration," position paper on ocean incineration, n.d., Box 5309 (Correspondence and Other Related Documents on Ocean Incineration, 1977–1978, 1981–1987, 1989), IISH, GIAA, including a response to the EPA's market study on ocean incineration.
108. Walter B. Jones Sr., chairman of the U.S. House of Representatives Committee on Merchant Marine and Fisheries, to William D. Ruckelshaus, letter, January 24, 1984, Box 5313 (Correspondence with Toxics Campaign Coordinator in the U.S. Jon Hinck, 1983–1986), IISH, GIIA.
109. Jack E. Ravan to Jon Hinck, letter, November 8, 1984, and Jon Hinck to Jack E. Ravan, Assistant Administrator for Water, U.S. EPA, letter, September 25, 1984, Box 5313, IISH, GIIA.
110. Northwest Indiana Coalition for the Environment, "Position Statement: Commercial Incineration of Hazardous Waste by Stauffer Chemical Co.," October 21, 1986, Box 5849 (Documentation of Jeff Barrett Howard [Great Lakes] Concerning Ocean Incineration, 1979, 1981, 1983, 1985–1986), IISH, GIAA.
111. Northwest Indiana Coalition for the Environment, "Position Statement: Commercial Incineration of Hazardous Waste by Stauffer Chemical Co."
112. Rae Tyson, "Report Says EPA Easy on Water Polluter," *USA Today*, September 20, 1984, Box 5851 (Clippings Concerning Ocean Incineration, 1984–1985, 1988, and n.d.), IISH, GIAA.
113. Pamela S. Zurer, "Incineration of Hazardous Wastes at Sea: Going Nowhere Fast," *C&EN News*, December 9, 1985, 36, 29–30, 42, Box 5853 (Clippings Concerning Ocean Incineration, 1984–1985, 1988), IISH, GIAA.

3. TRANSLOCAL ACTIVISM

114. Bruce Piasecki quoted in Zurer, "Incineration of Hazardous Wastes at Sea," 25, 36.
115. Andrew Szasz, "The Process and Significance of Political Scandals: A Comparison of Watergate and the 'Sewergate' Episode at the Environmental Protection Agency," *Social Problems* 33, no. 3 (1986): 202–17.
116. Joel A. Mintz, *Enforcement at the EPA: High Stakes and Hard Choices* (Austin: University of Texas Press, 2012), 41–61.
117. Patrick Allitt, *A Climate of Crisis: America in the Age of Environmentalism* (New York: Penguin, 2014), 297–99.
118. William Ruckelshaus quoted in Greenpeace USA, "Ocean Incineration of Toxic Waste—Chronology," 2.
119. Christina Duffy Burnett, "The Edges of Empire and the Limits of Sovereignty: American Guano Islands," *American Quarterly* 57, no. 3 (2005): 779–803.

3. TRANSLOCAL ACTIVISM

1. *The Rising Significance of World Opinion*, Reel 17, S-5-77, 1977, Part 1: Cold War Era Special Reports, Series B, 1964–1982, Records of the U.S. Information Agency, Roosevelt Institute for American Studies (RIAS), Middleburg, Netherlands; *The Importance of Foreign Public Opinion to U.S. Foreign Policy*, Reel 18, 0717 S-10-78, 1978, Part 1: Cold War Era Special Reports, Series B, 1964–1982, Records of the U.S. Information Agency, RIAS.
2. Frank Fischer, "Environmental Democracy: Participation, Deliberation and Citizenship," in *Environment and Society: Concepts and Challenges*, ed. Magnus Boström and Debra J. Davidson (Cham, Switzerland: Palgrave Macmillan, 2018), 257–279.
3. Robert. C. Mitchell, "Public Opinion and Environmental Politics in the 1970s and 1980s," in *Environmental Policy in the 1980s: Reagan's New Agenda*, ed. Norman J. Vig and Michael E. Kraft (Washington, DC: CQ Press, 1984), 51–74; Thomas Risse-Kappen, "Public Opinion, Domestic Structure, and Foreign Policy in Liberal Democracies," *World Politics* 43, no. 4 (1991): 479–512; Paul Burnstein, "Bringing the Public Back In: Should Sociologists Consider the Impact of Public Opinion on Public Policy?," *Social Forces* 77, no. 27 (1998): 62; Jon Agnone, "Amplifying Public Opinion: The Policy Impact of the U.S. Environmental Movement," *Social Forces* 85, no. 4 (2007): 1593–620.
4. Giovanna Di Chiro, "Living Environmentalisms: Coalition Politics, Social Reproduction, and Environmental Justice," *Environmental Politics* 17, no. 2 (2008): 276–98; Stephen Milder, "Thinking Globally, Acting (Trans-)Locally: Petra Kelly and the Transnational Roots of West German Green Politics," *Central European History* 43, no. 2 (2010): 301–26; Astrid Mignon Kirchhof and Jan-Henrik Meyer, "Global Protest Against Nuclear Power: Transfer and Transnational Exchange in the 1970s and 1980s," *Historical Social Research* 39, no. 1 (2014): 16. Jon Coburn has recently proposed the notion of the "interlocal" to combine the transnational and local dimensions; see Jon Coburn, "Everything Connected: The Interlocal Women's Peace Camp Movement," paper presented at

3. TRANSLOCAL ACTIVISM

"'Nuclear States': Science, Technology, and American Society in the Atomic Age, 2019," HOTCUS Winter Symposium, Lincoln, NE, February 2019.

5. Margarete S. Steinhauer and Christine E. Werme, *Ocean Incineration: Background and Status*, prepared for David P. Redford, U.S. Environmental Protection Agency (EPA), Office of Marine and Estuaries Protection, September 4, 1987, 5, 24, U.S. EPA National Service Center for Environmental Publications (EPA-NSCEP).
6. U.S. EPA, "Fact Sheet, Assistant Administrator for Water, Ocean Incineration Permits Decision, 1983," 1–2, Box 5764 (Correspondence and Other Documents of Andy Booth Concerning Ocean Incineration, 1981–1989), International Institute for Social History (IISH), Greenpeace International (Amsterdam) Archives (GIAA).
7. Russel Wyer quoted in Charlotte Garey, "Burning Wastes at Sea," *EPA Journal* 7, no. 3 (1981): 24–25, EPA-NSCEP.
8. "Russel Wyer, 1936–2020," *Tri-City Herald*, March 29, 2020.
9. Bruce Piasecki and Hans Sutter, *The Origins and Decline of Ocean Incineration in Europe: The German Example* (Berlin: Umweltbundesamt [Federal Environmental Agency], Federal Republic of Germany, 1988), Box 5762 (General Correspondence on Land and Ocean Incineration with Other Related Documents, 1988–1990), IISH, GIAA.
10. Elsa M. Bruton, *Banning the Burn: The Fight Against Ocean Incineration*, draft, report prepared for Dr. Ken Geiser, January 1989, 15, Box 5180 (Correspondence on Viewpoints and Background Information on Ocean Incineration, from the Archives of Lisa Bunin, 1989), IISH, GIAA.
11. Samuel P. Hays, *Explorations in Environmental History* (Pittsburgh: University of Pittsburgh Press, 1998), 303.
12. Steinhauer and Werme, *Ocean Incineration*, 5; Bruton, *Banning the Burn*, 2.
13. Desmond H. Bond, "At-Sea Incineration of Hazardous Wastes: The Risk Is Yet to Be Justified," *Environmental Science Technology* 18, no. 5 (1984): 148–52, quote on 148.
14. Richard W. Gossett, David A. Brown, and David R. Young, "Predicting the Bioaccumulation and Toxicity of Organic Compounds in Marine Organisms Using Octanol/Water Partition Coefficients," *Marine Pollution Bulletin* 14, no. 10 (1983): 387–92; G. A. Holton, C. Travis, and E. L. Etnier, "A Comparison of Human Exposures to PCB Emissions from Oceanic and Terrestrial Incineration," *Hazardous Waste and Hazardous Materials* 2, no. 4 (1985): 453–71; Peter S. Liss, "The Chemistry of Near-Surface Seawater," in *Dynamic Processes in the Chemistry of the Upper Ocean*, ed. James D. Burton, Paul G. Brewer, and R. Chessele (Boston: Springer, 1986), 41–51.
15. *Incineration of Hazardous Waste at Sea: Hearings Before the Subcommittee on Oceanography of the Committee on Merchant Marine and Fisheries, House of Representatives, Ninety-Ninth Congress, First Session on H.R. 1295, a Bill Entitled the "Ocean Incineration Research Act of 1985," November 11, 1985–December 3, 1985, San Francisco, CA*, Serial no. 99 (Washington, DC: U.S. Government Printing Office, 1986), 300.
16. Joseph Thornton, *Pandora's Poison: Chlorine, Health, and a New Environmental Strategy* (Cambridge, MA: MIT Press, 2001), 2–4.

17. T. A. Wastler, "Ocean Dumping Permit Program Under the London Dumping Convention in the United States," *Chemosphere* 10, no. 6 (1981): 665.
18. *Incineration of Hazardous Waste at Sea . . . 1985*, statement of Neil Shapiro, researcher, Environment and Policy, Cousteau Society, 33–34.
19. U.S. EPA, Office of Policy, Planning, and Evaluation, "Assessment of Incineration as a Treatment Method for Liquid Organic Hazardous Wastes: Summary and Conclusions," March 1985, 86, EPA-NSCEP.
20. "Key Observers Comment on Ocean Pollution," *EPA Journal* 10, no. 9 (1984): 3–6, EPA-NSCEP.
21. Andrew Szasz, *Ecopopulism: Toxic Waste and the Movement for Environmental Justice* (Minneapolis: University of Minnesota Press, 1994), 97; Andrew Hurley, *Environmental Inequalities: Class, Race, and Industrial Pollution in Gary, Indiana, 1945–1980* (Chapel Hill: University of North Carolina Press, 1995); Kelly D. Alley, Charles E. Faupel, and Conner Bailey, "The Historical Transformation of a Grassroots Environmental Group," *Human Organization* 54, no. 4 (1995): 410–16; David Naguib Pellow, *Resisting Global Toxics: Transnational Movements for Environmental Justice* (Cambridge, MA: MIT Press, 2007); Liam Leonard, *The Environmental Movement in Ireland* (Dordrecht, Netherlands: Springer, 2008), 11; Dorceta E. Taylor, *Toxic Communities: Environmental Racism, Industrial Pollution, and Residential Mobility* (New York: New York University Press, 2014).
22. Craig E. Colten and Peter N. Skinner, *The Road to Love Canal: Managing Industrial Waste Before EPA* (Austin: University of Texas Press, 1996).
23. Richard S. Newman, *Love Canal: A Toxic History from Colonial Times to the Present* (New York: Oxford University Press, 2016), 10–30; Ellen Griffith Spears, *Rethinking the American Environmental Movement Post-1945* (London: Routledge, 2019), 129–64. See also Kenneth Geiser, "One, Two, Many Environmentalists: The 1980's Transformation of the Environmental Movement," Department of Urban and Environmental Policy, Tufts University, Medford, March 1987, 4, Box 5315 (General Correspondence with Reports and Other Related Documents, 1985–1990)," IISH, GIAA.
24. Conner Bailey and Charles E. Faupel, "Out of Sight Is Not out of Mind: Public Opposition to Ocean Incineration," *Coastal Management* 17, no. 2 (1989): 89–102.
25. *Vulcanus II* captain interview in *Stern* magazine quoted in Greenpeace USA, "Ocean Incineration of Toxic Waste—Chronology," 1, Box 5320 (Documentation Office Concerning Ocean Incineration, 1985–1987), Folder "Chronology and Clippings, 1985," IISH, GIAA. The captain's comment is also reported in "Toxic-Waste Site Planned for Phila," *Philadelphia Inquirer*, December 6, 1982. See also "Waste-Burning 'Leper-Ship' Stalked by Controversy," *Montreal Gazette*, March 7, 1983.
26. Axel Goodbody, "From Egocentrism to Ecocentrism: Nature and Morality in German Writing in the 1980s," in *Nature in Literary and Cultural Studies: Transatlantic Conversations on Ecocriticism*, ed. Catrin Gersdorf and Sylvia Mayer (Amsterdam: Rodopi, 2006), 393–416; Gwen Ottinger and Benjamin R. Cohen, "Introduction: Environmental Justice and the Transformation of Science and Engineering," in *Technoscience and*

3. TRANSLOCAL ACTIVISM

Environmental Justice: Expert Cultures in a Grassroots Movement, ed. Gwen Ottinger and Benjamin R. Cohen (Cambridge, MA: MIT Press, 2011), 1–19; Karen Hoffman, "From Science-Based Legal Advocacy to Community Organizing: Opportunities and Obstacles to Transforming Patterns of Expertise and Access," in *Technoscience and Environmental Justice*, ed. Ottinger and Cohen, 41–62.

27. Patricia Matthews, "Scientific Knowledge and the Aesthetic Appreciation of Nature," in *Nature, Aesthetics, and Environmentalism: From Beauty to Duty*, ed. Allen Carlson and Sheila Lintott (New York: Columbia University Press, 2008), 188–204.
28. D. T. Kuzmiak, "The American Environmental Movement," *Geographical Journal* 157, no. 3 (1991): 265–78.
29. Lisbeth Miner, "Protectors of Marine Life," *New York Times*, September 4, 1977.
30. *Incineration of Hazardous Waste at Sea . . . 1985*, 361.
31. The Oceanic Society's most important allies were the American Littoral Society, the League for Environmental Action Now, the California League of Conservation Voters Campaign for Economic Democracy, the Chickasaw Community Affairs Group, the Clean Ocean Action, the Environmental Policy Institute, the Farm Labor Organizing Committee, the Farm Worker Education Project, the Fisherman's Environmental Defense Fund, the League for Coastal Protection, the Ocean Tourism Council, and the Whale Center. See "Joint Comments on EPA's Draft Ocean Incineration Research Burn Permit, Prepared by the Oceanic Society," February 15, 1986, 1–2, Box 5321 (Research of the Oceanic Society Concerning the Draft Regulations of the EPA Regarding Ocean Incineration, 1985–1987), IISH, GIAA; Sally Ann Lentz to Joe Retzer, U.S. EPA, Office of Policy, letter, December 3, 1984, Box 5309 (Correspondence and Other Related Documents on Ocean Incineration, 1977–1978, 1981–1987, 1989), IISH, GIAA.
32. Oceanic Society, "Memorandum: Coalition Comments on EPA's Draft Ocean Incineration Regulations and Update on Recent Events," July 3, 1985, attachment: "Joint Comments of Environmental and Other Citizen Organizations in Response to the Environmental Protection Agency's Draft Regulation on Ocean Incinerations," 19, Box 5321, IISH, GIIA.
33. Emma Shortis, "'Who Can Resist This Guy?' Jacques Cousteau, Celebrity Diplomacy, and the Environmental Protection of the Antarctic," *Australian Journal of Politics and History* 61, no. 3 (2015): 366–80.
34. Jacques A. Constans, "The Cousteau Society—Fondation Cousteau," *Environmental Conservation* 9, no. 1 (1982): 49–50.
35. *Hearing Before a Subcommittee of the Committee on Government Operations House of Representatives, Ninety-Eighth Congress, Second Session, July 12, 1984* (Washington, DC: U.S. Government Printing Office, 1985), statement of Jean-Michel Cousteau, Cousteau Society, Los Angeles, 81–84.
36. *Incineration of Hazardous Waste at Sea: Hearing Before the Subcommittee on Fisheries and Wildlife Conservation and the Environment and the Subcommittee on Oceanography of the Committee on Merchant Marine and Fisheries House of Representatives, Ninety-Eighth Congress, First Session on Oversight Regarding the Incineration of Hazardous Waste as Part of the*

3. TRANSLOCAL ACTIVISM

Overall Efforts of Congress to Confront the Problem of Managing Hazardous Waste, December 7, 1983 (Washington, DC: U.S. Government Printing Office, 1984), testimony by Jacques-Yves Cousteau, 221–22. The quote from Captain Cousteau is also reported in Piasecki and Sutter, *The Origins and Decline of Ocean Incineration in Europe*, 24.

37. Rex Wayler, *Greenpeace: How a Group of Ecologists, Journalists, and Visionaries Changed the World* (Emmaus, PA: Rodale, 2015).
38. "Greenpeace: IUCN's Unconventional Member," *IUCN Bulletin* 17, nos. 4–6 (1988): 80, Box 5180, IISH, GIIA. See also Frank Zelko, "Scaling Greenpeace: From Local Activism to Global Governance," *Historical Social Research/Historische Sozialforschung* 42, no. 2 (2017): 318–42.
39. Rémi Parmentier, "Greenpeace and the Dumping of Waste at Sea: A Case of Nonstate Actors' Intervention in International Affairs," *International Negotiation* 4, no. 1 (1999): 436.
40. Jon Hinck, Toxics Project Director, to Toxics Campaigners, Board Members, Directors, memo, "Progress on the Toxics Campaign, Action Plans, What Is Needed," March 27, 1985, 2, Box 5313 (Correspondence with Toxics Campaign Coordinator in the U.S. Jon Hinck, 1983–1986), IISH, GIAA.
41. Bruton, *Banning the Burn*, 2–3.
42. Eugene Stuik, Greenpeace Nederland, "Acties Greenpeace Tegen Verbrandin Van Afvalstoffen Op Zee: Gebaseerde Op Degelijke Argumenten en Wetenschappelijke Rapporten," September 1987, Box 1722–1724, Algemeen Rijksarchief, Archieven ven de Raad van Waterstaa en zijn taakvoorgangers, 1892–1992, Nationaal Archief, The Hague.
43. Pat Costner and Joe Thornton, *Playing with Fire: Hazardous Waste Incineration* (Washington, DC: Greenpeace USA, 1993), 4–5, Box 6648 (Various Publications—Toxics, 1989–2001), IISH, GIIA.
44. Costner and Thornton, *Playing with Fire*, 6; Michael R. Greenberg, *Siting Noxious Facilities: Integrating Location Economics and Risk Analysis to Protect Environmental Health and Investments* (London: Routledge, 2018), 36.
45. Parmentier, "Greenpeace and the Dumping of Waste at Sea," 433.
46. "Comments Presented to the Environmental Protection Agency. Review of Draft Permits for Incineration of PCBs, Organochlorine Wastes, and DDT Tentatively Approved for Chemical Waste Management, Inc.," prepared by Lisa Bunin, Jon Hinck, Elizabeth Otto, and Lesley Scheele, Greenpeace USA, January 20, 1984, 2, Box 5764, IISH, GIIA.
47. Ban the Burn, Minutes of the Meeting on Ocean Incineration, Amsterdam, February 26–27, 1986, Box 5809 (Proposals and Policy Documents Concerning Ocean Incineration, 1984, 1986–1987, 1989–1992), Folder "Correspondence and Documentation, 1984, 1986–1987," IISH, GIAA.
48. Steve McAllister quoted in Bruton, *Banning the Burn*, 7.
49. Jon Hinck to Lois Gibbs, President, Citizen's Clearinghouse for Hazardous Wastes, Inc., letter, August 27, 1984, Box 5313, IISH, GIIA.
50. Ban the Burn, Minutes of the Meeting on Ocean Incineration, Amsterdam, February 26–27, 1986, 2–3.

51. "Draft—Ocean Incineration Campaign Issue Paper," March 6, 1986, 1, Box 5809, Folder "Correspondence and Documentation, 1984, 1986–1987," IISH, GIAA.
52. Parmentier, "Greenpeace and the Dumping of Waste at Sea," 436.
53. "Organochlorines," 1986, 1, Box 5766 (Correspondence and Documentation Concerning Ocean Incineration in Europe, 1986), IISH, GIAA.
54. Greenpeace USA, "Report of the N.C.D.," May 3, 1984, 2, Box 5314 (Correspondence from the Archives of Lisa Bunin, Internal Correspondence of Office in Washington DC, 1984–1986), IISH, GIAA. See also "Greenpeace: Verbranding op zee Streng Aanpakken," *De Waarheid*, April 20, 1984.
55. "Questions to Be Answered Re. Ocean Incineration in Europe Before September 1st to Janus in the Danish Office," July 14, 1984, Box 5766, IISH, GIIA.
56. Janus Hillgaard to Toxic Committee, Jon Hinck, Alan Pickaver, and Monika Griefahn, letter, "Re: Incineration," July 14, 1984, Box 5766, IISH, GIIA.
57. "Summary of Public Comments on the Proposed Ocean Incineration Regulation (50 F.R. 8222, February 28, 1985)," in *Incineration of Hazardous Waste at Sea . . . 1985*, 118–19.
58. Bruton, *Banning the Burn*, 14.
59. Bruton, *Banning the Burn*, 2.
60. Luke W. Cole and Sheila R. Foster, *From the Ground Up: Environmental Racism and the Rise of the Environmental Justice Movement* (New York: New York University Press, 2000), 158.
61. Michele Perrault quoted in Larry B. Stammer, "Incinerator Ships: Toxic Waste—Are Seas the Answer?," *Los Angeles Times*, June 20, 1985.
62. *Hearing Before a Subcommittee of the Committee on Government Operations*, testimony by Peter P. Russell, Marin Conservation League, San Rafael, California, 122–23.
63. Northwest Indiana Coalition for the Environment, "Position Statement," October 21, 1986, Box 5849 (Documentation of Jeff Barrett Howard [Great Lakes] Concerning Ocean Incineration, 1979, 1981, 1983, 1985–1986), IISH, GIAA.
64. *Hearing Before a Subcommittee of the Committee on Government Operations*, statement of Sarah Kulungowski, finance officer, Gulf Coast Coalition for Public Health (GCCPH), 130–33.
65. GCCPH, "Proposal Summary," October 11, 1985, Box 149, Folder 9 "Organizations: Gulf Coast Coalition for Public Health, 1985–1987," Grant Records, 1950–2007, Public Welfare Foundation Records, Ruth Lilly Special Collections and Archives, Philanthropic Studies Archives, Indiana University—Purdue University, University Library, Indianapolis (hereafter GCCPH Records), 58 (items in GCCPH Records paginated consecutively).
66. GCCPH, "Proposed Budget for 1986, Structure and Administration," GCCPH Records, 87.
67. GCCPH, Harlingen, TX, "Proposal Comment Sheet," August 22, 1985, GCCPH Records, 74.
68. Nora Deyaun Boudreaux, Government and Political Liaison, GCCPH, to Larry Presley, Public Welfare Foundation, letter, August 14, 1985, GCCPH Records, 105. On the

3. TRANSLOCAL ACTIVISM

Ixtoc spill, see John Farrington, *Ixtoc I Oil Well: Cruise Summary and Report* (Woods Hole, MA: Woods Hole Oceanographic Institution, 1979), https://www.whoi.edu/fileserver.do?id=84384&pt=10&p=55633; and Arne Jernelöv and Olof Lindén, "Ixtoc I: A Case Study of the World's Largest Oil Spill," *Ambio* 10, no. 6 (1981): 299–306.

69. GCCPH, "1986 Year End Report," GCHPP Records, 8.
70. Joan B. Brotman, coordinator, to Larry Kressley, letter, October 19, 1987, GCCPH Records, 123.
71. GCCPH, "Proposal Comment Sheet," August 22, 1985, 74.
72. GCCPH, "1986 Year End Report," 8.
73. Sarah Kulungowski, President, GCCPH, to Larry Jensen, Assistant Administrator, Office of Water, U.S. EPA, letter, September 13, 1986, GCHHP Records, 29.
74. GCCPH, "Proposal Summary," October 11, 1985, GCCPH Records, 58.
75. GCCPH, "1986 Year End Report," 8.
76. Brotman to Kressley, October 19, 1987, 123.
77. "Comments Presented to the Environmental Protection Agency. Review of Draft Permits for Incineration of PCBs," January 20, 1984, 1.
78. U.S. EPA, "Fact Sheet, Assistant Administrator for Water, Ocean Incineration Permits Decision, 1983," 1, Box 5764, IISH, GIIA.
79. *Hearing Before a Subcommittee of the Committee on Government Operations*, statement of Ramon de Leon on behalf of the GCCPH, 134–37.
80. Bruton, *Banning the Burn*, 2, 14.
81. *Hearing Before a Subcommittee of the Committee on Government Operations*, statement of Ramon de Leon, 134–37.
82. *Hearing Before a Subcommittee of the Committee on Government Operations*, statement of Ramon de Leon, 134.
83. U.S. EPA, "40CFR Parts 220, 227, 228, and 234 (FRL-2698-5), Ocean Incineration Regulation," *Federal Register* 50, nos. 36–40 (February 28, 1985): 8223. See also Bruton, *Banning the Burn*, 14. Ken Geiser describes the varied group of people that participated in these meetings as "fisheries operators and employees, 'Republican ladies,' residents of coastal communities, migrant workers in the rural south (Texas, Louisiana, and Mississippi), church groups—a loose coalition of citizen groups spanning the economic spectrum" (Geiser, "One, Two, Many Environmentalists," 4).
84. U.S. Congress, Office of Technology Assessment, *Ocean Incineration: Its Role in Managing Hazardous Waste*, OTA-O-313 (Washington, DC: U.S. Government Printing Office, 1986), 182.
85. U.S. EPA, "Fact Sheet, Assistant Administrator for Water, Ocean Incineration Permits Decision, 1983," 1.
86. "News in Brief," *Christian Science Monitor*, November 8, 1983.
87. Bruton, *Banning the Burn*, 14.
88. Robin Alexander, Texas Rural Legal Aid, Inc., to Lisa Bunin, Greenpeace, letter, May 9, 1984, Box 5309, IISH, GIIA.

3. TRANSLOCAL ACTIVISM

89. *Hearing Before a Subcommittee of the Committee on Government Operations*, statement of Sue Ann Fruge, coordinator, on behalf of the GCCPH, 140–42.
90. U.S. EPA, Office of Water Programs, "Decision on Ocean Incineration Permits," May 1984, 5, EPA-NSCEP.
91. *Hearing Before a Subcommittee of the Committee on Government Operations*, statement of Sue Ann Fruge, 142.
92. U.S. EPA, Office of Policy, "Planning an Evaluation, Memorandum from Milton Russell to Al Alm," April 10, 1984, and "Planning an Evaluation, Memorandum: Science Advisory Board Review of Incineration, from Jean Caufield to Milton Russell," April 10, 1984, Box 5856 (Miscellaneous Documentation from the United States Concerning Waste, Land Incineration, and Ocean Incineration, 1986), IISH, GIAA.
93. U.S. EPA, *Environmental News*, press release (quoting and summarizing Schatzow's recommendations), April 23, 1984, in *Hearing Before a Subcommittee of the Committee on Government Operation*, 301–2.
94. Alexander to Bunin, May 9, 1984.
95. U.S. EPA, "Assistant Administrator's Determination on Applications of Chemical Waste Management, Inc. and Combustion Services, B.V. for Special and Research Ocean Incineration Permits," May 22, 1984, Box 5764, IISH, GIIA. See also "Greenpeace Calls EPA Push for Ocean Incineration 'Tragically Misplaced' as Agency Releases Draft Regulations," January 27, 1986, Box 5309, IISH, GIIA.
96. *Hearing Before a Subcommittee of the Committee on Government Operations*, statement of Jack Ravan, assistant administrator for water, U.S. EPA, accompanied by Steven Schatzow, Patrick Tobin, and Alan Rubin, and statement of Mr. Jack E. Ravan and U.S. EPA, *Environmental News*, May 23, 1984, 19, 28, 36.
97. *Hearing Before a Subcommittee of the Committee on Government Operations*, opening statement of Acting Chairwoman Barbara Boxer, 2.
98. "Greenpeace Calls EPA Push for Ocean Incineration 'Tragically Misplaced.'"
99. Jon Hinck to Toxics Campaigners, Trustees, NCD [National Campaign Director], AD [Administrative Director], Others, "Re: Campaign Updates," letter, June 12, 1984, Box 5313, IISH, GIIA.
100. See, for example, Hal Lancaster, "Down in the Dumps?," *Wall Street Journal*, October 4, 1983; and Cass Peterson, "EPA Faulted on Waste Incineration at Sea," *Washington Post*, December 8, 1983.
101. Philip Shabecoff, "Burning Toxic Chemicals at Sea Makes Waves on Shore," *New York Times*, December 25, 1983 (quotes); Shabecoff, "Area for Ships to Burn Wastes Is Found to Be Whale Habitat," *New York Times*, April 2, 1984; Shabecoff, "Gaps Seen in Data on Burning Toxic Wastes," *New York Times*, January 17, 1985.
102. Alan Rubin quoted in "Burning of Waste at Sea Closer," *New York Times*, November 30, 1986.
103. Jay D. Reed, "Environment: Destroying Toxic Wastes at Sea," *Time*, May 7, 1984.
104. Larry B. Stammer, "Incinerator Ships: Toxic Waste—Are Seas the Answer?," *Los Angeles Times*, June 20, 1985.

4. RELENTLESS COMMITMENT

105. *Incineration of Hazardous Waste at Sea . . . 1983*, comments by Representative John B. Breaux, 11.
106. Frederick W. Allen and Roy Popkin, "Environmental Polls: What They Tell US," *EPA Journal* 14, no. 1 (January–February 1988): 10–12.

4. RELENTLESS COMMITMENT

1. On the politicization of environmental science, see Tim O'Riordan, "Environmental Science, Sustainability and Politics," *Transactions of the Institute of British Geographers* 29, no. 2 (2004): 234–47.
2. In other words, anti-ocean-incineration campaigners took a political rather than an apolitical approach. See Paul Robbins, *Political Ecology: A Critical Introduction* (Malden, MA: Wiley, 2012), 13.
3. Robert Gottlieb, *Forcing the Spring: The Transformation of the American Environmental Movement* (Washington, DC: Island Press, 2005), 4; Vincent Ostrom, "Polycentricity (Part 1)" and "Polycentricity (Part 2)," in *Polycentricity and Local Public Economies: Readings from the Workshop in Political Theory and Policy Analysis*, ed. Michael D. McGinnis (Ann Arbor: University of Michigan Press, 1999), 52–74, 119–38.
4. Daniel Faber, "Building a Transnational Environmental Justice Movement," in *Coalitions Across Borders: Transnational Protest and the Neoliberal Order*, ed. Jackie Smith and Joe Bandy (Lanham, MD: Rowman & Littlefield, 2005), 45.
5. Andrew Rowell, *Green Backlash: Global Subversion of the Environmental Movement* (London: Routledge, 1996), 102–3.
6. Jack Ravan, in "The Job of Protecting the Seas: An Interview with Jack E. Ravan," *EPA Journal* 10, no. 9 (November 1984): 9, U.S. Environmental Protection Agency (EPA) National Service Center for Environmental Publications (EPA-NSCEP).
7. U.S. EPA, Office of Water, "Annual Report," December 1984, 10; "Update," *EPA Journal* 10, no. 5 (June 1984): 43, EPA-NSCEP.
8. "Incinerator Ship Apollo One Launched at Tacoma Boatbuilding," *Maritime Reporter/Engineering News*, April 1984, 21–22.
9. "EPA to Resume Burns at Sea," *Mobile Press Register*, September 16, 1984.
10. Jon Hinck to Jack E. Ravan, letter, "Re: Toxic Waste Research Burns at Sea," September 25, 1984, emphasis in original, Box 5313 (Correspondence with Toxics Campaign Coordinator in the U.S. Jon Hinck 1983–1986), International Institute for Social History (IISH), Greenpeace International (Amsterdam) Archives (GIAA).
11. Jack E. Ravan to Jon Hinck, letter, November 8, 1984, Box 5313, IISH, GIAA. On the November 13 meeting, see "Report to Congress on Administration of the Marine Protection Research and Sanctuaries Act of 1972 as Amended (P.L. 92–532) 1984–1986," 31–31, EPA-NSCEP; Oceanic Society, "Memorandum: Coalition Comments on EPA's Draft Ocean Incineration Regulations and Update on Recent Events," July 3, 1985, attachment titled "Joint Comments of Environmental and Other Citizen Organizations in

4. RELENTLESS COMMITMENT

Response to the Environmental Protection Agency's Draft Regulation on Ocean Incinerations," 7, Box 5321 (Research of the Oceanic Society Concerning the Draft Regulations of the EPA Regarding Ocean Incineration, 1985–1987), IISH, GIAA.

12. U.S. EPA, "Report on the Incineration of Liquid Hazardous Wastes by the Environmental Effects, Transport, and Fate Committee, Science Advisory Board," April 1985, iii, 1–2, 3–4, EPA-NSCEP. See also Margarete S. Steinhauer and Christine E. Werme, *Ocean Incineration: Background and Status*, prepared for David P. Redford, U.S. EPA, Office of Marine and Estuaries Protection, September 4, 1987, 6, EPA-NSCEP; and U.S. Congress, Office of Technology Assessment (OTA), *Ocean Incineration: Its Role in Managing Hazardous Waste*, OTA-O-313 (Washington, DC: U.S. Government Printing Office, 1986), 186.
13. Norton Nelson was the SAB's chairman, while Rolf Hartung was the head of the EPA's Environmental Effects, Transport, and Fate Committee.
14. Rolf Hartung and Norton Nelson to Lee M. Thomas, letter, April 5, 1985, attached to and introducing U.S. EPA, "Report on the Incineration of Liquid Hazardous Wastes."
15. U.S. EPA, Office of Policy, Planning, and Evaluation (OPPE), "Assessment of Incineration as a Treatment Method for Liquid Organic Hazardous Wastes: Summary and Conclusions," March 1985, EPA-NSCEP.
16. Milton Russell to James Barnes, letter, "Re: Final Report of the OPPE Incineration Study," March 25, 1985, 2, EPA-NSCEP. Concerning ocean incineration in Europe in 1986, see U.S. EPA, OPPE, "Assessment of Incineration," 5.
17. U.S. EPA, OPPE, "Assessment of Incineration," 1–4.
18. U.S. Congress, OTA, *Ocean Incineration*, 186.
19. U.S. EPA, Office of Water, "Incineration-at-Sea: Research Strategy," February 19, 1985, 13, EPA-NSCEP.
20. U.S. Congress, OTA, *Ocean Incineration*, 166.
21. H.R.2867—Hazardous and Solid Waste Amendments of 1984, 98th Cong. (1983–1984), https://www.congress.gov/bill/98th-congress/house-bill/2867. See also Daryl Ditz, "Interpretation of Need in US Ocean Incineration Policy," *Marine Policy* 13, no. 1 (1989): 47.
22. Greenpeace, "Proposal for Ocean Incineration: Contingency Plan and Budget," position paper, 1985, 1–2, Box 5853 (Clippings Concerning Ocean Incineration, 1984–1985, 1988, and n.d.), IISH, GIAA.
23. U.S. Congress, OTA, *Ocean Incineration*, 186.
24. Marc K. Landy, Marc J. Roberts, and Stephen R. Thomas, *The Environmental Protection Agency: Asking the Wrong Questions from Nixon to Clinton* (New York: Oxford University Press, 1994), 262.
25. Richard J. Lazarus, "The Neglected Question of Congressional Oversight of EPA: Quis Custodiet Ipsos Custodes (Who Shall Watch the Watchers Themselves?)," *Law and Contemporary Problems* 54, no. 4 (1991): 205–39.
26. Ditz, "Interpretation of Need in US Ocean Incineration Policy," 46.

4. RELENTLESS COMMITMENT

27. *Hearing Before a Subcommittee of the Committee on Government Operations, House of Representatives, Ninety-Eighth Congress, Second Session, July 12, 1984* (Washington, DC: U.S. Government Printing Office, 1985), opening statement of Acting Chairwoman Barbara Boxer, 2.
28. *Hearing Before a Subcommittee of the Committee on Government Operations*, Boxer opening statement, 1, 2.
29. *Hearing Before a Subcommittee of the Committee on Government Operations*, statement of Jack O'Connell, assemblyman, State of California Legislature, and vice chairman, Education Committee, 4.
30. *Hearing Before a Subcommittee of the Committee on Government Operations*, statement of Jean-Michel Cousteau on behalf of the Cousteau Society, 81–82, 83.
31. *Hearing Before a Subcommittee of the Committee on Government Operations*, statement of Michael J. Herz, PhD, senior vice president, Oceanic Society, 88.
32. *Hearing Before a Subcommittee of the Committee on Government Operations*, statements of Cathy Ryan and Elizabeth Otto, 111–15.
33. *Hearing Before a Subcommittee of the Committee on Government Operations*, exchange between Representative Tom Lantos and EPA officers Jack Ravan and Steven Schatzow, 65.
34. Jon Hinck to Toxics Campaigners, Trustees, NCD [National Campaign Director], AD [Administrative Director], Others, letter, "Re: Campaign Update," June 12, 1984, Box 5313, IISH, GIAA.
35. Larry B. Stammer, "Incinerator Ships: Toxic Waste—Are Seas the Answer?," *Los Angeles Times*, June 20, 1985; H.R. 1295—a Bill Entitled: "The Ocean Incineration Research Act of 1985," 99th Cong. (1985–1986), https://www.congress.gov/bill/99th-congress/house-bill/1295?s=1&r=7. The bill had twenty-nine cosponsors from across the country; see Lisa Bunin, "Update: Proposed Incineration Regulations and Moratorium Legislation," April 29, 1985, Box 5320 (Documentation Office Concerning Ocean Incineration, 1985–1987), IISH, GIAA. "Due to the lack of information on need, efficiency, and safety" of ocean incineration, even Governor Mark White of Texas endorsed the proposed bill; see Mark White to Jim Wright, U.S. House of Representatives, letter, March 15, 1985, Box 5320, IISH, GIAA.
36. "Draft," letter accompanying the bill introduced by Rep. Barbara Boxer (D-CA), August 31, 1984, Box 5309 (Correspondence and Other Related Documents on Ocean Incineration, 1977–1978, 1981–1987, 1989), IISH, GIAA.
37. Elsa M. Bruton, *Banning the Burn: The Fight Against Ocean Incineration*, a report prepared for Dr. Ken Geiser, January 1989, draft, 2, Box 5180 (Correspondence on Viewpoints and Background Information on Ocean Incineration, from the Archives of Lisa Bunin, 1989), IISH, GIAA.
38. *Hearings Before the Subcommittee on Environmental Pollution of the Committee on Environment and Public Works, United States Senate, Ninety-Ninth Congress, First Session, June 19 and July 17, 1985* (Washington, DC: U.S. Government Printing Office, 1985), opening statement of Senator John H. Chafee of Rhode Island, 1.

4. RELENTLESS COMMITMENT

39. *Hearings Before the Subcommittee on Environmental Pollution of the Committee on Environment and Public Works*, statement of Governor Mark White of Texas, 4–6.
40. *Hearings Before the Subcommittee on Environmental Pollution of the Committee on Environment and Public Works*, statement of Rick Gimello, executive director, New Jersey Hazardous Waste Facilities Siting Commission, 10–16. See also New Jersey Hazardous Waste Facilities Siting Commission, testimony before the U.S. Senate Subcommittee on Environmental Pollution, June 19, 1985, 1–6, Box 5309, IISH, GIAA.
41. *Hearings Before the Subcommittee on Environmental Pollution of the Committee on Environment and Public Works*, statement of Sue Ann Fruge, coordinator, GCCPH, 36; statement of Sharon Stuart, coastal resources chairman, Texas Environmental Coalition, 29; statement of Kenneth S. Kamlet, director, Pollution and Toxic Substances Division, National Wildlife Federation, 31; statement of Sally Ann Lentz, staff attorney, Ocean Policy Office, Oceanic Society, 33; Neal Shapiro, the Cousteau Society, letter, June 5, 1985, 565; statement of Zeke Grader, executive director, Pacific Coast Federation of Fishermen's Associations, 30; statement of D. W. Bennett, executive director, American Littoral Society, 34.
42. *Hearings Before the Subcommittee on Environmental Pollution of the Committee on Environment and Public Works*, statement of Howard Canter, president of governmental affairs, At-Sea Incineration, Elizabeth, NJ, 38.
43. *Hearings Before the Subcommittee on Environmental Pollution of the Committee on Environment and Public Works*, statement of William Brown, director of marine affairs, Waste Management, Inc., accompanied by George Vander Velde, 42–44.
44. *Hearings Before the Subcommittee on Merchant Marine and Fisheries, House of Representatives, Ninety-Ninth Congress, First Session, on H.R. 1295, a Bill Entitled the "Ocean Incineration Research Act of 1985," November 11, 1985–December 3, 1985, San Francisco, CA* (Washington, DC: U.S. Government Printing Office, 1986), opening statement of Representative Barbara A. Mikulski of Maryland, 441–43.
45. See these representatives' statements in *Hearings Before the Subcommittee on Merchant Marine and Fisheries*, 445–51.
46. *Hearings Before the Subcommittee on Merchant Marine and Fisheries*, statement of Representative Barbara Boxer of California, 451–52.
47. *Hearings Before the Subcommittee on Merchant Marine and Fisheries*, statement of Peg Stevenson, 85–88.
48. "Statement on Ocean Incineration of Toxic Waste and Proposed Regulations," submitted by Lisa J. Bunin, Jon Hinck, and Elizabeth Otto on behalf of Greenpeace USA, June 28, 1985, 2–11, 24–25, Box 5854 (Reports and Press Clippings Concerning Ocean Incineration, 1985–1986), IISH, GIAA.
49. *Hearings Before the Subcommittee on Merchant Marine and Fisheries*, statement of Joan Brotman, GCCPH, 88–89.
50. *Hearings Before the Subcommittee on Environmental Pollution of the Committee on Environment and Public Works*, statement of Senator Joseph R. Biden Jr. of Delaware, 401.

4. RELENTLESS COMMITMENT

51. Sally Ann Lentz to Environmental and Public Interest Groups Concerned with Ocean Incineration, letter, "Re: Update on Ocean Incineration," April 15, 1987, and Greenpeace USA, telegram, November 26, 1985, both in Box 5309, IISH, GIAA. See also Steinhauer and Werme, *Ocean Incineration*, 6.
52. Ramon Álvarez Larrauri quoted in Pedro Miguel, "Graves daños económicos causaría a México la quema de PCB en el Golfo," *El Día*, July 24, 1984, my translation.
53. José Garcia, Segura, "México puede impeder se descarguen desechos en aguas internacionales," *El Día*, July 25, 1984.
54. José Lizarraga quoted in Alejandra Sanchez Gavito, "Se violarían tratados caribeños en materia de protección marina," *El Día*, July 26, 1984, my translation.
55. Pedro Miguel, "Las inceneraciones oceánicas de desechos ponen en peligro la ecología del Continente," *El Día*, July 23, 1984; Luzmaria Mejia, "El gobierno debe tomar medidas para defender el patrimonio nacional," *El Día*, July 26, 1984; José Luis Camacho, "Desde hace 20 años Estados Unidos usa el Golfo como basurero: PPS," *El Día*, July 28, 1984.
56. SGD special session reported on in International Maritime Organization (IMO), Ninth Consultative Meeting of the Contracting Parties to the Convention on the Prevention of the Marine Pollution by Dumping of Wastes and Other Matter, September 23–25, 1985, "Report of the Scientific Group on Dumping," 8–15, esp. 13, https://wwwcdn.imo.org/localresources/en/KnowledgeCentre/ConferencesMeetings/LDC_LC_Documents/LDC%209%2012%20%E2%80%93%20REPORT%20OF%20THE%20NINTH%20CONSULTATIVE%20MEETING.pdf.
57. As reported in "Statement on Ocean Incineration of Toxic Waste and Proposed Regulations," 6.
58. Edward W. Kleppinger and Desmond H. Bond, *Ocean Incineration of Hazardous Waste: A Critique* (Washington, DC: EWK Consultant, 1983); David G. Ackerman, L. L. Scinto, C. C. Shih, and B. J. Matthews, *The Capability of Ocean Incineration—a Critical Review and Rebuttal of the Kleppinger Report* (Redondo Beach, CA: TWR Energy and Environmental Division, 1983). See also IMO, Scientific Group on Dumping (SGD), 8th Meeting, March 11–15, 1985, agenda item 7: "Incineration at Sea: Review of Incineration of Hazardous Wastes at Sea, Notes by the Secretariat," Box 5854, IISH, GIAA.
59. IMO, SGD, 8th Meeting, March 11–15, 1985, "Review of Waste Incineration at Sea, Part 1: Kleppinger Report," Box 5854, IISH, GIAA.
60. IMO, SGD, 8th Meeting, March 11–15, 1985, "Review of Waste Incineration at Sea, Part 2: Ackerman Report," Box 5854, IISH, GIAA.
61. European Toxics Campaign 1986, Box 5766 (Correspondence and Documentation Concerning Ocean Incineration in Europe, 1986), IISH, GIAA.
62. European Toxics Campaign 1986; "Future Needs to Incinerate at Sea, OSCOM Countries," 1984, Box 5809 (Proposals and Policy Documents Concerning Ocean Incineration, 1984, 1986–1987, 1989–1992), Folder "Correspondence and Documentation, 1984, 1986–1987," IISH, GIAA.

4. RELENTLESS COMMITMENT

63. European Toxics Campaign 1986.
64. *Hearings Before the Subcommittee on Merchant Marine and Fisheries*, "Joint Comments of Environmental and Other Citizen Organizations in Response to the Environmental Protection Agency's Draft Regulation on Ocean Incinerations," prepared by the Oceanic Society, June 28, 1985, submitted on behalf of a national coalition of thirty-five organizations, 352–55, also in Box 5321, IISH, GIAA. See also *Hearings Before the Subcommittee on Environmental Pollution of the Committee on Environment and Public Works*, Lentz statement, 33.
65. The two regional bodies merged in 1992 into the Convention for the Protection of the Marine Environment of the North-East Atlantic, or OSPAR Convention. See Dik Tromp and Koos Wieriks, "The OSPAR Convention: 25 Years of North Sea Protection," *Marine Pollution Bulletin* 29, no. 6 (1994): 622–26; and Jon Birger Skjærseth, "The Making and Implementation of North Sea Commitments: The Politics of Environmental Participation," in *The Implementation and Effectiveness of International Environmental Commitments: Theory and Practice*, ed. David Victor, Kal Raustiala, and Eugene B. Skolnikoff (Cambridge, MA: MIT Press, 1998), 327–80.
66. Rémi Parmentier, "Greenpeace and the Dumping of Waste at Sea: A Case of Nonstate Actors' Intervention in International Affairs," *International Negotiation* 4, no. 1 (1999): 438.
67. Bruton, *Banning the Burn*, 8; Convention for the Prevention of Marine Pollution by Dumping from Ships and Aircraft, Twelfth Meeting of the Standing Advisory Committee for Scientific Advice, Hamburg, March 19–22, 1985, 1, Box 5853, IISH, GIAA.
68. "Report of the Working Group on Incineration at Sea," March 11–15, 1985, 1–2, Box 5853, IISH, GIAA.
69. "Greenpeace Presentation to the SGD, Prepared by Lisa J. Bunin," April 25, 1988, Box 5180, IISH, GIAA.
70. Eugene [Stuik?] to All European Offices, telegram, "Re: Ocean Incineration," March 19, 1985, Box 5766, IISH, GIAA.
71. Greenpeace, "Ocean Incineration Fact Sheet," March 1985, Box 5180, IISH, GIAA.
72. Greenpeace, "Position Paper: Organochlorines," 1985, Box 5766, IISH, GIAA.
73. Desmond H. Bond, "Ocean Incineration of Hazardous Wastes: An Update," *Environment, Science & Technology* 19, no. 6 (1985): 486–87.
74. Lisa J. Bunin to Board Members, Toxic Campaigners, and Interested Others, letter, "Re: Legislative Year in Review," November 1, 1985, Box 5853, IISH, GIAA.
75. Jon Hinck to Toxic Campaigners, January 31, 1984, Box 5313, IISH, GIAA.
76. Jon Hinck to Offices of Greenpeace USA, letter, "Re: Monthly Report," March 1984, Box 5313, IISH, GIAA.
77. Matt Seiden, "Greenpeacenicks Restore Faith in New Generation," *Baltimore Sun*, October 26, 1984. See also Dario Fazzi, "The Nuclear Freeze Generation: The Early 1980s Anti-nuclear Youth Revolt Between 'Carter's Vietnam' and 'Euroshima,'" in *A European Youth Revolt in 1980–1981*, ed. Knud Andresen and Bart van der Steen (Basingstoke, U.K.: Palgrave, 2016), 145–58.

4. RELENTLESS COMMITMENT

78. Jon Hinck to Toxics Campaigners, Board Members, Directors, letter, March 27, 1985, Box 5313, IISH, GIAA.
79. Greenpeace, "Proposal for Ocean Incineration: Contingency Plan and Budget," position paper, 1985, 1–2, Box 5853, IISH, GIAA.
80. Bunin to Board Members, November 1, 1985.
81. Bunin to Board Members, November 1, 1985; see also Michael Holmes, "Texas Lawmakers Blast EPA Plan for Burning Waste in Gulf," *Dallas Morning News*, April 3, 1985.
82. Lisa Bunin, "Ocean Incineration Alert," March 18, 1985, Box 5180, IISH, GIAA.
83. Don Lee quoted in Holmes, "Texas Lawmakers Blast EPA Plan."
84. In this regard, the anti-ocean-incineration battle resembled many other locally driven antitoxics campaigns that were exposing the connections between environmental pollution and degradation, on the one hand, and racial and class exploitation, on the other. See, among other sources, Robert D. Bullard, *Dumping in Dixie: Race, Class, and Environmental Quality* (Boulder, CO: Westview Press, 1990); Dorceta E. Taylor, *Toxic Communities: Environmental Racism, Industrial Pollution, and Residential Mobility* (New York: New York University Press, 2014); Ellen Griffith Spears, *Baptized in PCBs: Race, Pollution, and Justice in an All-American Town* (Chapel Hill: University of North Carolina Press, 2014).
85. GCCPH, "Proposal Comment Sheet," August 22, 1985, Box 9, Folder 9 "Organizations: Gulf Coast Coalition for Public Health, 1985–1987," Grant Records, 1950–2007, Public Welfare Foundation Records, Philanthropic Studies Archives, Ruth Lilly Special Collections and Archives, University Library, Indiana University—Purdue University, Indianapolis (hereafter GCCPH Records), 75 (items in GCCPH Records paginated consecutively).
86. On the EPA in these areas, see U.S. EPA, "Chesapeake Bay Program: Findings and Recommendations," September 1983, 1–56, EPA-NSCEP; and U.S. EPA, "Puget Sound Monitoring Program: A Proposed Pan," November 1986, ix–xviii, EPA-NSCEP.
87. GCCPH, "1987 Public Welfare Grant Proposal," GCCPH Records, 142.
88. Greenpeace memo quoted in Brooks K. Tigner, "Europe's Growing Debate Over Ocean Incineration," *Management Review*, April 1986, 14–16.
89. Phil Gramm, U.S. Senator, to Deyaun Bodreaux, letter, August 22, 1985, GCCPH Records, 64; Solomon P. Ortiz, Member of Congress, to Larry Presley, Public Welfare Foundation, letter, September 19, 1985, GCCPH Records, 103; Jim Matton, Texas Attorney General, to Larry Presley, letter, "Re: Grant Application of the Gulf Coast Coalition for Public Health," September 20, 1985, GCCPH Records, 62; Jack E. Ravan, U.S. EPA, Regional Administrator, to Joan Brotman, GCCPH, September 25, 1985, GCCPH Records, 70.
90. Geert Heinemann quoted in Tigner, "Europe's Growing Debate Over Ocean Incineration," 15.
91. Freddy Gielen and Elke Jordan quoted in Tigner, "Europe's Growing Debate Over Ocean Incineration," 15. See also Greenpeace USA to Greenpeace Offices, telegram, November 21, 1985, Box 5309, IISH, GIAA; and Pamela S. Zurer, "Incineration of Hazardous

4. RELENTLESS COMMITMENT

Wastes at Sea: Going Nowhere Fast," *C&EN*, December 9, 1985, 38, Box 5853, IISH, GIAA.
92. "The Chicken Guarding the Foxes: U.S. Environmental Protection Agency's Record of Performance Controlling the Environmental Degradation of Chemical Waste Management, Inc.," testimony of Peter Montague before the U.S. EPA Public Hearing on Ocean Incineration, April 18, 1985, 3, Box 5854, IISH, GIAA; Ralph Blumenthal, "A Waste Hauler Under the Gun," *New York Times*, November 25, 1984.
93. Donald Carruth's opinion quoted in U.S. Congress, OTA, *Ocean Incineration*, 180–81.
94. U.S. Congress, OTA, *Ocean Incineration*, 183.

5. BAN THE BURN

1. Edward Broughton, "The Bhopal Disaster and Its Aftermath: A Review," *Environmental Health* 4, no. 6 (2005): 1–6; Tomás Mac Sheoin and Frank Pearce, "Introduction: Bhopal and After," in "Bhopal and After: The Chemical Industry as Toxic Capitalism," special issue of *Social Justice* 41, nos. 1–2 (2014): 1–27.
2. Ben A. Franklin, "Toxic Cloud Leaks at Carbide Plant in West Virginia," *New York Times*, August 12, 1985; "250 Flee Toxic Cloud as Train Derails in Arizona," *New York Times*, August 13, 1985; U.S. National Transportation Safety Board, *Special Investigation Report: Failure of Cargo Tank Transporting Hazardous Waste on the Washington, D.C. Beltway, I-95, Fairfax County, Virginia, August 12, 1985* (Washington, DC: National Technical Information Service, 1986); Robert D. McFadden, "A Toxic Chemical Spills in Camden," *New York Times*, August 13, 1985.
3. Chad Montrie, *The Myth of Silent Spring: Rethinking the Origins of American Environmentalism* (Berkeley: University of California Press, 2018), 1–21.
4. Patrick Allitt, *A Climate of Crisis: America in the Age of Environmentalism* (New York: Penguin, 2014), 225–28.
5. *99th Congress—2nd Session, January 21–October 18, 1986, House Reports 1037–1045, United States Congressional Serial Set, Serial Number 13716, Oversight Hearing of State Review of Offshore Oil and Exploration Development and Protection Under the Coastal Zone Management Act, Oversight Hearings on Ocean Incineration* (Washington, DC: U.S. Government Printing Office, 1988), 214. See also "Memorandum from Sally Ann Lentz to Environmental and Public Interest Groups Concerned with Incineration at Sea," November 27, 1985, 1, Box 5309 (Correspondence and Other Related Documents on Ocean Incineration, 1977–1978, 1981–1987, 1989), International Institute for Social History (IISH), Greenpeace International (Amsterdam) Archives (GIAA); and Cass Peterson, "EPA Allows Test Burning of Toxic Wastes off Coast," *Washington Post*, November 27, 1985.
6. "Ocean Dumping; Chemical Waste Incineration; Tentative Research Permit, Hearings," *Federal Register* 50, no. 241 (December 16, 1985): 51360.
7. U.S. Congress, Office of Technology Assessment (OTA), *Ocean Incineration: Its Role in Managing Hazardous Waste*, OTA-O-313 (Washington, DC: U.S. Government Printing Office, 1986), 183.

5. BAN THE BURN

8. Lisa Bunin to All Greenpeace Offices, telegram, "Greenpeace Wins Denial of Ocean Incineration Permit," May 28, 1986, 1, Box 5854 (Reports and Press Clippings Concerning Ocean Incineration, 1985–1986), IISH, GIAA.
9. Christopher Rootes and Liam Leonard, "Environmental Movements and Campaigns Against Waste Infrastructure in the United States," *Environmental Politics* 18, no. 6 (2009): 835–50.
10. Ellen Griffith Spears, *Rethinking the American Environmental Movement Post-1945* (London: Routledge, 2020), 144.
11. Greenpeace Policy Memo, "Ban the Burn," January 1986, 2, Box 5180 (Correspondence on Viewpoints and Background Information on Ocean Incineration, from the Archives of Lisa Bunin, 1989), IISH, GIAA.
12. Greenpeace, "Greenpeace Calls EPA's 'Research' Burn an Attempt to 'Justify' Permanent Ocean Incineration," press release, January 27, 1986, 1, Box 5854, IISH, GIAA.
13. Elsa Bruton, "Banning the Burn: The Fight Against Ocean Incineration," appendix to Ken Geiser, "Halogenated Hydrocarbons: Recommendations for a Phase Out Strategy," a project completed for Greenpeace International, Tufts University, Medford, MA, May 1989, 10, Box 5762 (General Correspondence on Land and Ocean Incineration with Other Related Documents, 1988–1990), IISH, GIAA.
14. Greenpeace, "Greenpeace Calls EPA's 'Research' Burn an Attempt to 'Justify' Permanent Ocean Incineration," 1.
15. Greenpeace, "Ban the Burn," leaflet, January 1986, 1, Box 5180, IISH, GIAA.
16. Greenpeace, "Greenpeace Calls EPA's 'Research' Burn an Attempt to 'Justify' Permanent Ocean Incineration," 1.
17. Lisa Bunin to Larry Jensen, letter, January 9, 1986, 1–2, Box 5320 (Documentation Office Concerning Ocean Incineration, 1985–1987), IISH, GIAA.
18. Greenpeace Ban the Burn, "Ocean Incineration of Toxic Waste Fact Sheet," *Ocean Ecology*, Spring 1986, Box 5764 (Correspondence and Other Documents of Andy Booth Concerning Ocean Incineration, 1981–1989), IISH, GIAA.
19. Public-service announcements, sixty seconds and thirty seconds, Box 5320, IISH, GIAA.
20. Lisa Bunin, memorandum, March 21, 1986, 1, Box 5314 (Correspondence from the Archives of Lisa Bunin, Internal Correspondence of Office in Washington DC, 1984–1986), IISH, GIAA.
21. Bunin, memorandum, March 21, 1986, 3.
22. Greenpeace Paper, "Public Outreach," Box 5314, IISH, GIAA.
23. Elsa M. Bruton, *Banning the Burn: The Fight Against Ocean Incineration*, a report prepared for Dr. Ken Geiser, January 1989, draft, 11, Box 5180, IISH, GIAA.
24. Sally Ann Lentz and Beth Millemann, "Danger in Burn," *Baltimore Sun*, February 14, 1986, Box 5321 (Research of the Oceanic Society Concerning the Draft Regulations of the EPA Regarding Ocean Incineration, 1985–1987), IISH, GIAA.
25. Oceanic Society, "Memorandum from Sally Ann Lentz to Environmental and Public Interest Groups Concerned with Incineration at Sea," February 6, 1986, Box 5321, IISH, GIAA. See also "Joint Comments on EPA's Draft Ocean Incineration Research Burn Permit, Prepared by the Oceanic Society," February 15, 1986, 4, Box 5321, IISH, GIAA.

5. BAN THE BURN

26. Robert L. Nadeau, *The Environmental Endgame: Mainstream Economics, Ecological Disaster, and Human Survival* (New Brunswick, NJ: Rutgers University Press, 2006), 66.
27. Greenpeace, "EPA Plans to Burn PCBs 150 Miles off New Jersey and Long Island Beaches—Toxins to Be Loaded in Philadelphia," press release, January 8, 1986, 1, Box 5320, IISH, GIAA.
28. David Rapaport and Jon Lax, "Special Report Submitted by Greenpeace Regarding Waste Management's Lack of Responsibility for the Proposed Research Burn," February 25, 1986, 1, 4, Box 5320, IISH, GIAA.
29. Blue Ridge Environmental Defense League, "WMI's Record: Environmental and Contract Crimes," October 2002, https://www.bredl.org/pdf/WMI_trackrecord2002.PDF; "Alabama Waste Company Fined $1 Million," *The Lantern*, November 1, 1984; "Waste Concern Is Said to Agree to Pay Fines," *New York Times*, November 1, 1984; Bill Boyce, "$2.5 Million Fine Settles Waste Suit," *Chicago Tribune*, April 6, 1985; David Beers and Catherine Capellaro, "Greenwash!," *Mother Jones*, March–April 1991.
30. Greenpeace, "State and Local Officials Join Environmentalists' Call for EPA to Deny Permit to Burn Toxic Waste off Atlantic Shore," press release, April 25, 1986, Box 5309, IISH, GIAA.
31. Barbara Boxer to Lee M. Thomas, letter, December 18, 1985, Box 5320, IISH, GIAA.
32. "Memorandum from Sally Ann Lentz to Environmental and Public Interest Groups Concerned with Ocean Incineration: Update on Ocean Incineration Activities—EPA Regulatory Action," September 15, 1986, 1, Box 5309, IISH, GIAA. Several federal lawmakers supported the Oceanic Society's views on ocean incineration by endorsing a report titled "Joint Comments of Environmental and Other Citizen Organizations in Response to the U.S. Environmental Protection Agency's Draft Regulations on Ocean Incineration," which the society prepared on behalf of thirty-five environmental and citizen organizations and submitted to the EPA on June 28, 1985, along with another document titled "Joint Comments of Environmental and Other Citizen Organizations in Response to the U.S. Environmental Protection Agency's Proposed Ocean Incineration Research Burn Permits," which the society prepared on behalf of forty-six environmental and citizens organizations. These joint comments, according to the Oceanic Society, would have helped the EPA to formulate its new regulation. See Sally Ann Lentz to Lawrence J. Jensen, letter, September 15, 1986, 1, Box 5309, IISH, GIAA; and "Memorandum from Sally Ann Lentz to Environmental and Citizen Organizations Members of Coalition on Incineration at Sea," with attachments, July 3, 1985, 1–2, Box 5321, IISH, GIAA.
33. "Summary of Public Comments on the Proposed Research Permit for Incineration at Sea to U.S. Environmental Protection Agency, by JT&A, Contract No. 68-01-6986, Work Assignment 1-19, Battelle, Washington Environmental Program Office, 2030 M St., NW, Washington, DC 20036," 25–28, U.S. Environmental Protection Agency (EPA) National Service Center for Environmental Publications (EPA-NSCEP).
34. Tim Eichenberg and Jack Archer, "The Federal Consistency Doctrine: Coastal Zone Management and 'New Federalism,'" *Ecology Law Quarterly* 14, no. 1 (1987): 9–68.

5. BAN THE BURN

35. Arnold W. Reitze and Andrew N. Davis, "Reconsidering Ocean Incineration as Part of a U.S. Hazardous Waste Management Program: Separating the Rhetoric from the Reality," *Boston College Environmental Affairs Law Review* 17, no. 4 (1990): 734.
36. "Memorandum from Sally Ann Lentz to Environmental and Public Interest Groups Concerned with Incineration at Sea," November 27, 1985, 1. See also Greenpeace USA, telegram, February 7, 1986, 1, Box 5309, IISH, GIAA; U.S. Congress, OTA, *Ocean Incineration*, 182.
37. Peter Dykstra (Greenpeace USA), "Unseaworthy Project," letter to the editor, *Wall Street Journal*, January 24, 1986; "Blocking Waste Disposal," *Wall Street Journal*, December 31, 1985, Box 5764, IISH, GIAA.
38. Greenpeace USA to All Offices, telegram, January 13, 1985, 1, Box 5309, IISH, GIAA. See also Greenpeace, "EPA Plans to Burn PCBs 150 Miles off New Jersey and Long Island Beaches—Toxins to Be Loaded in Philadelphia," press release, January 8, 1986, 1, Box 5320, IISH, GIAA.
39. Alfonso A. Narvaez, "Issue and Debate: Decision due on Burning Toxic Wastes Off Jersey," *New York Times*, May 8, 1986, quoting Ralph J. Gorga; "Greenpeace Joins Lavallette Group in Opposing Ocean Incineration," *Ocean County Review*, January 16, 1986.
40. "200 Protest Ocean Burning of Toxic Waste," *Asbury Park Press*, February 5, 1986, including quote from Edward Herman.
41. Greenpeace USA, "Ocean Incineration of Toxic Waste—Chronology," 1985, 2 (including quote from Rolando Powell), Box 5320, IISH, GIAA.
42. U.S. EPA, "Ocean Dumping Program, Final Determination to Deny a Research Permit for the Incineration of Chemical Wastes at Sea," 4–6, Box 5854, IISH, GIAA.
43. Lisa Bunin, "Self-Evaluation," December 5, 1986, 1–2, Box 5766 (Correspondence and Documentation Concerning Ocean Incineration in Europe, 1986), IISH, GIAA.
44. "Official Greenpeace Policy on Ocean Incineration," July 1986, 1–8, Box 5766, IISH, GIAA.
45. Narvaez, "Issue and Debate"; Philip Shabecoff, "U.S. Refuses Permit to Burn Toxic Wastes in the Atlantic," *New York Times*, May 29, 1986.
46. Narvaez, "Issue and Debate" (quoting Ken Brown); John Bacon, "Oceanic Toxic Burning Sparks Massive Outcry," *USA Today*, undated, Box 5853 (Clippings Concerning Ocean Incineration, 1984–1985, 1988, and n.d.), IISH, GIAA.
47. Patrick M. Tobin, *Hearing Officer's Report on the Tentative Determination to Issue the Incineration-at-Sea Research Permit* (1986), 1–37, EPA-NSCEP.
48. Tobin, *Hearing Officer's Report*, quoted in Sally Ann Lentz to Lawrence Jensen, May 14, 1986, 1, Box 5309, IISH, GIAA.
49. U.S. EPA, "EPA Denies Permit for Ocean Incineration of Toxic Wastes," *Environmental News*, May 28, 1986, 1–2, Box 5321, IISH, GIAA.
50. "Final Decision to Deny Chemical Waste Management's Application for a Research Permit to Burn Hazardous Waste at Sea, Statement of Lawrence J. Jensen, Assistant Administrator for Water, U.S. Environmental Protection Agency," May 28, 1986, Box 5854, IISH, GIAA; Narvaez, "Issue and Debate."

5. BAN THE BURN

51. Mark Jaffe, "EPA Rejects Toxic-Burn Test Offshore. Widespread Opposition to Plan Cited," *Philadelphia Inquirer*, May 29, 1986, quoting David Rapport, Greenpeace spokesperson.
52. "Memorandum from Sally Ann Lentz to Environmental and Public Interest Groups Concerned with Incineration at Sea: Update on Ocean Incineration Activities—EPA Permit Denial," June 5, 1986, 1, Box 5309, IISH, GIAA; and "Memorandum from Sally Ann Lentz to Environmental and Public Interest Groups Concerned with Incineration at Sea: Update on Ocean Incineration Activities—EPA Regulatory Action," September 15, 1986, 1.
53. "Memorandum from Sally Ann Lentz to Environmental and Public Interest Groups Concerned with Incineration at Sea: Update on Ocean Incineration Activities—Chem Waste Sues EPA," December 23, 1986, 1–2, Box 5309, IISH, GIAA; Sally Ann Lentz and Clifton Curtis to Lee Thomas, letter, December 23, 1986, 1, Box 5309, IISH, GIAA; "Memorandum from Sally Ann Lentz to Environmental and Public Interest Groups Concerned with Incineration at Sea: Update on Ocean Incineration Activities—Chem Waste Suit Against EPA," February 4, 1987, 1–2, Box 5321, IISH, GIAA.
54. House Subcommittee on Oceanography and Full Committee Staff, "Memorandum to Members," November 12, 1987, in *Hearing Before the Subcommittee on Oceanography of the Committee on Merchant Marine and Fisheries House of Representatives, One Hundredth Congress, First Session on H.R. 737, a Bill Relating to the Incineration of Hazardous Waste, November 17, 1987*, Serial No. 100-39 (Washington, DC: U.S. Government Printing Office, 1988), 52.
55. U.S. Congress, OTA, *Ocean Incineration*.
56. Greenpeace, "Greenpeace Blasts Contradictions in Agency's Views on Ocean Incineration," press release, August 15, 1986, 1, Box 5309, IISH, GIAA.
57. William Hughes quoted in "Critics Assail Report Backing Ocean Incineration," *Raleigh Times*, August 15, 1986.
58. Walter B. Jones, Robert M. Davis, Norman D. Shumway, Norman F. Lent, Tony Coelho, Arlan Stangeland, Sherwood L. Boehlert, Gene Snyder, David O'B Martin, and Mayor R. Owens to Lee M. Thomas, Administrator, U.S. EPA, August 20, 1986, 1–3, Box 5321, IISH, GIAA.
59. Jon Hinck, Advisory Panel Member, to Howard Levenson and Richard Denison, OTA, U.S. Congress, "Revision of OTA Draft Report," July 1, 1986, 1–4, Box 5320, IISH, GIAA.
60. Lisa Bunin said that two points of Hinck's criticism in particular disturbed her. First, Hinck said that "chlorinated hydrocarbons" were among the best candidates for "on-site treatment methods," but she did not understand what type of treatment Hinck was referring to. Second, Hinck considered "the possibility that ocean incineration could play some role in the response to the present toxic waste crisis," but, according to Bunin, such an open-minded approach was in utter contrast to Greenpeace's position, which "categorically oppose[s] ocean incineration" (Lisa Bunin to Jon Hinck, letter, July 21, 1986, Box 5314, IISH, GIAA).

5. BAN THE BURN

61. "Draft Proposal Ocean Incineration Campaign 1986 (and 1987)," 1–3, Box 5766, IISH, GIAA.
62. "Draft—Ocean Incineration Campaign Issue Paper," March 6, 1986, 1, Box 5809 (Proposals and Policy Documents Concerning Ocean Incineration, 1984, 1986–1987, 1989–1992), Folder "Correspondence and Documentation, 1984, 1986–1987," IISH, GIAA.
63. "Draft—Ocean Incineration Campaign Issue Paper," 7. See also Lisa Bunin and Ron van Huizen, "Greenpeace Campaign Against Ocean Incineration," August 1987, 6, Box 5782 (Correspondence Concerning Media Coverage on Ocean Incineration, 1987, 1990)," IISH, GIAA.
64. Veronica Frank, *The European Community and Marine Environmental Protection in the International Law of the Sea: Implementing Global Obligations at the Regional Level* (Leiden, Netherlands: Brill, 2007), 312. See also Commission of the European Communities, "Proposal for a Council Directive on the Dumping of Waste at Sea," COM (83) 373, final, July 12, 1985, http://aei.pitt.edu/8833/1/8833.pdf; and Commission of the European Communities, "Reducing Pollution of the Seas: Commission Proposes Stricter Rules for Burning and Dumping," press release, July 1, 1985, P/85/86, https://ec.europa.eu/commission/presscorner/detail/en/P_85_66.
65. Commission of the European Communities, "Proposal for a Council Directive on the Dumping of Waste at Sea," 2, 18. See also Declaration of the International Conference on the Protection of the North Sea, October 31–November 1, 1984, https://www.ospar.org/site/assets/files/1239/1nsc-1984-bremen_declaration.pdf; and Daniel Suman, "Regulation of Ocean Dumping by the European Economic Community," *Ecology Law Quarterly* 18, no. 3 (1991): 559–618, esp. 583–84.
66. Ocean Combustion Service (OCS), "Waste Incineration at Sea: Lidar Measurements of the Waste Gas Plume," research under the direction of Dr. C. Weitkamp, GKSS, Geesthacht, FRG, 9/86/5, September 1986, 1, Box 5762, IISH, GIAA.
67. OCS, "Waste Incineration at Sea: Pollutants and Influence on the North Sea Ecosystem," 9/86/5, September 1986, 1, Box 5762, IISH, GIAA.
68. H. Compaan, "Incineration of Chemical Wastes at Sea: A Short Review," Dutch Government Institute for Sewage and Wastewater Treatment, Amsterdam, February 27, 1986, 1–34, https://puc.overheid.nl/rijkswaterstaat/doc/PUC_16528_31/; "Summary of the Lecture Given by Mr. H. Compaan, Toegepast Natuurwetenschappelijk Onderzoek, Delft, on the Occasion of the Press Conference Given on 27th of February 1986 in Antwerp—Environmental Impact of Chemical Waste Incineration in the North Sea," February 27, 1986, 1–3, Box 5854, IISH, GIAA.
69. J. D. Bletchly, "Polychorinated Biphenyl (PCBs) Problems in the Members States of the European Communities," February 27, 1986, 1–22, Box 5854, IISH, GIAA. Further studies in favor of ocean incineration were listed in "Fact Sheet: The Safety of Ocean Incineration," February 27, 1986, 1, Box 5854, IISH, GIAA.
70. George Welham, Managing Director, Gavin Anderson & Company, to Carole Tongue, letter, April 16, 1986, 1–2, Box 5766, IISH, GIAA.

5. BAN THE BURN

71. Barry D. Ricketts, Gavin Anderson & Company, to Kenneth D. Collins, letter, August 8, 1986, 1–2, Box 5766, IISH, GIAA.
72. Andy Booth, Greenpeace UK Office, to Lisa Bunin, telegram, "House of Lords Select Committee on the European Communities Dumping of Waste at Sea," August 4, 1986, 1, Box 5766, IISH, GIAA.
73. OCS, "Fact Sheet: The Safety of Ocean Incineration," n.d. [c. April 1986], 1–2, Box 5766, IISH, GIAA.
74. OCS, *Facts About Ocean Incineration*, booklet (October 1985), 1, Box 5766, IISH, GIAA.
75. OCS, "Ocean Incineration in a Nutshell," 9/86/o, September 1986, Box 5762, IISH, GIAA.
76. "Association of Maritime Incinerators Established," press release, October 14, 1986, Box 5772 (Correspondence Concerning the Greenpeace Viewpoint Versus That of the Association of Maritime Incinerators [AMI], 1986–1989), IISH, GIAA.
77. AMI press release quoted in "New Association of Maritime Incinerators," *Marine Pollution Bulletin* 17, no. 12 (December 1986): 520.
78. Eugene Stuik to Lisa Bunin, telegram, "Re: Meeting in Amsterdam," February 18, 1986, 1, Box 5766, IISH, GIAA. The telegram also included a tentative agenda for the meeting. See also Ban the Burn, "Minutes of the Meeting on Ocean Incineration (O.I.), Amsterdam, 26–27 February, 1986," 1–8, Box 5809, IISH, GIAA.
79. Ban the Burn, "Minutes of the Meeting on Ocean Incineration (O.I.), Amsterdam, 26–27 February, 1986," 5–7.
80. Edward W. Kleppinger and Desmond H. Bond, *Ocean Incineration of Hazardous Waste: A Revisit to the Controversy* (Washington, DC: EWK Consultants, 1985).
81. International Maritime Organization (IMO), Scientific Group on Dumping (SGD), 9th Meeting, April 28–May 2, 1986, agenda item 4: "Incineration at Sea, Ocean Incineration of Hazardous Waste: A Revisit to the Controversy," submitted by Greenpeace International, Box 5856 (Miscellaneous Documentation from the United States Concerning Waste, Land Incineration, and Ocean Incineration, 1986), IISH, GIAA.
82. Greenpeace Netherlands to Greenpeace International, telegram, "Report on SGD Meeting London; the Need for Scientific Expertise; Future Actions in Europe," May 27, 1986, 1–4, Box 5766, IISH, GIAA.
83. Sally Ann Lentz, "Environmental Effects of Ocean Incineration: An Uncertain Science," n.d. [c. 1987], 1–28, Box 5854, IISH, GIIA.
84. Lisa Bunin to Eugene Stuik, letter, July 2, 1986, 1–2, Box 5766, IISH, GIAA.
85. Lisa Bunin to David Rapaport, memorandum, June 25, 1986, 1, Box 5766, IISH, GIAA.
86. Bunin to Rapaport, June 25, 1986, 2.
87. IMO, SGD, 9th Meeting, April 28–May 2, 1986, agenda item 4: "Incineration at Sea, Ocean Incineration of Hazardous Waste: A Revisit to the Controversy."
88. "Ocean Incineration Terms of Reference Submitted to the Scientific Group on Dumping, April 28–May 2, 1986 by Greenpeace International," May 1, 1986, 1, Box 5766, IISH, GIAA.

5. BAN THE BURN

89. Clif Curtis, Oceanic Society, memorandum, "Comments/Road Map on Environmental Issues Pending at LDC 10 (13–17 October 1986)," September 27, 1986, 4, Box 5321, IISH, GIAA.
90. IMO, SGD, 9th Meeting, April 28–May 2, 1986, agenda item 4: "Incineration at Sea, Terms of Reference Proposed for an Intersessional Working Group on Incineration at Sea," Note by the Secretariat, Box 6331 (Agenda and Documents of the 8th and 9th IMO Meeting on Dumping, 1985–1986), IISH, GIAA.
91. European Toxics Campaign 1986, 1, Box 5766, IISH, GIAA. On the Helsinki Convention, see Tuomas Räsänen and Simo Laakkonen, "Cold War and the Environment: The Role of Finland in International Environmental Politics in the Baltic Sea Region," *Ambio* 36, nos. 2–3 (2007): 229–36.
92. Rik Scarce, *Eco-Warriors: Understanding the Radical Environmental Movement*, updated ed. (London: Routledge, 2006), 47–56.
93. Monika Griefahn to All Greenpeace Offices, telegram, September 10, 1986, 1, Box 5768 (Correspondence Concerning the Ocean Incinerator Vulcanus II 1986–1990, Action in Belgium v. OI 1986–1987)), IISH, GIAA.
94. Greenpeace London to All Greenpeace Offices, "Ban the Burn," September 9, 1986, 1, Box 5768, IISH, GIAA.
95. Monika Griefahn to All Greenpeace Offices, telegram, September 14, 1986, 1, Box 5768, IISH, GIAA.
96. To All Toxic Campaigners, telegram, "Film Material Confiscated," September 15, 1986, 1, Box 5768, IISH, GIAA.
97. To All Toxic Campaigners, telegram, "Vulcanus Is to Live Tuesday," September 15, 1986, and to All Toxic Campaigners, telegram, "Vulcanus," September 16, 1986, 1–2, Box 5768, IISH, GIAA.
98. Greenpeace Belgium to All Toxic Campaigners, telegram, "Confiscated Film Material Re Vulcanus 2 Action," September 30, 1986, 1–2, Box 5766, IISH, GIAA.
99. Association of Maritime Incinerators, "A Response to the Submission of Greenpeace to the Tenth Consultative Meeting of the Contracting Parties to the London Dumping Convention," October 14, 1986, 4, Box 5854, IISH, GIAA. See also IMO, Tenth Consultative Meeting of Contracting Parties to the Convention on the Prevention of Marine Pollution by Dumping of Wastes and Other Matter, October 13–17, 1986, agenda item 4: "Incineration at Sea, Ocean Incineration, Comments on LDC 10/INF.12, Submitted by the Association of Maritime Incinerators (AMI)," 1, Box 5854, IISH, GIAA.
100. Curtis, Oceanic Society, memorandum, "Comments/Road Map on Environmental Issues Pending at LDC 10 (13–17 October 1986)," September 27, 1986. Upon the request made to the LDC secretariat, the Oceanic Society went to the barricades and asked the LDC members to support more, not less, NGOs' participation. More interestingly, the society highlighted the weird position of the U.S. delegation, which kept proposing ocean incineration and other environmentally unsound practices as "capping." For the U.S. government, indeed, capping of unacceptable dredged material was part of a long-term

5. BAN THE BURN

management strategy of dredged material and should continue on an experimental basis. Thus, the U.S. delegation, too, was trying to oppose any move to declare capping and ocean incineration prohibited by the LDC. See Curtis, Oceanic Society, memorandum, "Comments/Road Map on Environmental Issues Pending at LDC 10 (13–17 October 1986)," September 27, 1986.

101. "Greenpeace Geplet Tussen Wal en Schip," *De Morgen*, September 10, 1986; "Greenpeace Houdt Vulcanus II Van De Kaai," *Gazet van Antwerpen*, September 15, 1986; "Greenpeace Belemmerde Vulcanus II de Afvaart," *Gazet van Antwerpen*, September 17, 1986; "La guerre aux déchets: Greenpeace continue," *La libre belgique*, September 16, 1986; Richard North, "Fallout Fear Over Toxic Waste Ships," *The Independent*, September 16, 1986; "Aktionen in Ost und West," *Balster AZ*, September 16, 1986; "Greenpeace Hindert Vulcanus 2 in Antwerpen," *PZC*, September 15, 1986; "Greenpeace Hindrade Avfallsskepp Gå I Hamn," *Ingekomen*, October 19, 1986.
102. "Draft Proposal Ocean Incineration Campaign 1986 (and 1987)," 1–3, Box 5766, IISH, GIAA.

6. QUITTING SMOKING

1. U.S. Congress, Office of Technology Assessment, *Ocean Incineration: Its Role in Managing Hazardous Waste*, OTA-O-313 (Washington, DC: U.S. Government Printing Office, 1986), 9.
2. "Testimony of Greenpeace before the U.S. Environmental Protection Agency Regarding the Proposed Research Permit for Ocean Incineration of Hazardous Waste by Chemical Waste Management, Inc.," January 27, 1986, prepared by Lisa J. Bunin and David Rapaport, 1, Box 5180 (Correspondence on Viewpoints and Background Information on Ocean Incineration, from the Archives of Lisa Bunin, 1989), International Institute for Social History (IISH), Greenpeace International (Amsterdam) Archives (GIAA).
3. Jonathan Symons, *Ecomodernism: Technology, Politics, and the Climate Crisis* (Cambridge: Polity Press, 2019), 3.
4. International Maritime Organization (IMO), Tenth Consultative Meeting of Contracting Parties to the Convention on the Prevention of Marine Pollution by Dumping of Wastes and Other Matter, October 13–17, 1986, agenda item 15: "Report of the Tenth Consultative Meeting," 20–21, https://www.imo.org/en/KnowledgeCentre/ConferencesMeetings/Pages/LDC-LC-Reports-of-Consultative-Meetings.aspx.
5. In London, Greenpeace called for a rapid phaseout of ocean incineration in Europe and a ban on the use of the technology in new areas. Greenpeace delegates also requested the LDC to take note of Greenpeace's own terms of reference, which had been submitted to the SGD in May 1986, and were pleased to report that their statements had been included in the general terms of reference proposed by the SGD. See "Greenpeace International Submission on Ocean Incineration to the Tenth Consultative Meeting of

6. QUITTING SMOKING

Contracting Parties London Dumping Convention, London, October 13–17, 1986," 2, Box 5854 (Reports and Press Clippings Concerning Ocean Incineration, 1985–1986), IISH, GIAA. See also IMO, Tenth Consultative Meeting of Contracting Parties to the Convention on the Prevention of Marine Pollution by Dumping of Wastes and Other Matter, October 13–17, 1986, agenda item 4, annex 8: "Incineration at Sea," 96, https://www.imo.org/en/KnowledgeCentre/ConferencesMeetings/Pages/LDC-LC-Reports-of-Consultative-Meetings.aspx, and Box 6332 (Agenda and Documents of the 10th Consultative Meeting of the IMO Concerning Ocean Incineration, 13–17 October 1986), IISH, GIAA.

6. See "Greenpeace International Submission on Ocean Incineration to the Tenth Consultative Meeting of Contracting Parties London Dumping Convention, London, October 13–17, 1986," 1–7.
7. Oceanic Society, "Environmental Effects of Ocean Incineration: An Uncertain Science, by Sally Ann Lentz, Staff Attorney, the Oceanic Society," n.d., esp. 13–14, Box 5854, IISH, GIAA.
8. IMO, Tenth Consultative Meeting of Contracting Parties to the Convention on the Prevention of Marine Pollution by Dumping of Wastes and Other Matter, October 13–17, 1986, agenda item 4: "Incineration at Sea, Adoption of Provisions for the Surveillance of Cleaning Operations Carried Out at Sea on Board Incineration Vessels," submitted by the United States, 2–4, Box 6332, IISH, GIAA.
9. Clif Curtis, Oceanic Society, memorandum, "Comments/Road Map on Environmental Issues Pending at LDC 10 (13–17 October 1986)," September 27, 1986, 5–6, Box 5321 (Research of the Oceanic Society Concerning the Draft Regulations of the EPA Regarding Ocean Incineration, 1985–1987), IISH, GIAA.
10. "Greenpeace Internal Memo: Ocean Incineration Campaign 1987—Roles and Responsibilities," prepared by Lisa Bunin, November 5, 1986, and Lisa Bunin to Alan Pickaver, memorandum, "Re: LDC/OSCOM Meeting on OI," February 8, 1987, Box 5766 (Correspondence and Documentation Concerning Ocean Incineration in Europe, 1986), IISH, GIAA.
11. Lynn Squires, "Striving for Sustainability: Paul Johnston's Contributions to Conservation Biology," *Earth Common Journal* 2, no. 1 (2012): 1–11.
12. Lisa Bunin to Toxics Campaigners, memorandum, "Re: Ocean Incineration Campaign Update," May 8, 1987, 1, Box 5785 (Miscellaneous Correspondence of Lisa Bunin Mainly on Ocean Incineration, 1984–1987), IISH, GIAA.
13. IMO, Joint London Dumping Convention (LDC) / Oslo Commission (OSCOM) Group of Experts on Incineration at Sea—2nd Meeting, April 27–May 1, 1987, agenda item 4: "Comparative Assessment of Available Alternatives to Incineration at Sea: Hazardous Waste Reduction—the Best Approach to Hazardous Waste Management," submitted by Greenpeace International, April 7, 1987, 1–15, Box 5180, IISH, GIAA.
14. Lisa J. Bunin to Brian Leslie, Conventions Committee and Toxics Campaigners, confidential memorandum, "Re: Ocean Incineration Political Game Plan," March 29, 1987, 1–2, Box 5785, IISH, GIAA.

6. QUITTING SMOKING

15. To be sure, Lisa Bunin was not satisfied with Henk Kersten's work and results. See Lisa Bunin to Henk Kersten, memorandum, July 16, 1987, 1, Box 5775 (Correspondence Concerning a Spill Study Regarding Ocean Incineration, 1987), IISH, GIAA.
16. Lisa Bunin to Toxics Campaigners, memorandum, February 13, 1987, 1, Box 5776 (Correspondence Concerning Direct Action with Regard to Ocean Incineration, 1987), IISH, GIAA.
17. IMO, Joint LDC/OSCOM Group of Experts on Incineration at Sea—2nd Meeting, April 27–May 1, 1987, agenda item 1: "Adoption of the Agenda, Draft Working Arrangements and Timetable," April 27, 1987, 1–2, Box 5774 (Correspondence and Working Group Reports on Ocean Incineration, 1987), IISH, GIAA.
18. IMO, LDC/OSCOM Working Group 1, "Effects on the Environment of Emissions from Incineration at Sea and on Land," May 1987, 1–5, Box 5774, IISH, GIAA.
19. IMO, LDC/OSCOM Working Group 2, "Report of the Working Group on Incineration Technology: Combustion and Destruction Efficiencies: Formation of New Compounds; Control Mechanism," May 1987, 1–6, Box 5774, IISH, GIAA.
20. IMO, LDC/OSCOM Working Group 3, "Report of the Working Group on Alternative Technologies for the Treatment and Disposal of Hazardous Wastes, Including Their Risks and Costs," May 1987, 1–5, Box 5774, IISH, GIAA.
21. "A Response by the Association of Maritime Incinerators to Comments by Greenpeace on the Subject of the Incineration at Sea of Organohalogen Wastes," March 2, 1987, AMI/7/G, 1–8, Box 5774, IISH, GIAA.
22. "A Response by the Association of Maritime Incinerators," 5.
23. "Comments on AMI and US Submissions to Joint LDC/OSCOM Experts Meeting on at-Sea Incineration," prepared by Sally Ann Lentz, Oceanic Society, on behalf of Friends of the Earth, International, n.d., 1–10, Box 5774, IISH, GIAA.
24. Lisa J. Bunin and Ruth Stringer, "Incineration at Sea: Unneeded Technology Poses Unacceptable Environmental Hazards," Greenpeace International Submission to the Joint LDC/OSCOM Meeting of Scientific Experts on Ocean Incineration, April 27–May 1, 1987, London, 1–22, Box 5786 (Miscellaneous Correspondence of Lisa Bunin Concerning Ocean Incineration and the London Dumping Conference, 1987–1988), IISH, GIAA. See also IMO, Joint LDC/OSCOM Group of Experts on Incineration at Sea—2nd Meeting, April 27–May 1, 1987, annex 8: "Wastes Incinerated at Sea and Some Land-Based Alternatives," 1–2, Box 5782 (Correspondence Concerning Media Coverage on Ocean Incineration, 1987, 1990), IISH, GIAA.
25. "Greenpeace International's Submission to the Oslo Commission's Working Group on Incineration at Sea," IMO, May 4–6, 1987, 1, Box 5776, IISH, GIAA.
26. Eugene Stuik to Toxic Campaigners Europe, telegram, "Re: Ocean Incineration," May 23, 1986, 1, Box 5766, IISH, GIAA.
27. A. Klingenberg, *Incineration at Sea* (Utrecht, Netherlands: Stichting Natuur en Milieu, January 1988), 6, Box 5762 (General Correspondence on Land and Ocean Incineration with Other Related Documents, 1988–1990), IISH, GIAA; Rijkswaterstaat, "Decision on Application Vulcanus I," September 17, 1987, and IMO, "Form of Approval of the

6. QUITTING SMOKING

Incineration Vessel Vulcanus I Issued by the Netherlands Authorities," December 24, 1987, Box 5771 (Correspondence Concerning the Vulcanus I and II, 1987–1989), IISH, GIAA.
28. Lisa Bunin to Alan Pickaver, telegram, "Re: Ocean Incineration," May 1, 1986, 1, Box 5766, IISH, GIAA.
29. Lisa Bunin to José Luis, letter, December 9, 1986, 1, Box 5766, IISH, GIAA.
30. "Spain Authorizes at-Sea Incineration," *Chemical Engineering*, June 22, 1987, 20, Box 5769 (Correspondence Concerning Legal Matters—Vulcanus II, September–December 1987), IISH, GIAA.
31. "Synthesis Document on Alternative Means of Disposal of Organochlorine Wastes," presented by the Netherlands, OSCOM, Cardiff, June 8–10, 1987, 1–5, esp. 4, Box 5854, IISH, GIAA.
32. "Greenpeace Campaign Against Ocean Incineration, International Political Situation," August 1987, 3–4, Box 5782, IISH, GIAA.
33. "Greenpeace International's Submission on Incineration at Sea to the Oslo Commission, Cardiff," June 8–10, 1987, 1, Box 5776, IISH, GIAA.
34. "Greenpeace Campaign Against Ocean Incineration," appendix II: "Oslo Commission Overview," August 1987, 1, Box 5782, IISH, GIAA.
35. "Greenpeace Campaign Against Ocean Incineration, Greenpeace Involvement in the Ocean Incineration Debate," August 1987, 5, Box 5782, IISH, GIAA.
36. "Greenpeace International's Submission on Incineration at Sea to the Oslo Commission, Cardiff," 5.
37. Lisa Bunin to Toxic Campaigners in OSCOM countries, telegram, June 1, 1987, 1–2, Box 5785, IISH, GIAA; Convention for the Prevention of Marine Pollution by Dumping from Ships and Aircraft, Thirteenth Meeting of the OSCOM, Cardiff, June 8–10, 1987, "Proposal for an OSCOM Decision on the Incineration of Wastes at Sea," OSCOM 13/4/1-E, Box 5786, IISH, GIAA.
38. Bunin to Toxic Campaigners, May 8, 1987, 1–2.
39. Frank Zelko, *Make It a Green Peace! The Rise of Countercultural Environmentalism* (New York: Oxford University Press, 2013), 319–20.
40. "Greenpeace Voert Actie Tegen Gifschip," *PZC*, May 29, 1987, https://www.krantenbankzeeland.nl/issue/pzc/1987-05-29/edition/0/page/17?query=; Greenpeace Germany to All Offices, telegram, "Re: Symbolic Blockade of the Tank-Motor-Ship 'Wedau' in the Rheinau Hafen (Harbour) Mannheim," May 26, 1987, 1, 2 (quote), Box 5777 (Correspondence Concerning the Action Against the Tanker Ship Wed(d)au on the Rhine with a Poisonous Cargo Destined for Ocean Incineration, 1987), IISH, GIAA.
41. Greenpeace Netherlands to All Toxics Campaigners, telegram, "Re: North Sea Update," August 12, 1987, 1, Box 5775, IISH, GIAA.
42. The joint press statement called for a ban on ocean incineration and an end to the discharge of radioactive materials and other harmful chemical pollutants in the North Sea. See Greenpeace International to All Toxics Campaigners, telegram, August 14, 1987, 1,

6. QUITTING SMOKING

Box 5768 (Correspondence Concerning the Ocean Incinerator Vulcanus II 1986–1990, Action in Belgium v. OI 1986–1987), IISH, GIAA.

43. Andy Booth to All Toxics Campaigners, telegram, "Re: O.I.," August 14, 1987, 1, Box 5768, IISH, GIAA. See also Aviv, Onderzoek en Advisering Veiligheids- en Mileuvraagstukken, "Risicoanalyse Westerschelde, Fase II, Brongerichte Maatregelen," Project 9515, January 1997, Onderzoek en Adviesgroep van Ingenieurs, "Zeeverbranding van Afval: Transportrisico's Westerschelde," Rijkswaterstaat Rapportendatabank and Aviv, Nationaal Archief, The Hague, and p. 2, Box 5775, IISH, GIAA.

44. Greenpeace Netherlands/Andy Booth to All European Offices, Greenpeace International, Greenpeace Communication, telegram, "Re: Ocean Incineration," August 17, 1987, 1, Box 5768, IISH, GIAA.

45. Greenpeace Netherlands/Andy Booth to All European Offices, Greenpeace International, Greenpeace Communication, telegram, "Re: Ocean Incineration," August 19, 1987, and Greenpeace Netherlands to All Euro-Offices, International, telegram, "Re: Updated 4 Ocean Incin. Camp.," August 21, 1987, Box 5768, IISH, GIAA. See also Greenpeace, "Greenpeace Intercepts Poisonous Waste Incineration Ship," press release (embargoed), August 21, 1987, Box 5776, IISH, GIAA.

46. Andy Booth to All Offices, Toxic Campaigners, Greenpeace International, Greenpeace Communication, telegram, "Re: Update no. 6 Ocean Incineration Action," August 8, 1987, Box 5768, IISH, GIAA.

47. Andy Booth to All Offices, Toxic Campaigners, and Major US and NewZea Land [sic] Offices, telegram, "Re: Update no. 7 Ocean Incineration," August 22, 1987, Box 5768, IISH, GIAA.

48. The activists chained to the stack and subsequently arrested were Rune Erikson from Sweden, Benoit Molineaux and Helene Bours from Belgium, Achim Loehdorf and Harold Zindler from Germany, and Heather Holve from the United States. See Andy Booth to All Offices, Toxic Campaigners, and Major US and NewZea Land [sic] Offices, telegram, "Re: Update no. 8 Ocean Incineration," August 22, 1987, Box 5768, IISH, GIAA; and Andy Booth to All Offices, International, Communication, telegram, "Re: Update no. 9 Ocean Incineration," August 22, 1987, Box 5768, IISH, GIAA.

49. Andy Booth to All European and Major Overseas Offices, Greenpeace International, Greenpeace Communication, telegram, "Re: Update no. 10 Ocean Incineration," and Andy Booth to Toxic Campaigners, All European Offices, telegram, "Re: Update no. 11 O.I.," August 22, 1987, Box 5768, IISH, GIAA.

50. Greenpeace, "Greenpeace Intercepts Poisonous Waste Incineration Ship After Twenty Four Hour High Speed Chase," press release (no embargo), August, 23, 1987, Box 5768, IISH, GIAA; Andy Booth to Toxic Campaigners, telegram, "Re: O.I.," August 24, 1987, Box 5768, IISH, GIAA; Greenpeace Netherlands to Toxic Campaigners, telegram, "Re: O.I.," August 24, 1987, Box 5768, IISH, GIAA; Paul Verschuur, "Greenpeace Ends Three-Day Protest Against Waste-Burning," Associated Press, August 24, 1987, Box 5769, IISH, GIAA.

6. QUITTING SMOKING

51. See, for example, "Greenpeace-Aksjon Mot Skip Med Gift," *Norske Argus*, August 24, 1987; "Greenpeace Oppga Aksjon," *Norske Argus*, August 25, 1987; "Greenpeace Wins Tactical Victory," *The Guardian*, August 25, 1987; "Greenpeace Storms Waste Ship," *The Times* (London), August 24, 1987; "Disposing of the Chemical Waste Issue," *The Independent*, August 24, 1987; "Misslyckad Aktion av Greenpeace," *Sydsvenska Dagbladet*, August 23, 1987; "Svensk Aktivist Stoppade Fartyg med Miljögifter," *Aftonbladet*, August 23, 1987; "Greenpeace-Aktion Abgebrocher," *Darmstädter Echo*, August 25, 1987; "Greenpeace: Gift-Fartyg Tvingades Återvända," *Sita Helsinki*, August 23, 1987; "Greenpeace in Actie tegen Giftschepen," *Haarlem Dagblad*, August 24, 1987; "Greenpeace Entert Schepen voor Verbranding Chemisch Afval," *De Volkskrant*, August 24, 1987: all in Box 5860 (Press Clippings Concerning the Action Against the Ocean Incinerators Vesta and Vulcanus, August 1987), IISH, GIAA.
52. "OCS Statement to the Murderous Threat by Greenpeace on the Incineration Vessel Vulcanus II on 24 August 1987," Box 5768, IISH, GIAA.
53. "Greenpeace Translation of an Article in a Belgian Newspaper of August 27, 1987," Box 5768, IISH, GIAA.
54. Greenpeace Denmark to Janus Hillgaard, Andy Booth, and Lisa Bunin, memorandum, "Re: Recap of the Campaign Against Spanish Ocean Incineration," June 16, 1988, 1–6, Box 5783 (Correspondence Concerning Ocean Incineration of Lisa Bunin, Janus Hillgaard, and Andy Booth, 1987–1990), IISH, GIAA.
55. Greenpeace Denmark to Hillgaard, Booth, and Bunin, June 16, 1988, 2 (quoting Spanish minister); Paul Mollet, "Spain in Talks on Burning Site," *Lloyd's List*, April 26, 1988, Box 5783, IISH, GIAA.
56. Jesus Delgado, "El buque incinerador 'Vulcanus II' zarpa de Santander tras cargar 1.000 toneladas de residuos tóxicos," *El País*, October 8, 1987; Greenpeace Denmark to Hillgaard, Booth, and Bunin, June 16, 1988, 2.
57. "Toxic Waste Ship Denies [sic] Attempt to Enter UK Port," Universal News Service, October 14, 1987, Box 5769, IISH, GIAA; "US-Owned Waste Ship Reportedly Leaves Its Intended Location Off the English Coast After Objectors Threaten to Interfere with It," Associated Press, October 11, 1987, Box 5770 (Correspondence Concerning the Ocean Incinerator Vulcanus II, 1986–1990), IISH, GIAA.
58. "Incinerator Ship Vulcanus II Is Detained at Antwerp," *Chemical Week*, October 21, 1987, 5, Box 5769, IISH, GIAA.
59. "Vulcanus and Greenpeace," Universal News Service, October 15, 1987, Box 5769, IISH, GIAA.
60. Notes of a brief meeting between Duncan Currie and Lisa Bunin, "Re: Ocean Incineration Beluga Action—Belgium," October 15, 1987, 1, Box 5769, IISH, GIAA.
61. Greenpeace Belgium to Greenpeace International—Marine Division, telegram, "Re: Beluga/Vulcanus, Action Wednesday 14 October 1987, Antwerp Harbour," October 19, 1987, 1–2, Box 5770, IISH, GIAA.
62. "Greenpeace Activists Board Incinerator Ship, Scuffle with Crew," Associated Press, October 17, 1987, Box 5769, IISH, GIAA.

6. QUITTING SMOKING

63. Civil Court of Rotterdam, Case No. 743-87, October 16, 1987, 1, Box 5769, IISH, GIAA.
64. "Danish Fishermen Reportedly Back Greenpeace Protest," Associated Press, October 18, 1987, Box 5769, IISH, GIAA.
65. Shyama Perera, "Fishermen Sabotage Waste Ship," *Manchester Guardian Weekly*, October 20, 1987, and Perera, "The World," *Los Angeles Times*, October 20, 1987, Box 5769, IISH, GIAA.
66. Greenpeace Denmark to Lisa Bunin, confidential memorandum, November 18, 1987, 1, Box 5769, IISH, GIAA.
67. The fishermen against whom the claim was filed were Jesper Larsen of the *Sand Kirk* for his role as ringleader of the action, Svend Christensen of the *Sonja Doris* for having fired distress-signal flares, and Christian Nielsen of the *Pacific* for having maneuvered in such a way as to ensnare the propeller of the *Vulcanus II*.
68. "Report on Incineration at Sea Submitted by Greenpeace International to the Scientific Group on Dumping, London Dumping Convention, London, April 10–14, 1989," Box 5180, IISH, GIAA. For the press coverage, see "Vulcanus II BLE Tauet Til Havn," *Norske Argus*, October 20, 1987; "Buque Vulcanus II a la deriva tras accidente," *El Díario*, October 20, 1987; "Fiskekuttrar Släckte Ena Avfallsbrasan," *Hufvudstadsblades*, October 20, 1987; "Fiskebåtar på Vakt Mot Giftfartyg," *Dagens Nyheter*, October 17, 1987; "Danish Fishing Nets Halt Waste Burning," *Milwaukee Journal*, October 19, 1987; "Trawlers Clash with Toxic Waste Ship," *Daily Telegraph* (London), October 19, 1987; "Trawlers and Waste Ship in Fire Hose Duel," *The Guardian*, October 19, 1987; "Danish Fishermen Spray Waste Vessel," *The Independent*, October 19, 1987; "Über 100 Schiffe Mobilisiert," *Nidwaldner Volksblatt*, October 19, 1987; "Gangway Greenpeace," *International Herald Tribune*, October 17–18, 1987; "Pollution Battle Hots Up," *Fishing News International*, November 3, 1987: all in Box 5861 (Press Clippings Concerning the Action of Danish Fishers and Greenpeace Against Vulcanus II, October 1987), IISH, GIAA.
69. OCS quoted in "Greenpeace Lie and the Vulcanus," Universal News Service, August 24, 1987, Box 5769, IISH, GIAA.
70. "Greenpeace Terrorism Disables Vulcanus," statement by Ocean Combustion Service, October 19, 1987, Box 5769, IISH, GIAA.
71. Association of Maritime Incinerators to IMO Secretariat, letter, October 21, 1987, 1, Box 5769, IISH, GIAA.
72. Lisa Bunin to Janus Hillgaard, memo, "Re: Ocean Incineration Legal Situation—Update," November 9, 1987, 1, Box 5769, IISH, GIAA; Duncan Currie to Greenpeace International, telegram, "Re: OCS," November 9, 1987, 1–2, Box 5770, IISH, GIAA.
73. Bunin to Hillgaard, November 9, 1987, 2.
74. Monika Griefhahn, Duncan Currie, and Lisa Bunin, "Meeting to Discuss the Legal Situation with Regard to Ocean Incineration," draft letter to AMI, November 10, 1987, 1, 2, Box 5770, IISH, GIAA.
75. Andrew Parnell to Duncan Currie, second draft letter to AMI, "Re: Vulcanus II Defamation," November 12, 1987, 1–2, 3, Box 5770, IISH, GIAA.

6. QUITTING SMOKING

76. Waste Management Inc., "The Greenpeace Report: A Commentary," September–October 1987, 1–29, esp. 26, Box 5769, IISH, GIAA.
77. Duncan Currie to Lisa Bunin, telegram, "Re: OCS Press Release," December 6, 1987, 1–2, Box 5770, IISH, GIAA.
78. Klaus Weber and Sara B. Soderstrom, "Social Movements, Business, and the Environment," in *The Oxford Handbook of Business and the Natural Environment*, ed. Pratima Bansal and Andrew J. Hoffman (New York: Oxford University Press, 2011), 248–68.
79. Jim Vallette to Duncan Currie, letter, November 13, 1987, 1, Box 5770, IISH, GIAA.
80. "Greenpeace Translation of an Article in a Belgian Newspaper of August 27, 1987," 1–2.
81. Jim Valette, "Author's Responses to Waste Management, Inc.'s Rebuttal (Undated) to Waste Management, Inc.: The Greenpeace Report (June 1987)," November 1987, 1–35, esp. 12, Box 5770, IISH, GIAA.
82. Sally Ann Lentz (Oceanic Society) to Environmental and Public Interest Groups Concerned with Incineration at Sea, telegram, "Re: Update on Ocean Incineration Activities, Coalition Memo, December 10, 1987, Page Two, Congressional Hearings," January 13, 1988, 2, and Lisa J. Bunin to Sally Ann Lentz, memorandum, "Re: Political Situation with Respect to Ocean Incineration," September 1, 1987, 1–2: both in Box 5784 (Correspondence of Lisa Bunin with the Oceanic Society in Washington Concerning an Analysis of Regulations Regarding Ocean Incineration in the United States, Made by the EPA, 1987–1988), IISH, GIAA.
83. Lentz to Environmental and Public Interest Groups Concerned with Incineration at Sea, telegram, January 13, 1988; Second International Conference on the Protection of the North Sea, London, November 24–25, 1987, Draft Ministerial Declaration, "Marine Incineration: Agreed Text," Box 5784, IISH, GIAA.
84. Second International Conference on the Protection of the North Sea, London, Final Declaration, November 24–25, 1987, Box 5854, IISH, GIAA. The Final Declaration reaffirmed the necessity of using common Environmental Quality Objectives and Uniform Emission Standards and decided "to phase-out the dumping in the North Sea of industrial wastes by 31 December 1989" and to "reaffirm the status of marine incineration as an interim method of waste treatment."
85. Lentz to Environmental and Public Interest Groups Concerned with Incineration at Sea, telegram, January 13, 1988.
86. Lentz to Environmental and Public Interest Groups Concerned with Incineration at Sea, telegram, January 13, 1988, 2, quoting *Inside EPA*.
87. Elsa M. Bruton, *Banning the Burn: The Fight Against Ocean Incineration*, report prepared for Dr. Ken Geiser, January 1989, draft, 15, Box 5180, IISH, GIAA; Lisa Bunin to All Toxics Campaigners, telegram, "Re: Return of OI Vessels, Apollo I & II, Built in the USA but Never Used," October 6, 1989, Box 5408 (Miscellaneous Correspondence of Lisa Bunin, 1987–1990), IISH, GIAA; U.S. EPA to Interested Congressional Members and Staff, memorandum, "Re: Ocean Incineration," February 1, 1988, 1, Box 5781 (Correspondence Concerning the Hamburg Meeting on Ocean Incineration, 1988), IISH, GIAA.

6. QUITTING SMOKING

88. Lisa Bunin, "Ocean Incineration: Banned in the North Sea and Bound for Developing Nation? Or Ocean Incineration in Europe: A Lesson to Be Learned from Not to Be Replicated [sic]," draft, December 23, 1987, 2, Box 5836 (Documentation on Waste Management International [WMI]), IISH, GIAA; Lisa J. Bunin, "Ocean Incineration in Europe: A Lesson to Be Learned but Not Replicated," *IUCN Bulletin* 19, nos. 1–3 (December 1987): 9–10, Box 5836, IISH, GIAA.
89. IMO, Scientific Group on Dumping (SGD)—11th Meeting, April 25–29, 1988, agenda item 13: "Consideration and Adoption of the Report," 1–3, Box 5127 (Documents Concerning the Ocean Incineration, the London Dumping Conference, and the Scientific Group on Dumping, 1988), IISH, GIAA.
90. Leo Spaans, "Incineration of Chlorinated Waste at Sea: Process and Emissions," Marien eco publication 1, Marien Eco Consult, 1987.
91. IMO, SGD—11th Meeting, April 25–29, 1988, agenda item 2: "Consideration of the Report of the Joint LDC/OSCOM Group of Experts Incineration at Sea; Incineration at Sea—an Interim Method of Waste Disposal," submitted by Denmark, and agenda item 2: "Consideration of the Report of the Joint LDC/OSCOM Group of Experts Incineration at Sea, List of Substances About Which Doubts Exist as to Their Incinerability," submitted by the Federal Republic of Germany, Box 5127, IISH, GIAA.
92. Sean Moloney, "Denmark Lashed on Chemical Waste Plan," *Lloyd's List*, April 26, 1988, and Sean Mac Connell, "Spanish to Burn Waste at Sea, Fishermen Claim," *Irish Times*, April 27, 1988, Box 5783, IISH, GIAA.
93. Greenpeace Denmark to Hillgaard, Booth, and Bunin, June 16, 1988, 6.
94. Janus Hillgaard to Lisa Bunin and Andy Booth, telegram, "Re: Campaign Against Spanish Ocean Incineration," June 16, 1988, 1, Box 5783, IISH, GIAA.
95. Janus Hillgaard to Lisa Bunin, Andy Booth, and Martin Besieux, telegram, "Re: Danish Action Finished," June 17, 1988, 1, Box 5783, IISH, GIAA.
96. Janus Hillgaard to Greenpeace Europe, telegram, "Re: Greenpeace Action in Santander Against the Presence of Vulcanus II," June 18, 1988, Box 5787 (Miscellaneous Correspondence of Lisa Bunin Concerning Ocean Incineration and the London Dumping Conference, 1987–1988 [sic]), IISH, GIAA.
97. Janus Hillgaard to European Toxics Campaigners, letter, "Very Brief Summary on the European Situation," March 1, 1988, 3, Box 5781, IISH, GIAA.
98. Greenpeace Denmark to Hillgaard, Booth, and Bunin, June 16, 1988, 4.
99. Janus Hillgaard to Greenpeace Offices, telegram, "Re: Ocean Incineration," March 2, 1988, 1, Box 5783, IISH, GIAA; "Greenpeace Campaign Against Ocean Incineration, International Political Situation," August, 1987, 2, Box 5782, IISH, GIAA; IMO, SDG—11th Meeting, April 25–29, 1988, agenda item 2: "Consideration of the Report of the Joint LDC/OSCOM Group of Experts Incineration at Sea; Incineration at Sea—an Interim Method of Waste Disposal," 2; IMO, SGD—11th Meeting, April 25–29, 1988, agenda item 2: "Consideration of the Report of the Joint LDC/OSCOM Group of Experts Incineration at Sea, Draft Resolution on the Phasing Out of Incineration at Sea," submitted by Denmark, 1–3, Box 5781, IISH, GIAA. In Denmark, a huge majority in

6. QUITTING SMOKING

Parliament instructed the government to call for a ban on ocean-incineration permits starting December 31, 1981. Such a national political statement was translated into an internationally binding agreement during the OSCOM meeting in Lisbon on June 22–24, 1988; see Greenpeace Denmark to Hillgaard, Booth, and Bunin, June 16, 1988, 3 (quoting Dutch delegation).

100. Greenpeace, internal memo, "Position of the [Dutch] Government," n.d., 1–4, Box 5783, IISH, GIAA; Lisa Bunin, "Overview Situation in the Netherlands," n.d., 1–2, Box 5781, IISH, GIAA.
101. Janus Hillgaard to Lisa Bunin, telegram, "Re: FRG/B/NL," February 7, 1988, 1–2, Box 5781, IISH, GIAA.
102. IMO, SGD—11th Meeting, April 25–29, 1988, agenda item 2: "Consideration of the Report of the Joint LDC/OSCOM Group of Experts Incineration at Sea, Comments on Section 2 of the Report (LDC/OSCOM/IAS 2/9)," submitted by Greenpeace International, and annex 2: "Ocean Incineration Theory: An Inaccurate Representation of the Practice," prepared by Lisa J. Bunin and Janus Hillgaard, 1–3, Box 5127, IISH, GIAA.
103. IMO, SGD—11th Meeting, April 25–29, 1988, agenda item 2: "Consideration of the Report of the Joint LDC/OSCOM Group of Experts Incineration at Sea, 'A Discussion of Ocean Incineration for Chlorinated Waste' and 'Chlorinated Environmental Pollutants Emitted from Ocean Incineration Stacks,'" submitted by Greenpeace International, Box 5127, IISH, GIAA; Greenpeace, "Greenpeace Calls Existing Ocean Incineration Theory Invalid," press release (embargoed until April 1, 1988), April 6, 1988, 1, Box 5094–95 (The Denouncement of Greenpeace Against Ocean Incineration for the London Dumping Conference, 1988), IISH, GIAA.
104. Greenpeace Communication to Greenpeace Offices, telegram, "Re: OI Press Release, May 2, 1988, Greenpeace Research Denounces Ocean Incineration: LDC Scientists Ask for Details of New Evidence," May 2, 1988, 1–2, Box 5094–95, IISH, GIAA.
105. In their presentation, Bunin and Hillgaard defined ocean incineration as "an archaic method." See Greenpeace, "Greenpeace Calls Existing Ocean Incineration Theory Invalid," 1; Greenpeace Communication to Greenpeace Offices," May 2, 1988, 1–2.
106. Studsvik Energiteknik reports quoted in Greenpeace, "Scientists Consider Worldwide Future of Ocean Incineration: Greenpeace Releases Further Evidence of Pollution from North Sea Burns," press release, April 25, 1988, emphasis in original, Boxes 5783 and 5854, IISH, GIAA.
107. Lars Strömberg quoted in IMO, SGD—11th Meeting, April 25–29, 1988, agenda item 2: "Consideration of the Report of the Joint LDC/OSCOM Group of Experts Incineration at Sea, Comments on Section 2 of the Report (LDC/OSCOM/IAS 2/9)," and annex 2: "Ocean Incineration Theory," 4.
108. "Report on Incineration at Sea Submitted by Greenpeace International to the Scientific Group on Dumping, London Dumping Convention, London, April 10–14, 1989," Box 5180, IISH, GIAA.
109. Janus Hillgaard to Lisa Bunin, telegram, "Re: AMI Press Release, Studsvik Reports," April 14, 1988, 1–2, Box 5772 (Correspondence Concerning the Greenpeace Viewpoint

6. QUITTING SMOKING

Versus That of the Association of Maritime Incinerators [AMI] 1986–1989), IISH, GIAA; Greenpeace Belgium to Janus Hillgaard and Lisa Bunin, telegram, "Re: Press Release AMI, Greenpeace Is Drawing a Smoke-Screen Around Ocean Incineration," April 13, 1988, 1–2, Box 5772, IISH, GIAA.

110. Hillgaard to Bunin, April 14, 1988, 1–2.
111. "Greenpeace's Reply to AMI's Press Release, Studsvik Reports," n.d., 4, Box 5772, IISH, GIAA.
112. The paper was originally titled "Transport Mechanism of Organochlorine Residues After Incineration to Air, Water Microlayer, and Organism," Department of Ecology, Ecotoxicology, University of Lund, S-223, 62 Lund, summary 1, Box 5836, IISH, GIAA. The study was then published as Anders Södergen, Per Larsson, Johan Knulst, and Carina Bergqvist, "Transport of Incinerated Organochlorine Compounds to Air, Water, Microlayer, and Organisms," *Marine Pollution Bulletin* 21, no. 1 (1990): 18–24.
113. Lars Strömberg, "A Discussion of Ocean Incinerators for Chlorinated Waste," Studsvik Arbetsrapport-Technical Note, EP-88/10, February 2, 1988, 1–22, Box 5836, IISH, GIAA.
114. Joachim Lohse, "Ocean Incineration of Toxic Wastes: A Footprint in North Sea Sediments," *Marine Pollution Bulletin* 19, no. 8 (1988): 366–71; Robin J. Law, Colin R. Allchin, and John Harwood, "Concentrations of Organochlorine Compound in the Blubber of Seals from Eastern and North-eastern England, 1988," *Marine Pollution Bulletin* 20, no. 3 (1989): 110–14; Roy E. Lewis and Andrew M. Riddle, "Sea Disposal: Modelling Studies of Waste Field Dilution," *Marine Pollution Bulletin* 20, no. 3 (1989): 124–29.
115. IMO, Twelfth Consultative Meeting of Contracting Parties to the Convention on the Prevention of Maine Pollution by Dumping of Wastes and Other Matters, October 30–November 3, 1989, agenda item 7: "Matters Relating to the Incineration of Wastes and Other Matters at Sea, Clean Technology/Source Reduction Contact and Reference List to Facilitate the Phase-out of Ocean Incineration," submitted by Greenpeace International, Beverly Thorpe, and Lisa J. Bunin, October 30, 1989, introduction, 1, Box 5762, IISH, GIAA. See also "Greenpeace Meeting on Ocean Incineration/Kommunekemi, Denmark," August 24, 1989, Box 5762, 1–3.
116. "The Thirteenth Consultative Meeting of the Contracting Parties to the London Dumping Convention (LDC), October 29–November 2, 1990," press brief, October 29, 1990, 1, Box 5762, IISH, GIAA.
117. Lisa Bunin to Ricardo Wilson-Grau, telegram, "Re: Special Projects," June 21, 1990, 1, Box 5787, IISH, GIAA.
118. "The Thirteenth Consultative Meeting of the Contracting Parties to the London Dumping Convention (LDC)," press brief, October 29, 1990, 2.

CONCLUSION

1. Author's interview with Sue Ann Fruge, January 2022.
2. Elsa Bruton, "Banning the Burn: The Fight Against Ocean Incineration," appendix to Ken Geiser, "Halogenated Hydrocarbons: Recommendations for a Phase Out Strategy,"

a project completed for Greenpeace International, Tufts University, Medford, MA, May 1989, Box 5762 (General Correspondence on Land and Ocean Incineration with Other Related Documents, 1986–1990), 18, International Institute for Social History (IISH), Greenpeace International (Amsterdam) Archives (GIAA); "1989 Joint GPUSA and GPA Toxics Campaign Proposal," Box 5308 (Minutes of Meetings with Other Related Documents, 1989–1990), 2, IISH, GIAA; Michael Stewart Foley, *Front Porch Politics: The Forgotten Heyday of American Activism in the 1970s and 1980s* (New York: Hill & Wang, 2013).
3. Sherilyn MacGregor, *Beyond Mothering Earth: Ecological Citizenship and the Politics of Care* (Vancouver: University of British Columbia Press, 2006), 5. On women homemakers' radicalism, see also Emily E. LB. Twarog, *Politics of the Pantry: Housewives, Food, and Consumer Protest in Twentieth-Century America* (New York: Oxford University Press, 2017).
4. W. Jeffrey Bolster, "Opportunities in Marine Environmental History," *Environmental History* 11, no. 3 (2006): 567–97; Helen M. Rozwadowski, "The Promise of Ocean History for Environmental History," *Journal of American History* 100, no. 1 (2013): 136–39.
5. Fruge interview, January 2022.
6. Stephen J. Macekura and Erez Manela, introduction to *The Development Century: A Global History*, ed. Stephen J. Macekura and Erez Manela (New York: Cambridge University Press, 2018), 8–9.
7. David Schlosberg, *Environmental Justice and the New Pluralism: The Challenge of Difference for Environmentalism* (New York: Oxford University Press, 2002), 159–60.
8. Robert Gordon, "'Shell No!': OCAW and the Labor–Environmental Alliance," *Environmental History* 3, no. 4 (1998): 460–87; Kenneth Gould, Tammy Lewis, and J. Timmons Roberts, "Blue–Green Coalitions: Constraints and Possibilities in the Post 9-11 Political Environment," *Journal of World-Systems Research* 10, no. 1 (2004): 91–116; Victor Silverman, "Sustainable Alliances: The Origins of International Labor Environmentalism," *International Labor and Working-Class History* 66 (2005): 118–35; Matthew Hilton, "Social Activism in an Age of Consumption: The Organized Consumer Movement," *Social History* 32, no. 2 (2007): 121–43; Brian Mayer, *Blue–Green Coalitions: Fighting for Safe Workplaces and Healthy Communities* (Ithaca, NY: ILR Press, 2009); Dan Jakopovich, "Uniting to Win: Labor–Environmental Alliances," *Capitalism Nature Socialism* 20, no. 2 (2009): 74–96; Thomas Estabrook, *Labor-Environmental Coalitions: Lessons from a Louisiana Petrochemical Region* (Boca Raton, FL: CRC Press, 2018); Jean-Baptiste Paranthoën, "From Opposition to the GATT to the Creation of AMAPs: The Birth of a Movement That Has Become Representative of the SSE," *RECMA* 356, no. 2 (2020): 50–67; Paul Adler, *No Globalization Without Representation: U.S. Activists and World Inequality* (Philadelphia: University of Pennsylvania Press, 2021); Shana Bernstein, "'True Sustainability': An Environmental, Worker, and Consumer History of Organic Strawberry Farming in 1990s California," *Agricultural History* 95, no. 3 (2021): 500–531.
9. United Nations (UN) General Assembly, *Report of the United Nations Conference on Environment and Development (Rio de Janeiro, 3–14 June 1992)*, annex I: Rio Declaration on Environment and Development, esp. principle 6, https://www.un.org/en/development

CONCLUSION

/desa/population/migration/generalassembly/docs/globalcompact/A_CONF.151_26_Vol.I_; White House, "Executive Order 12898 of February 11, 1994: Federal Actions to Address Environmental Justice in Minority Populations and Low-Income Populations," *Federal Register* 59, no. 32 (February 16, 1994), https://www.archives.gov/files/federal-register/executive-orders/pdf/12898.pdf.

10. Charles Lee, "Evaluating Environmental Protection Agency's Definition of Environmental Justice," *Environmental Justice* 14, no. 5 (2021): 332–37.
11. Vivien Hamilton and Brinda Sarathy, "Introduction: Toxicity, Uncertainty, and Expertise," in *Inevitably Toxic: Historical Perspectives on Contamination, Exposure, and Expertise*, ed. Brinda Sarathy, Janet Brodie, and Vivien Hamilton (Pittsburgh: University of Pittsburgh Press, 2019), 3–21.
12. Arnold W. Reitze and Andrew N. Davis, "Reconsidering Ocean Incineration as Part of a U.S. Hazardous Waste Management Program: Separating the Rhetoric from the Reality," *Environmental Affairs Law Review* 17, no. 4 (1990): 688–798, esp. 690.
13. U.S. Congress, Office of Technology Assessment, *From Pollution to Prevention: A Progress Report on Waste Reduction—Special Report*, OTA-ITE-347 (Washington, DC: U.S. Government Printing Office, 1987), 19, https://repository.library.georgetown.edu/bitstream/handle/10822/708371/8709.PDF?sequence=1&isAllowed=y.
14. "Chemical Industry Waste Down 20 Percent, CMA Says," International Environmental Report (BNA) 361, July 8, 1987.
15. Iris Borowy, "Hazardous Waste: The Beginning of International Organizations Addressing a Growing Global Challenge in the 1970s," *Worldwide Waste: Journal of Interdisciplinary Studies* 2, no. 1 (2019): 11; National Intelligence Council and DCI Environmental Center, *The Environmental Outlook in Russia* (1999), https://fas.org/irp/nic/environmental_outlook_russia.html; National Toxics Campaign Fund, *The National Toxics Campaign: Some Reflections, Thoughts for the Movement* (1993), https://www.ejnet.org/ej/ntcf.pdf.
16. European Environment Agency, *Environment in the European Union at the Turn of the Century* (Copenhagen: European Environment Agency, June 1999), chap. 3.7, "Waste Generation and Management," 203–27, https://www.eea.europa.eu/publications/92-9157-202-0/3.7.pdf/view.
17. Max Liboiron, *Pollution Is Colonialism* (Durham, NC: Duke University Press, 2021).
18. Laura A. Pratt, "Decreasing Dirty Dumping? A Reevaluation of Toxic Waste Colonialism and the Global Management of Transboundary Hazardous Waste," *William & Mary Environmental Law and Policy Review* 35, no. 2 (2011): 581–623; Amitav Ghosh, *The Great Derangement: Climate Change and the Unthinkable* (Chicago: University of Chicago Press, 2016).
19. Finn Arne Jørgensen, "The Backbone of Everyday Environmentalism: Cultural Scripting and Technological Systems," in *New Natures: Joining Environmental History with Science and Technology Studies*, ed. Finn Arne Jørgensen, Dolly Jørgensen, and Sara B. Pritchard (Pittsburgh: University of Pittsburg Press, 2013), 69–86; Michael Lewis, "And All Was Light? Science and Environmental History," in *The Oxford Handbook of Environmental History*, ed. Andrew C. Isenberg (New York: Oxford University Press, 2014),

CONCLUSION

207–26; Nikolaos Voulvoulis and Mark A. Burgman, "The Contrasting Roles of Science and Technology in Environmental Challenges," *Critical Reviews in Environmental Science and Technology* 49, no. 12 (2019): 1079–106; William San Martín, ed., "Technology and Expertise," Environment and Society Portal, https://www.environmentandsociety.org/arcadia-collection/technology-and-expertise.

20. Timothy O'Riordan and Andrew Jordan, "The Precautionary Principle in Contemporary Environmental Politics," *Environmental Values* 4, no. 3 (1995): 191–212; Philippe H. Martin, "'If You Don't Know How to Fix It, Please Stop Breaking It!' The Precautionary Principle and Climate Change," *Foundations of Science* 2 (1997): 263–92; Martin Ashley, "Science: An Unreliable Friend to Environmental Education?," *Environmental Education Research* 6, no. 3 (2000): 269–80; Brian Mayer, Phil Brown, and Meadow Linder, "Moving Further Upstream: From Toxics Reduction to the Precautionary Principle," *Public Health Reports* 117, no. 6 (2002): 574–86; David Vanderzwaag, "The Precautionary Principle and Marine Environmental Protection: Slippery Shores, Rough Seas, and Rising Normative Tides," *Ocean Development & International Law* 33, no. 2 (2002): 165–88; Kerry H. Whiteside, *Precautionary Politics: Principle and Practice in Confronting Environmental Risk* (Cambridge, MA: MIT Press, 2006); Douglas A. Kysar, *Regulating from Nowhere: Environmental Law and the Search for Objectivity* (New Haven, CT: Yale University Press, 2010).

21. Iris Borowy, "Negotiating Environment: The Making of the OECD Environment Committee and the Polluter Pays Principle, 1968–1972," in *The OECD and the International Political Economy Since 1948*, ed. Matthieu Leimgruber and Matthias Schmelzer (Cham, Switzerland: Palgrave Macmillan, 2017), 311–34; Daniel H. Henning and William R. Mangun, *Managing the Environmental Crisis: Incorporating Competing Values in Natural Resource Administration* (Durham, NC: Duke University Press, 1989); Bernardo Heisler Motta, "The Community's Right to Know About Toxic Spills in American Legislation," in *Engaging with Environmental Justice: Governance, Education, and Citizenship*, ed. Matthew Cotton and Bernardo Heisler Motta (Leiden, Netherlands: Brill, 2011), 11–22.

22. Matthew J. Hoffmann, *Ozone Depletion and Climate Change: Constructing a Global Response* (Albany: State University of New York Press, 2005); Brian J. Gareau, *From Precaution to Profit: Contemporary Challenges to Environmental Protection in the Montreal Protocol* (New Haven, CT: Yale University Press, 2013); Michael Mortimore, *Adapting to Drought: Farmers, Famines, and Desertification in West Africa* (New York: Cambridge University Press, 1989); Roy H. Behnke and Michael Mortimore, eds., *The End of Desertification: Disputing Environmental Change in the Drylands* (Berlin: Springer, 2016); Stephan Schwartzman, Ane Alencar, Hilary Zarin, and Ana Paula Santos Souza, "Social Movements and Large-Scale Tropical Forest Protection on the Amazon Frontier: Conservation from Chaos," *Journal of Environment & Development* 19, no. 3 (2010): 274–99; Neville Brown, *History and Climate Change: A Eurocentric Perspective* (London: Routledge, 2001); Spencer R. Weart, *The Discovery of Global Warming: Revised and Expanded Edition* (Cambridge, MA: Harvard University Press, 2008); Rupert Darwall, *The Age of Global Warming: A History* (London: Quartet Books, 2013);

CONCLUSION

David Ciplet, J. Timmons Roberts, and Mizan R. Khan, *Power in a Warming World: The New Global Politics of Climate Change and the Remaking of Environmental Inequality* (Cambridge, MA: MIT Press, 2015); Sverker Sörlin and Melissa Lane, "Historicizing Climate Change: Engaging New Approaches to Climate and History," *Climatic Change* 151 (2018): 1–13; Ann Byers, *Reuse It: The History of Modern Recycling* (New York: Cavendish Square, 2018); Erica Cirino, *Thicker Than Water: The Quest for Solutions to the Plastic Crisis* (Washington, DC: Island Press, 2021).

23. U.S. Environmental Protection Agency (EPA), Office of Pollution Prevention and Toxics, "1990 Toxics Release Inventory: Public Data Release, May 1992 (Updated September 1992)," 1992, U.S. EPA National Service Center for Environmental Publications (EPA-NSCEP).

24. U.S. EPA, "2011 Toxics Release Inventory: National Analysis Overview," 2011, https://www.epa.gov/sites/default/files/documents/complete_2011_tri_na_overview_document.pdf.

25. Marquita K. Hill, *Understanding Environmental Pollution*, 3rd ed. (New York: Cambridge University Press, 2010), 351; UN Environment Programme, "UN Report: Time to Seize Opportunity, Tackle Challenge of E-Waste," January 24, 2019, https://www.unep.org/news-and-stories/press-release/un-report-time-seize-opportunity-tackle-challenge-e-waste; UN Environment Programme, International Environmental Technology Centre, "Future E-Waste Scenarios," 2019, https://www.unep.org/ietc/resources/publication/future-e-waste-scenarios?_ga=2.164204287.1565843659.1643899846-274067025.1642234194; UN Environment Programme, "The Growing Footprint of Digitalization," November 22, 2021, https://www.unep.org/resources/emerging-issues/growing-footprint-digitalisation.

26. The World Counts, "Household Hazardous Waste Statistics," updated 2023, https://www.theworldcounts.com/stories/household-hazardous-waste-statistics.

27. Jolanta Dabrowska, Radosław Stodolak, Marcin Sobota, Małgorzata Swiader, Paweł Borowski, Andrzej Moryl, Ewa Kucharczak, et al., "Marine Waste: Sources, Fate, Risks, Challenges, and Research Needs," *International Journal of Environmental Research and Public Health* 18, no. 433 (2021): 1–17.

28. Elisabet Van Wymeersch, Thomas Vanoutrive, and Stijn Oosterlynck, "Unravelling the Concept of Social Transformation in Planning: Inclusion, Power Changes, and Political Subjectification in the Oosterweel Link Road Conflict," *Planning Theory & Practice* 21, no. 2 (2020): 200–217.

29. Syed Hasan, "Public Awareness Is Key to Successful Waste Management," *Journal of Environmental Science and Health, Part A: Toxic/Hazardous Substances and Environmental Engineering* 39, no. 2 (2004): 483–92.

30. Travis Wagner, "Hazardous Waste: Evolution of a National Environmental Problem," *Journal of Policy History* 16, no. 4 (2009): 306–31.

31. Lisa Bunin to OI [Ocean-Incineration] Campaigners, letter, November 17, 1989, Box 5761 (General Correspondence on Land and Ocean Incineration with Other Related Documents, 1986–1990), IISH, GIAA.

CONCLUSION

32. Dave Rapaport, Pat Costner, Ken Gelser, and John Mitchell to Peter Bahout, GPUSA [Greenpeace USA] Board of Directors, "Re: Draft GPUSA Proposal 1990, Long Term Goals," August 15, 1989, Box 5308, IISH, GIAA. On environmental democracy as participation, inclusion, deliberation, and social engagement, see Michael Mason, *Environmental Democracy: A Contextual Approach* (London: Routledge, 1999); and Joshua C. Gellers and Chris Jeffords, "Toward Environmental Democracy? Procedural Environmental Rights and Environmental Justice," *Global Environmental Politics* 18, no. 1 (2018): 99–121.
33. Dayna Nadine Scott, Jennie Haw, and Robyn Lee, "'Wannabe Toxic-Free?' From Precautionary Consumption to Corporeal Citizenship," *Environmental Politics* 26, no. 2 (2017): 322–42.

INDEX

accidents, environmental, 27–28, 47, 59–60, 79–80; in Bhopal, 17–18, 131; hazardous waste and, 131, 168–69; at Love Canal, 11, 46, 75, 131; Waste Management and, 139

accountability: enforcement and, 32; EPA and, 104–5; military-industrial complex and, 68

Ackerman, David, 120–23

activism, 173–74; in communities, 82–85, 100, 134–35, 171; direct actions and, 18, 193; of Fruge, 1–2, 4; gender and, 13–14, 75–76, 186; Greenpeace and, *155*; incinerator vessels and, *167*, *174*, 258n48; intersectionality of, 84–85; opposition to ocean incineration and, 122–29; terrorism and, 175–78

Agent Orange, 45–46; destruction efficiency for, 51–53; Johnston Atoll and, 49, *50*, 51–52; TCDD and, 49; Vietnam War and, 49, 68

agreements, international, 15, 21–22, 30, 37

Air Force, U.S., 49–52, 225n39

air pollution, 36, 98

Alexander, Robin, 87

allies, of U.S., 54, 102

alternatives, to ocean incineration, 79, 85–86, 95, 163, 183; chlorinolysis as, 33; dismissal of, 110–12; disposal and, 11, 217n69; land-based, 38, 56, 66–67

Álvarez Larrauri, Ramon, 119

AMI. *See* Association of Maritime Incinerators

anger, in communities, 8, 185

anti-ocean-incineration campaigns, 84–85, 124–28, 133, 166, 192; in Europe, 83, 150, 180; Oceanic Society and, 77–78, 151; press and, 136; strategy of, 9, 16–17, 72, 84–85, 102, 160–61

antitoxics campaign, 12, 72, 75–76, 123, 190; environmental justice and, 245n84; women in, 13–14

Antwerp, Belgium, 34, 121, 148, 150, 181; blockade in, 154, 156, 168–69, 172

Apollo I and *Apollo II* (ships), 65, 103

INDEX

Army, U.S., 47–48
Association of Maritime Incinerators (AMI), 149; Greenpeace and, 175–76, 183; LDC/OSCOM meeting and, 163–64
atmospheric pollution, 42, 75, 110, 118, 169, 190
At-Sea Incineration, Inc., 65, 128
authority, of OSCOM, 30

ban, on ocean incineration, 262n19; campaigns for, 150, 192–93; consensus and, 117, 179; Greenpeace and, 83, 146, 254n5; international, 55–56, 179; LDC and, 178–79; OSCOM and, 178–79; press and, 257n42
Ban the Burn campaign, 17–18, 184; Bunin and, 133–36, 150–52; direct actions for, 153–54, 155, 156–57; education and, 150–52; as environmental democracy, 191–93; EPA and, 142–43, 157; grassroots initiatives and, 185–86; Greenpeace and, 135–36, 137, 153–54, 155, 156–57; Oceanic Society and, 136, 138; press and, 141–42, 154, 156; protests and, 131–32, 149–50; public hearings and, 134–35, 149–52, 252n78
Basel Convention, 190
Belgium, Antwerp, 34, 121, 148, 150, 181
Beluga (ship), 125, 172
Bennett, Deryl, 115
benzene, 23, 33–34, 210n8
Bhopal, India, accident in, 17–18, 131
Biden, Joseph, 19, 118
Biglane, Kenneth, 59
biochemical weapons, U.S., 45–47, 220n6
bipartisan opposition, to ocean incineration, 117
blockades, 125; in Antwerp, 154, 156, 168–69, 172; Europe, 168–73; of incinerator vessels, 169–74; OCS and, 170; press and, 168–70
Blum, Barbara, 60

Bond, Desmond H., 74; *Ocean Incineration of Hazardous Waste*, 120–23, 151
Boxer, Barbara, 62, 96, 229n94; public hearings and, 109, 117
Brotman, Joan, 87, 91; public hearings and, 115, 118
Brown, William, 116
Brownsville, Texas, 91–93, 96–97, 99
buffer, oceans as, 33, 36, 73
Bunin, Lisa, 80–81, 96, 182, 263n105; Ban the Burn and, 133–36, 150–52; Kersten and, 162, 256n15; LDC/OSCOM meeting and, 161–62, 165–66; on protests, 176; on regulations, 144–46, 179, 250n60
burns: mismanagement of, 53; observation of, 81, *82*; of PCBs, 62–63, 164–65; permits for, 34, 58, 65–66, 94, 106, 171; problems and, 34–35; test, 62, 73
Bush, George H. W., 61–62
business interests. *See* commercial interests

California, 42, 78, 103, 109–10; activism in, 85
campaigns: anti-ocean-incineration, 72, 77–78, 83–85, 124–28, 133, 192; antitoxics, 12–13, 72, 75–76, 123, 190; for ban, 150, 192–93; Ban the Burn, 17–18, 184; funding for, 89–90, 136
Cantabrian Sea, direct actions in, 165, 171
Canter, Howard, 115–16
"capping," 253n100
Carruth, Donald, 127–28
Carter, Jimmy, 56, 60
CBWs. *See* chemical and bacteriological weapons
CCMS. *See* Committee on the Challenges of Modern Societies
CEQ. *See* White House Council on Environmental Quality
Chafee, John, 113–14
challenges: to EPA, 1, 92–93, 100, 112–13, 143–44; to military-industrial complex, 14

272

INDEX

chemical and bacteriological weapons (CBWs), 46, 49; Nixon and, 47, 222n12; U.S. Army and, 47–48
chemical industry, U.S., 24–25, 103, 121, 159
chemical warfare agents, 45, 220n6; criticism of, 46–47, 221n8
Chemical Waste Management (CWM), 64, 73, 127, 178; Greenpeace and, 176–77; insurance and, 138; OCS and, 61; permits for, 96, 128, 132–33, 139, 143–44; public hearings and, 116, 139; studies of, 62–63; test burns of, 108–9
chemical weapons, Vietnam War and, 221n8
chlorinated hydrocarbons, 25–26, 34, 145, 182; treatment of, 250n60
chlorinolysis, 33, 50, 163
claims, by EPA, 67, 114–15, 127–28
class, pollution and, 21, 86, 88, 133
Clean Air Act (1970), 27, 49–50
Clean Water Act (1972), 27
climate crisis, 19, 190
Clinton, Bill, 188
coalitions, 18, 133–34, 187; GCCPH, 17, 86–88; Gulf Initiative and, 89; Northwest Indiana Coalition for the Environment, 86
coastal communities, 17, 19, 103
coastal zone management (CZM), 140
coastal zones, in LDC, 216n61
colonialism, U.S. and, 5, 119, 189
combustion efficiency, 42, 220n102; of Agent Orange, 53; destruction efficiency and, 58–59, 182
commercial interests, 61–62, 185, 187; EPA and, 80–81, 97, 109, 128, 138–39, 227n68; Gorsuch and, 67–68; Greenpeace on, 80–81; scientific data and, 74
Committee on the Challenges of Modern Societies (CCMS), 38
communities: activism in, 82–85, 100, 134–35, 171; anger in, 8, 185; coastal, 17, 19, 103; concerns of, 115, 135–36, 141–43; dismissal of, 92–93, 97–98, 107, 109, 185; marginalized, 2, 13, 19, 85, 187–88; pollution in, 86–87
Compaan, H., 148
Comprehensive Environmental Response, Compensation, and Liability Act (1980) (Superfund), 67–68
compromise: LDC and, 31, 38–39, 56; strategy and, 17–18, 133–34
concentrations, of pollution, 53, 177, 182, 225n39; PCBs and, 26, 57, 60–61, 81, 183, 220n102
concerns: community, 115, 135–36, 141–43; international, 54–55, 121, 184; for jobs, 84
Conference on the Human Environment (1972), UN (Stockholm Conference), 6; ocean dumping and, 28–29; U.S. and, 214n49, 214n51
confidentiality, secrecy and, 45–46, 66
Congress, U.S., 11, 98–99; investigations by, 101–2; legislation of, 21–22, 113, 190, 241n35; OTA of, 108; public hearings of, 1–2, 109–19; scrutiny from, 67, 109
consensus, 28–29, 72, 79, 120, 126; ban and, 117, 179; in science, 31–32, 146, 159–60
controversy, 13, 187; ocean incineration and, 46, 58, 101–3, 150–52; studies and, 62–63, 123, 150–51
Convention for the Prevention of Marine Pollution by Dumping from Ships and Aircraft (1972) (Oslo Convention on Dumping), 6–7, 214n53, 226n56; debate and, 39; western Europe and, 29–30
Convention for the Prevention of Marine Pollution from Land-Based Sources (Paris Convention), 6–7, 214n53
Convention for the Protection of the Marine Environment of the North-East Atlantic (OSPAR Convention), 122, 244n65
Convention on the Prevention of Marine Pollution by Dumping of Wastes and Other Matter (1972). *See* London Dumping Convention

273

INDEX

cost, of waste disposal, 11, 33, 48, 63, 211n32
Costle, Douglas, 57, 60
Cousteau, Jacques-Yves, 78
Cousteau, Jean-Michel, 110
Cousteau Society: independent studies and, 78; public hearings and, 110–11
crisis: climate, 19, 190; of hazardous waste, 9–15, 21, 32–33, 59–60, 183
criticism, 128; of chemical warfare agents, 46–47, 221n8; of EPA, 66–67, 118–19, 125–26, 134; of Greenpeace, 156; of ocean incineration, 75–76
CWM. *See* Chemical Waste Management
CZM. *See* coastal zone management

dangers, 73, 211n32; CBWs and, 48–49; of PCBs, 212n35
data, 39, 52, 90–91; EPA and, 58–59, 65–66, 114–15; NGOs and, 76; SAB and, 105–6; scientific, 55–56, 71
Davies, Tudor, 121, 126
debate, 94, 116–17, 129; in Europe, 147–50; LDC and, 38–40, 161; OSCOM meeting and, 165–66; Oslo Convention on Dumping and, 39; public, 71–72; reports and, 120–21
de Leon, Ramon, 92
democracy, environmental, 14, 72, 84–91, 269n32
demonstrations. *See* protests
Denmark, 165; fishing boats of, 173, *174*, 175, 260n67; Greenpeace and, 152–53; opposition to ocean incineration of, 38, 124–25, 180–81, 262n99
Department of Defense, U.S., 26, 47
deregulation, 4; Reagan and, 46. *See also* regulation, of hazardous waste disposal
designation of sites, for ocean incineration, 41, 109–10
destruction efficiency, 42, 55, 105–6; for Agent Orange, 51–53; combustion efficiency and, 58–59, 182; Lentz on, 136

dioxin, 73–74, 183; Agent Orange and, 51–52; Gulfport and, 49; Johnston Atoll and, 52–53; PCBs and, 37; TCDD and, 49, 225n39
direct actions, 18, 193; for Ban the Burn, 153–54, *155*, 156–57; in Cantabrian Sea, 165, 171; of Greenpeace, 124–25, 166, *167*, 168–73, *174*. *See also* protests
discrimination, 2, 102
dismissal: of alternatives to ocean incineration, 110–12; of communities, 92–93, 97–98, 107, 109, 185
disposal, of hazardous waste, 10, 12, 26, 68–69; alternatives for, 11, 217n69; CBWs and, 47–49; chlorinolysis and, 33, 50; cost of, 11, 33, 48, 63, 211n32; in Gulf of Mexico, 73, 86; land-based, 25, 32–33, 189; regulation of, 43–44
distributive justice, 15
Dow Chemical, 24, 210n8
dumping, 189; illegal, 60–61, 118; ocean, 10, 21, 26, 212n37; permits for, 30–32; race and, 13–14
DuPont, 24

Earth Day, 26–27
education: Ban the Burn and, 150–52; GCCPH and, 90–91; Greenpeace and, 82–83, 123–24, 135, 153; OCS and, 147–49
EEC. *See* European Economic Community
efficiency, of ocean incineration, 36–37, 182; destruction and combustion, 42, 58–59, 220n102
EIS. *See* Environmental Impact Statement
Eisenhower, Dwight D., 45–46
emissions, 36–37, 53, 151, 161; dioxin in, 51, 73–74; microlayer and, 74, 152, 163; monitoring of, 58–59, 105–6, 108, 146, 181–82; of PCBs, 181–82
enforcement: accountability and, 32; LDC and, 217n66; ocean dumping and, 29

INDEX

environmental accidents, 27–28, 47, 59–60, 79–80
environmental consciousness, 7, 15–16, 192
environmental democracy, 14, 72, 84–91, 269n32; Ban the Burn as, 191–93
environmental history, 4, 202n7
Environmental Impact Statement (EIS), 140; EPA and, 117; Gulf of Mexico and, 35–36, 41, 219n98; permits and, 110
environmentalism, 177, 212n40; global approaches to, 16–17, 202n7, 203n9; military-industrial complex and, 26–27; politics and, 101–2, 126–27, 190, 239n1–2; reduction of hazardous waste and, 183, 192–93
environmental justice, 8, 13–15, 102, 187; antitoxics campaigns and, 245n84; EPA and, 188; GCCPH and, 126
environmental organizations, 42–43, 100, 186, 219n98; antitoxics campaign of, 72, 75–76; strategy of, 102, 122. *See also specific organizations*
environmental policy, of U.S., 4–5, 7, 186–87, 193
Environmental Protection Agency (EPA), U.S., 5, 27, 77, 190, 211n23; accountability and, 104–5; Ban the Burn and, 142–43, 157; challenges to, 1, 92–93, 100, 112–13, 143–44; claims of, 67, 114–15, 127–28; commercial interests and, 80–81, 97, 109, 128, 138–39, 227n68; criticism of, 66–67, 118–19, 125–26, 134; data and, 58–59, 65–66, 114–15; EIS and, 117; GCCPH and, 89–90, 93–94; Gulf Initiative and, 89; international regulations and, 6, 112, 136; investigations by, 139; Johnston Atoll and, 51–54, 225n39; market analysis and, 63–64; mistrust of, 110–11, 118, 128; MPRSA and, 34; neoliberalism and, 62, 186–87; Office of Environmental Justice of, 188; Office of Water of, 94, 96–97, 107–8; OPPE of, 106–9; permits from, 57,
95–97, 103, 117, 132–33, 136, 138; public hearings and, 91–93, 109–14; public opinion and, 179; Reagan and, 68; regulations and, 49–50, 58–59, 144–46; reorganization of, 62; SAB of, 74–75; scientific research and, 34, 57–58; site designation and, 41, 109–10; studies and, 11, 101–2; support for ocean incineration of, 1, 71–73, 101–2, 107–8; transparency of, 97, 109–10, 127–28; *Vulcanus I* and, 218n78
environmental safety, 16–17, 131, 134
environmental science, 101, 239n1
EPA. *See* Environmental Protection Agency
ethylene, 23–24, 26
Europe, 132; anti-ocean-incineration campaigns in, 83, 150, 180; blockades in, 168–73; debate in, 147–50; direct action in, 153–54, *155*, 156–57; permits in, 150; phase out of ocean incineration in, 254n5. *See also* western Europe
European Economic Community (EEC), 147–49
e-waste, 191
ExxonMobile, 24

farmers, 84, 88
findings, 52–54, 107–8, 183; of public hearings, 95–96; of SAB, 105; of SGD, 58–59, 161
fishers, 15, 84, 88, 115; protests and, 173, *174, 175*, 260n67
flag state, port-loading state and, 32, 39–40, 217n66
frameworks, for regulation, 30, 66
Fruge, Sue Ann, *3*, 86–87, 185; activism of, 1–2, 4; public hearings and, 93–94, 115
funding, 24, 128; for campaigns, 89–90, 136; taxpayer, 138

gas scrubbing, 36, 73, 90, 177–78
GCCPH. *See* Gulf Coast Coalition for Public Health
gender, activism and, 13–14, 75–76, 186

275

INDEX

Germany, ocean incineration and, 33–34, 74
Gielen, Freddy, 127
Gimello, Richard, 114–15
global approaches, to environmentalism, 16–17, 202n7, 203n9
Gorsuch, Anne, 62, 109; commercial interests and, 67–68
Grader, Zeke, 115
grassroots initiatives, 4, 17, 87–88; Ban the Burn and, 185–86
Greenpeace, 17–18, 77, 78–79, 84, 126; AMI and, 175–76, 183; ban on ocean incineration and, 83, 146, 254n5; Ban the Burn and, 135–36, 137, 153–54, 155, 156–57; *Beluga* of, 125, 172; burn observation of, 81, 82; on commercial interests, 80–81; criticism of, 156; CWM and, 176–77; Denmark and, 152–53; direct actions of, 124–25, 166, 167, 168–73, 174; education and, 82–83, 123–24, 135, 153; independent studies and, 168–69, 183; LDC/OSCOM meeting and, 162–63; legal action and, 173, 175; neoliberalism and, 182–83; ocean incineration ban and, 83; OCS and, 175–76; public hearings and, 111–12, 118; reports of, 123, 150–51; SACSA and, 122–23; scientific data and, 151–52; strategy of, 79, 156–57; UN observer status and, 83; in Western Europe, 83
groups, transnational, 187–88, 231n4
Gulf Coast Coalition for Public Health (GCCPH), 1, 17, 86–88; education and, 90–91; environmental justice and, 126; EPA and, 89–90, 93–94; public hearings and, 115
Gulf Initiative, 89
Gulf of Mexico, 57; disposal in, 73, 86; EIS and, 35–36, 41, 219n98; Incineration Site in, 3, 34, 35, 41–42, 73; organochlorines in, 55; PCBs and, 120
Gulfport, Mississippi: Agent Orange and, 51; dioxin and, 49; TCDD in, 52

Hamblin, Jacob Darwin, 32
Harris, Paul, 5, 214n49
hazardous waste, 43–44, 63–64, 124, 192; crisis of, 9–15, 21, 32–33, 59–60, 183; disposal of, 10, 12, 26, 68–69; environmental accidents and, 131, 168–69; industrial, 211n23; production of, 8–9, 22, 65–66, 107–8, 115–16, 143, 188–89; reduction of, 66, 82, 90, 118, 144–46; transportation of, 36, 139; treatment of, 11, 36, 79, 107, 163, 250n60; U.S. policy for, 2, 98–99
health, 2, 5, 75, 192; human, 25, 53–54, 89, 115–18, 169–70, 181; of oceans, 28, 132, 144, 190–91; public, 12–13, 60–61, 81, 89, 115; reports and, 105–8, 145, 181, 190; of workers, 15, 77–78, 87, 172, 175
hearings, public, 17, 237n83
heavy metals, 24–25
Heinemann, Geert, 127, 149
Herz, Michael, 111
Hillgaard, Janus, 83–84, 182, 263n105
Hinck, Jon, 80–81, 92, 96; Ravan and, 103–5; on regulations, 144–46, 250n60
history, environmental, 4, 202n7
House Committee on Merchant Marine and Fisheries, U.S., 1, 144; Subcommittee on Fisheries and Wildlife Conservation and the Environment of, 93, 98; Subcommittee on Oceanography, Fisheries, and Wildlife Conservation of, 178; Subcommittee on Oceanography of, 117–19; Subcommittee on the Environment of, 178
House Subcommittee on Environment, Energy, and Natural Resources, U.S., 109–13
Hughes, William, 144
human health, 25, 53–54, 89, 115–18, 169–70, 181
hydrochloride, 36

INDEX

illegal dumping, 60–61, 118
IMCO. *See* Inter-Governmental Maritime Consultative Organization
IMO. *See* International Maritime Organization
impartiality, in regulations, 32, 40, 46, 81, 102, 186–87
imperialism, 5–6; law of the sea and, 215n57
inaccuracy, of monitoring, 71–72, 120–21
incineration. *See* burns
incinerator vessels, 33, 108; activism and, *167*, *174*, 258n48; *Apollo I* and *Apollo II*, 65, 103; blockades of, 169–74; inspection of, 63; Netherlands and, 34, 39–40; *Vesta*, 74, 150, 154, 169, *174*; *Vulcanus I*, 34, 38, 138, 164–65; *Vulcanus II*, 73, 76, 81, *82*, *167*
independent studies, 79, 160; Cousteau Society and, 78; Greenpeace and, 168–69, 183; LDC/OSCOM meeting and, 151–52
India, Bhopal, 17–18, 131
Indiana, activism in, 86
industrial hazardous waste, 211n23
industrialization, of oceans, 189
industrial liquid waste, pollution and, 28
industry, 177; chemical, 24–25, 103, 121, 159; petrochemical, 21, 24–26, 189; of waste management, 61–62, 103
initiatives, 89; grassroots, 4, 17, 87–88. *See also* campaigns
inspection, of incinerator vessels, 63
insurance, ocean incineration and, 114, 138
interests: commercial, 61–62, 185, 187; national, 29, 39–40, 187; public and private, 16
Intergovernmental Conference on the Marine Pollution by Dumping of Wastes and Other Matter (1972), 30
Inter-Governmental Maritime Consultative Organization (IMCO), 42–43, 54

international agreements, 15, 21–22, 30, 37
international ban, on ocean incineration, 55–56, 179
international concerns, 54–55, 121, 184; Mexico and, 119–20
International Convention for the Prevention of Pollution from Ships (MARPOL) (1973), 6, 184, 214n53
International Convention for the Prevention of Pollution of the Sea by Oil (1954), 27
International Maritime Organization (IMO), 12, 182
international negotiations, 12, 83
international perspective, on pollution, 28–29
international regulations, 38, 146, 179, 213n43; EPA and, 6, 112, 136; U.S. policy and, 6, 102
international waters, ocean incineration and, 22, 37, 169
intersectionality, of activism, 84–85
investigations: by EPA, 139; by U.S. Congress, 101–2
investment, in ocean incineration, 56–57, 227n68

Japan, 34, 41, 54, 79
Jensen, Lawrence, 142–43
job concerns, 84
Johnson, Ayana Elizabeth, 18–19
Johnston, Paul, 162
Johnston Atoll: Agent Orange and, 49, 50, 51–52; dioxin and, 52–53; EPA and, 51–54, 225n39
Jordan, Elke, 127
justice: distributive, 15; environmental, 8, 13–15, 102, 187; social, 2, 87

Kersten, Henk, 162, 256n15
Kissinger, Henry, 30–31
Kleppinger, Edward W., 67, 120–23, 151
Kulungowski, Sarah, 86–87, 90

277

INDEX

land-based disposal, 25, 32–33, 189; as alternative, 38, 56, 66–67
landfills, 10–11, 21, 211n32
Lantos, Tom, 112–13
lawmakers, reports from, 125–26, 248n32
law of the sea, 12, 31, 37; imperialism and, 215n57
LDC. *See* London Dumping Convention
LDC/OSCOM meeting, 160, 164; Bunin and, 161–62, 165–66; Greenpeace and, 162–63; independent studies and, 151–52; report of, 165–66
Lee, Don, 125–26
legacies, translocal movements and, 18, 186, 192
legal action, Greenpeace and, 173, 175
legislation, on ocean incineration, 113, 190, 241n35; Greenpeace and, 125; MPRSA, 28, 34, 49–50
legislation, on pollution, 21–22; Clean Air Act, 27, 49–50; Clean Water Act, 27; Resource Recovery Act, 27; Superfund, 67–68; Water Pollution Control Act, 27; WQIA, 27
Lentz, Sally Ann, 115, 151, 164; on destruction efficiency, 136
liability, ocean incineration and, 67, 98, 114, 118, 151
Lizarraga, José, 119–20
London Dumping Convention (LDC), 6, 30, 32, 122; ban on ocean incineration and, 178–79; coastal zones in, 216n61; compromise and, 31, 38–39, 56; enforcement and, 217n66; meetings of, 38–42, 160, 164, 220n102; SGD of, 58–59, 120–21, 150–51, 161; U.S. and, 40–42
Love Canal, New York, 11, 46, 75, 131
Lower Rio Grande Valley, U.S., 1–2, 86, 185

marginalized communities, 2, 13, 19, 85, 187–88

Marine Protection, Research, and Sanctuaries Act (1972) (MPRSA), 28, 34, 49–50; Ocean Incineration Research Bill of, 113
Maritime Administration, U.S., 65, 124, 128
market analysis, EPA and, 63–66
MARPOL. *See* International Convention for the Prevention of Pollution from Ships
Martini, Edwin, 49
McAllister, Steve, 81, *82*
meetings, of LDC and OSCOM, 38–42, 160–64, 220n102. *See also* public hearings
Mexico, 102; international concerns and, 119–20
microlayer, of oceans, 108; emissions and, 74, 152, 163; scientific research on, 75; studies on, 100, 183
Mikulski, Barbara, 117
military exemption, 31, 216n59
military-industrial complex, 9, 14, 16; accountability and, 68; environmentalism and, 26–27
mismanagement, of burns, 53
mistrust, of EPA, 110–11, 118, 128
mobilization, 8, 17, 85, 185; Bunin and, 133
monitoring, of ocean incineration, 35–36, 40, 190; emissions and, 58–59, 105–6, 108, 146, 181–82; inaccuracy of, 71–72, 120–21; *Vulcanus I* and, 52–53
Montague, Peter, 127–28
moratorium, on ocean incineration, 113, 241n35
movements: for environmental justice, 8, 13–15, 102, 187; translocal, 4, 9, 82–84, 184. *See also* campaigns
MPRSA. *See* Marine Protection, Research, and Sanctuaries Act
Murphy, Thomas, 59

national interests, of U.S., 29, 39–40, 187; Kissinger and, 30–31; secrecy and, 45–46

INDEX

national security, of U.S., 56–57
NATO. *See* North Atlantic Treaty Organization
natural resources, 5, 91, 100, 214n53
necessity, of ocean incineration, 45, 65–66, 101, 115–16; reduction of hazardous waste and, 165–66
negotiations, 30, 161, 169; international, 12, 83
neoliberalism, 4; EPA and, 62, 186–87; Greenpeace and, 182–83; Reagan and, 69
Netherlands, 24, 147–48, 150, 180–81; incinerator vessels and, 34, 39–40; ocean incineration sites of, 41, 164–65, 168; protests and, 156, 169–70, 172–73; regulations and, 55, 74
New Jersey, 85, 114–15, 140; accidents in, 131; public hearings in, 141
New York, Love Canal, 11, 46, 75, 131
NGOs. *See* nongovernmental organizations
Nixon, Richard, 30–31; CBWs and, 47, 222n12; CEQ and, 28; Vietnam War and, 214n49, 223n27
nongovernmental organizations (NGOs), 76, 156; Oceanic Society and, 253n100; translocal movements and, 7–8, 16–17
North Atlantic, 132–33; Incineration Site in, *43*, *104*, 219n101; OSPAR Convention and, 122, 244n65
North Atlantic Treaty Organization (NATO), 38
North Carolina, Sunny Point Military Ocean Terminal, 48
North Sea, 153, 164–65; PCBs in, 148; test burns in, 81, *82*
Northwest Indiana Coalition for the Environment, 86

observer status, UN, Greenpeace and, 83
Ocean Combustion Service (OCS), 34, 127; blockades and, 170; CWM and, 61; education and, 147–49; Greenpeace and, 175–76; permits for, 57

ocean dumping, 10, 21, 26, 212n37; of CBWs, 48; enforcement and, 29; Stockholm Conference and, 28–29
Oceanic Society, 15, 18, 234n31; anti-ocean-incineration campaigns and, 77–78, 151; Ban the Burn and, 136, 138; LDC and, 122; NGOs and, 253n100; public hearings and, 111; research and, 77
ocean incineration. *See specific topics*
Ocean Incineration of Hazardous Waste (Kleppinger and Bond), 120–23, 151
Ocean Incineration Research Bill, of MPRSA, 113
ocean incineration sites, 12, 39, 131–32, 180; designation of, 41, 109–10; Gulf of Mexico as, *3*, 34, *35*, 41–42, 73; of Netherlands, 41, 164–65, 168; North Atlantic, *43*, *104*, 219n101
oceans, 5, 9, 143; as buffer, 33, 36, 73; health of, 28, 132, 144, 190–91; industrialization of, 189; microlayer of, 108
OCS. *See* Ocean Combustion Service
Office of Environmental Justice, EPA, 188
Office of Policy, Planning, and Evaluation, EPA (OPPE), study of, 106–9
Office of Technology Assessment (OTA), 108
Office of Water, of EPA, 94, 96–97, 107–8
OPPE. *See* Office of Policy, Planning, and Evaluation, EPA
opposition, to ocean incineration, 7–9, 91–92, 98–100, *99*, 102, 146; activism and, 122–29; bipartisan, 117; campaigns for, 72, 77–78, 83–85, 124–28, 133, 192; communities and, 84–85; of Denmark, 38, 124–25, 180–81, 262n19; polycentric, 126–29; strategy of, 159; support and, 116–17, 121–22; Texas and, 125–26
organochlorines, 25–26, 186; in Gulf of Mexico, 55
organohalogen compounds, 33, 54, 56, 74, 91, 146

INDEX

OSCOM. *See* Oslo Commission

Oslo Commission (OSCOM), 12; authority of, 30; ban on ocean incineration and, 178–79; debate and, 165–66; meetings of, 160–64; SACSA of, 122–23

Oslo Convention on Dumping. *See* Convention for the Prevention of Marine Pollution by Dumping from Ships and Aircraft

OSPAR Convention. *See* Convention for the Protection of the Marine Environment of the North-East Atlantic

OTA. *See* Office of Technology Assessment

Otto, Elizabeth, 111–12

Pacer HO, 51–52

Paris Convention. *See* Convention for the Prevention of Marine Pollution from Land-Based Sources

PCBs. *See* polychlorinated biphenyls

Pennsylvania, Philadelphia, 135, 140–42

permits, for burns, 34, 58, 65–66, 94, 106, 171; for CWM, 96, 128, 132–33, 139, 143–44; EIS and, 110; from EPA, 57, 95–97, 103, 117, 132–33, 136, 138; in Europe, 150; for OCS, 57; public opinion and, 95–96

permits, for dumping, 30–32

Perrault, Michele, 85

petitions, 94, 141

petrochemical industry, 21, 189; toxic by-products of, 24–26; U.S., 10, 43–44; World Wars I and II and, 23, 210n8

phase out, of ocean incineration, 147, 166, 178, 183–84, 261n84; in Europe, 254n5

Philadelphia, Pennsylvania, 135, 140–42

Pickaver, Alan, 162

PICs. *See* products of incomplete combustion

plastics, 21, 23–25, 31, 191

POHCs. *See* principal organic hazardous constituents

policy, U.S., 192, 203n8; environmental, 4–5, 7, 186–87, 193; for hazardous waste, 2, 98–99; International regulations and, 6, 102

politics, environmentalism and, 101–2, 126–27, 190, 239n1–2

pollution: air, 36, 98; atmospheric, 42, 75, 110, 118, 169, 190; class and, 21, 86, 88, 133; in communities, 86–87; concentrations of, 53, 177, 182, 225n39; heavy metals and, 24–25; industrial liquid waste and, 28; international perspective on, 28–29; legislation on, 21–22; soil contamination and, 49, 52–53, 88; stack gas and, 42, 51, 57–59, 66, 74, 151–52; on *Vulcanus I*, 53–54

polycentric opposition, to ocean incineration, 126–29

polychlorinated biphenyls (PCBs), 12, 65; burns of, 62–63, 164–65; concentrations of, 26, 57, 60–61, 81, 183, 220n102; dangers of, 212n35; dioxin and, 37; emissions of, 181–82; Gulf of Mexico and, 120; in North Sea, 148; in studies, 81

port-loading state, flag state and, 32, 39–40, 217n66

power, of U.S., 4–5, 43–44

precaution, 102–4, 117, 183, 190

press, 192; anti-ocean-incineration campaigns and, 136; bans and, 257n42; Ban the Burn and, 141–42, 154, 156; blockades and, 168–70; on ocean incineration, 82, 97–98, 127; protests and, 260n68

principal organic hazardous constituents (POHCs), 37, 57

private interests, public and, 16

problems, with ocean incineration, 22, 36–37; burns and, 34–35

production: of hazardous waste, 8–9, 22, 65–66, 107–8, 115–16, 143, 188–89; of weapons, 23, 210n8

INDEX

products of incomplete combustion (PICs), 37, 57, 105–6, 121
profits, from ocean incineration, 16, 61, 65, 77–78
protests, 27, 99, 135–36, 180; Ban the Burn and, 131–32, 149–50; blockades as, 125, 168–69; Bunin on, 176; direct actions as, 18, 193; fishers and, 173, *174*, 175, 260n67; in Mexico, 120; Netherlands and, 156, 169–70, 172–73; press and, 260n68; *Vulcanus II* and, 123–24, 171–73
public comments, 95, 133
public debate, 71–72
public health, 12–13, 60–61, 81, 89, 115; GCCPH and, 1, 17, 86–88
public hearings, 17, 72, 140, 178, 237n83; Ban the Burn and, 134–35, 149–52, 252n78; CWM and, 116, 139; EPA and, 91–93, 109–14; findings of, 95–96; Fruge and, 93–94, 115; Greenpeace and, 111–12, 118; in New Jersey, 141; public opinion and, 142; of U.S. Congress, 1–2, 109–19; waste management industry and, 115–16
public interests, private and, 16
public opinion, 7, 128–29, 184, 188; Ban the Burn and, 132; EPA and, 179; permits and, 95–96; public hearings and, 142

race, dumping and, 13–14
Rapaport, David, 138, 153
Ravan, Jack E., 66, 94, 112–13; findings and, 95–96; Hinck and, 103–5
Reagan, Ronald, 61–62, 109; deregulation and, 46; EPA and, 68; neoliberalism and, 69
reduction, of hazardous waste, 66, 82, 90, 118, 144–46; environmentalism and, 183, 192–93; necessity of ocean incineration and, 165–66; research on, 84, 113, 162–63
regulation, of hazardous waste disposal, 43–44; frameworks for, 30, 66; ocean incineration and, 114, 203n8; by western Europe, 38–39
regulations, 80, 248n32; Bunin on, 144–46, 179, 250n60; EPA and, 49–50, 58–59, 144–46; impartiality in, 32, 40, 46, 81, 102, 186–87; international, 38, 146, 179, 213n43; Netherlands and, 55, 74; secrecy and, 16; U.S. and, 186–87
reorganization, of EPA, 62
reports: of Ackerman, 120–23; of Greenpeace, 123, 150–51; health and, 105–8, 145, 181, 190; from lawmakers, 125–26, 248n32; of LDC/OSCOM meeting, 165–66
research: Oceanic Society and, 77; on reduction of hazardous waste, 84, 113, 162–63; scientific, 189–90; test burns and, 108–9
Resource Recovery Act (1970), 27
rifts, of U.S., 54–55, 145–46
risk assessment, in studies, 94, 106–7, 110, 117
Royal Dutch Shell, 34, 57
Rubin, Alan, 94, 97
Ruckelshaus, William, 67–68
Runnels, Gayle, 87
Russell, Milton, 106–7
Ryan, Cathy, 111–12

SAB. *See* Science Advisory Board, EPA
SACSA. *See* Standing Advisory Committee for Scientific Advice, OSCOM
safety, 67, 74, 105, 118, 149–51; environmental, 16–17, 131, 134; of workers, 15, 77–78, 87, 172, 175
Schatzow, Steven, 94–96, 112–13
science, 183–84; consensus in, 31–32, 146, 159–60; environmental, 101, 239n1
Science Advisory Board, EPA (SAB), 74–75; burn permits and, 94–95; data and, 105–6
scientific data, 55–56, 71; commercial interests and, 74; Greenpeace and, 151–52

281

INDEX

Scientific Group on Dumping (SGD), 120–21, 150–51; findings of, 58–59, 161; support for ocean incineration of, 179–81
scientific research, 189–90; EPA and, 34, 57–58; on microlayer, 75
scrutiny, from U.S. Congress, 67, 109
seawater, 1, 35–36, 86
secrecy: confidentiality and, 45–46, 66; regulations and, 16
Senate Subcommittee on Environmental Pollution of the Committee on Environment and Public Works, 113–16
Senate Subcommittee on Merchant Marine and Tourism, U.S., 59
SGD. *See* Scientific Group on Dumping
Shabecoff, Philip, 97
Shell, *See* Royal Dutch Shell
ships. *See* incinerator vessels
Sierra Club, 85
Sirius (ship), 168–69, 171–72
sites, for ocean incineration, 12, 39, 131–32, 180; designation of, 41, 109–10
social justice, 2, 87
soil contamination, 49, 52–53, 88
solidarity, 15, 88
sovereign immunity, 31
Spaans, Leo, 179–82
Spain, 171–72, 180
stack gas, 42, 51, 57–59, 66, 74, 151–52; gas scrubbing and, 36, 73, 90, 177–78
Stammer, Larry, 98
Standard Oil, 23
Standing Advisory Committee for Scientific Advice, OSCOM (SACSA), 122–23
Stockholm Conference. *See* Conference on the Human Environment (1972), UN
strategy, 192–93; of anti-ocean-incineration campaigns, 9, 16–17, 72, 84–85, 102, 160–61; compromise and, 17–18, 133–34; of environmental organizations, 102, 122; grassroots, 185–86; of Greenpeace, 79, 156–57; of opposition to ocean incineration, 159; of support for ocean incineration, 160; of transnational groups, 72
Stringer, Ruth, 162, 164
Strömberg, Lars, 182
studies, 33, 38, 81; controversy and, 62–63, 123, 150–51; of CWM, 62–63; EPA and, 11, 101–2; independent, 78–79, 151–52, 160, 168–69, 183; on microlayer, 100, 183; of OPPE, 106–9; risk assessment in, 94, 106–7, 110, 117; Studsvik Energiteknik and, 181–83; support for ocean incineration and, 62–63
Studsvik Energiteknik, 181–83
subsidies, 5, 65; for waste management, 46
Sunny Point Military Ocean Terminal, North Carolina, 48
Superfund. *See* Comprehensive Environmental Response, Compensation, and Liability Act
support, for ocean incineration, 6–7, 33–36, 64, 68–69, 106; AMI and, 163–64; EPA and, 1, 71–73, 101–2, 107–8; Europe and, 132; opposition and, 116–17, 121–22; of SGD, 179–81; strategy of, 160; studies and, 62–63; by U.S., 44, 59–60, 63–64, 161

taxpayer funding, 138
TCDD. *See* tetrachlorodibenzo-p-dioxin
technical aspects, of ocean incineration, 51, 93, 163, 203n8; flaws and, 8, 22, 122–23, 182
temperature control, 37, 40–41, 98, 121, 163
terrorism, activism and, 175–78
test burns, 55, 62, 73; of CWM, 108–9; North Sea, 81, *82*
tetrachlorodibenzo-p-dioxin (TCDD), 49, 225n39; in Gulfport, 52
Texas, 185; Brownsville, 91–93, 96–97, *99*; opposition to ocean incineration and, 125–26

282

INDEX

Thomas, Lee, 106, 139, 144
Tobin, Patrick, 142–43
toxic by-products, of petrochemical industry, 24–26
toxic waste. *See* hazardous waste
Train, Russell, 28–29, 31–32, 214n51
translocal movements, 4, 9, 82–84, 184; legacies and, 18, 186, 192; NGOs and, 7–8, 16–17
transnational groups, 187–88, 231n4; strategy of, 72
transparency, in policy, 54, 93, 138, 192; EPA and, 97, 109–10, 127–28
transportation, of hazardous waste, 36, 139; EIS and, 140
treaties, violation of, 102, 119–20
treatment, of hazardous waste, 11, 36, 79, 107, 250n60; chlorinolysis and, 33, 50, 163

UN. *See* United Nations
Union Carbide, 17–18, 131
unions, 135, 154, 171; environmental justice and, 14–15
United Kingdom, petrochemical industry in, 24
United Nations (UN): observer status and, 83; Stockholm Conference of, 6
United States (U.S.): Air Force of, 49–52, 225n39; allies of, 54, 102; Army of, 47–48; biochemical weapons of, 45–47, 220n6; chemical industry of, 24–25, 103, 121, 159; colonialism of, 5, 119, 189; Congress of, 11, 98–99; Department of Defense, 26, 47; environmental policy of, 4–5, 7, 186–87, 193; hazardous waste policy of, 2, 98–99; House Committee on Merchant Marine and Fisheries, 1, 144; House Subcommittee on Environment, Energy, and Natural Resources, 109–13; LDC and, 40–42; Lower Rio Grande Valley, 1–2, 86, 185; Maritime Administration, 65, 124, 128; national interests of, 29, 39–40, 187; national security of, 56–57; petrochemical industry of, 10, 43–44; power of, 4–5, 43–44; regulations and, 186–87; rifts of, 54–55, 145–46; Senate Subcommittee on Merchant Marine and Tourism, 59; Stockholm Conference and, 214n49, 214n51–52; support for ocean incineration by, 44, 59–60, 63–65, 161; White House CEQ, 27, 28

Vallette, Jim, 177–78
Vander Velde, George, 116
vessels: *Beluga*, 125, 172; incinerator, 33, 108; *Sirius*, 168–69, 171–72
Vesta (ship), 74, 150, 154, 169, *174*
Vietnam War: Agent Orange and, 49, 68; chemical weapons and, 221n8; Nixon and, 214n49, 223n27
violation, of treaties, 102, 119–20
violence, activism and, 175–78
Vulcanus II (ship), 73, 76, 81, *82*, *167*; direct actions and, 153–54, *155*; protests and, 123–24, 171–73
Vulcanus I (ship), 34, 38, 138, 164–65; EPA and, 218n78; monitoring and, 52–53; pollution on, 53–54

Warren County controversy, 13
waste, hazardous, 63–64, 124, 192
Waste Management, Inc., 61; accidents and, 139
waste management, industry of, 61–62, 103; public hearings and, 115–16; subsidies for, 46
Water Pollution Control Act (1948), 27
Water Quality Improvement Act (WQIA) (1970), 27
weapons, 26; biochemical, 45–47, 220n6; CBWs, 46, 49; chemical, 221n8; production of, 23, 210n8

INDEX

Wells Diaz, Margaret, 87
western Europe, *43*, 54–55, 120–21; Greenpeace in, 83; ocean incineration and, 22, 102; Oslo Convention on Dumping and, 29–30; petrochemical industry in, 24; regulation by, 38–39
whaling, 6, 176
White, Mark, 93, 114, 241n35, 242n39
White House Council on Environmental Quality (CEQ), 27; Nixon and, 28

women: activism and, 75–76, 186; in antitoxics campaign, 13–14
workers, health and safety of, 15, 77–78, 87, 172, 175
World Wars I and II, petrochemical industry and, 23, 210n8
WQIA. *See* Water Quality Improvement Act
Wyer, Russel, 73

Zurer, Pamela, 67

GPSR Authorized Representative: Easy Access System Europe, Mustamäe tee 50, 10621 Tallinn, Estonia, gpsr.requests@easproject.com

www.ingramcontent.com/pod-product-compliance
Lightning Source LLC
Chambersburg PA
CBHW022040290426
44109CB00014B/919